HUBERT R.

HARMON

HUBERT R.
HARMON

AIRMAN, OFFICER, FATHER OF THE AIR FORCE ACADEMY

PHILLIP S. MEILINGER

FULCRUM
GROUP

Golden, Colorado

Library of Congress Cataloging-in-Publication Data

Meilinger, Phillip S., 1948-
  Hubert R. Harmon : airman, officer, father of the Air Force Academy / Phillip S. Meilinger.
    p. cm.
  ISBN 978-1-56373-184-6 (hardcover) -- ISBN 978-1-56373-185-3 (pbk.)
  1. Harmon, Hubert Reilly, 1892-1957. 2. Generals--United States--Biography. 3. Air pilots, Military--United States--Biography. 4. Aeronautics, Military--United States--History. 5. United States. Army. Air Corps--History--20th century. 6. United States Air Force Academy--Biography. 7. United States Air Force Academy--History. I. Title.
  UG626.2.H355M45 2009
  358.40092--dc22
  [B]
                                             2008048494

0 9 8 7 6 5 4 3 2 1

Interior design by Patty Maher
Cover and jacket design by Phil Meilinger

Fulcrum Group
4690 Table Mountain Drive, Suite 100
Golden, Colorado 80403
800-992-2908 • 303-277-1623

To all Air Force Academy cadets
Past, Present, and Future

THE FRIENDS OF THE
UNITED STATES AIR FORCE ACADEMY LIBRARY

The Friends of the United States Air Force Academy Library is a tax-exempt charitable foundation established in 1987 to enhance the quality of the Academy Library as an educational, research, scientific, and cultural institution. The Friends enable the library to acquire materials, to pursue projects, to create publications, and to implement services beyond those made possible through funds allocated by the United States Air Force.

The Friends sponsored this biography, and are pleased to commemorate, with its release, the 50th anniversary of the first Air Force Academy graduating class.

Table of Contents

Acknowledgments ix

Foreword xi

Preface xiii

Chapter 1—Beginnings 1
    The School on the Hudson 7
    "Doodle, Doodle ..." 13

Chapter 2—The Young Officer 25
    Winning Wings 28
    Staff and Command...34
    Over There..37
    Occupation Duty 41

Chapter 3—Learning the Ropes 47
    Air Staff Duties..51
    The Courtship of Rosa-Maye 61
    An Extended Honeymoon 69
    A Return to the Hudson 74

Chapter 4—Education and Preparing for the Test 81
    "Horses have Right of Way"...88
    Operational Command 91
    The School for Senior Officers 97
    A Return to the Air...104

Chapter 5—The War Years 113
    Combat Command 124
    The Personnel Expert..139

Chapter 6—Transitioning to Peace and then to Cold War..........................145
    A Return to the Tropics...149
    The Sinecure, not the Cynosure 155
    Unification and Disunity...160

Chapter 7—The Man and the Idea
    Hubert Harmon and the Academy Dream....................................167
    The Quest for an Air Academy...174
    Congress and the Special Assistant 185

Chapter 8—Frustration and Triumph 191
    Stagnation in Congress...200
    Finalizing the Initial Site and Generating Momentum...................205
    "Enthusiasm, Gloom and Despair—but Never Lethargy"................216

Chapter 9—Preparing the Academy Home 221
    A Site of Grandeur 230
    Selecting the Team 242

Chapter 10—Finalizing the Program 249
    A Quality Faculty 256
    The Pace Quickens 261

Chapter 11—"Instruction, Experience, and Motivation" 269
    Discipline and Cadet Activities 274
    "We Will Not Lie …"..278
    The First Stumble...283
    "Our Goal is to the Stars" 292

Chapter 12—"The Academy is his Monument" 297
    Retrospective 304

Endnotes 311
Glossary..339
Bibliography..341
Appendix One: Key Staff Personnel, Academic Year 1955–56.....349
Appendix Two: Class of 1959 Graduating Class 351
Appendix Three: Air Training Officers, Academic Year 1955–56.................353
Appendix Four: Academic Curriculum, Academic Year 1955–56.............355
Index..357
About the Author..374

Acknowledgments

Many individuals made this project possible. First and foremost, I would like to thank The Friends of the Air Force Academy Library who sponsored this effort. Specifically, Duane Reed, the former archivist in the McDermott Library and old friend, convinced me of the need for a biography of Hubert Harmon; he then served as the point man in all dealings with The Friends. Lieutenant General Albert P. Clark (Retired), the president of The Friends, then put his considerable influence behind the idea to make this biography a reality. The executive committe of The Friends also enthusiastically supported this effort.

As all writers know, it is the numerous archivists and librarians at locations all over the country who make any work of history or biography a reality. This project could never have been completed without their expertise and assistance. Most of the research for this work was completed in the Clark Special Collections branch of the McDermott Library, and the help of Dr. Mary Elizabeth Ruwell, John Beardsley and Trudy Pollok was essential. Their friendly and gracious response to any and all requests has been greatly appreciated. Invaluable help was given by Joan Philips, Joe Caver and Sylvester Jackson at the Fairchild Library and Historical Research Agency, both located on Maxwell AFB; Cynde Georgen at the *Trail End* state historical site in Sheridan, Wyoming; Valerie Dutdut at West Point; Kathy Bunker at Fort Leavenworth, Kansas; and James Tobias at the US Army Center of Military History on Fort McNair in Washington DC. Special thanks are due to the reference personnel at the West Chicago Public Library who responded quickly and professionally to the several dozen interlibrary loan requests I made of them. The Friends and I also thank the class of 1959 for their generous encouragement and support.

In addition, I owe an un-payable debt to Rosa-Maye Harmon, the devoted wife of General Harmon. She saved all his letters, plus those she and others wrote to him over the decades. Her daily diaries, covering her entire adult life, were also invaluable. Eula Harmon Hoff and Kendrick Harmon, the general's children, have similarly proved a valuable source of memories and written material. Eula selflessly sent me box upon box of materials and photos from her files regarding her father's life and career. Kendrick provided the oil portrait that serves as the book's dust jacket. This biography could not have been possible, at least not with the depth of personal insight provided, without the unfailing help of the Harmon family.

I want to thank Dr. Dave Mets and Dr. Jim Gaston who took the time to read parts of the manuscript and offer critical comments. Especially, however, I owe an enormous debt of gratitude to Dr. Elliott Converse. It was Elliott who volunteered the time and effort needed to do a close edit of the entire manuscript. His knowledge of the subject matter is enormous, and he educated me on a number of historical issues. In addition, his technical expertise as an editor is humbling. During all those classes in English grammar where I was obviously not paying attention, Elliott was taking careful notes. His labors have made this a far better book.

Finally, I thank my wife Barbara for her constant encouragement and support. She read every page and listened for hours; she makes my life complete.

Foreword

Members of the Air Force of the last fifty years and the many followers of its lore know of Hubert Reilly Harmon more as vague myth than person. He does not enjoy shelves of books and quick name recognition, as do of many classmates from his West Point Class of 1915 (Eisenhower, Bradley, Van Fleet, McNarney, Stratemeyer), or his associates in combat (Twining, Halsey, Stearns, Kenney, Whitehead), or peacetime flying mates (Arnold, Yount, Eaker) or his poker circle (again Arnold, Eaker and Whitehead, Spaatz, Andrews).

For most of us, Lieutenant General Hubert R. Harmon is, simply, Father of the Air Force Academy—despite his long and productive service and rich collection of earlier achievements. Seeing General Harmon as Mister Academy is not unreasonable. Achievements during his first thirty years were shadowed by more memorable events and names. During those years General Harmon was building the skills and reinforcing the native talents that came together and peaked with the challenges of creating the Academy. That final achievement stands alone, like Cathedral Rock on the Academy site; the immediate surrounding terrain has nothing to compare.

To cadets in that first year 1955–1956 General Harmon was, officially, inaccessibly remote, the ultimate omnipotent authority behind and above the entire phalanx of visible and often much too intrusive authorities that were part of daily life. At the same time, when he was present and involved in conversation or dialogue, he was warm, personable, completely present. The one image somehow did not illuminate the other, although both began to plant useful seeds in young minds searching to understand what "commander" should mean. Our first yearbook dedication—"He brought us through selfless example to the true meaning of honor and devotion to country"—is our early collective insight to the measure of the man.

Returning for duty to the Academy thirty one years after my commissioning—as General Harmon's eleventh successor—did not make the man any less mythical to me; if anything, he became more so. A simple but important fact became evident in the early weeks of that tour of duty: the Academy is different from other Air Force commands in at least one important way. Other commands are organizations that can and should flex and change like putty to meet the demands of their time: the needs of the nation, and the judgment of their commander how best to fulfill the mission in current circumstances. The Academy is all that, but it also is an institution. It is founded on enduring fundamental elements that shape, form and ultimately make possible what it does for the Air Force and the country. Those fundamental elements limit the authority of any effective superintendent to alter the shape of the Academy, their command. As this realization crystallized, my personal admiration for the officer who somehow managed to create such a working institution from scratch only grew stronger. Mythic, indeed.

How this could and did happen is a powerful, personal narrative that exposes the strong bones behind the vague myth. We see the growth of the special talents and exceptional human skills that became essential tools in the tremendous organizational challenges of World War II. Those same tools then enabled General Harmon to create a functioning institution of higher learning out of thin air (and copious previous studies)—in fifteen months from the Congressional "go"!

Examples abound of the confidence and trust General Harmon won from hostile critics and the loyalty he routinely earned from those with whom he served. Many are enduring, and some appear decades after his retirement—including, in one case, a campaign to promote him posthumously.

Far more a man of deeds than of words, the written official record of General Harmon's thinking is sparse. The research invested in this narrative is remarkable, extensive and rewarding. The impulse behind events, their consequence, and many telling details would not be visible without it. The web of decisions and opportunities that shaped the Air Service, then Air Corps, then finally Air Force, is clearly the same web that shaped the Hubert R. Harmon who was capable of creating the Academy when handed the task.

Lieutenant General Hubert R. Harmon was indeed The Right Man. He may well have been the only man.

Bradley C. Hosmer
Class of 1959

Preface

*I*t was a Colorado morning in January. It had snowed the day before, but this morning was bright and clear. As is common here, the storm was followed by a brilliant day of sun, melting the snow on the streets and pavement. But all else was covered in a dazzling blanket of white.

As I drove up to the Cadet Area for the first time in many years, I saw several familiar sights. Five deer foraged in a snowy pasture near the road, oblivious to the cars going by. The stadium stared back at the highway, part of the block AIR FORCE letters peaking through the snow on its bleachers. T-41s—light Cessna trainers flown by cadet student pilots and their officer instructors—buzzed in the traffic pattern overhead. The behemoth B-52 jet bomber sat menacingly on its steel and concrete pedestal. The cadet parking lot was jammed, although unlike in my day when Corvettes, MGs and Jaguars were the preferred choices, now there were large numbers of pickup trucks and SUVs. And then I started to see the real changes.

The Cadet Area was ringed by a black steel fence, and gate guards stopped all vehicles. These were a product of the terrorist attacks of 11 September 2001 and the heightened security requirements in its aftermath. The cadets themselves looked even younger than I had remembered—and then it occurred to me that my grandson was but a year younger than I was upon signing in as a Doolie. There were other changes of course—entirely new buildings appeared where none had existed before, and a laundromat was visible on the ground floor of Vandenberg Hall. The cadets themselves, though as cocky and self-assured as always, now wore camouflage fatigues instead of blue uniforms.

The purpose of my visit was only partly to trip down the memory path of my youth; it was also to begin research on this book.

Hubert R. Harmon was a semi-mythic figure to cadets of my era. A building was named in his honor. Besides the fact that this building was where the

Almighty—the superintendent—lived during the day; it was also compelling that other buildings in the Cadet Area were named after Air Force icons: Billy Mitchell, Henry "Hap" Arnold, Hoyt Vandenberg, and Muir "Santy" Fairchild—this was fine company. In truth, however, most cadets of my time knew little of Harmon—he had been "the Soup" a decade earlier—a previous century for teenagers of 18 or 19. We knew he had been the first leader of our Academy and that as a West Point graduate he had patterned our school on his alma mater, complete with an Honor Code that was the core of the cadet experience. We were told that he had loved the Academy, and although cancer would claim him before the first class graduated, he had nonetheless left an indelible stamp on the institution that he had done so much to establish.

My goal was to discover this man who had played such a key role in shaping an Academy that had such a profound influence on my own life and that of thousands of other men and women. Why did he come out of retirement to take the job? Why was he chosen in the first place? What was his vision?

The answers to these questions were to be found in Harmon's nearly four decades in uniform before he ever became associated with the Air Force Academy.

His father had been a West Point graduate and career soldier, as had his two older brothers. Harmon followed in their footsteps. He was not a particularly impressive cadet, either academically or militarily, but he was a gifted athlete. Despite his small size—5'8" and 140 lbs.—Hubert Harmon played football, baseball, hockey and tennis, lettering as the backup quarterback on undefeated Army football teams in 1913 and 1914. The cadet experience, as with most, was formative. The friends made, memories shared, and character traits strengthened would stay with Harmon his entire life. For these reasons, I have spent a great deal of time describing West Point in the first two decades of the twentieth century, and Harmon's time there as a cadet.

Hubert Harmon began commissioned service in the Coast Artillery, his father's branch, but after less than two years and based on the advice of his brother Millard, he transferred to the Aviation Section of the Signal Corps and became a pilot in 1917. Initially posted to Texas in the flying training program as the nation began mobilizing for war, Harmon pulled strings—Millard was stationed in Washington—and headed for France. Near-fatal bouts with influenza and pneumonia kept him from combat, but he stayed in Europe for two years in occupation duty and then in disposing of war surplus material. In 1921 he returned to the States, and was posted to the Air Service Staff in Washington DC. He remained there for the next six years—with one year off to attend engineering school in Dayton, Ohio—learning the intricacies of airpower and the organization and administration of a large military unit. He testified for the defense at the Billy Mitchell court-martial of 1925; served as an executive officer for two Air Service chiefs, Major Generals Charles Menoher and Mason Patrick; and was Hap Arnold's deputy in the Information Division. He also met and pursued one of the most difficult challenges of his life, a challenge that did not result in victory for five years. Her name was Rosa-Maye Kendrick, daughter of a US senator from Wyoming. She stole Hubert's heart from the moment he met her and continued to do so for the next four decades.

After marriage in 1927, a tour as an air attaché in London, and duty as a tactical officer at West Point, Harmon went back to school in 1931: the Air Corps Tactical School at Maxwell Field, Alabama; Command and General Staff School at Fort Leavenworth, Kansas; and the Army War College at Washington Barracks, Washington DC (now Fort McNair). His academic performance at these three important schools was no more brilliant than it had been at West Point, but it nonetheless solidified his professional knowledge and abilities as a staff officer, administrator and airman.

Upon graduating from the War College, Harmon served a stint in the Personnel Division on the War Department General Staff. In 1940, Colonel Harmon took command of Kelly Field and the Advanced Flying School in San Antonio, Texas. After one year he received his first star and was named commander of the Gulf Coast Training Center. In this position he oversaw the flight training of thousands of young men mobilized for war. As in the First World War, Harmon's talents were initially seen as more valuable in a major training role. In 1942, however, he was awarded a second star and named commander of the Sixth Air Force, headquartered in the Panama Canal Zone. This was a frustrating assignment, largely because the Canal, although vital to US security, was in no real danger from either German or Japanese attack. Harmon craved a more meaningful combat tour.

In late 1943 he received his wish: he was named commander of the Thirteenth Air Force in the Solomon Islands. Significantly, his immediate Army Air Forces supervisor was his brother Millard, the same "Miff" who had talked him into becoming an airman in the first place back in 1916. This was, however, a profoundly disappointing assignment for Harmon. Although he believed

he had done an excellent job and proved his mettle at commanding a major
air unit in combat, he was relieved after less than six months. Hurt but not
deterred, he returned to the Air Staff, again in Personnel, and worked tirelessly
in this essential but arcane world for two years. In 1946 he was sent back to
Panama to head the Caribbean Air Command, and after eighteen months was
posted to New York City where he became the senior US airman on the United
Nations Military Staff Committee. Although now a lieutenant general, he was
very restive in this position—international politics ensured that agreements
were seldom reached between the erstwhile allies, the US and the Soviet Union.
Harmon was bored and asked the Joint Staff in the Pentagon for additional
duties to keep him gainfully employed.

One of these projects was a highly classified investigation into the ability
of the US Air Force to carry out its role in the national warplan: could it successfully conduct an atomic air offensive against the Soviet Union? Harmon's
conclusion was a highly unpopular and controversial "partly." Although many
of his fellow airmen were no doubt stunned and irritated by this conclusion,
one man was not. The Air Force chief of staff, General Hoyt S. Vandenberg,
appreciated Harmon's honesty and candor. In December 1949, Vandenberg
gave Harmon a new job, a task that required someone of unquestioned integrity—he was to be his Special Assistant for Air Academy Matters.

Over the next five years Harmon would become an expert on military education and the requirements for an Air Force academy. Unfortunately, because
the nation was embroiled in the Korean War six months after his appointment,
Congress did not deem it appropriate to establish a new academy at that time.
In September 1953 Harmon retired, and he, Rosa-Maye and his daughter—his
son was a cadet at West Point—moved to San Antonio. His retirement was
short-lived. With the war ending, the White House made it plain that the time
had come, and Congress finally looked favorably on legislation establishing
an air academy. President Dwight Eisenhower, Harmon's West Point classmate
and football teammate, brought his old colleague "Doodle" out of retirement
once again, to be the first superintendent of the new Air Force Academy.

The problems encountered in establishing a military academy from scratch
were enormous. Required were an entire academic curriculum and a faculty to
teach it; a commandant's office that would be responsible for housing, feeding,
clothing, training and disciplining the cadets; an athletic department to administer a full slate of physical education classes, as well as an intramural program and

intercollegiate athletics; and the design and building of an entirely new institution with dozens of buildings and facilities. In addition to these major tasks, there were countless details: designing new uniforms and flags, determining a mascot, ensuring cadets had things to do on weekends, and establishing a Cadet Honor Code. The list was almost endless. Yet, Hubert Harmon did all of this with seeming ease. He had done it before during the war. At the same time, he had a facility for dealing with people, military of all ranks, as well as civilians, which bordered on genius. He made no enemies; indeed, he was beloved by virtually everyone who knew him.

Hubert Harmon, the Father of the Air Force Academy, was the perfect man for the job.

Phillip S. Meilinger
West Chicago, IL

CHAPTER 1

Beginnings

*H*ubert Harmon liked to say that he came from a military family, but then he would add that it was not an *old* military family. By that he meant the roots of the Harmon family's involvement in the US military did not stretch back much further than his own father. Research indicates, however, that Harmon military history is both broad and deep.

In 1976 one of the Harmon clan's members, John Honeycutt (a nephew of Hubert) noted that in the entire extended family, no less than thirty-one men had graduated from West Point. Those attending the Academy included fathers, sons, grandsons, and many in-laws. For example, Hubert Harmon's father, Millard Fillmore Harmon, was a West Point graduate of the Class of 1880. Hubert's two older brothers also graduated from the Military Academy— Kenneth in 1910 and Millard, Jr., in 1912. Hubert's two sisters married West Point graduates: Margaret wed Francis W. Honeycutt (Class of 1904), and Edith married John W. Lang (Class of 1907). And so it went. Among those thirty-one Academy graduates were one general, four lieutenant generals, six major generals and four brigadier generals.[1]

This is an astonishing record for a single family. More to the point, it speaks to the profound sense of duty and service that permeated the entire extended Harmon family. These qualities were not lost on Hubert Harmon.

Little is known about the Harmon ancestry. The family today believes that the Harmons came from Alsace-Lorraine in France, although one branch originated in Ireland. The first Harmons about whom we know anything are George Washington Harman—as he originally spelled his name—and his wife Ann. George was born in Berrysburg, Pennsylvania, in 1824 and came from humble origins; he made his living as a plasterer. In 1854 he moved to Altoona and married Ann Blackburn. The couple had three children, the oldest being Millard Fillmore Harmon, born in 1856. On December 4, 1862, Ann died in childbirth along with her fourth child, a baby girl. George then took his three children, ages 2 through 6, to Bedford where they were to live with Ann's parents. Thomas Blackburn, whose ancestors came from Ireland around 1745, was a prosperous farmer. He and his wife, Jane, were Quakers, and apparently were not pleased about having to raise their grandchildren. Their irritation increased when George remarried a woman twenty years his junior, had two more children, and then moved to Kansas—leaving Millard, Edith and John Bell behind.[2] It appears the children did not see their father again after he left for Kansas, and neither did they have much contact with the rest of the Harmon side of the family. Essentially orphaned, Millard and his younger brother and sister had a difficult childhood.

Millard was a young boy during the Civil War, and with Gettysburg only seventy miles from Bedford, he must have been aware of the climactic events that occurred in his home state. These memories no doubt played a role in his decision to become a soldier and to apply for a position at West Point. He was offered an appointment and entered the Academy the month following his twentieth birthday. He was always deeply appreciative of the opportunity given him to serve his country and to do so with such an important start at West Point. Perhaps because of this he did well at the Academy, graduating fourteenth in a class of fifty-three. He served as a cadet lieutenant—one of fourteen in his class—and went two of his four years without earning a single demerit. During his senior

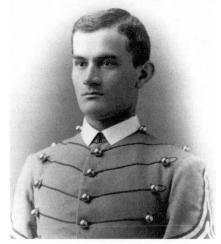

Madelin Kendig Harmon at the time of her marriage in 1881.

Millard Fillmore in his West Point graduation photo, 1880.

year he garnered a perfect score in military professionalism and was ranked first in his class in discipline.[3] His graduation photograph of 1880 shows him to have been an unusually handsome young man.

A year out of school, the second lieutenant of the 1st Artillery married his high school sweetheart, Madelin Kendig, who was born in Orrstown, Pennsylvania, but raised in Bedford. Her father, Henry Kendig, had served as a first lieutenant in a Pennsylvania cavalry regiment during the Civil War and was wounded in action. He returned home after the war to work for the railroad as a clerk. He remained with the Pennsylvania Railroad for the rest of his working life. It is believed that the Kendigs had come originally from Berne, Switzerland.[4]

Hubert Harmon at age two, before his first haircut.

For seven years, Lieutenant and Mrs. Harmon lived at a number of posts on the Pacific coast: Fort Canby, Washington; Fort Stevens, Oregon; the Presidio at San Francisco; and Fort Mason, California. Millard was an avid sportsman and relished these years for the time he had to hunt, fish, and enjoy his growing family. Margaret and Edith were born at Fort Stevens; Kenneth arrived when the Harmons were stationed at the Presidio; and Millard, Jr. was born while the family was assigned to Fort Mason.

In 1888 Harmon was promoted to first lieutenant and attended the Artillery School at Fort Monroe in Virginia where he was an honor graduate. Here the Harmon's fifth child, Madelin, was born. In 1890 Harmon was assigned as an instructor of military science and tactics, while also serving as commandant, at the Pennsylvania Military Academy in Chester.[5] During this three-year tour, the Harmons had their sixth and final child, Hubert Reilly, born April 3, 1892.[6]

As a child, Hubert's nickname was "Buzzie," given him by his next oldest sister, Madelin, who died as a child of scarlet fever.[7] The five remaining children grew up as Army "brats" following their father to various posts around the country. "Papa" as his kids called him, was assigned to the US Proving Ground at Sandy Hook, New Jersey, upon leaving Chester. From there it was to Fort Wadsworth on Staten Island, followed by Fort Barrancas in Florida. After this, Harmon was the regimental quartermaster at Sullivan's Island, South Carolina.

A long-awaited promotion to captain in 1899 also resulted in a move to Fort McHenry, Maryland (of "Star Spangled Banner" fame). When the Spanish-American War broke out, Harmon commanded a company of artillery that he eventually took to Cuba for occupation duty at Cabana Barracks. The Harmons lived in the Havana area for two years before returning to Fort Monroe where Millard served as adjutant of the Artillery School. This was followed by more postings: Fort Hamilton (New York), Fort Adams (Rhode Island)—where Harmon was promoted to major in 1905—and Fort Caswell (North Carolina).

After an eighteen-month stint as member of the Ordnance Board, Major Harmon chose the Coast Artillery when that branch was split away from the Field Artillery in 1907. Harmon made this choice largely because the coastal artillery posts offered better educational opportunities for his five children. In 1910, Lieutenant Colonel Harmon was posted to the Philippines where he commanded the island fortress of Corregidor off the Bataan Peninsula—places that would gain infamy and glory three decades later. Harmon returned to the US as a colonel in 1912, but the tour overseas had not been good for his health. He was named commander of the artillery defenses of Narragansett Bay, headquartered in Rhode Island—a highly desirable assignment—but this tour was cut short by an unfortunate and embarrassing error. While assigned at Fort Adams as commander in 1913, he failed to keep an appointment with Rear Admiral Charles J. Badger of the Atlantic Fleet. Harmon said in his defense that the meeting had simply slipped his mind. Badger complained to Harmon's superior of the perceived snub, and although the *New York Times* noted that the colonel was one of "the best known officers in the Coast Artillery Service," Harmon was relieved of command and transferred to Fort Du Pont in Delaware.[8]

Colonel Harmon never really recovered from this blow, and his health continued to deteriorate. In March the following year he retired for medical reasons, and he and Madelin moved to Washington DC. He lived for eight more years, and saw all three of his sons graduate from West Point and both daughters marry West Point graduates. He died at his home in Washington on March 27, 1922.[9] He and Madelin, who died in 1947, are buried beneath the spreading branches of a cedar tree in Arlington Cemetery.

For Hubert, growing up as the youngest in a large family stationed at various Army posts around the country was a wonderful experience. This type of life—moving from place to place, starting new schools, saying goodbye to friends and making new ones—forced youngsters to adapt and have a flexible nature. It also often resulted in children who grew up with an unusual degree of openness and affability. They made friends easily throughout life for the simple reason that they were conditioned to do so from an early age.

The family was Episcopalian, but did not appear to be devout. Later, Hubert would marry in a Unitarian Church—his bride's preference—but the hundreds of extant letters from his adult life almost never mention religion or even attendance at church services. In fact, his wife kept daily diaries throughout her life, but she seldom recorded attending church services on Sunday, and even then, she generally went alone as Hubert often went golfing. Yet, he was a man of rigid integrity. The Honor Code of the Military Academy would never be a challenge for him— he had already been raised in adherence to its principles. In my view, it was his sense of integrity and doing what he thought right that led to his appointment in 1949 to be the Special Assistant for Air Academy Matters. But more on that later.

Growing up near the seacoast in artillery forts meant a great deal of time spent fishing, swimming, snake hunting, crab digging and boating. On one prank, while the family was at Fort Barrancas in Florida, Hubert fell down the cellar steps and cut a deep gash in his forehead. He was rescued by the post doctor, but ever after had a bit of a "dent" in his head where he had fallen. While the family was stationed in Cuba, Hubert took a fancy to the special type of guava jelly produced there. Years later his wife would write that she attempted to make the jelly herself using a variety of recipes, but it was never deemed as good as that he had had as a child. In Brooklyn (Fort Hamilton) the boys got in trouble for removing the lead weights from gun carriages and selling them to a junk dealer. This was standard behavior for rambunctious boys, but they were also intelligent and curious. Millard and Madelin understood the importance of education, and it was standard practice for the children to be required to read up on a topic from history and then be prepared to discuss what they had read over dinner.[10]

Hubert and his siblings at Fort Barrancas, Florida, in 1898. From left to right: Millard, Edith (in rear) and Margaret, Hubert, and Kenneth.

Oldest brother Kenneth was very mechanically inclined. It was his chore as a youngster to start the coal fireplace in the kitchen each morning. He soon figured out that he could build the fire the night before, and he then rigged a device that connected the fireplace to his bedroom. When he woke up in the morning, he merely needed to flip a switch near his bed that would trigger a starter in the fireplace in the kitchen. Later, while a cadet at West Point, Kenneth rigged a secret panel in his room. When he pressed a spot on a leg of his table, the panel would swing open revealing a stash of detailed plans for airships, submarines, torpedoes, automobiles, motorcycles and other inventions "that he would one day set fire to a startled world."[11] He would spend his entire Army career in the Ordnance Corps, retiring as a colonel.

Millard, Jr., would transfer to the Aviation Section of the Signal Corps early in his Army career and serve in a number of important operational assignments. He was a born leader. On two occasions he would be younger brother Hubert's commander. He rose to the rank of lieutenant general and was one of the Army Air Forces' senior commanders, serving as the Army commander in the South Pacific Area. Tragically, on a flight to Hawaii in early 1945 his aircraft disappeared over the ocean.

As a student, Hubert showed early promise, especially in mathematics. At Brooklyn Polytechnic Preparatory School, he had a good teacher who pushed him to develop these skills. While at "Poly Prep," he solved a particularly difficult geometry theorem, causing quite a stir, especially when it was discovered that he had employed an entirely original method of solution. This facility for solving mind games, word puzzles, and mathematical problems was to stay with Hubert for life. Brother Kenneth later recalled a formidable puzzle that he had posed to Hubert: arrange thirty-five girls in a column, five abreast and seven deep, for each day of the week so that no girl occupied a line of five girls in which there were other girls she had been with, or would be with, on other days. According to Kenneth, his brother was the only person he knew who had ever solved this problem.[12]

The constant transferring to different schools took a toll on Hubert's education, which is why he attended "Poly Prep" for two years—he wanted to hone his mathematical and engineering skills prior to a bid to enter one of the service academies. Once he decided on West Point, he also moved to Highland Falls outside the Academy's gates for the specific purpose of preparing for the entrance exam. He even worked as a draftsman with the Corps of Engineers in New York City for a summer as a way of improving his practical skills.[13] In a letter to his father, Hubert recounted how he had to fire nearly all of the workers on a power house project he was supervising, while then hiring twenty-three new laborers to replace them. The results were satisfactory, and the project was now almost finished. He was fifteen years old at the time.[14] Such efforts were to prove worthwhile.

The School on the Hudson

As the US entered the twentieth century great changes were afoot. The country was about to emerge from its "splendid isolation" and gain an empire. The proximate cause of this imperial notion occurred in Havana harbor, but in truth, the force behind the impulse had been part of the American spirit for decades and saw its apotheosis in a sense of Manifest Destiny as it pushed inexorably to the Pacific, while butting up against, not always benignly, its neighbors north and south. There was even a bit of an overseas impulse at work, as evidenced by the purchase of Alaska in 1867 and the forcible annexation of Hawaii in 1898. The explosion of the USS *Maine* on February 15, 1898, ostensibly at the hands of Spanish colonial officials, pushed the country into war. Unfortunately, the Army was unprepared for action.

Still led by men who had fought in the Civil War more than three decades earlier, the Army was ill-prepared strategically, tactically and logistically to take on a first-rate opponent. Luckily, Spain was not a first-rate military power, so the nation and its Army muddled through to victory.[15]

In the aftermath, Congress, the public, and even the Army itself realized that major reforms were necessary. Slowly, but measurably, those changes began to occur. A new secretary of war, Elihu Root, was instrumental in instituting reforms such as a general staff, rotation of officers between staff and line, reduced emphasis on seniority, an improved National Guard, and an enhanced emphasis on military education.[16]

This last was to impact the US Military Academy at West Point in a significant way. First, the increasing size of the Army meant that in order to keep a stable percentage of the officer corps as West Point graduates, the size of the cadet battalion would need to expand beyond its then-371 members.[17] In 1900, Congress authorized growth to 481 cadets, and three years later increased it again to 523. As the number of cadets grew, it was equally necessary to expand the facilities for their housing and education, as well as increase the size of the faculty and staff. A new superintendent, an unusually young officer, First Lieutenant Albert L. Mills (he was promoted to colonel upon his appointment), arrived at the Academy as these changes were looming. He was a good choice in some ways. His energy, drive and vision were of great importance, because it was during his tenure that a massive building program was conceived, a building program that Mills decided should employ a distinctive architectural style befitting the Academy's illustrious past. The result was the impressive and instantly recognizable "Collegiate Gothic" motif that was popular across the country in the second half of the nineteenth century and that remains the Academy's hallmark today.

It was under Mills's successors, Colonel Hugh L. Scott until 1910 and then Major General Thomas H. Barry, that the building program, approved by Secretary of War Root, was actually carried out. In 1908 the barracks and stables for the artillery and cavalry troops were completed. The following year saw the construction of the heating and generating plant, as well as a new cadet barracks. In 1910 a new administration building and the iconic Cadet Chapel were finished, the latter destined to be the venue for countless weddings of newly graduated lieutenants in the decades ahead. (The old chapel was moved to the cemetery.) 1910 also heralded the erection of more faculty quarters and a new gymnasium; a riding hall (the largest in the world) was added the year thereafter and an academic building in 1914. Construction would continue for another two decades as the cadet corps expanded again during the First World War.[18]

To go with the new buildings, the Academy also instituted a new approach to military training. Before the Spanish-American War this training consisted almost entirely of drill, in-ranks-inspections, and menial administrative matters. There was little insight provided as to the point of the endless drill—which culminated in a parade most days, weather permitting. As an observer noted, "professional education in military history, weaponry, political economy, and leadership was nearly nonexistent."[19] After the war, military training improved to include an emphasis on small-unit tactics, marksmanship, exercises and unit maneuvers. Superintendent Mills even requested Congressional funds for the erection of a coastal artillery position on Academy grounds so as to provide cadets with realistic experience of actual military equipment. Although the request was denied, the search for more realism in cadet training continued.

Athletically, the Academy also began to participate in intercollegiate competition, forming squads in football, baseball, basketball, hockey, lacrosse, track, fencing and polo. It was during this period that the perennial contests with archrival Navy—especially in football and baseball—took on mythic proportions. One famous West Point graduate and athlete, Omar Bradley, later recalled that the Academy was "sports-oriented to a feverish degree. The most esteemed cadets were star athletes."[20]

Although the Academy's physical appearance changed sharply with the dawn of the new century and much-needed reforms were made in the areas of military training and athletics, one institutional aspect changed hardly at all. Specifically, the academic curriculum and its educational philosophy remained mired in the previous century.

West Point was founded in 1802 as an engineering school; indeed, it was the first such school in the country. As a consequence, its curriculum was based largely on mathematics, engineering and science. For that time, it was a solid and useful model. In fact, a new school in Cambridge, the Massachusetts Institute of Technology, modeled its curriculum on that of West Point when it opened in 1865. Regrettably, the curriculum on the Hudson barely changed over its first century of existence, so that by 1902, 75 percent of the course work was devoted to mathematics, engineering and science; the remainder was military studies, foreign languages and law. By then, even for an engineering school this curriculum was dated.[21]

The pedagogical philosophy behind the teaching of this fading curriculum similarly had not kept pace with the times. While an educational revolution was spreading through universities across the country, West Point continued an archaic system. The curriculum was prescribed for all cadets, regardless of their abilities or whether they had attended prior college: all cadets took exactly the same courses through all four years. There were no electives. There were no academic majors. The classroom instructors were exclusively military officers—all were West Point graduates, usually with between three to eight years of commissioned service—and most had no further academic education beyond that they had received as cadets. The engineering courses were a bit better off, because they generally plucked their instructors from the Corps of Engineers; these officers at least had some practical experience under their belts.[22] Generally arriving only a week or two prior to the start of the fall semester, line officers with no prior teaching experience "had to work day and night" merely to stay ahead of their students.[23] The textbooks used were ordinarily written by the department heads, and over time these texts assumed the status of sacred writ, and any change required the approval of the secretary of war.[24] Among the eleven departments, there were seven headed by "permanent professors"— men who had been appointed for life, or until the mandatory retirement age of

64.[25] Although most permanent professors had advanced degrees, there was no requirement for them to continue their studies or to stay abreast of the latest developments in their field. There also was little likelihood they would return to operational duty. In 1902, for example, of the seven permanent professors at West Point, five would serve in their positions until age 64; a sixth died in office a few months prior to his 64th birthday.[26]

Because the military instructors knew little about the subjects they were teaching beyond what they had learned as cadets, they were often unable to impart much insight to their students. Instead, classes would begin with an instructor blandly asking if there were any questions. One contemporary account, written by a graduate and former instructor, noted that the cadets would often attempt to out-fox the officers by spending the entire lesson asking questions. A clever instructor would see through this ruse and refuse to take any questions! Instead, he would proceed to call on each cadet in turn—class sizes averaged twelve men—to "recite" their lesson.[27] In mathematics or engineering classes, cadets would work pre-determined problems at the blackboards for the entire period. One observer wrote gloomily: "In most cases, there was no room for discussion or exploitation of new answers to old problems. English was composition, never literature; history was fact, never inquiry. It was all rote learning."[28]

Every cadet was graded on his performance daily in every class. Grades accumulated and were posted each week for all to see. Academic rankings, which to a great extent determined the graduation order of merit, were tallied over four years of class recitations and end-of-semester examinations. The graduation order of merit determined how cadets selected the branch they would join in the Army. Most of those graduating at the top of their classes selected the few openings available in the prestigious Corps of Engineers—the branch that offered the best chance for a lucrative civilian career after an officer hung up his uniform. Graduates at the bottom of their classes were generally relegated to the Infantry.

Overall, one expert observer stated that by 1900 the education provided at West Point was barely advanced beyond the high-school level.[29] The main stumbling block to reform—but not the only one—was the dominance of the Academic Board. This Board was composed of the eleven department heads (both the permanent professors and the "detailed" officers), as well as the commandant of cadets; the superintendent served as the *ex officio* president. This meant that any academic change had to be approved by the majority of the aged permanent professors. This was unlikely to occur for the simple reason that although many of these men realized that some type of change was inevitable, they were determined that it should occur in someone else's department. Thus, for example, when Superintendent Mills suggested that new courses be offered in the emerging discipline of political science, as well as new courses in history and an increased emphasis in foreign language—especially Spanish given America's new responsibilities in the Caribbean and the Philippine Islands—no permanent professor was willing to reduce his own department's course load to make room for these new offerings. Moreover, if such new courses were offered, who would teach them? The existing permanent professors lacked the expertise to do so, and because they hired only Academy graduates with no academic training beyond West Point, neither were those officers competent. The solution would first and foremost require the broadening of the educational purview of the permanent professors, and that was unlikely to occur.

This adamantine stance was exemplified by Colonel Charles Larned, the Professor of Drawing (of the mechanical and topographical variety) who pontificated that the "genius of West Point" was "its grounding in the three fundamentals: every man in every subject; every man proficient in everything; and every man every day." As for change, Larned lauded the Academic Board's basic operating principle: "There is a disposition to make haste slowly in all matters involving change." In other words, Larned held firm to the principle of a set curriculum for all cadets regardless of their abilities or educational level. He also insisted that every cadet pass each class with no exceptions. And he favored the daily recitations that emphasized rote learning and memorization rather than originality or creative thought.[30] This system had been installed by the great Sylvanus Thayer in 1837, and for Larned, there was no need to change it. This was a remarkably depressing and antiquated educational vision.

There were, however, mechanisms for change if skillfully employed. The Board of Visitors, for example, could make recommendations to the secretary of war to force reform, but all "knowledgeable educators" were deliberately eliminated from the Board's membership in 1908 so as to forestall academic innovation.[31] In addition, Colonel Mills pushed the Academic Board to offer new courses as noted, but it resisted. Mills pushed harder. One of his ploys was to convince the War Department to grant him *three* votes on the Academic Board as a way of trying to sway the majority—obviously hoping that the commandant and temporary "detailed" department heads would be more amenable to reform.[32] Finally, the professors agreed to increase the amount of Spanish taught to cadets, while also approving the formation of a Department of English and History to teach new courses, but the professors still maintained that none of the present curriculum could be cut. In order to make room for these new offerings the professors insisted that the entire course of study be lengthened by three months. New cadets would therefore be required to report for duty in March of each year instead of June![33] It was a quirk of fate that Hubert Reilly Harmon would be one of those selected to report for duty in March 1910—with unexpected results.

Despite these failings, this creaking military and academic edifice produced the vast majority of senior Army officers, commanders, and combat leaders throughout the country's history. In the Civil War, for example, the vast majority of senior officers, on both sides, were West Point graduates.[34] Looking ahead to the near future, this same ossified structure would produce a number of truly remarkable airmen, including General of the Air Force Henry "Hap" Arnold (Class of 1907), and the first four chiefs of staff of an independent Air Force.[35] Clearly, the Military Academy was doing something right. The Academy itself was well aware of its dominance within the Army, and lest anyone forget it, each year the "Official Register" (what today we would call a college catalog) began with a page or more of quotations from famous men—many of them presidents—extolling the great deeds of the Academy and its illustrious graduates. The "Register" of 1911, for example, quotes Andrew Jackson: "This institution has already exercised the happiest influence upon the moral and intellectual character of our Army."[36] It was a fair assessment.

A young Hubert dreams of being a soldier.

The seemingly short-sighted and muddle-headed thinking of the old guard professors was not without some justification. To these men, West Point was not supposed to be a liberal arts college that produced broadminded thinkers. Nor was it meant to be a professional school, as were medical or law schools, which turned out competent practitioners of a specific discipline. Rather, the mission of West Point was to produce men of character who would then devote their lives to serving the country. (I would also note that the use of the term "*men* of character" was chosen deliberately. This was a totally male environment.) If character building was the goal, than it called for a curriculum—and indeed an entire structure—that stressed hard work, thoroughness, close supervision, technicism (the emphasis on science and mathematics), mental discipline, preparedness, duty, and obedience.[37] This was not an unworthy goal, and these were not trivial or mean character traits. Many argued then and since—including high-ranking alumni who were among the most vocal opponents of change—that West Point was achieving its purpose.

"Doodle, Doodle ..."

By the early twentieth century, the Harmon clan was on its way to becoming a military family. As noted, Millard Fillmore Harmon, Sr. had graduated from West Point in 1880 and served thirty-four years as an officer. His eldest son, Kenneth, also attended the Academy, joining the Class of 1910. The next son, Millard, Jr., then received an appointment, joining the Class of 1912.

In order for a young man to attend West Point, he had to receive a nomination from his congressman, senator, or the President of the United States. Each senator and representative could have one cadet in the Academy at a time; the president had forty slots each year that he could use for nominating young men from the country at large. Obviously, such nominations were an important form of patronage, so politicians guarded them carefully. In practice, the politicians would nominate one primary candidate and two alternates. These three men would then be required to take a physical and an academic examination, the test being drawn up by West Point professors and administered throughout the country under Army auspices on a set day each April. It was not a very challenging exam, but as the "Register" noted, the prospective cadet needed to be well-versed in algebra—quadratic equations and progressions—plane geometry, English grammar, geography, and history.[38] If the primary candidate passed the physical and academic exams, he was offered an appointment. If he did not pass, or if he had changed his mind about wanting to be a cadet, then an alternate would take his place.

Hubert had initially considered attending the Naval Academy, but upon seeing his older brothers come home on furlough wearing their traditional, snappy gray uniforms, he elected to try for the Military Academy instead. In 1910, Hubert, who was living with his parents on Governor's Island in New York harbor where his father was stationed, received an appointment. Recall that in order to accommodate new courses in English, history, and Spanish the Academic Board had decreed an early start date. As a consequence, Hubert signed in on March 10, while both of his brothers were still cadets—although Kenneth was due to graduate three months hence. A week into the basic training referred to as "Beast Barracks," Cadet Harmon was summoned to the office of the superintendent, Colonel Hugh L. Scott. For a cadet, especially a basic cadet, to be called to the superintendent's office was unusual, and Hubert must have had some apprehension. He had cause to be worried. Scott got immediately to the point, holding up a cadet roster and noting that there were two other cadets listed on it that were also named Harmon. Were they of any relation? "Yes," Hubert replied; "those are my brothers." Scott then stated, "In that case, you will have to leave. You cannot expect American tax-payers to pay for the education of three boys from the same family."[39]

Hubert was dumbfounded. His father was outraged and wrote the Army chief of staff, General Leonard Wood. His appeal was unsuccessful. Colonel and Mrs. Millard Harmon were on a ship headed to their assignment in the Philippines when Hubert received a reply from General Wood. He regretted to inform him that he had spoken to the president (William Howard Taft), who had declined to intercede. (The Harmons had hoped Taft would either overrule Colonel Scott or tender Hubert a presidential appointment.) Wood added that he would bring the subject up with the president again, "if there is an opportunity." In the meantime, he advised, "go on with your work, and be ready for whatever turns up."[40]

Dismayed, Hubert pondered his future from the Brooklyn boarding house on Clairmont Avenue where he was now living. The family lore has it that Hubert told his sad tale to his landlady, an Irish woman with a big heart. She said that they ought to speak with her husband, but they needed to be clever about it. They would wait until himself was home from work, had enjoyed his supper, and was sitting in his favorite chair with a cup of coffee and a cigar. At the appropriate time she and Hubert sat down, and he told his story. The husband was moved. He had friends. Off he and Hubert went to speak to a politician of his acquaintance, the local ward boss. Hands were shook; drinks were drunk. Hubert was told not to worry. Sure enough, a few months later he received *another* Congressional appointment from Representative William M. Calder of Brooklyn.[41] The timing was propitious. Kenneth had graduated. The ill-advised experiment of having new cadets arrive three months early had just ended, and just before Hubert re-arrived at West Point on June 14, 1911, Colonel Scott had left. His replacement, Major General Thomas H. Barry, knew nothing of the previous year's incident. No questions were asked of Hubert this time about his brothers.

When Hubert took the oath in June along with 251 other young men, he was two months past his nineteenth birthday. Upon entry he stood 5'8" and weighed 134 lbs. with brown hair and hazel eyes.[42] The next four years would be among the most important and formative of his life.

"Beast Barracks" was the first three weeks of basic training for all new cadets; it was a rite of passage at West Point. Taking place on Academy grounds, it began with the storied arrival of hundreds of young men from all over the country wearing civilian clothes and apprehensive smiles. They were immediately set upon by stern and immaculately dressed upperclassmen who proceeded to shout and berate the new recruits. Now began the running everywhere, answering all queries in a loud voice, assuming an exaggerated posture of attention termed "bracing," and to memorize trivial facts. One source gives a typical and absurd example of the sort of things new cadets were required to memorize. If a cadet did not know the answer to a particular question, he was required to respond:

> Sir, my cranium consisting of Vermont marble, volcanic lava and African ivory, covered with a thick layer of case-hardened steel, forms an impenetrable barrier to all that seeks to impress itself upon the ashen tissues of my brain. Hence the effulgent and ostentatiously effervescent phrases just now directed and reiterated for my comprehension have failed to penetrate and permeate the somniferous fences of my atrocious intelligence. In other words, I am very, very dumb and I do not understand, sir.[43]

This was all very foolish, but the new cadets would endure it for another year. The newcomers were issued bedding, uniforms, and shown to their barracks—blessedly, the new building (unlike the old) had indoor plumbing. Training began with a rigorous regimen of physical conditioning, drill, manual of arms, and military indoctrination—how to make a bed properly, shine shoes, clean a room, fieldstrip a rifle, and salute. Everything had its place and its own unique method of storage—and virtually everything they had learned at home was wrong. In this regard, Hubert must have been ahead of his peers, having learned the ropes from his father and brothers, but this may also have worked to his disadvantage—new cadets sought anonymity, not name recognition. Hubert was quickly identified as Millard's little brother.[44]

After three weeks, the new cadets moved out of the barracks to join the rest of the cadet battalion in the summer encampment. They were no longer termed "beasts"; they had graduated to become "plebes."[45] Training continued of course—and now with more upperclassmen around to watch their every move. There were still the endless drill and manual, along with castrametation (tent-camp techniques). One should note, however, that in addition to all this infantry training, plebes also received instruction in swimming and dancing. The cadets practiced the latter with their tent-mates because women were not available for this purpose![46] Except for the dancing classes, which employed a civilian teacher, the training and instruction were generally administered by upperclassmen, overseen by officers. Occasionally, cadets would go too far, and unseen by their officer supervisors, would subject plebes to excessive physical stress. Such treatment—hazing—was and still is officially forbidden, but it occurred nonetheless.[47] Omar Bradley later wrote, surprisingly, that hazing was actually a "great leveler" because it quickly identified the "pampered boys" among them.[48] Perhaps, but it is difficult to see the point at this distance. For example, one of the silly drills required of Millard Harmon as a plebe had been to crawl around on all fours, "like a doodle bug" while reciting: "Doodle Bug, Doodle Bug your house is on fire." He apparently was quite good at this questionable skill and earned the nickname of "Doodle." When Hubert arrived, he too was often directed to emulate insects. Like his brother, he became proficient at it, earning him the nickname of "Little Doodle."[49] The sobriquet for Millard was eventually lost—for the rest of his life he would be called "Miff." With Hubert, however, the name stuck; henceforth, his classmates—as well as colleagues throughout his Air Force career—would know him as Doodle.

Academic classes began in September, and for the plebes it was a welcome respite. Although they were still closely watched and "corrected" by upperclassmen, the fact that all cadets were now in the classroom most of the day and studying in their rooms after dinner limited the exposure of the plebes to harassment. Cadet rooms were designed to house two men, but three plebes often occupied a room—at least until attrition drove the numbers down. The rooms were austere in the extreme: hot in the summer and cold in the winter. There was one washstand with mirror and towel racks; a desk and chair for each man, as well as a cot—rolled up during the day—and accompanying mattress and sheets. Hooks were available to hang clothes. No pictures, banners, carpets, rugs or any other decoration was permitted. Plebe rooms were inspected daily, and any amount of dust or items out of place would result in an infraction punishable by demerits or worse.[50]

Classes were held six days per week, and lasted from 0755 to 1545, with a seventy-five minute break for lunch. Cadets formed up in front of the barracks;

roll was taken; and they marched off to the academic building. After classes, there was generally drill, followed by a parade. On Saturdays, the parade was usually attended by tourists and other visitors. Sunday began with mandatory chapel services, but the rest of the day was generally devoted to study or cleaning up shoes, uniforms and the room.

Doodle Harmon's academics during his plebe year included mathematics (algebra, geometry and trigonometry);[51] English and history, which alternated throughout the year (English consisted of rhetoric, composition and an introduction to "selected literary masterpieces"; history was world political and economic events from the Middle Ages to the present with special emphasis on the US); surveying, and drill regulations. He was an average student, ranked 90th overall in his class of 212 (forty cadets had resigned or been dismissed during his plebe year). His best class was in mathematics where he ranked 60th; his worst was drill regulations where he stood at 159. Cadets also took physical education classes during the academic year, and for Harmon these included boxing and wrestling. (Intramural sports held after classes did not become part of the cadet schedule until Brigadier General Douglas MacArthur inaugurated them during his tenure as superintendent from 1919 to 1922.) Harmon's military conduct was far below average: his 112 demerits put him at number 171 in his class.[52] Infractions—or "skins" in cadet parlance—earned demerits, and these he received for a variety of standard offenses: late for dinner, dirty bucket (parade hat), late for chapel, towel not neatly placed on wash stand, late for parade, dust in rifle chamber at inspection, late for reveille, etc.[53] Of note, Hubert received more demerits during his plebe year than his father had earned in all four years as a cadet.

Normally, there was no opportunity for cadets to leave the Academy on furlough during their first two years. For the two upper classes, summer leaves were permitted, with the rest of the summer spent in military training, and also in breaking in the new class of plebes. In addition, those upperclassmen not academically or militarily deficient could expect a week or so off at Christmas.[54] If a cadet were academically deficient, than over the holiday break when upperclassmen went home, he would take what was termed a "turnout exam." If he passed, he could continue with his studies. If he failed, he would either be dismissed, or, if he showed military promise, be "turned back" to the next class and forced to begin the year over—in all academic courses, including those he had already passed![55]

In his sophomore or third-class year (plebes now became "yearlings"), Doodle Harmon took more mathematics (plane and solid geometry, calculus), French, drawing (blocks, objects, lettering), military hygiene (physical training principles, foods and their preparation in the field, camp sanitation, etc.), surveying, and drill.[56] Harmon was second in his class (now down to 177 members) in drawing—his best performance as a cadet, and possibly adding meaning to his nickname. He was terrible in military hygiene, and his conduct continued to be sub-par—he was ranked 157th in his class with 176 demerits, which put him near the "top" of the class in that category.[57]

During his junior year, Harmon dropped to number 137 of 171 in his class. Academic work included natural and experimental philosophy (essentially physics, which included topics such as sound, light, hydraulics, and mechanics), chemistry, Spanish, drawing, and drill. He again excelled in drawing, ranking fourth in his class. In all other subjects he did poorly, finishing in the bottom third. In military conduct he remained near the bottom at number 160, with a further 117 demerits on his record.[58]

Then, finally, he became a senior—a first classman. Life for firsties was quite good—at least in comparison to the lower three classes. There was a First Class Club where they could lounge about, smoke, drink cider, play chess and listen to the phonograph. The seniors had more off-post privileges on weekends, and also more money to spend. All cadets were paid $600 per year—$709.50 including rations—and from this was deducted most of the cost of their meals plus their uniforms, room furniture, textbooks, athletic gear, and other items—the Army picked up the tab for building maintenance and utilities. Most of the remainder was deposited into a savings account that was presented to the cadet upon graduation. This windfall was necessary because it went mostly towards the cost of buying a full complement of officer uniforms. A small stipend was given to cadets

The West Point and the Class of 1915 shields, samples of Harmon's art talent, found in his 1915 scrapbook.

each month for purchases in the Cadet Store—toiletries, stationery or other personal items. This stipend was increased during the first-class year. Cadets were prohibited from receiving money or any other supplies from outside sources.[59] In this sense, West Point was an egalitarian society; a man's family wealth and background meant little inside cadet walls simply because it was not permitted to play a role. All cadets were theoretically equal, and as President Theodore Roosevelt phrased it: "And of all the institutions in the country, none is more absolutely American; none more absolutely democratic than this. Here we care nothing for the boy's birthplace, nor his creed, nor his social standing."[60]

During his senior year, Harmon took civil and military engineering, ordnance and the science of gunnery, law, Spanish (his worst class, ranking 153 out of 168), drill regulations, and practical military engineering—where he did quite well, finishing sixth in the class. His military performance remained dismal; he finished his final year ranked 160 out of 168, garnering an impressive 154 demerits—fourth in his class! His infractions this year remained largely the same as those for all four years—he was late, his room and uniform were dirty or items were out of place, he was dinged for "not standing still in parade formation," and, ominously, for "combining with other cadets for the purpose of raising sums of money to wager on outcome of Army-Navy game."[61]

It was athletics that Doodle enjoyed most as a cadet. Despite his diminutive size, Harmon played football, baseball, hockey and tennis. He was most proud of his football experience, playing backup quarterback on an outstanding Army team that went undefeated during both his junior and senior years.[62] One story has it that on one play Harmon attempted a quarterback sneak by diving over the top of his offensive line. Unfortunately, an opposing lineman caught him in midair and held him there until the whistle blew.[63] The highlight of each year was the Navy game—there were no post-season bowl games back then. *The Howitzer*, the cadet yearbook, devoted four pages to the 20-0 victory over the midshipmen during his senior year. The same was true for baseball—with five pages devoted to the 8–2 win over Navy. Harmon won the coveted "A" for his sweater, one of only fourteen men in his class to do so. Of importance, two of his football teammates and fellow letter-winners were Dwight Eisenhower and Omar Bradley—Bradley also lettered in baseball.[64]

As for military training, after plebe year the upperclassmen participated in an encampment on the grounds at West Point each summer where they not only helped train the new class of plebes, but also learned progressively more about the

Army's combat branches—Infantry, Cavalry, Field and Coastal Artillery, and Signals. Maneuvers and exercises became increasingly more complex as the cadets grew in rank and experience. In addition, more advanced stages of "equitation" (horseback riding) were included, with seniors learning the fine points of polo— a social activity for peacetime Army officers not dissimilar to the role played by golf in later generations. In truth, these encampments seemed a far cry from the real thing, and several years later Douglas MacArthur derided them as "a ludicrous caricature of life in the field," and he would move them to Fort Dix in New Jersey, where cadets could witness and participate with active-duty officers and non-commissioned officers in the use and employment of actual field and coastal artillery, cavalry units, aviation, and infantry maneuvers. Surprisingly, MacArthur encountered strong resistance to this seemingly logical reform.[65] Faculty, staff and even the cadets themselves resented the move off Academy grounds—and they resented it for interesting and not completely illogical reasons.

Besides being a training period, summers at West Point also inaugurated the cadet social season. During the academic year cadets seldom received approval to leave Academy grounds. Given that classes lasted six days per week and newspapers were not readily available, cadet life was astonishingly boring—staying busy with endless drill and parades kept cadets out of mischief. Thus, when the summer finally arrived, the opportunities to meet women at cadet dances and outdoor concerts and engage in the mating rituals along Flirtation Walk were a much-needed and important diversion and socializing experience. Removing the Cadet Battalion to Fort Dix severely curtailed these romantic activities.[66]

The heart of this summertime social process was the thrice-weekly cadet "hop" when women would be brought on-post from the local area. Many of these young ladies were the daughters, nieces, sisters and friends of faculty and staff members—which is why they also opposed the removal of the traditional encampments. Doodle Harmon was particularly keen about this activity. He was a "Hop Manager" during his senior year, which meant he helped arrange these popular events. He was also a member of the "Spoonoid Club," an unofficial group of ten cadets who fancied themselves lotharios. *The Howitzer* defined the term spoonoid as follows: "A bear with ladies; a social whirlwind who constitutes himself a committee of one to show off the library to every femme who visits the post."[67] The root word of course is "spoon," a now-archaic verb that referred to "amorous behavior, such as kissing and caressing." Doodle and his ilk had no desire to head off to an Army post each summer in order to spend even more time hanging around with men!

Harmon was also a member of the yearbook staff as an artist. His drawings, both architectural and cartoons, can be seen throughout the 1915 *Howitzer* as well as the creative and attractive "Hop Cards" used for the dances. Finally, and not insignificantly, Harmon was an "Expert" rifleman, one of only twenty-one in his class. This was a distinction, along with the Army "A" on his sweater, of which he was enormously proud.

This four-year period was one of the most important and formative of Hubert Harmon's life. The unique, monastic seclusion of the Military Academy meant that Harmon was forced to communicate and relate to his classmates, as well as superiors and subordinates, on a daily basis. One of his classmates noted that the constant contact with classmates forged unbreakable bonds that lasted a lifetime.[68] As a consequence, Academy graduates shared a common and indelible experience, one that shaped their personalities and characters for life. West Point inculcated beliefs, opinions and values—albeit not always good ones or those officially fostered by the Army—that would stick with these men for decades. In one sense, Harmon and his classmates were fortunate. The reforms that swept through the Army in the aftermath of the Spanish-American War were dramatic. Change also drifted out to the Military Academy. Although not revolutionary in scope or vision, there were nonetheless significant improvements in the military and educational systems, and, not a small point, the Academy itself underwent a significant and beautiful transformation as new construction changed the face of West Point.

Harmon's class, the Class of 1915, was one of the most illustrious in West Point history. It was later termed "the class that stars fell on" because so many of its members eventually rose to general officer. There were two five-stars—Eisenhower and Bradley, both of whom were also athletic teammates of Harmon; two four-stars—James Van Fleet and Joseph McNarney; and seven others who reached three-star rank: Henry Aurand, Tom Larkin, George Stratemeyer, Joseph Swing, Stafford Irwin, and Hubert Harmon. (McNarney and Stratemeyer would also become airmen; Van Fleet and Larkin were football teammates.) All together, sixty members of the 1915 class of 164 wore stars—an impressive achievement.

Harmon himself clearly enjoyed the cadet experience, despite not doing all that well during his four years either academically or militarily. Except for military engineering and drawing, at which he excelled and which may have contributed to his life-long nickname, Harmon did poorly in almost all of his classes. Militarily, he was similarly well below average, garnering an unusually large number of demerits each year. To his credit, most of his infractions were trivial. Even so, Harmon managed to go through his entire cadet career without ever achieving rank. He never wore chevrons—not even as a corporal—and was thus known as a "clean sleeve"—a buck private for all four years. On the face of it, this is a remarkable underachievement. Yet, it is also a notable coincidence—and not altogether comforting—that three other cadets who were destined for great careers as airmen were also "clean sleeves": Hap Arnold, "Tooey" Spaatz, and Hoyt Vandenberg—the first three commanders of the modern US Air Force. Perhaps Harmon was correct when he later commented that those who graduated in the middle of their class were "well rounded."

Through it all, Harmon maintained a delightful disposition and sense of humor, due partly to his innately affable and optimistic personality, and partly to athletics that served as a pressure valve, relieving much of the frustration that came with the dreary cadet existence. He was held in affection by most of his classmates throughout his life. *The Howitzer* refers to his infectious sense of humor by noting that upon turning twenty-one during his third-class year, he awoke and yelled to his roommate: "Wake up, Buddy, there's a *man* in the room!"[69] There was indeed.

One anecdote, recalled by a classmate, refers to Harmon's sense of humor, but also his notoriety for tardiness. During his second-class year, Harmon served as the "D" company clerk and was responsible for preparing the payroll report and muster roll each month. As the deadline approached, the company first sergeant, his classmate Jake Meneely, would begin pestering Doodle for the reports. Harmon would put him off day after day. Finally, in exasperation, Meneely would burst into his room and scream, "Doodle, where the hell is that payroll?!" Our man would smile sweetly and calmly reply that he would have it to him "by the crack of dawn" the following day. The man telling the story, Hume Peabody (who was Meneely's roommate), was convinced that Harmon's dilatory habits were part real—although he never turned the reports in late—and part mischief: he loved to see Jake work himself into a dither.[70]

Another story told by a classmate even more effectively sums the man. Harmon and seven of his friends had rooms close together on the third floor of the South Barracks. They referred to themselves as "the squirrels." One of this cohort, Ed McGuire, lived in New York City and invited the others to spend Christmas

leave at his home. In order to enjoy leave, a cadet needed
not only to be academically proficient, but also had
to be below a certain number of demerits. Doodle
was within ten demerits of the limit; if he was
gigged for a serious infraction, he would have to
remain in the barracks over the holidays. One
day in mid-December one of the eight, John
Wogan, was serving as Cadet Officer of the Day.
In this capacity, he was honor-bound to report
all breaches of discipline witnessed at the noon
formation. His good friend, Doodle, went past him
and uttered an obscenity—"Wog, God damn, I hope
I make that Christmas leave." Profanity was a
reportable offense—worth ten demerits—and
Wogan of course heard it. Later that evening

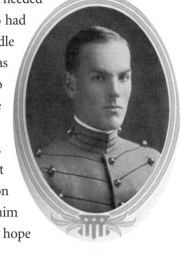

*Hubert R. Harmon as a West Point
graduate in 1915.*

Harmon asked his compatriot if he had reported him for his infraction. Wogan
said that he had. Harmon replied, "That's all I wanted to know. If you hadn't, I
wouldn't speak to you again."[71] This strong sense of integrity would also remain
with Harmon throughout his life, and it too would be a character trait for which
he was known and respected.

The speaker at Harmon's graduation exercises on June 11, 1915, was Secretary of War Lindley M. Garrison. In a short but memorable address, Garrison
spoke of the importance of tradition, especially as it applied to the men of West
Point. Men, he said, learn things by education, through an intellectual process; but, they also learn things that have been imbibed through tradition. The
knowledge coming from tradition, if it takes root, becomes like instinct and it
is of vast importance in our lives. This is so because it is during times of crisis,
when there is no time to deliberate a course of action, that the instinct formed
by tradition unconsciously guides our actions. As officers in the US Army, concluded the secretary, you have been give a higher trust than most, the traditions
of duty and service that you have absorbed must now be your pole-star.[72]

The traditions of West Point were indeed absorbed by Cadet Harmon,
and he would endeavor to pass on those life-guiding principles when he led the
Air Force Academy four decades later.

CHAPTER 2

The Young Officer

A cadet's order of merit at the time of graduation determined which branch of the Army he would enter: cadets selected in rank order. At number 103 of 164, Hubert Harmon's options were limited. In his cadet records is a notation stating that whichever branch he selected, "he should be assigned to an organization under a strict commanding officer."[1] Clearly, Harmon was viewed as having some maturity issues. Traditionally, the top cadets invariably chose the Corps of Engineers. In Harmon's class, the first nineteen cadets and twenty-three of the top twenty-five selected the Engineers. The Field Artillery went next, followed by the Coast Artillery and then the Cavalry; the Infantry brought up the rear. In fact, the last twelve men in the class had no choice—the Infantry was the only branch remaining. Harmon wished to follow in his father's footsteps and listed his preferences as Coast Artillery, Field Artillery and Infantry. He received Coast Artillery.

After three months of graduation leave, Second Lieutenant Harmon reported to Fort Monroe, Virginia, for coastal artillery school. He was joined by several of his classmates, and Harmon later recalled that all bought bicycles, "and it was an inspiring sight full of charm and solemn pathos, to see us twenty little shave-tails, resplendent in our new uniforms, the light glancing from our pink puttees, peddling up the street in a column of fours to Mess."[2] His commander noted that he was excellent in drilling and handling enlisted men, that he had a facility for drawing, was a very good horseman, and an excellent marksman.[3] Harmon completed school in late November, in time to hurry up to New York City to attend the Army-Navy football game.

From there, Harmon reported on 4 December 1915 to his first operational assignment—the five coastal gun batteries at Fort Andrews. Located on a rocky patch of ground (Peddocks Island) in Boston Harbor, this was not a particularly desirable place to be in the middle of a New England winter. The young lieutenant recalled that his "most stirring duty" was to "inspect each morning the breech-blocks of a couple of six-inch cannings to ascertain that no German soldier had come and pocketed them during the night." It was so bitterly cold that winter, his hands often stuck to the guns.[4]

There was, however, something else to be remembered about this assignment that affected him. He shared quarters with the post commander, Lieutenant Colonel William Chamberlaine, who insisted that they put on their dress blue uniforms when sitting down to dinner each night. The colonel would then put on the phonograph and play classical records. This sense of dignity and elegance struck Harmon deeply; he would witness such conduct again in England, and it would move him.[5]

He performed his duties as part of a 12" mortar company and as adjutant at Fort Andrews successfully. Again, his supervisor called attention to his skill at drawing and in drilling enlisted troops. Colonel Chamberlaine concluded his evaluation: "This is a capable, intelligent and active young officer, who lacks experience, and in some degree a sense of responsibility."[6] Not an untypical report for a new second lieutenant.

At this point in his young career as an Army officer, Harmon was not enamored with his position or his duties. In May 1916, his skill in the drilling and handling of men was required elsewhere. He received orders of an unusual nature, and it was during this four-month period in upstate New York that he made a momentous decision.

In 1913 General Leonard Wood, Army chief of staff, conceived the idea of a training camp where young men would learn the rudiments of military service. The nation was at peace, but Wood believed that it was the responsibility of all able-bodied American males to acquaint themselves with the military so that in the event of a crisis there would be a pool of officer material available for mobilization. To those who accused him of attempting to militarize American society, Wood responded that his intent was precisely the opposite. He wanted to civilianize the military by ensuring that if war broke out and the Army expanded, knowledgeable and well-educated civilians—who also understood military fundamentals—would form the heart of the officer corps. It is important to note that Wood's emphasis was on the training of future officers—not enlisted men. He did not want the camps to engage in basic training for the masses—he therefore targeted college students and businessmen.[7]

The first camps were held in 1915, and initially this strictly volunteer program was for college students. The students had to provide their own transportation to and from the camp, and they also had to pay for their food and uniforms—$27.50. In 1916, businessmen under the age of 45 were also included in the program. Under pressure from the US Chamber of Commerce, many employers agreed to grant these men a month's leave of absence "without prejudice to their advancement and without loss of salary."[8] Wood's idea of camps, which soon spread nationwide, came to be known as "The Plattsburg Movement," named after the largest camp located in Plattsburg, New York, about 150 miles north of Albany on Lake Champlain. Hundreds of men, some of them quite distinguished and including the mayor of New York City and two sons of Theodore Roosevelt, attended the four-week encampment. At the camp in California, the commandant exclaimed: "I saw more Rolls-Royces and other fine cars around there then I have ever seen collected."[9] In 1916 the number of men flocking to the camps quadrupled, with over 16,000 attending the camps nationwide. The numbers grew even larger in the war years that followed.

In May 1916, Second Lieutenant Harmon was detailed to Plattsburg to serve as an instructor—he was promoted to First Lieutenant on 1 July and served as the assistant adjutant to the camp commander. West Point graduates were the obvious choice for such duties—six of Harmon's classmates joined him at Plattsburg. They had been extensively trained in drill, the use of firearms and camp life, and they had also spent their years as cadet upperclassmen teaching these skills to plebes. Moreover, as graduates of prestigious West Point, they were able to deal with the highly literate and in some cases wealthy volunteers who flocked to Plattsburg. In Harmon's case, he had also displayed a facility for such activities in his assignments in the Coast Artillery.

The classes that Harmon trained ranged in size from 1,387 to 3,281 volunteers, divided into companies of around 150 to 200 men each. One regular officer was assigned to each company. Whether college students or businessmen—termed "juniors" and "seniors" respectively—the basic routine was much the same.[10] Bugle sounded reveille at 0545 and all turned out for calisthenics, followed by breakfast. Lieutenant Harmon and his officer colleagues then spent the rest of the morning instructing their charges in setting-up exercises, close and extended-order drill, manual of arms, care and use of regular

Army rifles, target practice, personal and camp hygiene, use of the shelter tent, and elements of tactics. After lunch there were tactical exercises, discussions of the organization of the Army and its various branches, athletics, and recreation activities. After dinner, the men were generally left to themselves.[11] An exception to this schedule was at Plattsburg where General Wood liked to visit. He came up to the camp frequently after dinner to sit by a campfire near the lake and talk to those gathered around about military history, campaigning, and famous military leaders.[12]

The highlight of the camp experience was the hike. For the final week or so, all volunteers loaded up with 30 lb. backpacks and began to march, covering as much as fifteen miles each day. Along the way, the "army" engaged in maneuvers: "cemeteries were stormed and farmhouses captured."[13] The volunteers clearly appreciated the entire experience—numbers bloomed. Somewhat surprisingly, the biggest complaint registered about the camps initially was that "the discipline was not sufficiently rigorous." The officers had been reluctant to lean too heavily on these volunteers, especially the older businessmen. Later camps were more strict.[14]

When the United States went to war in April 1917, the camps expanded to ninety days in duration. In essence, the Plattsburg Camps became the origin of Officer Candidate School; upon completion of the three-month course, men received commissions and were inducted into the vastly expanding US Army. By June 1918, over 57,000 camp graduates were commissioned into the Army.[15]

Harmon enjoyed the experience and received a letter of commendation for his efforts from General Wood. More importantly, while in Plattsburg he also made a big decision—he transferred out of the Coast Artillery. He received a letter from Miff, by then a pilot in the air service, who wrote his younger brother that he too should join the Signal Corps and win his wings. As he phrased it, Hubert should transfer to the only branch in the Army that had a future. Hubert seldom ignored his brother's advice.[16]

Winning Wings

Orville and Wilbur Wright had made their first flight on December 17, 1903, at Kitty Hawk, North Carolina. After three more flights that day a heavy gust of wind blew the airplane over and damaged it severely. The brothers packed up their things and the pieces of their air machine and headed back to Dayton, Ohio.[17] For more than a year they labored in secrecy, fearful that their design would be stolen by other nascent aviation engineers. In January 1905 they offered their "Flyer" to the Army, but were ignored. They offered again in October, but the Army was still not interested. In frustration, the brothers began discussing their invention with the French and Germans.

If the brothers' intention was to apply pressure on the US Army to revisit their suggestion, they were successful. The Army issued a specification in December 1907 for an air machine. Although there were several dozen responses, the Wright brothers were the only serious contenders.[18] In August 1908 the brothers brought their airplane to Fort Myer on the Virginia side of the Potomac River across from Washington DC. Flying trials began on 3 September and all went well for the first two weeks, but then disaster struck. On 17 September Orville Wright took off with First Lieutenant Thomas E. Selfridge as his passenger. While flying at around 100 feet, the right propeller cracked, throwing the engine out of balance. The resulting vibration loosened the engine mounts, which then moved the propeller just enough to strike and cut a guy wire bracing the rudder. The rudder shifted severely and Orville lost control; the plane crashed. Selfridge was killed and Orville was seriously injured.[19]

The Wrights returned to Fort Myer the following July with a better design. This time the trials went smoothly, and the US Army bought its first airplane.

Now the Army needed some pilots and a place to train them. The Signal Corps, the branch under which aviation was then located, considered several sites, but few had the requisite environmental conditions that would allow training in the temperamental aircraft of that day. Initially, the Signal Corps established its one training airdrome at College Park, Maryland. The first three Army pilots taught by the Wrights at College Park were Frank Lahm, Frederic Humphreys, and Benjamin Foulois. Not long after, Hap Arnold and Thomas Milling learned how to fly from the Wrights at their home base in Dayton, Ohio.[20]

In 1913 the Signal Corps' training facility moved to a location with better weather, North Island—a sandy islet four miles long and two miles wide in San Diego Bay. In early 1913 there was nothing much on the island except thousands of jack rabbits. Initially, officers assigned to the school stayed in San Diego while enlisted men boarded at Fort Rosecrans. All then reached the island via motor boat or ferry. The island did not receive electricity from the mainland, but it was supplied to selected buildings by portable generators.[21] North Island (later named Rockwell Field) was where another pioneer aviator,

Glenn Curtiss, had first set up his business. Curtiss aircraft, which employed directional controls far superior to those of the Wright planes, soon became dominant within the Signal Corps. In fact, the Wrights' method of "wing-warping" was quickly supplanted worldwide by the far more practical aileron system used by Curtiss.

Army pilots at the Curtiss airfield, officially termed the Signal Corps Aviation School, first learned how the airplane and its engine were built, for the imminently practical reason that they malfunctioned so frequently a thorough grounding in mechanics and aerodynamics was essential. As for learning to fly the planes themselves, training progressed from taxiing, to short hops, to gradually higher, faster and more complex air maneuvers. Due to the extremely small numbers of Army officers chosen for flight duty, it was not until 1915 that the Army published the first regulations governing the administration of the flying school. Some of these rules are illuminating:

- Dogs without collars or muzzles will be shot.
- Horses will be tied on the picket line provided for mounts and not to trees, fences, water pipes or buildings.
- Officers are required to spend at least six hours per week on professional study or reading.
- Don't enter this branch of the Army lured by hopes of increased pay.
- If you hate work, don't take up aviation.
- If you expect to be married soon or are in love, don't take up aviation.[22]

Those who were not deterred proceeded with flight training. Soon, procedures and aircraft became more standardized, and the remaining Wright models were phased out as being too dangerous to fly.[23] In the summer of 1915, the Aviation School purchased its first Curtiss JN series aircraft, a plane that would soon evolve into the JN-4 "Jenny," the finest training aircraft in the country through the end of the World War. In fact, Curtiss sold more than 6,000 of these wonderful planes to the US and Britain.[24]

It was at North Island that Miff Harmon learned to fly in 1916. Other airmen, who would later become famous and were there at the same time, included Hap Arnold, Carl Spaatz, Frank Lahm (the Army's first pilot), George Brett, Ralph Royce, and Jack Curry.[25] All of these men would play significant roles in Hubert Harmon's career. It was also here that Miff wrote his younger brother to come join him and become a pilot.

When First Lieutenant Hubert Harmon received the letter suggesting he transfer to the Aviation Section of the Signal Corps, Army airpower was still in its infancy. Congress had authorized a total of 60 officers and 260 enlisted men, but the numbers actually in the Aviation Section did not approach those figures. There were reasons for these shortages: only volunteers were sent to the risky business of learning to be a pilot. In addition, there was as yet no career path established in the Army for aviators. This meant that volunteers had to apply to their branches for a transfer, but such a transfer was only temporary. Officers would be detailed to the Signal Corps for flight training, but Army rules stated that after four years they would be returned to their original branches. Even so, personnel officers at these branches, which were under-strength themselves, were reluctant to let their people go, even temporarily. The result was a chronically undermanned Army air arm. In his annual report to the secretary of war, the chief of the Signal Corps' Aviation Section, Colonel George Squier, wrote that on July 1, 1916, there were twenty-three pilots in the Army with twenty-six more under instruction. One year later the number of pilots had jumped to ninety-two.[26] This was a pitiful situation for the nation that had invented the airplane, but America's entry into the World War would soon change things.

Regrettably, Harmon's flight records from his training at North Island have been lost. We know that he arrived at the airfield on December 8, 1916, after a long drive across the country. To most people, the flying field locale would have appeared unimpressive. One contemporary related how he arrived at North Island to find "little to match my visions of a military aerodrome— just a few wooden hangars alongside the dusty field and some airplanes lined up in front of a crude operations office, where men in flying gear were lounging on benches in the shade."[27] No matter, to Harmon it must have looked magical. There were a number of old friends at the Aviation School during his five months there, including some twenty-five of his West Point classmates— there were fifty-one students at North Island at the time. Especially welcome sights were buddies Tom Hanley, Bill Boots, Hume Peabody, Sammy Cousins and Earl Naiden. Peabody later noted that the "washout" rate for student pilots was quite low—if you survived the training you won your wings![28]

As Harmon later remembered it, just prior to his arrival a visiting dignitary had been taken up for an orientation flight. The plane and its occupants soon disappeared, generating an extensive search. The result was that Harmon arrived for flying training just as most of the other students—those who possessed automobiles—were sent off on search parties. He therefore was able to get more training and more personalized attention than was normally the case.[29] In truth, there was more involved here than young Harmon had known. The visitor who had gone missing was Lieutenant Colonel H.G. Bishop from the Field Officers' School—a program designed to give senior ground officers an introduction to the flying business. Bishop and the pilot, Lieutenant W.A. Robertson, went down in Baja, Mexico. In one observer's judicious phrasing: "either due to a defective compass or not being furnished with proper maps on starting, the pilot got off course."[30] In other words, he was lost. The men were found nine days later. The problem: the flight school's commander, Colonel William Glassford—who was not a flyer—had delayed initiating search operations for four days, causing several instructors at North Island to become openly rebellious. As a result of the investigation that followed, Glassford was relieved, but several of the young pilots who had been most vocal about his dilatory actions were reassigned as well.[31] One of these young Turks was Hap Arnold. It was the first meeting between the future commanding general of the Army Air Forces and Hubert Harmon, but it would not be the last.

For personnel at North Island, the day began before dawn, so as to get the planes airborne at first light before winds and turbulence began to pick up. Flying usually occurred only in the morning; afternoons were reserved for airplane inspections and maintenance, and ground school. Instruction was given by both military pilots and civilians, due to the shortage of uniformed instructors. This training generally included forty to fifty hours of flying time over a period of several months. In ground school the student pilots learned about aerodynamics, engines, meteorology, map reading, and flight characteristics. The flights themselves grew increasingly more challenging and included stalls, spins and aerobatics. The curriculum also included cross-country flights—an exercise more sporting than it would ordinarily seem. There were no aeronautical charts available yet, nor were there weather stations, navigation aids or ground-to-air radios. Instrument flying had not yet been invented, so if a pilot inadvertently—or foolishly—entered clouds, he would usually be in trouble. Given the rudimentary nature of the existing "Jennies," even moderately windy or gusty conditions could play havoc with a pilot's directional control.[32]

Accidents in these early aircraft were frequent, and becoming disoriented while in flight—things certainly looked different from the air—was common. Stories of early aviators flying low enough to read street signs in towns below so as to determine their location were not completely apocryphal. In fact, Harmon later related that as a member of the 5th Aero Squadron at Kelly Field in 1918, he prepared for a cross-country flight with Carl Spaatz—then his squadron operations officer and later the first chief of staff of the US Air Force. The two prepared using Rand-McNally road maps. However, when Spaatz copied the directions for Harmon he omitted one of the key checkpoints—a railroad crossing. Harmon became—as pilots like to term it—"temporarily disoriented" when his view of the ground did not agree with his directions. He landed in a field when his gas finally ran low. Townspeople gathered to see the "flying machine"—this was 1918 and such sights were still extraordinary. Harmon needed gasoline but was broke. No problem: the obliging people passed the hat around to buy the young aviator his fuel. When Harmon later told the story he would say that folks were so generous he got a full fuel tank plus $100 for his pocket.[33]

Instruction in the actual tactical employment of aircraft—how to use airplanes in conjunction with ground forces—was barely discussed at this early stage. To learn how to actually employ aircraft in a military operation, pilots would need to continue training at their operational unit.[34]

Amazingly, despite the fact that aircraft had been used in Europe for the previous three years in a variety of combat roles including strategic bombardment, interdiction, close air support and air superiority, the US Army had no plans to use its own air arm in such activities. To ground officers, airplanes were to be used solely for reconnaissance—hence their placement in the Signal Corps—and that was that.[35]

Despite such organizational myopia, Army pilots were well aware of combat reports from Europe. Yet, there was little that could be done to train for war—the Army would not even acknowledge the growing roles of combat aviation, much less allocate the money and resources to begin realistic combat training. When the United States entered the war in April 1917, there was still only one regular Army flying school, at North Island, and the number of pilots and aircraft was pitifully small—perhaps 100 pilots scattered throughout the Army and around the same number of aircraft. None of these aircraft were suitable for combat. The US had fallen a long way from December 1903 when heavier-than-air flight had been born on the sands at Kitty Hawk.[36]

Upon completion of pilot training, Harmon took the test for his FAI Certificate (Fédération Aéronautique Internationale), which was standard for all US Army pilots. It included both a written and flight-test portion. Harmon passed both and received his FAI certificate, number 717, on May 9, 1917. He was the 149th Army pilot to complete training. With new wings sewn to his tunic, he left San Diego for Texas.

Staff and Command

In April 1917 the US entered the war, and a rapid expansion of the Army and its air arm, soon to be termed the Air Service, began. Harmon would remain in Texas for eighteen months, serving initially at the new Kelly Field near San Antonio as the commandant of the Ground Officers' Training School and president of the Air Service Examining Board. In December 1917 he was transferred to Fort Sam Houston, also in San Antonio, and was appointed Aeronautical Officer of the Army's Southern Department. In February 1918 he returned to Kelly as the engineer officer.[37]

Harmon's performance during this period was not all that impressive. He was a young man as well as a young officer, and the old charge that the time spent at West Point did not eliminate youthful mistakes in judgment but merely deferred them to a later date, seems to be true in this case. Hubert's wife would later recall, for example, that when reminiscing about his time in Texas, his thoughts would most often stray to the lovely ladies of San Antonio.[38] His superiors apparently noticed this tendency at the time as well. Brigadier General John

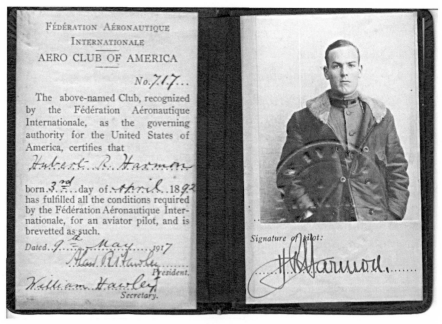

The F.A.I. (flight license) of 1Lt Hubert Harmon in May 1917.

W. Ruckman noted on Harmon's efficiency report that he "apparently has not yet found himself" but continued, hopefully, that "he will rise above the poor judgment he showed in allowing himself to be influenced by bad influences." In the block where the rating official is asked if he would desire to have him in his command in the future, Ruckman wrote tellingly: "not especially." Over the next two months while at Kelly Field, Harmon's performance improved a bit, although his new commander noted that he "does his best when pushed."[39]

Ruckman's report was the tip of the iceberg. In fact, Harmon had received an "adverse report" written by his immediate supervisor the previous month concerning his duties as the engineer officer. This report stated Harmon was "very inefficient; takes no interest whatever in his work, very seldom ever find him around the hangars or machine shops." This lack of involvement led to an extremely poor maintenance record. The supervisor wrote that when he visited the shops he found aircraft grounded with only minor problems that could have been repaired in an hour—but which had not been looked at in days: "However, I don't think Major Harmon is aware of this for I don't think he came around and inspected the machines himself." The anonymous rating official (his name is not given in the documents) recommended that Harmon be relieved of his duties and transferred from Kelly Field. His final statement was a real knife-twister: "From what I can gather, his social standing is too high in San Antonio, Texas, to prove an efficient officer while he is stationed near that city."

Harmon was incandescent. Clearly, he saw this as a hatchet job, coming from a rival—either at Kelly Field or perhaps in San Antonio. He demanded a Court of Inquiry to establish the facts of the situation and to clear his name. In the meantime, he wrote down his side of the story: it was all an "unscrupulous lie and could not have been based on any reliable information or on conversations with anyone at this field in a position to know the truth." Harmon argued that there were twenty-five hangars and fifteen other buildings that he supervised, so it was quite possible that two persons could visit each one of them frequently and never see each other. In fact, he did visit each shop and every hangar at least daily; furthermore, the head of these divisions and shops visited his office for a conference each day. He noted that he rarely left the office before 1700 and on some occasions did not complete his work until three in the morning. One of the major problems, and one well known to all, was the acute shortage of spare parts, tools, and trained mechanics. Even so, Harmon defended himself against the charge of inefficiency by noting that of 190 engines turned in for repair the previous month, 176 had been fixed and returned to service. He provided other statistics on flying hours, overhaul hours, and in-commission rates to make his case.

As for the last shot regarding his social standing, Harmon contrived to take it as a compliment. He went on to outline his social calendar—which was hardly impressive—and concluded that his moral conduct had been "exemplary."

Harmon cited the Manual for Courts Martial to demand a Court of Inquiry to examine these baseless charges and to clear his name.

Cooler heads prevailed. Major Harvey Burwell, the officer in charge of flying at Kelly Field, wrote that Harmon was "one of the brightest and most capable officers of his rank in the Aviation Service." He had done great work in running the Ground Officers' Training School at Kelly—which was why he had been chosen for engineer officer. He took that position "at its most critical period," and Burwell confirmed Harmon's complaints regarding shortages of materiel and qualified personnel. He also confirmed that he personally saw Harmon in the shops every day, and that he was well aware of the magnitude of the unit's maintenance problems. As for alleged inefficiency, Burwell scoffed, stating that Harmon was "an admirable organizer" who was well-suited for this type of work. He concluded that the proximity of Kelly Field to San Antonio had "no effect whatsoever on Major Harmon's efficiency."

Major Jack Heard, the Kelly Field executive officer, concurred with Burwell, stating that the problems stemmed from Harmon's subordinates. Since these officers were replaced, "the Department has been developed wonderfully, the credit for it going to Major Harmon. I have entire confidence in him."

Given the supportive endorsements of Burwell and Heard, the commander (his signature is illegible on the document) elected to refuse Harmon's demand for a Court of Inquiry.[40] The offending efficiency report was removed from his record, and Harmon was transferred to Taliaferro Field near Hicks, Texas, to become the executive officer.

It appears the entire incident was a shock to Harmon. If there was any kernel of truth to the allegations that he was living a wild existence—and the efficiency report signed by Ruckman intimates that there was—the resulting dust-up as engineer officer caught his attention.[41]

After a brief stay at Taliaffero, Harmon was named the officer in charge of flying and training at Barron Field just south of Fort Worth, Texas, and in April was promoted to be the field's commander. Barron Field was a Primary

Flying Training base for the surge to generate pilots for France, and it was here where the young major began to find himself. His superior, a Marine Corps exchange officer, wrote that Harmon was "extremely capable" and had a head for details and sound organization. He concluded: "I consider him without exception the best officer in charge of flying that I have seen."[42]

This was Harmon's first command, and he relished the experience. As a young bachelor on a relatively isolated post he bonded quickly with his personnel. As the Air Service mobilized for war, there was a feeling among all of excitement and the realization that they were part of a Great Event. The flying was especially exciting. Fairly isolated from close supervision, pilots often did things neither sanctioned nor wise. For example, Harmon later related that when out flying with aviation pioneer Eddie Stinson, the barnstormer suddenly asked Harmon if he liked ice cream. Hubert said that he did. Stinson then abruptly dropped out of the sky, landed in a city park and taxied up to an ice cream stand.[43] Harmon remained at Barron Field until September. By that point he began to fear that the war and its glory were passing him by. He wrote Miff, who had recently returned to Washington from France, and pleaded with him to pull strings so he could be sent overseas. He received his wish.

Upon leaving Barron Field, his fellow officers presented their major with an engraved watch. Harmon was deeply moved and kept the watch with him for the rest of his life. He also stayed in touch with some of these officers for years, and when he returned to Texas for extended duty in World War II, he renewed these friendships. This had been an important interlude.[44]

Over There

Hubert had his wish; on 8 September 1918 he left Hoboken for France via England on the troop transport SS *Minekahda*. He was to fly pursuit aircraft—fighter planes—in France. Because he was a field grade officer, his accommodations were reasonably comfortable—given the nature of the ship and in comparison to the enlisted men packed like cattle on decks below. Even so, conditions on board were poor, and when Harmon arrived at St. Maixent on 29 September, he was a very sick man. During the ocean crossing he had come down with the flu.

The influenza pandemic of 1918 was the worst plague in history. Estimates of the numbers who died worldwide vary, but the lowest figure is 21 million; most sources say the toll was 50 million, with some estimates running as high as 100 million. In the United States—where the flu originated—there

were 675,000 fatalities. To put these numbers, already horrendous, in a modern perspective, given the current world population, a similar pandemic today
would kill 350 million people; in the US, the death toll would be nearly 3 million—and it would all occur in the period of a few months.

The influenza probably originated in Haskell County, Kansas—likely
originating in swine—and rapidly spread east where it hit the 56,000 Army
recruits at Camp Funston. From there it continued on to the troop ships that
carried the American Expeditionary Force to France. It then hit the trenches;
soon it had spread worldwide. In the US Army alone the Spanish Influenza
struck over one million men—26 percent of the army—killing 30,000 before
they ever got to Europe. All told, the flu killed over 48,000 US soldiers, sailors
and marines—50,280 more died in combat.[45]

Several aspects of this plague made it especially insidious, devastating,
and appalling. First, like all flu viruses, it mutated extremely rapidly—adapting,
growing stronger, more deadly, and more resistant to antibodies and medicines.
Second, it was contagious before symptoms appeared; thus, when the onset of
the disease became obvious, it was already too late to prevent its spread. Third, it
was one of the unique aspects of this particular influenza strain that it attacked
a person's immune system most viciously. This meant, paradoxically, that those
who had the strongest immune systems—the young and those who appeared
most fit—were often infected first and hit the hardest. Finally, it is now realized
but was not fully appreciated in 1918, that influenza almost invariably leads to
pneumonia. It was this pneumonia that was the true killer, and it was an unusually ghastly death: high fever of 103–104 degrees was closely followed by intense
muscle aches, delirium, profuse bleeding (from the nose and mouth), and suf-
focating chest congestion. It would usually kill its victim within twenty-four to
forty-eight hours.[46] If, however, the person survived these first two days—and if
there was not a subsequent relapse into pneumonia a month or so later, which
would also claim its victim very quickly—then the patient would live.[47] Even so,
the effects of the plague would usually linger for years if not for life.

The influenza hit its peak ferocity in fall 1918. Because of the crowded
nature of military camps where young men lived in huge compounds in close
proximity and with virtually no privacy, the disease spread like wildfire. When
it got aboard troop ships, it was even worse. When the symptoms first appeared
the transports were already at sea, the spaces even more confined—men shared
the same air, mess facilities and latrines, and touched the same tables, chairs

and handrails. Prevention and treatment were virtually impossible. Some of these troop transports became death ships.[48]

Harmon, who had had influenza as a child, fell sick aboard ship, but he made it through this first test and was sent to the hospital at St. Maixent. He was there for one month before being allowed to leave for the major aviation training base at Issoudun on 23 October. Experience had shown that American pilots arriving in France had been poorly trained. The obsolescent "Jennies" used to teach the rudiments of flight were inadequate to allow the new pilots to fly frontline combat aircraft. In most cases, arriving American flyers had to be re-trained in French methods and in French aircraft—most of the aircraft these men would fly in combat would be French designs.

Issoudun, located around 140 miles south of Paris, was usually referred to as "the largest mudhole in France" by those assigned there. Issoudun was actually a huge facility consisting of a dozen different airfields, 90 hangars, and 150 barracks. All American pilots arriving in France, regardless of their prior experience, had to attend the training school there before being sent to the Front. Students began with a small Morane aircraft with clipped wings that was used for taxi practice. Although seemingly elementary, the Morane was used because it, like the combat Nieuports to which the pilots were aspiring, had a rotary engine. This unique design—which was not used in the US—featured a stationary crankshaft around which the entire engine rotated—thus inducing a large amount of torque. To unsuspecting American pilots, the tendency was to ground-loop planes with rotary engines, which often broke their landing gear.

Pilots began at Field 1 and progressed through a series of more advanced flying areas. The length of stay at each field—the aircraft became increasingly more powerful and the flight maneuvers more complex—depended on the skill of the pilot. It was expected, however, that the average officer would need forty flying hours before his certification as a pursuit pilot ready for combat.[49] It should be noted that this was serious business. Pursuit planes, especially the temperamental French-built Nieuports, claimed many lives. The fatality rate for the Pursuit School at Issoudun was five times that of the schools for bombardment and observation pilots. Indeed, one out of nine pursuit pilots at Issoudun ended up in "Field 13"—the cemetery.[50]

At some point early in this process, Harmon reported for a check ride that would move him on to the next phase. Arriving at the flight line, his check pilot saw that Harmon looked miserable. Was the major all right? Did he really want to fly on such a cold and rainy morning? Of course he did. Harmon wanted to get the flight over with so he could move ahead, be certified, and sent into combat before the war ended. The men climbed into their cockpits. By the time they landed, Harmon was clearly in distress—although he had passed the check ride. He was immediately sent back to the hospital, and this time the diagnosis was even more severe—double pneumonia.

The hospital commander had seen this syndrome far too frequently in the previous few months—influenza followed by pneumonia—and he feared the worst. He was a friend of Kenneth Harmon, who was then stationed at an ordnance depot in southern France. He called Kenneth and told him the diagnosis: he did not expect Hubert to live and advised that he begin thinking about the disposition of his brother's remains. Kenneth jumped in an auto and rushed north, but arrived just as the crisis point had passed. Hubert awoke to puzzlement: what was his brother doing here?

Hubert remained in the hospital for another month and was then transferred to Nice on convalescent leave for three weeks. He was there when the war ended.[51]

This was a period of great disappointment for Harmon. He had wanted to serve in combat and prove his mettle, but bad luck and a bit of bad judgment—his decision to rush his recuperation—conspired against him. It was no doubt particularly frustrating because Harmon had always been a good athlete and was undoubtedly stunned to be felled by illness—twice. He, along with millions of others, did not yet understand the nature of the influenza plague that was then sweeping the world, and it was precisely men like him who were so often its victims.[52] For the rest of his career, efficiency reports written by superiors would often downgrade Harmon in the "physical energy and endurance" block. His health never really recovered from the near-fatal bouts with influenza and pneumonia in 1918; he suffered from severe cases of bronchitis once or twice each year for the rest of his life. Experience would show that flu/pneumonia survivors often suffered from weakened hearts, central nervous system disorders, and respiratory track infections for years thereafter.[53]

Upon release from the hospital, Harmon returned to Issoudun to complete his training and graduated from the Pursuit School in late December. After celebrating New Year's in Paris—the first in peacetime that France had enjoyed in four years—Harmon headed for Coblenz, Germany, as part of the American Occupation Forces.

Occupation Duty

The war ended on November 11, 1918, before Harmon had a chance to get into combat. He was not finished in Europe, however. Because of the clamor to return the boys home, there was devised a practical and reasonably fair system to ship back and demobilize personnel based largely on time already spent overseas or in combat. Harmon was low on the list, so he would spend the next two years in Europe, serving first in Coblenz, Germany, as part of the American occupation force, and then moving to England to help dispose of surplus property.

The relations among the Allies were strained before the Armistice. General John J. Pershing, commander of the American Expeditionary Force, fought to ensure that US forces remained as a separate entity with their own section of the Front—the British and French wanted to use the new and fresh American troops as replacements for their own severely depleted units. Pershing dryly noted that he was "decidedly against our becoming a recruiting agency of either the French or British."[54] Pershing's decision—backed by Washington—meant that American units and their commanders flooding into France were in sore need of more training. While they were thus engaged, the situation at the Front remained precarious. The French believed, not without justification, that had Pershing not been so stubborn, the American doughboys could have easily been assimilated into already existing units where their training could have been handled much faster by the veterans serving next to them. Combat effectiveness for the entire Allied force would thus have been enhanced. But, as always, political considerations play major roles in war; the American people wanted a separate American Army.[55]

As American strength grew and the new troops took their place in the front lines, the Germans were inexorably pushed back. By the early fall of 1918 it seemed apparent that the tide had turned. At that point, the issue of a postwar settlement began to receive serious discussion among the Allies. Once again, however, they were sharply divided. The British, Belgians, Italians and French—and especially the last—were in the mood for harsh conditions. After four arduous years, France had no mind to go easy on Germany. The US, which had not had the war fought on its own soil or lost a generation of men in the trenches, spoke instead of reconciliation and lofty "principles." France wanted the Rhineland—the huge area east of the Rhine River and up to the traditional French border—separated permanently from Germany. They wanted a buffer zone so a future invasion of France would not be so easy. (Germany had invaded France in 1870 and 1914—they would do so again in 1940.) The US objected. The compromise reached was a demilitarization of this area, with an Allied army of occupation stationed there for a number of years—perhaps as many as fifteen—to ensure among other things that the Germans made their required reparations payments, and they would be unable to launch a surprise attack into France.[56]

On 18 November, one week after the Armistice went into effect, 750,000 Allied troops under the command of Marshal Ferdinand Foch entered German territory. The US part of that force, around 240,000 men, was allocated the 2,500 square-mile territory centered on the city of Coblenz, located at the confluence of the Rhine and Mosel Rivers. The approximately 900,000 Germans who lived in the American sector were understandably apprehensive at first— as were the American troops. Wartime propaganda had led both sides to expect the worst from each other.[57] All were pleasantly surprised.

The passivity of the German populace meant that US occupation forces could let down their guard. In one sense, this made the job of the officers more difficult. As the American commander, Major General Henry T. Allen noted, allowing "fraternization" between the soldiers and the German women resulted in "a striking increase in the venereal disease rate among the troops." Commanders devised other activities to keep the troops busy. There was the usual endless drill, cleaning and exercises, but there was also an effort to organize athletic events. Allen was especially supportive of the athletics initiative, believing it led to increased discipline and "contentment of the men."[58]

Not all was boredom and play. There were also regulations and Armistice stipulations that needed to be enforced. Germany was required to make not only heavy reparations payments to the Allies—in gold—but also to turn over vast stocks of war goods and other industrial materials.[59] At the beginning of the occupation there was still concern that a war party in Berlin might attempt to re-start the fighting after having had a breather. The occupation and disarmament of the Rhineland were major steps in preventing the renewal of hostilities. Collecting the required material was not, however, always easy. Some hardcore elements attempted to hide weapons and industrial machinery for future use. Moreover, the rules also stipulated that the arms and equipment turned over were to be in good working order. This was often not the case. The Germans protested, not without some validity, that after four years of war, *nothing* was in good working order any longer. And so, compromises were reached. The Armistice had called for the surrender of 2,000 aircraft, including the highly praised Fokker D.VII pursuit planes and the heavy night bombers that had so troubled England. In the event, many of these aircraft were not forthcoming—in many cases the Germans had simply destroyed them. Instead, the Allies accepted twenty draught horses in exchange for every airplane not surrendered.[60]

Harmon joined the US Third Army in the Rhineland in January 1919 after recovering from his bouts with influenza and pneumonia. His title, chief of staff of Air Service Command headquartered at Coblenz, was by his own admission, grander sounding than was actually the case. He later wrote that he had a "glorious time" in Germany, running into many old friends and drinking a great deal of wine.[61] His wife later recalled that the only thing she heard him talk about regarding that period was the magnificent officers' club at Coblenz with its lighted fountain out front—the site no doubt of those epic drinking parties. The city itself was in remarkably good condition with business as usual, cafes open, and opera or symphony every night.[62] In addition, it also appears that Hubert was busy in other activities. He gave his West Point class ring to a female telephone operator, an American, whom he met in the officers' club. She said she just wanted to wear it for the evening; it was never returned.[63]

Major Harmon did a bit more than this, and he did it fairly well. His main duties involved securing and disposing of excess property, and, presumably, getting hold of the German aircraft demanded by the Armistice agreement. The procedure was for the Germans to deliver the required airplanes to the airdrome south of Coblenz. There they would be uncrated and assembled by German mechanics under the watchful eye of American officers like Harmon. After assembly, German pilots would give the planes a test flight, again under the supervision of American pilots. If the plane had no serious deficiencies, it was accepted. Of the 200 planes accepted at Coblenz, over half were Fokker D.VIIs, most of them fresh from the factory. Other planes received were an assortment of used Rolands, Albatrosses, Pfalzes, and Halberstadts.[64]

It is also probable that Harmon was active in setting up the athletic program and drilling the troops—activities that he performed not only at West Point but also during his months at Plattsburg in 1916.[65] His commander thought that he performed his duties "in a very satisfactory manner." He was rated "above average" in all categories but one—an "average" check in the "physical energy and endurance" block. A follow-up evaluation three months later was largely the same.[66]

It is significant that Harmon's performance as a staff officer and administrator were lauded by his superiors. The serious deficiencies in these areas, especially among airmen, had been frequently noted during the war. These problems were magnified in Germany when officers had to engage with the Germans. The official Army history of the occupation noted this shortcoming: "It is extremely unfortunate that the qualifications necessary for a civil administration are not developed among officers in times of peace."[67] Harmon's abilities in this area were important.

In January 1920, Harmon moved from Coblenz to London where he worked in the area of surplus war equipment. During the war a mountain of materiel had been shipped to Britain for American use. Regarding aviation gear, these supplies included not only aircraft and engines, but also armaments, ammunition, airplane instruments, and spare parts. Some of this equipment was sold, but in truth, the Allies had their own surplus stocks to dispose of, and the goods offered for sale by the US held little interest. As a result, some of this gear was shipped back to the US, including 2,000 aircraft and an additional 1,000 engines. The serviceable aircraft remaining were assigned to the occupation forces. All else was destroyed.[68]

Harmon enjoyed this assignment even more than he had Coblenz, but for different reasons. During his eight months in England he spent a great deal of

Harmon in the cockpit of a DH-4 with West Point classmate Sammy Cousins standing alongside.

time with Royal Air Force (RAF) officers, and was greatly impressed. First, he quickly realized that these boys knew how to party. He later recalled the game played in the RAF mess, usually late at night and after many, many drinks that was called "sink the ship." (From his description, Americans would probably call this "game" Buck Buck.) It involved one team lining up, wrapping their arms around the waist of the person in front of them, and then all bending over. The other team would then, one at a time, start running from across the room and leap onto the bent backs of the other team. Whichever team could remain intact with the most number of the opponents poised upon their collective backs would be declared winner—entitling them, no doubt, to more drinks.[69] And then of course, there were the ladies. In a scrapbook that Harmon kept of his time in Europe, there is a prized possession: a telegram from legendary actress Mary Pickford. She wrote Harmon that she would be unable to accept his gracious invitation because of a previous commitment.[70] There must be a story there.

On a more prosaic note, Harmon's wife later said that this was the beginning of a strong belief in Harmon that air officers should not only be well-educated, but that education should be broadly based. He was stunned and impressed at his hosts' ability to discuss politics, art, literature, music, military affairs, and air tactics with equal facility.[71] His own narrowly focused technical education while at West Point simply had not prepared him for such topics. In some ways he would attempt to emulate this model—taking graduate courses in literature, art, and architecture upon his return to the US. In addition, he would file this lesson away for future use.

Professionally, his performance rose to the example set before him. Although again marked only "average" in "leadership" and "physical energy and endurance," he received—for the first time—a number of "superior" ratings. His commander also wrote that he was "well informed, intelligent and capable" with a pleasing personality.[72]

Overall, it had been an exciting and educational tour for Harmon. He had spent a great deal of time in three foreign countries and been exposed to a host of new experiences and stimuli. Although there were still indications of an immaturity not atypical for someone his age, he also displayed gradual but steady growth.[73] His final months in London were especially useful in developing his maturity. He would return seven years later for a refresher.

CHAPTER 3

Learning the Ropes

*T*he top American combat air commander during the World War had been Brigadier General William L. Mitchell. The son of a Wisconsin senator and the grandson of a Civil War hero, "Billy" Mitchell was an unusually forceful and charismatic officer. He was also opinionated, pushy, egotistical and driven. In France he had quarreled bitterly, and childishly, with his superior, Brigadier General Benjamin Foulois. The commander of the American Expeditionary Force, General John J. Pershing, watched this mess and in May 1918 finally decided that the Air Service needed adult leadership. He summoned to his office an old friend and West Point classmate, Mason Patrick. Pershing told Patrick that there were some fine officers down there in the Air Service, but they were running around in circles; he wanted him to make them go straight. Patrick, a member of the Corps of Engineers his entire career and at that point in charge of all construction projects in France for the American Army, protested that he knew nothing about airplanes or aviation. That was not the point said Pershing, he needed a leader and an effective administrator.[1]

Major General Patrick proved able to calm the roiling waters between his two airmen. Foulois—who had won his rating in 1909 as the Army's third pilot—managed the administrative and logistics functions, while Mitchell remained at the Front. Both men worked effectively and efficiently for Patrick.[2]

When the war ended and the troops headed back home for demobilization, Pershing requested that Patrick remain temporarily in Europe to close things down, dispose of the surplus equipment, secure the items received from the defeated Germans, and organize the air portion of the American occupation.[3] Back in the US, Major General Charles T. Menoher, who had commanded the famous 42nd Division (Rainbow) during the war and who was also one of Pershing's West Point classmates, was appointed as the new chief of the Air Service. He knew little of aviation and never learned to fly; as for his new command, it quickly began to dissolve between his fingers. From a high of 190,000 personnel on Armistice Day, numbers plummeted to 81,000 by January 1919 and to 27,000 by June. The free fall continued for several more years: in 1926 the Air Service consisted of a mere 996 officers, about two-thirds of whom were pilots.[4]

Most of those who remained on duty reverted to their "permanent" rank. Major General Patrick, for example, left France in July 1919 to return to the Corps of Engineers with an assignment in New Orleans. Stepping off the boat he reverted to colonel. Hap Arnold went from colonel to major overnight. Others, however, were more fortunate.

Although Billy Mitchell had expected to be made chief of the Air Service, Pershing instead installed Menoher, but allowed Mitchell to return from France as Menoher's deputy.[5] This posting meant that Mitchell would retain the star of a brigadier general as long as he remained in that position. In essence, this temporary rank was dependent on his job, and if he were to be transferred to a position that was not a general officer's billet, he too would revert to his permanent rank.

Billy Mitchell was a believer in airpower and its ability to revolutionize war. He had watched the trench slaughter that had killed millions and knew there had to be a better way. He argued incessantly with anyone who would listen—airmen, ground officers, politicians, newsmen and the public in general—that warfare as exemplified by the hecatomb of the World War was insane. There could be no victors in such a prolonged slaughter. Instead, it was necessary to apply pressure on the vital centers of an enemy nation—the industry, armaments factories, transportation nodes and government buildings where true power resided. In centuries past this had always been the goal, but in practical terms it meant a bloody and prolonged force-on-force engagement between opposing armies. Only when one army was destroyed could the opponent finally march towards the interior of the enemy country, where those vital centers were located, and apply pressure on the population and its government to force a peace. In the World War this had taken four years and cost millions of lives.

The airplane allowed a different strategy by flying over the ground forces locked in battle below. Mitchell preached these beliefs continuously and wrote prolifically. His major themes stressed the growing dominance of airpower in war, and thus the need for an air force independent of control by ground-oriented soldiers.[6]

Not everyone agreed with Mitchell's vision of the future, especially his Army superiors or the Navy.

Mitchell not only attacked the ground officers who dominated the Army, but also the admirals. In the case of the senior officers in his own service, Mitchell's stance was somewhat understandable. These soldiers often seemed to go out of their way to insist that warfare had not changed, that infantry would continue to be the only decisive factor in war, and that aviation could never be more than a supporting arm to that infantry. The priority given to aviation throughout the interwar period made it clear that Army leaders felt adamantly about this. The Air Service (the Air Corps after 1926) was perennially under-manned in comparison to the other combat branches—80 percent compared to the Army as a whole that was manned at 95.7 percent of its authorized strength. The share of the Army budget devoted to aviation averaged a paltry 12 percent per year for that twenty-year span.[7] As for leadership positions, it was not until mid-1939 that the first airman achieved the permanent rank of brigadier general.[8]

Mitchell's attacks on the Navy had a more parochial bent. The Navy had its own air arm—also strongly subordinated to the surface officers in dominance. The Navy began to experiment seriously with aircraft carriers in the early 1920s, a development that Mitchell did not like. Sailors tended to have a broader and more strategic view of war, seeing it on a more global scale than did tactically-oriented soldiers. With its claim as America's first line of defense, the Navy was a threat to the strategic mission envisioned by Mitchell for aviation. As a consequence, he attacked surface ships as highly vulnerable to air attack. One of his favorite claims was that a thousand aircraft could be purchased for the cost of a single battleship, but one airplane could sink that battleship.[9] The Navy vigorously contested Mitchell's claim.

In July 1921, Mitchell was given the chance to prove his allegations regarding the vulnerability of ships to airpower. Several captured German vessels, ranging in size from a submarine through a destroyer and light cruiser and up to a battleship, were anchored fifty miles off the Virginia coast as targets. Mitchell put together a group of aviators who practiced dropping bombs on silhouettes in the shape of ships painted on the ground. When Mitchell turned his bombers against the ships themselves, the smaller vessels went down quickly, some sinking in only a few minutes after being struck by bombs. Still, the Navy was certain that the battleship *Ostfriesland* with its thick armor plate and watertight compartments would withstand Air Service attacks.

On the morning of July 20, Mitchell took his personal plane out to survey the targets in the water. In the rear seat taking notes was his aide, First Lieutenant St. Clair Streett. In another aircraft, Major Hubert Harmon also watched the proceedings.[10] Five Martin MB-2 bombers approached the hulking battleship, a survivor of the 1916 Battle of Jutland, and dropped a number of small bombs. Some hit and caused obvious damage. Onlookers claimed the damage was superficial, but naval inspectors who went on board saw otherwise. Near misses that landed in the water next to the ship had, as Mitchell predicted, done the most damage. Acting as "water-hammers" due to water's incompressibility, the bombs pummeled the sides of the ship below the waterline, opening seams much like a mine would. The surveyors doubted the ships would long survive. The next day the bombers dropped 1,000 lb. bombs and severely damaged the ship even more. Shortly after noon the Martins, as well as even larger Handley Pages, dropped bombs weighing a ton each. The *Ostfriesland* rolled over and sank. As it did so, another bomb landed in the foam left on the surface by the sinking ship, as one account phrased it, "as if to tamp down the dirt over its grave."[11]

It was a stunning triumph. Navy diehards would nonetheless dispute the tests, arguing that Mitchell "cheated" by dropping too many bombs too quickly—as if an enemy would have worried about such things. Even so, Mitchell's victory proved bittersweet. Instead of forcing the Navy to surrender to his ideas on airpower, it would simply adopt them. After watching the *Ostfriesland* go belly up, General Menoher commented presciently that this probably meant the Navy would get its "airplane carriers" now, and he was correct.[12] The aircraft carrier would become the new capital ship, and Navy aviation would grow stronger despite Mitchell's humiliation of the battleship admirals. Time would prove that the Navy would take Mitchell's claims regarding the emerging dominance of aviation far more seriously than would the Army, and more seriously than Mitchell would like.

In the immediate aftermath of the *Ostfriesland* test, the Joint Army and Navy Board put out a bland and disingenuous report that admitted the ships had indeed been sunk by air attack, but the battleship was still king of the seas and backbone of the American fleet.[13] Mitchell, not surprisingly, was outraged, and he countered by leaking his own report to the newspapers, a report that was far more demonstrative regarding the now-obvious (to him) dominance of airpower over ships.

It was now Menoher's turn to be outraged. He went to his superior and gave a "him or me" ultimatum. To his surprise, Menoher's transfer was quickly arranged back to the Real Army.[14] His place was taken, not by Mitchell, but by Mason Patrick, who once again was called in to fix things. The change took place in September 1921, and Patrick immediately confronted Mitchell, who uncharacteristically backed down; things then proceeded in a relatively benign fashion for many months.[15] Patrick well understood Mitchell's personality and abilities and would later write: "Mitchell is very likeable and has ability; his ego is highly developed and he has an undoubted love for the limelight, a desire to be in the public eye. He is forceful, aggressive, spectacular. He had a better knowledge of the tactics of air fighting than any man in the country."[16]

Mitchell was in some respects beyond the control of his superiors, but Patrick handled him better than most, seeing his abilities and vision without ignoring the less desirable traits. One of the ways he kept Mitchell out of trouble was by sending him on lengthy inspection and fact-finding trips to both Europe and the Pacific. In addition, Patrick enrolled in pilot training school and won his wings—at the tender age of 59. He was not much of a pilot to be sure, and he always went up with another pilot actually at the controls, but the signal his effort sent to the Air Service was an important one.

Air Staff Duties

Hubert Harmon had sailed from England on the SS *Northern Pacific* and arrived in Washington in October 1920 to serve on the Air Service staff; specifically, he was to be the assistant executive officer for Major Generals Menoher and then Patrick. This was an important post, which gave Harmon an excellent purview of the entire Air Service operation. As an "exec," he was privy to almost everything that crossed his boss's desk—training, operational matters, procurement, budgeting, personnel, logistics and legislative matters to name but some.[17] The other assistant executive in the office, Ira Eaker, later detailed their duties. They were to prepare drafts of the chief's speeches and reports to the War Department and Congress; they would read the *Congressional Record*, marking items of Air Service interest; they would prepare short briefs of the many reports that came across the chief's desk. The guidance from Patrick was straightforward:

never equivocate or guess. If they did not know the answer to a question asked, they should simply say so, and then try to find the answer.[18]

This assignment was a tremendous learning experience. Harmon's office was situated between those of Patrick and Mitchell so that he was privy to the conflicts that arose between the two generals. Another of his additional duties, and one of some pleasure, was working as a White House aide. In this role he attended social functions at the White House, serving as an escort for visiting dignitaries and helping with arrangements. For one of these events, for example, he was appointed the military aide to the Duke of Sutherland.[19] This type of duty also introduced him to many politicians and other notables—good contacts for a member of the Air Service staff.

Harmon worked on Menoher's staff for over a year, spending his days immersed in paperwork. Here he began to perfect the administrative and organizational skills that would stand him in such good stead later in his career. Even so, at this point he was not yet a bright star in the emerging galaxy of air leaders. Menoher consistently ranked him as an "average" officer with "average ability."[20] When Mason Patrick took over as chief of the Air Service in late

Captain Harmon at his desk in civilian clothes while on the Air Service staff, ca. 1924.

1921, Harmon remained in the position of assistant executive officer. Harmon's immediate supervisor, Major W.H. "Tony" Frank, also rated him as "average" in most categories, though "above average" in "attention to duty," "tact," "intelligence," and "common sense." In describing his subordinate, Frank wrote that Harmon was "painstaking and thorough, although a bit slow." He lauded his judgment and intelligence, but then wrote that his "initiative and leadership are not as prominent as they should be in an officer of his general make up." This was a serious criticism, and such a characterization would resurface as a theme later in Harmon's career.[21]

During this period, budget cuts caused personnel turmoil, and in November 1922 Harmon again reverted to captain; he did not get back his oak leafs until March 1925. The year before, in his fourth year as the assistant exec, Harmon's stock went up in the eyes of his superiors. Part of this was due to his handling the onerous job of preparing the annual Air Service report to the Army chief of staff for Patrick's signature. This chore involved a great deal of work in compiling and organizing the data, and writing a lengthy narrative. By the time he finished this report, he was well-versed on all aspects of the Air Service. Patrick appreciated the effort, as did the Army deputy chief of staff, Major General John L. Hines, who wrote Harmon telling him how favorably impressed he was with the "excellent preparation" of the annual report. Hines acknowledged that this was generally looked upon as a thankless task, but it was essential nonetheless.[22] Partly as a result of his increasing proficiency, Harmon received a much better efficiency report at the end of his tour on the Air Service staff. Frank not only rated his overall performance as "excellent—above average," but also checked all qualification blocks as "above average," with a lone "superior" in the category of "tact." This may refer to the tussle between Billy Mitchell and the secretary of war that resulted in Mitchell's "exile" to Texas, to be discussed below. Frank's ranking of Harmon as tactful may have reflected a belief that the young captain was conducting himself properly in a very difficult situation. As we shall see, not all airmen were judged as having done so. In addition, Frank also added that Harmon "had developed a great deal of self assurance and confidence in the last year." More importantly, he noted that Harmon was "thoroughly dependable and has excellent judgment, a pleasing personality and is absolutely loyal." This was high praise, and the report was endorsed by General Patrick.[23]

While serving on the staff, Harmon also was required to fly each month. Usually, this was a fairly unexceptional event, but not always. In October 1922 Harmon and several others from the Air Staff, including General Patrick, flew to New Haven, Connecticut, to attend the Army-Yale football game. Harmon, coming into land just after Patrick's plane had touched down, realized that he was too close. He applied full power to go around, but was slow to react: he clipped several trees at the end of the runway. The impact also broke his propeller. He knew his plane was going down, so Hubert quickly picked out an emergency landing spot situated on an upward-sloping rise of ground. Unfortunately, he failed to pull the nose up sufficiently and hit the ground hard—nose first. He and his passenger walked away, but the aircraft was a mess. Patrick stood nearby and saw it all. The general was flustered, but pleased to see his young exec was still in one piece. He patted him on the back, tut-tutted, and jumped in a staff car to head off to the game. Harmon was lucky.[24]

In August 1924 Harmon was sent to the Air Service Engineering School at McCook Field in Dayton, Ohio. In one sense this was a surprise—other than in drawing classes Harmon had not distinguished himself academically at West Point. On the other hand, he had impressed his superiors with his intelligence over his first decade of service. It could also be that Patrick's career as an engineer and the fact that Tony Frank was a graduate of the Engineering School were factors in the decision. For his part, Harmon was clearly interested in more schooling. While working on the staff he attended night classes at George Washington University beginning in 1922. He went to class two or three nights each week and spent a great deal of his off-duty time studying. Initially, his tastes ran towards art and architecture, and he began by taking courses in free-hand drawing and "Beau Arts."[25] After discussion with the dean, it appeared he could get an architectural degree in two years. To his disappointment, this proved impossible. Soon, his tastes shifted towards English composition, and he signed up for courses in creative writing and journalism. This academic interest dovetailed nicely with his office duties. In 1924, for example, he wrote a lengthy press release announcing the famous Round the World Flight of Air Service aircraft.[26] He enjoyed night school a great deal but found that he could not devote the time to his studies that he would have liked. In one letter he even mused about the possibility of resigning his commission—"the idea has a great deal of charm"—and instead pursue a career as an architect or in journalism.[27] In the event, resignation would not be necessary. The Army would send Harmon to school, although not quite in the discipline he would have chosen.

The purpose of the Engineering School was to give Air Service officers "an understanding of technical matters relating to airplanes and motors and their maintenance." The school also hoped to distribute its graduates throughout the Air Service so as to "improve the operations of the flying stations."[28] To gain admission to the Engineering School, an officer had to be a pilot with a good record and have a technical degree from a recognized college—or be a West Point graduate. It was a rigorous, year-long school that tested Harmon's intellectual abilities. Yet, he enjoyed the academic environment a great deal. The curriculum was practical, with academic classes in the morning and experimental lab work in the afternoons.[29] There were classes in mathematics and mechanics—in which Harmon excelled gaining a score of 98.5 percent—business administration, applied mechanics (another good course), aerodynamics, airplane design, photography, thermodynamics, electricity, and several other technical subjects. Overall, Harmon did very well—far better than he had as a cadet—and graduated fourth of thirteen students.[30] Harmon had shown that he had the intelligence and perseverance to perform well in a graduate-level academic environment. It was a good show, and even more so when considering the quality of the competition. Three of his classmates were to make general officer, including Bart Yount. In fact, of the 197 officers who graduated from the Engineering School prior to World War II, 79 became generals—an astounding 41 percent.[31]

At the same time, he had the opportunity to do a good deal of flying. Part of the Engineering School's curriculum was to flight-test various new aircraft and instrument components. Most of these flights tended to be short hops around the local area, but others were of longer duration. On one cross-country to Wyoming taken for the alleged purpose of testing out a new compass, Harmon ran into bad weather. In a way, this was good—it gave him the opportunity to test the compass—but it was also bad because he was not certain where he was. A hole in the overcast soon confirmed that he was indeed on course, but it also revealed that unexpected headwinds meant he could not make it to Sheridan. He put the aircraft down in a field and almost immediately a group of young boys arrived to gawk. They had never seen an airplane up close before. Then their parents arrived, and they were similarly curious. The problem: Harmon needed gas. The spectators were glad to oblige, but the only containers available were a number of relatively small gas drums. Hubert was, after all, an engineering student trained in organizational matters: he arranged a chain with the boys carrying out the cans and lifting them up to the oldest lad on the wing who poured the gas in and passed back the empty drum. Harmon supervised. All worked nicely; the boys and their parents were glad to help, and the major was on his way to Wyoming.[32]

In August 1925, Harmon returned to the Air Service staff in Washington—this time to serve in the Information Division. The turmoil he had left the year before now had reached a peak. In January 1925, Mitchell had testified before a Congressional committee looking into the matter of a separate air arm. Several investigations of military aviation were conducted during the two decades between the wars, but other than stir up matters for a few weeks, the end results were generally minor. The Lampert Committee of early 1925 was one of these inquiries, which Mitchell used as a forum to expound his ideas on airpower. On this particular occasion Mitchell was more blunt than usual, noting that "conservatism in the Army and Navy" was responsible for the poor state of affairs in military aviation. This testimony contradicted the more moderate testimony of Mason Patrick, and that in turn irritated Secretary of War John Weeks. As a consequence, when Mitchell's tenure as deputy chief of the Air Service came up for reappointment a few weeks later, Weeks simply declined to approve it. The result: Mitchell, whose star as a brigadier general was dependent on his position in Washington, reverted to his permanent rank of colonel.[33] As noted earlier, this was a common occurrence for most officers after the end of the war—witness Patrick, Arnold and Harmon—but Mitchell had been able to deflect that fate for over five years. Now, what others saw as a normal reversion to permanent rank, Billy and his supporters saw as a demotion and an attempt to gag him. He was transferred to Fort Sam Houston in San Antonio, Texas, to become the senior air officer in the Army's VIII Corps area.

If the Army and Secretary Weeks thought that Mitchell would accept his fate in silence, they were mistaken. The powder keg may have been moved to Texas, but it had not been defused. The spark leading to detonation occurred in September 1925—the month after Harmon returned to Washington. On 3 September the Navy airship *Shenandoah* broke up in a thunderstorm over Ohio and crashed with a heavy loss of life. Among the dead was the *Shenandoah's* skipper, Commander Zachary Lansdowne, a friend of Mitchell's. Without waiting for the results of the accident investigation, Mitchell called a press conference in which he railed against the Navy for ordering the airship, which he claimed was an experimental craft (it was not), into marginal weather as a publicity stunt. Warming to the subject, Mitchell then painted a dismal picture of US military aviation in general. He referred to the leadership of both the Army and Navy in brutal terms, accusing it of "incompetency, criminal negligence and almost treasonable administration of the national defense." To ensure he would not be misquoted, Mitchell handed out copies of his 6,000-word statement to the assembled newsmen.[34] He was immediately recalled to Washington to be court-martialed; the charges were preferred by President Calvin Coolidge himself.

The Information Division combined the functions of public affairs, foreign military intelligence and legislative liaison. It was a pivotal division on the Air Service staff, and in mid-1925 it was headed by one of the air arm's most brilliant officers—Major Hap Arnold. Harmon had known Arnold since 1917 and thought most highly of him. Arnold saw his task as helping to promote the airpower agenda. He was a protégé of Mitchell's, and so he and the entire Information Division extended much help to Mitchell in preparing his defense. Patrick did not forbid this assistance—he was in his own way a true believer in airpower as well—but he warned his people to be careful and not go too far.[35] Eaker later recalled that Patrick told him that Mitchell could have any files and statistical studies necessary to help in his defense—but to ensure he got it back at the end of the trial.[36]

Arnold testified as a defense witness at the court-martial, as did other noted airmen Carl Spaatz, Hal George, Bert Dargue, Horace Hickam, Orville Anderson, Eddie Rickenbacker, and Hubert Harmon.

Fortunately for Harmon, his testimony did not generate much controversy. He was questioned about agreements reached between the Army and Navy regarding the air races of 1924. He read a letter from Assistant Secretary of the Navy Theodore Roosevelt (the former president's son), to General Patrick stating that their respective air arms should be considered as "sister services." Roosevelt suggested that rather than compete against one another, they should divide the races up with the Navy taking one and the Army the other. Patrick responded that he agreed heartily with the idea of being "sister services," stating that he sought "generous rivalry and not destructive competition." Yet, he had reservations about Roosevelt's proposal, and instead countered with the idea that "all of the high speed airplanes now in the possession of the Army or the Navy be divided equally and that the Army and Navy Air Services share equally in the expense of development of high speed airplanes." Roosevelt eventually responded that he concurred.[37] After reading the letters Harmon was dismissed. This was hardly inspiring stuff, and although he was testifying for the defense, the prosecutor had no questions in cross examination. The entire testimony was apparently designed to illustrate that the Navy had deliberately tried to conclude an agreement to retard aircraft development, thus supporting Mitchell's claims of misconduct. Patrick's response nudged the Navy away from this proposal, but the letters did not paint him in an overly favorable light. One interpretation—and Harmon wisely offered no commentary at the trial—

could be that Patrick was in collusion with the Navy in this effort to hold back aircraft and engine advancement. In other words, Harmon was on thin ice. In any event, the incident passed quietly, and Harmon suffered no damage.

The same could not be said for Arnold. The month following Mitchell's guilty verdict, Arnold was relieved as chief of the Information Division and sent to Fort Riley, Kansas. At the time, it was assumed that Arnold was fired by Patrick in retaliation for his vocal support of Billy Mitchell, but Arnold and Patrick biographers argue otherwise. There was a separate issue that occurred around the same time that caused the problem. In early 1926 a bill before Congress provided that more money would be sent to the Air Service and also grant it greater autonomy. Airmen certainly supported the bill, but Arnold and Bert Dargue went a step further, mimeographing circulars arguing for the bill's passage that they then distributed on Capitol Hill. This was going too far. There were strict rules about military officers lobbying Congress, and when Secretary Weeks caught wind of the incident he sent a strong message to Patrick ordering him to look into it. The culprits were quickly identified. Because Arnold was the senior man, he was called on the carpet where Patrick offered him an ultimatum: resign quietly or face a court-martial. Arnold was dismayed, but after thinking it over that night, called Patrick's bluff—and bluff it was—and asked for a court-martial. In truth, the last thing the Air Service needed was another messy court-martial where its dirty linen would be aired in public, so Patrick backed down and instead sent Arnold to Kansas.[38]

Harmon took his place as chief of the Information Division. In the final efficiency report of his subordinate, Arnold rated Harmon as "above average" overall and in most of the specific characteristics as well; however, he did downgrade him in the areas of "force" and "leadership." Patrick rated Harmon about the same; however, in his written comments, Patrick noted that Harmon was "absolutely loyal." When Harmon departed the division eight months later, Patrick raised all grades to "above average" and wrote blandly that the major was "an excellent officer, conscientious and efficient."[39] In a personal note, Patrick thanked Harmon for his efforts on the Air Staff. He wrote: "I am certain you will acquit yourself in your new post … as creditably as you have filled the various positions of responsibility in my own office."[40]

Professionally, Harmon had served in an important staff position at the heart of the Air Service for over five years. He had learned much about the administrative and organizational workings of the air arm, while also becoming acquainted with many of its top officers—as well as those who would be the top commanders in the future. It had not always been an enjoyable assignment, and as we have seen, he had even contemplated resigning his commission. But he worked his way through these challenges and came out the end a stronger and more committed officer.

There were also some good times. It was during this period that Harmon began to participate in a weekly poker game with Ira Eaker, Tony Frank and Idwal Edwards. Over the years, this poker group, depending on who was available or stationed in the area, included Horace Hickam, Tooey Spaatz and Frank Andrews.[41] This was a very important group of officers for Harmon to associate with.

In April 1926, Harmon flew up to Wright Field in Dayton for the annual Air Service maneuvers. Brigadier General James Fechet, Mitchell's replacement as Patrick's deputy, was in charge of the maneuvers and Harmon was his aide for the exercises. Among others on Fechet's temporary staff were Carl Spaatz, Conger Pratt and Ira Eaker. Over dinner one evening, Fechet told his staff of the time he bailed out of an airplane. He then asked impishly if any of them

At the Wright Field air maneuvers of April 1926. From left to right: Clayton Bissell, Ira Eaker, Harmon, Caleb Haynes, Carl Spaatz, Brigadier General James Fechet.

Harmon and Ira Eaker before the
parachute jump.

Harmon on the wing of a Martin MB-2 prior to
takeoff and his first (and only) parachute jump.

had ever used a parachute. No one had, but several got the impression that the
Old Man wanted somebody to enjoy that experience. Harmon and Eaker volunteered to do the deed the next day. Fechet smiled wolfishly and said, "I will
be down to watch you boys do it."

As "the boys" were putting on their parachutes, Harmon said, "if you don't
mind, I would like to jump first; I am superstitious." Eaker merely shrugged.
They climbed onto the wing of a Curtiss B-2 bomber piloted by C.V. Haynes
and grabbed a wing strut—Harmon was on the right side and Eaker on the left.
While circling the field at around 1,500 feet, Eaker glanced over and saw that
Harmon was looking elsewhere, so he immediately jumped off and deployed
his chute. When Doodle looked back and saw he was alone, he too jumped off.
Eaker recalled: "As he passed me I saw he was somersaulting end over end, and
his right hand was reaching over his chest looking for the ring. Doodle did
not find the ring and release the chute until he was but some 400 feet off the
ground." There was a strong wind blowing, and because Harmon had delayed
opening his chute for so long, he landed awkwardly and the wind pushed him
over on his back where he smacked his head, knocking him out cold. By the
time a truck arrived, however, he was up and doing fine.

Fechet was beside himself. He later said that he had "died a thousand
deaths when I saw Doodle Harmon tumble towards the ground with his chute
unopened, knowing I had inspired this effort on the part of you two boys."[42]
For his part, Harmon later denied that he had been frantically grabbing for the
ring; rather, he was deliberately counting to ten as he'd been told!

Even more important than this near-death experience, Hubert Harmon
met a most remarkable woman while stationed in Washington DC.

The Courtship of Rosa-Maye

On January 20, 1922, Harmon went to St. Margaret's Church in Washington for the wedding of a friend, an event that would change his life. The groom was Gene Vidal and the bride Nina Gore. Family lore has it that Harmon knew Nina, and was chosen by her to be a member of the wedding party, although it would seem more likely that he knew the groom, who was also an Air Service pilot and West Point graduate who had quarterbacked the football team after Harmon. At the wedding rehearsal, Harmon met one of the bridesmaids named Rosa-Maye Kendrick. Hubert took one look at her and said: "I'm going to walk down the aisle with you." Rosa-Maye took him to mean as members of the wedding party. Perhaps that is what Hubert meant, or perhaps he was coyly telling her that he had found the woman of his dreams. His following actions could justify either interpretation. When Rosa-Maye demurred at his suggestion, Hubert spoke to the bride and groom and had the lineup changed: he walked Rosa-Maye down the aisle.[43]

Rosa-Maye, then 23 years old, was the only daughter of John B. Kendrick, Democratic senator from Wyoming, and his wife, Eula Wulfjen Kendrick. John Kendrick had also been the governor of Wyoming and owned a sizeable cattle ranch of over 200,000 acres north of Sheridan, spread over four counties in Wyoming and Montana.[44] Rosa-Maye came from a wealthy and prestigious family. She was well educated, having graduated from Goucher College, a liberal arts school north of Baltimore. She had a great love for literature and poetry gained from her mother—Rosa-Maye's diaries and scrapbooks often contained verses from her favorite poems and references to novels she had read. She was also an accomplished writer, with her features appearing in the *Denver Post* and the *Sheridan Press*.[45] Photographs show her to have been a handsome woman—petite, but with strong features, curly chestnut hair, and dancing eyes. She spent most of the year in Washington with her family—living in a hotel at 2400 16th Street—and worked in her father's Senate office. Rosa-Maye loved the Washington social and cultural scene and frequently attended plays, academic lectures and concerts. Active with volunteer groups, she also worked at the White House, where Mrs. Harding and Mrs. Hoover enjoyed her company and used her talents for social functions, especially those involving the Girl Scouts. She was very politically aware, given her father's position, and also well informed on financial matters.[46]

Rosa-Maye was an excellent equestrian. During the summers she would return to Wyoming where she would divide her time between the family home,

Trail End, in Sheridan, and one of their cattle ranches, the *OW*. She and her brother, Manville, would often do range work and rope cattle; she was an excellent rider. Given this delightful combination of Washington socialite and tomboy, she must have been irresistible. She hit Major Hubert Harmon like a ton of bricks.

The day after meeting her, Hubert began to write and call on Rosa-Maye. Because he owned two horses that were stabled in Rock Creek Park, he often invited her to ride with him.[47] "Bobby" was a gelding that Rosa-Maye usually rode, and "Rummy Mare" was taken by Hubert. (Harmon had won "Rummy" in a poker game.) Supposedly, "Bobby" was the more sedate of the two, but occasionally he would get carried away when Harmon would lead them on trip around the park jumping over the benches. Fortunately, Rosa-Maye was able to keep the horse under control.

Almost immediately, Hubert's letters to this beautiful and vivacious young woman spoke of love and adoration. He missed her desperately when he was not with her, especially when she was out of town. She was the only woman in the world for him. He enjoyed the charm of her company more than life itself. His letters often began with a line such as "Dear precious most beloved darling sweetheart," and were peppered with literary allusions, which he knew she would like and understand, and also a good deal of wit. He sometimes accompanied his letters with cartoons and drawings, most of them nicely done. He even tried his hand at poetry:[48]

> *If I were a fellow of gentle persuasion,*
> *If Time would but offer a proper occasion,*
> *If I could boast wealth and wit and good looks,*
> *And erudite learning I'd gathered from books;*
> *If hope and Ambition were aught but a creed*
> *And throbbing desire could be changed into deed;*
> *And could I discern in a nod or a sigh*
> *Encouragement given so bold a design,*
> > *The stars that ride high*
> > *In the night's purple sky*
> *Would smile their approval—and the world would be*
> > *Mine!*
> > *A Young Man*
> > *(with a fancy!)*

Hubert was totally besotted.

Early in their courtship, Hubert discovered a book titled *Redcoat Captain*, a
copy of which he gave to Rosa-Maye.
It was not a particularly memorable
or impressive novel, but for some
reason it struck a chord in both of
them.[49] The two main characters and
lovers, "Captain Tiny" and "Baby,"
became the nicknames that our
couple took to calling each other for
many years thereafter. Rosa-Maye also
called him Doodle in her diary, seldom
Hubert, although he often signed his letters
to her in that fashion.[50] The childish
language used in the book was often
adopted by Hubert in his letters to
Rosa-Maye; for example, he often

*Rosa-Maye Kendrick ca. 1920. Photo
courtesy of Cynde Georgen at the Trail End
State Historical Site, Sheridan, Wyoming.*

referred to her as "most booful"—as Tiny did to Baby. He also named his
car, an old Haynes, *Goliath*, or *Golly*, after the elephant character in the book.
Hubert gave *Redcoat Captain* to Rosa-Maye in July 1922 with the inscription:
"Der Baby, send u this for u kno and because i lub you so." Still pressed into
the book eighty-five years later is a rose bud. One line in the book is under-
lined: "Then one evening after tea, as Tiny lay flat in a fat chair with his legs
out, and slept aloud, which he always did till bedtime, when he woke up very
spry and wanted to lecture on his favorite subject, …"[51] One suspects this
would be how Rosa-Maye would often describe Hubert's conduct. It was all
quite romantic.

For her part, Rosa-Maye liked Hubert immediately, and in one letter
early in their courtship she wrote: "although I have known you a comparatively
short time, it seems that we must have been friends for all along. You have come
into my life as a sudden realization of an old hunger, never quite realized or
satisfied. But I know that 'hunger' must have been the joy I have of you."[52] Yet,
she did not assume—as did Hubert—that their relationship was unbreakable.
On the contrary, this girl had options. She refers to several men in her diary. On
January 4, 1922, she spent the day with Bob Finley; the next day she talked with

Harry Kay about "past, present and future." On the 10th, she attended a wedding with Bob and afterwards engaged in "some promiscuous kissing." Three days later Bob was over for tea "and we visited more or less successfully." On 15 January, Lem came over, and she displayed "unpardonable weakness." Two days later she broke things off with Lem. A few days after that Doodle took her out to Bolling Field (in Anacostia on the east side of the Potomac River), and showed-off for her in an airplane. A week later she was back with Lem—and then out riding with Doodle where "they bared their souls to each other." The next day was Lem again.[53]

And so it went for several more years. Doodle/Tiny was always in the picture, but Lem continued to pop in and out as well, although that June she "closed the book on our friendship with bitter tears." A month later Lem announced his engagement to someone else.[54]

She seemed to miss Doodle most when away in Wyoming, although she dearly loved the ranch and the West in general. Her diary is lyrical when she discusses the "opulent sky," vast spaces and beautiful mountains. In September 1922, Doodle came to visit. They rode, played golf, and sometimes just read together in the living room "in undisturbed bliss."[55] In December, Rosa-Maye was back in Washington for the holidays where "Doodle told me of his unabated interest in me."[56] And yet, but a few days later she was out with Lem again—who apparently had broken off his engagement—where she "sat with heavily beating heart and was strangely elated." In January, a new character entered the scene, George, "who plead with me for a chance to win me."[57]

The following March, Doodle took her flying at Bolling Field. When she later had to break a riding date with him, she wrote that she "was surprised at the extent of my disappointment."[58] Upon returning to Wyoming, she missed him—and vice versa—so he flew out there again to visit. But on 30 December 1923, Rosa-Maye wrote in her diary that she and Doodle had

Harmon in his DH-4 while visiting Rosa-Maye in Wyoming. This photo was taken before he went through the fence.

Trail End, *the Kendrick mansion in Sheridan, Wyoming. Photo courtesy of Cynde Georgen at the* Trail End *State Historical Site in Sheridan.*

gone riding that morning and "he asked me for my answer—which I gave."[59] Apparently, the answer was "no," because the next day Hubert went over and "begged again." Nonetheless, our boy is still in the picture come March: "we sat up reading and talking but avoiding the serious."[60]

The summer of 1924 found Rosa-Maye home in Wyoming, and again Doodle flew out to see her. These trips were ostensibly taken for official purposes—to fulfill periodic flying training requirements or to test certain pieces of aircraft equipment. The rules were far more lax about such things in those days. The peacetime Air Service was a decidedly laid-back organization in most regards, and the time Harmon spent flying around the country—or for that matter riding his horses with Rosa-Maye around the District—was not considered unusual. The Army during these years enjoyed a period of exceptional peace: there were no Indians or Filipinos to fight, and the Marines were sent to Latin America if there was trouble. In Washington, officers seldom even wore their uniforms to work. It was not a bad life—except during the Depression when all military pay was cut by 15 percent and no checks were issued at all for one month in 1933![61]

On Harmon's 1924 trip to Sheridan, however, things went astray. Rosa-Maye's diary entry says it all—or most of it: "And then the take off—which failed. The huge plane burdened with its load of gas failed to leave the ground and plunged through the Country Club fence smashing a wing and almost turning over. The rest of the day spent in dismantling the plane for shipment, sending telegrams and fixing fence."[62] Doodle was in trouble. The obvious mistake was "pilot error" in attempting to take off at high altitude (Sheridan was at 4,800 feet) while fully loaded. The main problem was that Harmon had agreed to take a passenger—and his baggage. This was a serious error, but Harmon was lucky: the crash could have been much worse. Ten days later he was luckier still, writing Rosa-Maye that his accident would be treated "with toleration."[63]

In September 1925 Rosa-Maye wrote a letter that "tried to sever our friendship," but that same November she changed her mind and told him "yes." In January 1926 she spoke with her mother who told her to plan on getting married "this summer." Perhaps in order to plan for such a domestic existence, Rosa-Maye attempted to bake a cake for Hubert's birthday, but "succeeded only in disrupting the entire kitchen force—spoiling both icing and cake which were terrible."[64] Two weeks later she told her father of her marital plans. That summer Doodle again visited Sheridan, and all was bliss. But on 6 September she told Hubert that "I felt I could not be happy married to him."[65]

He refused to accept that decision; yet, he is not mentioned in Rosa-Maye's diary for the next six weeks. Obviously, she was in the process of washing that man right out of her hair. In November 1926, however, Rosa-Maye wired Hubert to suggest that they meet in Chicago and talk things over.

Three months later Hubert and Rosa-Maye were married. What happened?

Throughout this five-year courtship Hubert never wavered in his devotion to Rosa-Maye. From the moment he laid eyes on her in January 1922 he was a goner. His professions of undying love never diminished in the scores of letters he wrote to her. He craved her company continually, and he was adrift whenever she went back to Wyoming or when he was attending Engineering School. For her part, Rosa-Maye obviously thought highly of him and much enjoyed his company. Yet, there were several other men courting her during those years, and it was difficult for her to make up her mind and commit to Hubert. Partly, this may have been due to the social/economic gap between her family and his. She was the daughter of a wealthy and powerful US senator and cattle baron. John Kendrick was of the American aristocracy—in fact, in 1924 and 1928 he was mentioned as a possible vice presidential candidate.[66] Hubert came from more humble origins, although it must be said that being a military officer in those days had its own form of prestige. This was a practical and not at all unworthy consideration for Rosa-Maye. She could have had her pick of men from the important families of Washington or the West; she needed to ensure her heart did not overrule her head. In the event, her heart and head were in agreement.

Hubert never gave up. The catalyst for the wedding was a fortuitous and unexpected event. Major Clarence Tinker was the air attaché to London. He had been injured in an aircraft accident and needed to be brought back to the US for extended treatment.[67] The Personnel Division asked Harmon if he would want such a short-notice posting. He replied he would get back to them on that; he then went to see Rosa-Maye. He told her that he was due for an overseas assignment. Would she go with him to the Philippines? She was stunned, and "as usual, I asked him for time to think but my heart was heavy and the world looked dark and empty." A few days later Hubert called on her again, and this time confessed that his previous announcement had been a hoax. It was true that he had been tapped for an overseas assignment, but it was to England, not the Philippines. Rosa-Maye "cried for sheer relief and joy." She told her mother, and "her mind leaped to overcome the obstacles." Those obstacles presumably centered on the fact that if she agreed to Doodle's proposal, the two of them would be on a boat to England in one month! Rosa-Maye then told her

Rosa-Maye's parents, Senator John B. Kendrick and Eula Wulfjen Kendrick. Photo courtesy of Cynde Georgen at the Trail End State Historical Site in Sheridan.

Major and Mrs. Hubert R. Harmon.

father who was caught by surprise, but his voice was "husky with tenderness and with tears in his eyes." The wedding was on.

Yet, it was hard in some ways for Rosa-Maye to fully grasp the step she was about to take. The next day she saw George, who invited her out for a ride in his auto. He mentioned Doodle and the fact that he would be going overseas, poor chap. Ah well, his number was up, and he had to go sooner or later. Obviously, George saw this as a positive development for his own prospects, because he then insisted that they go look at a house that was up for sale in Washington. When touring the house, the owner asked if they were married. George replied with a smile, "not yet." Rosa-Maye said nothing; she was simply unable to break the news to him that morning.[68]

The engagement was announced by Rosa-Maye and her mother at a luncheon in Chevy Chase on 20 January. Later that afternoon, the betrothed couple went for tea at the home of Mrs. Herbert Hoover. She sat on the couch next to Rosa-Maye and told amusing stories—"as was her wont." As they were leaving, Mrs. Hoover put her arm around Rosa-Maye and said: "why didn't you bring him to call long ago? I could have told you what to do *then*."[69]

The wedding took place at All Souls Unitarian Church on 16th Street in Washington DC on Saturday evening, 19 February 1927. The matron of honor was Rosa-Maye's cousin, Eula Cumming; the best man was Miff. Nina Gore, the woman who started it all five years before, was a bridesmaid.[70]

The bride was, as all brides are, radiant. In her shoe, Rosa-Maye carried a gold dollar given to her by the president's wife. The *Washington Post* described her dress:[71]

She wore a gown of white bide's satin, simply made and draped at the front, where the drapery was held with a rhinestone ornament, and the ends of the drapery falling below the bottom of the skirt, lined with pale flesh color. A deep V in the front of the bodice, reaching to the waist, was filled in with Venetian rose point lace over pale flesh, making a round neckline. A coronet of rose point lace was held at either side with orange blossoms. The lace, falling down each side of the coronet to the waist, was set into a tulle veil, which fell over the court train, and was finished at the bottom with a deep flounce of the same lace. She carried a bouquet of orchids and white lilacs, with a shower of lilies of the valley.

Major Hubert Harmon wore his dress uniform.

The wedding was a major Washington social event, and attendees included President and Mrs. Coolidge, Vice President and Mrs. Dawes, Secretary of Commerce and Mrs. Hoover, and several senators, congressmen and high-ranking military officers. It was a beautiful ceremony, and Rosa-Maye wrote that they spoke their vows "clearly and beautifully"; their kiss was "not too brief." The reception after was at the home of Senator and Mrs. Kendrick at 2400 16th Street, where the newlyweds cut the cake using the sword of the late Colonel Millard Fillmore Harmon, Sr. and drank a toast with cherry wine—made by the bride's mother. The Harmons then departed to the ringing of cowbells—a Wyoming tradition—and went back to what was now *their* apartment. As they crossed the threshold, Hubert put his arms around his new bride.

Three days later the newlyweds sailed for England on the SS *Republic* to begin a two-year honeymoon.

An Extended Honeymoon

When the Harmons arrived in London after their ten-day voyage, they were met by the outgoing air attaché, Major Clarence Tinker and his wife, who had them to dinner and explained what their tour of duty would be like. It would be a delightful assignment. Rosa-Maye and Hubert were Anglophiles—she had been to England on numerous occasions in the past, and he had been stationed there after the war—both loved the people, the scenery, the architecture and the history. Rosa-Maye kept a diary of these two years in England, while also sending frequent letters to her parents. These letters, later published by her mother, tell of a spirited and happy bride who was inquisitive and enchanted by everything she saw and did.[72] She loved to describe the people and the way they spoke, what they read and what movies they saw. She found, for example, that the educated class tended to have a much better knowledge of American literature than she herself did![73] She especially loved to watch the Royal Family, writing in detail of their clothes, expressions and mannerisms.

The Harmons had brought over a new Buick—a wedding present from the Kendricks—which was used for weekend forays into the countryside. They enjoyed driving through the quaint villages, where they sought out antiques, especially silver dining pieces, as well as, to use Hubert's later description, "worm-infested furniture."[74] He joined the Ranleagh Country Club and went golfing as often as possible. Of interest, Rosa-Maye always took special interest in English horses and livestock, noting their general condition, looks and attributes. She was, after all, a rancher's daughter. During the week, Hubert used the car—named *Marwy* after a lamb in *Redcoat Captain*—for work. Rosa-Maye usually had a chauffeur to take her around to the many parties, teas and shopping excursions in and around London. All of this enjoyable travel and sight-seeing did, however, cause Major Harmon to become a bit distracted. He received a letter from the War Department that began: "Unofficial information has reached the Department of your recent marriage." Harmon was directed to fill out and forward the appropriate paperwork, IAW Paragraph 14B, AR 605-120, as amended, forthwith.[75]

The Harmons lived for one year at 37 Chelsea Park Gardens, an upscale neighborhood on London's southwest side. Centuries earlier it had been the area where Sir Thomas Moore had lived. After one year, they lost their lease and moved to a house at 15 Argyll Road. Rosa-Maye enjoyed the service of a maid, cook, and chauffeur, and these proved especially useful when entertaining house guests—who included "Mother and Father," "Banny" (Harmon's mother) and relatives from Wyoming.

There was a great deal of socializing involved with an attaché assignment, and Harmon, as a member of the US Embassy staff, received a variety of interesting invitations. The Harmons sat in the Royal Enclosure at Ascot for the annual races and attended tea parties at Buckingham Palace. Rosa-Maye's status as the daughter of a prominent US senator also led to engagements with British politicians who knew her parents. Hubert's duties took him to various military airfields around England, while also allowing him to meet with high-ranking RAF officers and officials in the Air Ministry. On some occasions, Rosa-Maye accompanied him on these visits—as when the major drove to Ilford to inspect a shipment of aircraft instruments purchased by the Air Corps.[76] At the annual air maneuvers at Hendon, just north of London, she witnessed the air shows that included the air bombardment of a cardboard town.[77]

Rosa-Maye was perfect for this type of life. Wives were always important to an officer's career, but few had Rosa-Maye's qualities. As one observer noted: "A good wife and mother, a charming hostess and guest, and a woman who clearly understood the place of the Army in her husband's life, was a definite asset."[78] In Hubert Harmon's case, that was an understatement.

The Harmons were often called upon to entertain visiting dignitaries. In July 1927 they met Clarence Chamberlain and Charles Devine, aviators who had recently crossed the Atlantic.[79] Of even greater import of course was the earlier flight of Charles Lindbergh who had made the trans-Atlantic flight solo. After landing in Paris and enduring the subsequent celebrations, Lindbergh flew *The Spirit of St. Louis* to London where he thrilled British crowds. The Harmons were at Croydon Airfield when he arrived and then met with him at a reception at the US Embassy. Rosa-Maye found Lindy "astonishingly natural and at ease" with a smile as winning and infectious as that of the Prince of Wales—whom they also met on several occasions. Soon after, Harmon would be responsible for crating and shipping *The Spirit* for a sea passage back to New York.[80] In August, the

Chelsea Park Gardens—Where the Harmons first lived during their assignment in London in 1927.

Harmons attended a luncheon hosted by the Italian air attaché, Colonel Alessandro Guidoni, for his guests, the Italian Air Minister Italo Balbo and General and Mrs. Billy Mitchell. Although retired, Mitchell still enjoyed the respect of aviators worldwide. Rosa-Maye loved his "unquenchable enthusiasm."[81] In June 1928 they met Amelia Earhart at an Embassy luncheon following her trans-Atlantic flight. Rosa-Maye found her "slender, sandy and quite reserved."[82]

At a dinner hosted by the Aeronautical Engineers of England, Harmon was asked, unexpectedly, to give some remarks on the state of American aviation. He was a bit upset by the rudeness of this surprise invitation, but, according to Rosa-Maye, handled himself well. It also taught him to always prepare remarks in advance for any such event so as not to be caught with his flaps down in the future.[83]

For more formal events, he was well prepared. When asked to give a talk at the RAF Staff College at Andover, he gave a lengthy accounting of the organization and administration of the Air Corps.[84] Given his extensive service on the staff in Washington, one would have expected a more theoretical discussion of airpower doctrine and strategic bombardment—subjects then of enormous interest in both Britain and the US. Surprisingly, he did not discuss these topics.

Before finishing his tour as attaché, Harmon traveled to the Middle East to witness RAF operations in imperial policing duties. Britain had a huge colonial empire during the 1920s, made even larger by absorption of German and Turkish territories after the World War. Attempts to maintain control in these tribal areas using British ground troops was enormously expensive and labor intensive. In the austere financial situation of postwar Britain, these costs were a great concern. In mid-1919, therefore, General Sir Hugh Trenchard, the chief of air staff, suggested to his civilian superior, Air and War Minister Sir Winston Churchill, that the RAF be given the opportunity to subdue a festering uprising in Somaliland. Churchill agreed and the results were dramatic. The RAF chased the rebel ringleader, "the mad mullah," out of the area and pacified Somaliland at a cost of £77,000 rather than the £6 million it would have cost for the two army divisions originally planned.

As a consequence, the demand for air policing grew quickly, and over the next decade the RAF deployed—with varying degrees of success—to Iraq, Afghanistan, India, Aden, Transjordan, Palestine, Egypt, and Sudan. The strategy employed in these campaigns involved patrolling the disputed areas, flying political representatives around to the various tribes to discuss problems and devise solutions, issuing ultimatums to recalcitrants if persuasion failed, and as a last resort, bombing selected rebel targets to compel compliance.[85]

It was a valuable experience for Harmon to visit Iraq, Palestine and Egypt to witness these operations; it was especially enjoyable because Rosa-Maye was able to go with him. Soon after their return to England, Rosa-Maye's parents arrived and the four then took off for the Continent for a six-week tour of France, Spain, Germany, Italy, the Netherlands, Switzerland and Austria. Upon arriving in Bremen, they embarked for a voyage back to the United States.[86]

Harmon sent periodic reports back to the Washington on what he saw, heard and did. Given the close relations between Britain and the US, and especially between the RAF and the Air Corps, these reports did not have the type of secretive power that similar reports from Germany, Italy and Japan had during the same period. Instead, Harmon wrote of aircraft accidents, as well as the RAF's annual maneuvers, exercises and airshows.[87] In April 1928, Harmon did, however, file an unusually detailed and insightful report regarding the status of the RAF within the British defense establishment. He offered that the RAF was still very much resented by the other services, that craved its budget share and control over its air assets. He stated that all three services had fundamentally different views on what a future war would be like and how it would be fought—they could not even agree on who the main enemy might be. The RAF was fortunate in that several key politicians, as well as the public and the press, had a favorable view of the air service, and this was an important factor. Harmon also argued, controversially, that the RAF did not pay enough attention to its Fleet Air Arm—which in Britain was part of the RAF. Worse, the RAF short-changed the Army as well. Finally, Harmon gave an overview of British commercial aviation and the aircraft industry, arguing that the health of these two sectors was vital to the health of the RAF.[88]

Harmon's performance throughout his tour as air attaché was excellent. His superior, the US military attaché, rated him as "above average" or "superior" in all categories for both years. Especially appropriate for his duties in this assignment, Harmon was noted to have "a pleasing personality" and was "a good mixer."[89] Once again, one of Hubert Harmon's defining characteristics—his ability to get along with everyone, make friends, and serve as an effective mediator and coordinator among peoples of diverse personalities and backgrounds—was recognized and applauded. At the same time, he was able to witness firsthand and at close range an officer corps that possessed an unusual breadth of vision and strategic insight. He remained enormously impressed with the education and breeding of RAF officers.[90] He knew it would serve as a good role model for American air officers as well.

In the summer of 1929 the Harmons left Britain for a new assignment— West Point. He had received word of this move in January and was pleased. Initially, Rosa-Maye was not, but soon warmed to the idea and would much enjoy her time there.

A Return to the Hudson

When Major Hubert Harmon reported for duty at West Point in August 1929, it was the first time he had been back to his alma mater since graduation. When he and Rosa-Maye drove through the gates he would have noticed several changes. First was the new construction that had taken place over the previous fourteen years. A new barracks had been built in 1921; a new hospital was completed in 1923; the football stadium was finished in 1924; and a new mess hall had been added in 1926. This new construction, in the traditional Gothic style, was necessary to accommodate the larger Cadet Corps. The number of cadets now approached 1,300—more than twice the total in 1915. While he was stationed at West Point for the next three years, Harmon would also see a new barracks built on the site of the old building.

Despite these exterior alterations, Harmon soon discovered that little had changed in military training and even less in the curriculum. There was, however, an introduction to aviation included in the cadet program, and this was held at Langley Field, Virginia. In 1929 the superintendent, Major General William R. Smith, asked Congress to appropriate the funds to purchase 15,000 acres adjacent to Academy property. This additional land would allow the cadets to remain on–post for artillery and aviation instruction during the summer.[91] In 1931 these funds were indeed authorized, and the extra land was purchased. It was Major Hubert Harmon who surveyed the land and made the recommendation to Smith to purchase it.[92]

Cadet military training was essentially the same as it had been fifteen years earlier. Cadets still endured "Beast Barracks," endless drill, parades and inspections, and the rigid discipline of inflexible rules and regulations. The reason for this continuity was no doubt the result of the Academy's mission statement:

> The mission of the Military Academy is to train a cadet to think clearly
> and logically and to do so habitually; to teach him discipline and the

basic principles applicable to the various arms in the Military Service; to develop his physique and above all his character; and to teach him to approach all of his problems with an attitude of intellectual honesty, to be sensible of the rights of others, to be inspired by a high sense of duty and honor, and unhesitatingly to lay down his life in the service of his country should the occasion arise.[93]

Although such a statement had not been so clearly articulated when Harmon was a cadet, the principles behind it had been in effect for over a century.

Academically, there were minor corrections and additions, of a predominantly cosmetic nature. The curriculum was still fixed for all cadets regardless of their abilities or prior schooling. There were still neither electives nor majors. The permanent professors remained in charge of their departments and the curriculum in general. The instructors continued to consist almost exclusively of military officers who had little academic training beyond the baccalaureate.[94] Yet, there were glimmerings of hope. The permanent professors and even some faculty members now occasionally traveled so as to study academic procedures elsewhere and broaden their knowledge. In 1930, for example, the professor of civil and military engineering and the professor of drawing "were sent abroad for one year of detached service in order that they might improve themselves professionally and improve the courses under their jurisdiction."[95]

There had been a few minor academic changes in the previous fifteen years. In 1919 the Department of Chemistry and Electricity had been split in two. More laboratories and practical exercises were included in the science and engineering courses—although daily recitations and board work remained classroom staples. Mathematics was still the cornerstone of the curriculum, occupying more class time than any other subject by far. In 1929 there were also two new courses that Harmon had not taken: one in economics and government (taught by the old English and History Department, which was still under the leadership of Lucius Holt), and another in physics. In fact, the realization that the Department of Natural and Experimental Philosophy was archaic finally occurred to its head in 1931 when he renamed it the Physics Department. In English, there was a slight turn as well, with more emphasis placed on literature at the expense of rhetoric.[96]

There had been a serious attempt to reform and revitalize the curriculum during this period, but it had failed. That attempt was made by Brigadier

General Douglas MacArthur during his tenure as superintendent between 1919 and 1922. MacArthur, the top graduate in the Class of 1903, had returned from the World War as a hero. At age 39, he was the youngest officer to lead West Point in a century. His experiences on the Western Front had convinced him that American officers were deficient in dealing with allies and in understanding the political context of military operations. MacArthur therefore arrived on the Hudson with the intent of modernizing West Point—its curriculum, military training system, and athletics. Regarding the curriculum, he pushed for new courses in social sciences, economics and government, history, foreign languages, and even aeronautics and the workings of the internal combustion engine. To make room, the offerings in mathematics and drawing were cut back. French was given more importance than Spanish, and MacArthur directed the use of Intelligence Branch reports from the late war to be used in the classroom. As for military history: the campaigns of the Civil War were replaced by those of the war just ended.

These were small changes dearly won. The overall curriculum changed by barely 10 percent, the Academic Board fighting MacArthur at every turn. At one point he exclaimed in exasperation: "The professors are so secure, they have become set and smug. They deliver the same schedule year after year with the blessed unction that they have reached the zenith in education." The Board was unmoved. It simply out-waited the aggressive superintendent. When MacArthur left in 1922, things quickly returned to what passed for normal at West Point.[97]

Harmon was not detailed to West Point to be an academic instructor, however, and so the changes—or their lack—on this side of the house were of little direct interest to him, although he certainly noted them. The intransigence of the permanent professors who dominated the Academic Board would linger in his memory. Two decades later when establishing the Air Force Academy he would labor to ensure the professors were not so powerful.

Harmon was to be a "tactical officer," the officers who actually commanded the cadet companies. In a letter to his mother-in-law, Harmon explained his new job, writing that his real duty title should be "watchdog" or "nursemaid," because the bulk of his activity involved the disciplining of cadets. He recounted for "Muvver" the cadets' daily schedule—which was little different from what his own had been: up at 0600 for reveille, clean up room, breakfast, class all morning, lunch, class till 1515, and then "outside work" consisting of either drill or athletics. At 1630 there was a full-dress parade, which was followed by forty minutes of free time (!) This period of relaxation, when cadets could do "as they jolly well please," led to dinner. "Call to quarters," when cadets were expected to be in their rooms studying or at the library, lasted until 2200.[98]

Harmon then described the organization of the Academy and his own duties. At the top was the superintendent, and below him was the academic side run by the professors—at this time West Point did not have an academic dean to coordinate and rationalize the courses of the various departments to ensure a coherent whole or to remove redundancies and plug gaps—and the commandant's office. Lieutenant Colonel Robert C. Richardson, a cavalryman, was the commandant of cadets and below him were several staff officers and the tactical officers. There was a "battalion tac" for each of the three cadet battalions—Harmon was one of these (Third Battalion)—and also a "company tac" for each of the twelve cadet companies. Due to under-manning, Harmon was one of these as well (I Company). Each year Harmon would move offices, becoming the Second Battalion tac in 1930 and then taking over First Battalion in 1931. After the first year he was not required to serve as a company tac.[99]

As the I Company tactical officer, Harmon inspected each cadet room daily, as well as the company common rooms. (He would later remark that a good tac knew what *not* to see during an inspection.) He monitored closely each cadet's academic performance (which was still graded daily), and if someone was having difficulty he would assign another cadet to tutor him. He handled administrative matters such as the daily reports, money accounts, guard rosters, drill and athletics, efficiency reports, and, perhaps most famously, the delinquency slips known as "skins." He assigned punishments for minor infractions, while also keeping records of them. Harmon added that he also conducted drill each day, helped coach the lacrosse team, and, when inclement weather prevented drill, taught afternoon classes on military subjects. Because he was the senior airman on post—in fact, he was the only aviator on the commandant's staff—he also taught lessons on airpower. Finally, and most importantly, his job was to guide and mentor cadets.[100] Cadets often established enduring and important relationships with their tactical officers. These men, who often came from operational assignments, served as role models for cadets in a way that academic instructors—despite their intellectual achievements—could seldom match. Moreover, the tacs saw the cadets every day for months on end, and did so in a variety of settings. Many would argue that the tactical officers, and

their counterparts at the other service academies, were the true backbone of
the unique Academy system.

Major Harmon's position as a battalion tac imposed other duties, mostly
of an administrative and supervisory nature. One of the most visible of these
was to serve on the "Supreme Court," the disciplinary board that sat in judgment
on the more serious cadet offenses. This duty earned him special recognition
from the Cadet Corps. The 1930 *Howitzer* contains a full-page watercolor of
the Battalion Board (its real name) composed of the three battalion tacs sitting
at a desk with a hapless cadet standing at attention before them. Harmon is easily recognizable because of his receding hairline and the Air Corps insignia and
wings on his uniform blouse. In the 1932 *Howitzer*, the cadet editors described
the Battalion Board, mixing humor, apprehension and perhaps even a little dis-
taste. A cadet arrives at the "Chamber of Justice." He "stands rigidly before this
formidable trio, trembling a little in anticipation of their sharp reprimands and
startling queries." The cadet has prepared a written report, noting the extenu-
ating circumstances surrounding his infraction. It lies unread. Moreover, "his
offense may be ludicrous but the humor is wasted on his audience; his plea
for clemency is dashed to pieces by the stony trio he faces." The triumvirate
administers their brand of justice and then "jokingly" disband, oblivious to the
pain they have caused.[101]

It is not a favorable portrait. The battalion tacs, unlike their company
subordinates, were more removed by rank and position from the cadets. Worse,
too often their main contact with cadets was in the disciplinary environment
noted above. Battalion tactical officers had difficulty bonding with cadets under
such circumstances.

During Harmon's final year at West Point he was also the assistant commandant. In this role he accompanied the second classmen on their tours to
operational posts, including the trip to Langley Field for aviation demonstra-
tions, while also commanding plebe training and going on the summer hike.
He enjoyed all of this immensely. He liked being around cadets, and often had
them over for dinner on holidays. One of these was his nephew, John Honeycutt—his sister Margaret's son. Harmon often played chess with the cadets
and talked to them about his career in the Air Corps. The environment was
pleasant, the pressure was low, he and Rosa-Maye had the time and inclination
to socialize with friends, shop, and enjoy the theater in New York City, and in
the fall there was Academy football.[102] It was a custom of the times that most

Sunday afternoons were reserved for "calling." Couples would dress up and pay a social visit to their friends and superiors. In the latter case, they would leave their calling cards on the silver plate inside the door. It was a quaint custom that died with World War II.

The Harmons had brought with them their maid and cook from London, and they also enjoyed the services of a laundress, seamstress and "striker"—a handyman who was usually a young soldier. This freed up considerable time for the newlyweds to enjoy life and each other.[103] Often in the evenings, the couple would simply sit and talk, play cards, go for walks, or read to each other. There were numerous visits from family and friends—many of Hubert's classmates and colleagues from Washington stopped through to stay a day or two. On such occasions there was always time for a round of golf or a game of bridge after dinner. More important than all of this, on April 17, 1931, Eula Wulfjen Harmon was born in Washington DC—the medical facilities were far superior there—and the mother and child then convalesced with the Kendricks before returning home to West Point the following month.[104]

Harmon's efficiency reports for all three years were a mixture of "excellent" and "superior" marks. He was generally ranked highest for his administrative and executive duties. The commandant, Lieutenant Colonel Richardson, wrote that Harmon "has a good mind which is not warped but sees above the military groove, bringing a broad view to all questions. Thoroughly honorable, dependable and just."[105] These last were certainly excellent characteristics for any officer to possess. The following year Richardson wrote that Harmon was "the hardest worker I have met in the Army."[106]

This was an important assignment for Harmon, not because it led immediately to promotion, but because it once again immersed him in an academic environment. Significantly, this role was not that of either student or teacher—at least not in the traditional meaning of those terms—but rather as an administrator and one who was intimately involved with the disciplinary and logistical facets of cadet life. This balanced view was crucial. He had already been a student, at West Point, the Engineering School, and at night school in Washington DC, and he would soon be again—on three more occasions during the next decade. His tour at West Point gave him a different perspective, and one that he would remember.

Rosa-Maye Harmon would later remark that this assignment also helped solidify in her husband's mind the importance of a broad education and an internationalist outlook. His previous two years working with Royal Air Force officers had illustrated for him the stark contrast between their education and worldview and that of the still-cloistered Corps of Cadets.[107] This was another lesson he would file away for future use.

In the summer of 1932 the Harmons left West Point a year earlier than planned in order to attend the Air Corps Tactical School. This was an essential professional step for an air officer, and Harmon worried that he was getting too senior. He noted that nearly all his classmates who were airmen had already attended the school, and he feared he would be left behind. He lobbied his superiors to release him early from his assignment so he could attend the Tactical School and not be penalized on future promotion lists. Major General Benjamin Foulois, the Air Corps chief, wrote directly to Colonel Richardson also requesting the early move. The request was granted.[108]

En route, they took a long detour and drove out to Sheridan. Harmon, always clever with his hands and a good carpenter, built a special crib for the rear seat of the car that could be converted into a regular crib for use in a hotel room. Still, it was a grueling drive, lasting twelve days, and little Eula was sick much of the way. Yet, being a father had its own magical wonder, and in November he wrote to Rosa-Maye's cousin that his daughter was "the most fascinating creature in the world. She still toddles around on her toes with her little shoulders and arms hunched way up for balance. Jabbers like a magpie and knows dozens of words."[109] Despite his hectic schedule, for the rest of his life Hubert Harmon enjoyed being a father as much as anything else he did.

CHAPTER 4

Education and
Preparing for the Test

illy Mitchell had not been alone in arguing that the airplane had revolutionized war. Others in the US as well as in Great Britain (notably Air Marshal Hugh Trenchard and Group Captain John Slessor) and in Italy (Brigadier General Giulio Douhet), were then saying much the same thing. The difference in America was that Mitchell's position after the World War as the deputy chief of the Air Service, combined with his dominating personality, made him the unquestioned intellectual leader of Army airmen.

In 1920 the Air Service took an important step by opening its own branch school at Langley Field—what would soon be called the Air Service Tactical School. Very quickly the Tactical School began teaching—although preaching may not be too strong a term—the ideas that Mitchell was expounding at the same time. In 1926, Major William Sherman, an instructor at Langley, wrote *Air Warfare*, a book based on his Tactical School lectures that echoed the thoughts of Mitchell. Significantly, Sherman discussed the importance of selecting strategic targets. Just because aircraft now had the ability to fly over enemy armies, as well as geographic obstacles like oceans, mountains and deserts that inhibited ground forces, and could then strike at virtually anything in an enemy country, that did not mean aircraft could or should strike everything. Instead, air planners would need to select targets that would cause the most disruption for the least effort. Sherman focused on the key aspects of an enemy's industrial infrastructure.[1]

Others followed in Sherman's footsteps, and by the early 1930s there was a group of energetic and original thinkers at the Tactical School—now called the Air Corps Tactical School (ACTS) and located at Maxwell Field, Alabama.

Officers like Ken Walker, Don Wilson, Hal George, Haywood "Possum" Hansell, Larry Kuter, and others formulated a unique theory of strategic bombing that was termed the "industrial web." This concept postulated that a modern economy was tied together in a complex and symbiotic manner. All aspects of a nation's transportation, industrial, communications, and power-generating infrastructures were connected, and, like a spider's web, a disturbance in one sector would reverberate throughout the entire system.

One of those quirks of fate that sometimes leads to unexpected results helped shape this revolutionary theory. One day the instructors and students at the Tactical School went out to the flightline to get in some flying, when they were told that the planes were grounded. A small spring in the propeller governing mechanism of one of the planes had broken, causing the propeller to "run away." When checking other aircraft they found other springs that were defective. The planes were grounded until new springs could be procured. However, only one factory in the US, in Pittsburgh, made the required springs, and it was closed due to flooding. The springs were on back order. This seemed important: no factory, no springs, no flying. The implication seemed obvious: if an enemy wished to gain air superiority over the United States, perhaps it was not necessary to shoot down every aircraft in the Air Corps; perhaps it was merely necessary to destroy one factory in Pittsburgh.[2]

This was, admittedly, a feeble example upon which to build a theory of war, but the underlying concept was intriguing. Specifically, what if an air force were to attack and destroy, say, a nation's power grid, and this destruction had a cascading and massive effect throughout the economy of the entire country? The objective was to select the bottlenecks—like the propeller spring—the key targets whose neutralization would most effectively and efficiently result in a system-wide collapse.[3]

The main problem with the theory was that it was based on almost no experience. Strategic bombing had barely been conducted during the World War, so airmen could not give solid historical examples to support their predictions. Worse, the "industrial web" theory required the use of bombers large enough, fast enough, and accurate enough, to find and obliterate those key targets. In the decade following the World War, such bombardment planes simply did not exist. But help was on the way.

February 1932 saw the first flight of a new bomber, the Martin B-10. This airplane was a dramatic leap over its predecessors. It was an all-metal

cantilever monoplane with retractable landing gear and enclosed cockpits. It entered
Air Corps service six months after a new
fighter, the Boeing P-26. The "Peashooter"
was an open-cockpit monoplane with a
wire-braced wing and fixed landing gear.
Although marginally faster than the B-10,
this new fighter was technologically inferior
to the new bomber. To underline this growing dominance of bombers over fighters,
the Boeing B-17 made its maiden flight in
1935. The "Flying Fortress" would become
a legendary airplane during World War II. It
was, as Hap Arnold commented, "Air Power
you could put your hand on."[4]

Rosa-Maye in the 1930s.

Major Hubert Harmon arrived at Maxwell Field in the summer of
1932—a few months after the B-10 and P-26 had made their first flights. The
Tactical School had just moved to Maxwell from Langley Field the year previously, and so much construction was still on-going to complete the academic
buildings and family housing. Even so, Maxwell was one of the more beautiful airbases in the Air Corps. One of the benefits for Harmon was the fact
that old friend and classmate Hume Peabody was the assistant commandant
of the School. Hubert arrived for the start of class, but Rosa-Maye and Eula
lingered in Wyoming with the family until October enjoying relatives, while
Rosa-Maye also busied herself helping out on the ranch by "cutting cows and
calves" and "working the herd." Upon their arrival in Alabama, Hubert took
wife and daughter to the house they would be renting in Montgomery and
introduced them to the staff: Roger the butler, Annie the cook, and Flossie the
maid and baby tender.[5]

Because ACTS was an Army branch school, the curriculum discussed
not only the specifics of the air branch, but also the other branches as well,
so that students would understand how the pieces fit together to work as an
effective Army team. As a result, during Harmon's year at Maxwell, more than
half of the curriculum was devoted to non-air subjects. Some of these were of
a general nature, such as logistics, signals, military intelligence and staff duties.
Several courses covered the other Army branches: Infantry, Cavalry, Field and

Coastal Artillery, Chemical Warfare, Ordnance, and the Medical Corps. There were also guest speakers for maritime operations.[6]

The 43 percent of the ACTS curriculum that dealt with air matters included Air Force, Air Navigation, Balloons and Airships, International Air Regulations, and the heart of the matter: Bombardment, Attack, Pursuit, and Observation Aviation.[7] Most of these air topics were taught in the second half of the year. In addition, both students and faculty were expected to fly frequently. The aircraft available at Maxwell were generally observation and training aircraft—there were no front-line combat planes except, arguably, some rapidly obsolescing P-12 biplanes.[8] Because classes were generally held five days each week in the mornings, afternoons were usually set aside for flying (students were expected to accumulate about eighty flying hours during the year) and, surprisingly, equitation.[9]

Classes began each morning with a lecture, given in a long and narrow room, not an auditorium, which had poor acoustics and no microphone. One instructor later recalled that one usually had nearly to shout in order to be heard by everyone.[10] After a question-and-answer period, the students would break up into smaller seminars where they would discuss the subject of the lecture or work tactical problems. These tactical problems typically involved determining the number and type of aircraft needed, the ordnance they would carry, and the tactical formation used by a strike force to hit a specific target— and conversely the size and composition of the defensive force that would be needed to thwart such an attack.[11] These detailed and complex tactical problems took several hours to complete.

The faculty members were usually ACTS graduates who had been kept on for another tour, not always willingly. Although this practice—which was standard at most Army schools—was somewhat incestuous, the quality of the officers chosen for the ACTS faculty was unusually high. Six of the men who served as instructors during the two decades between the world wars later rose to the rank of full general, while a dozen others would wear three stars—one of those was Millard Harmon.[12]

The students varied in rank. In Hubert Harmon's class were ten majors, nineteen captains and twelve first lieutenants. All but ten of these forty-one students were airmen. There were no naval officers in the class, but there was a marine.[13]

When Harmon and his classmates began their instruction on airpower after Christmas, they were exposed to strategic bombing theories then being formulated by the faculty members. Although Harmon had served several years on the Air Staff in Washington and been exposed to the revolutionary ideas of Billy Mitchell at close range, the heady ideas then being taught at ACTS must have been a bit surprising.

The thrust of this airpower thinking can be illustrated by a lecture given by First Lieutenant Ken Walker, an instructor at the Tactical School while Harmon was a student. Walker began by stating that bombardment was "the backbone of any air force." As such, it must be the dominant arm of the Air Corps, with pursuit and observation units acting in support. Given the defensive posture of the United States, Walker argued that the first and most obvious target for the bombers would be an enemy fleet that would approach our coast. Such a fleet would never be able to land an invading army as long as we could control the air over the ocean approaches to our shores—naval vessels were helpless in the face of air attack.

In the event of war against a land power, Walker then made a statement that would be echoed by fellow airmen repeatedly thereafter: "a determined air attack, once launched, is most difficult, if not impossible to stop when directed against land objectives." Walker and his colleagues were writing before the invention of radar; as a consequence, they postulated that aircraft could attack from any direction, any altitude, and at any time, thus achieving tactical surprise. Once again assuming that the US would be on the strategic defensive, Walker argued that enemy airbases near the US—in Central or South America—would present the greatest threat to the US. The mission of our bombers would be to destroy those airbases before they could be used against us.

Walker then noted that although antiaircraft fire was a threat to a bomber formation, it could never stop a determined attack. Pursuit aircraft would be a greater danger, but given that new bombers (like the B-10) had a performance nearly equal to that of enemy fighters, and that bombers would be equipped with their own defensive guns, even this threat could be discounted.

In summary, Walker argued that long-range airpower had now become the first line of defense for the US—not the Navy. It would therefore logically follow that an independent Air Force should be created that was coequal to the Army and Navy, and this Air Force should be built around bombardment aviation.[14]

This was typical of the arguments used by the bomber advocates at the Tactical School during the interwar period. They were long on passion and theory, but short on proof. It should also be noted that not everyone at ACTS subscribed to this belief in the primacy of bombardment. Captain Claire Chennault, a pursuit instructor at Maxwell during this period, argued just as vehemently that the bomber would *not* always get through, and that a well organized and capable defense armed with first-rate interceptor planes and backed by a ground-observer corps (of the kind used by the British in the World War), *would* be able to meet and then defeat an enemy air attack. In one of his lectures he dismissed the overly-optimistic thinking of those like Walker by sniffing: "this lack of regard for hostile opposition is a theory which has no foundation in experience."[15] Chennault, who would later organize and command the *Flying Tigers* in China during World War II, was ignored, with devastating results.[16]

Classes ended in early May 1933, and the class flew out to March Field, California, to participate in aerial maneuvers. This was a thoroughly enjoyable and rewarding experience for Harmon and his classmates. Because he had finished the pursuit course at Issoudun in 1918, Harmon was still considered a pursuit pilot; he therefore was permitted to fly a P-12 out to California and back. The maneuvers themselves were extensive and unusually realistic. Their purposes were to concentrate air force units over long distances; exercise staff efficiency; test radio control of aircraft; practice rendezvousing of units from dispersed locations; attack land and sea targets; employ camouflage techniques; test interception of "enemy" bombardment forces; and practice night operations. Besides the contingent from Maxwell, units also flew in from Kelly, Langley, Barksdale, Chanute, and several other airfields around the country.

Harmon was assigned to the G-3 (Operations) division for the maneuvers, working for Major Ralph Royce. More important, Miff was there, as was old friend Walt Krause from the Engineering School. It was a thorough and professionally-run exercise. For the debrief, Brigadier General Oscar Westover, the deputy chief of the Air Corps, singled out Miff for praise, no doubt swelling Hubert with pride.[17]

After this lengthy trip, Harmon and a few other students were sent to Fort Du Pont, Delaware, to participate in a command-post exercise. These were practical and useful conclusions to a stimulating and intellectual year.[18] Unlike most Army schools, ACTS did not rank-order its graduates, so we do not know how Harmon fared vis-à-vis his classmates, but it does not appear he expended a great deal of extra effort. Rosa-Maye later recalled that their year at Maxwell Field was relaxing and enjoyable. Her diary notes often that Hubert was golfing—it seldom mentions him buried in books and doing his homework.

Harmon's efficiency report for that year was unusually bland. Although the blocks on the front of the form were all checked "superior"—except for "physical activity"—the word description on the back of the form said simply: "An intelligent, conscientious, hard working officer, superior in every respect."[19] Still, the importance of this year should not be under-estimated. ACTS was the intellectual heart of the Air Corps between the wars. It labored to turn platitudes into plans and to codify the amorphous ideas and theories of Billy Mitchell and others that had been circulating in the ether for more than a decade. There were shortcomings with the Tactical School and its approach to air doctrine, but its impact was enormous. Of the 320 airmen who were general officers at the end of World War II, 261 were ACTS graduates. The three full generals in the Army Air Forces—Carl Spaatz, Joe McNarney and George Kenney—were all graduates (and the last two had been on the faculty), and eleven of thirteen lieutenant generals were also graduates.[20]

More to the point: when Hap Arnold formed a war plans division on the Air Staff in 1941 and sought a blueprint for a strategic bombing campaign against Germany, he turned to four men—Hal George, Ken Walker, "Possum" Hansell and Larry Kuter to write it. All four had been instructors at the Tactical School. Their effort, AWPD-1, not surprisingly read much like the lectures they had given at Maxwell the previous decade. ACTS had been the incubator for the doctrine of high altitude, daylight, precision bombing of industrial targets that the Army Air Forces employed in World War II.

Harmon listened to what was taught at Maxwell Field, and in later years he would give speeches and write letters regarding the role of airpower in war that were echoes of what he had heard at the Tactical School.

In the summer of 1933, Harmon received orders for more school; he was to attend the Command and General Staff School at Fort Leavenworth, Kansas. Because classes did not begin until the end of August, he and the family remained in Montgomery for six weeks after graduation. He was assigned "casual duties," but was pretty much left alone to enjoy a vacation.[21] Once again, the family drove out to *Trail End*; Rosa-Maye and Eula remained there until September while Hubert went on ahead to Leavenworth for the beginning of class. There was a tragic note here, although it was not realized at the time. When Rosa-Maye said goodbye to her father, it was for the last time—he would die of a cerebral hemorrhage in November.

"Horses have Right of Way"

Harmon arrived at the Command and General Staff School in late August 1933. He found housing and then hired a cook, maid and striker prior to Rosa-Maye's arrival. As for the curriculum, the Staff School focused almost exclusively on the ground-combat arms. Because the Air Corps was a branch of the Army, however, air officers hoping for promotion were expected to attend Fort Leavenworth to become well-rounded and learn more about their parent organization. Attendance at the Staff School was virtually essential for an officer who wished to be selected for command. As a result of the School's ground focus, the curriculum was often boring and routine for airmen, especially because the Staff School lasted a full two years when Harmon was in attendance—it would revert to a one-year school for those coming after him.[22]

Students spent an enormous amount of time on ground tactics and map exercises, many of which were "trite, predictable, and often unrealistic."[23] The School's mission was to produce staff officers whose function was to assist their commanders. They were expected to administer, advise, prepare orders, and ensure the commander's wishes were followed. Leavenworth did not seek to develop officers who would "operate independently without direction," but instead to be members of a team and most especially an extension of the commander. Staff officers were to strive for a "well-oiled machine with all parts working together harmoniously."[24]

Rosa-Maye with "Bob," while stationed at Fort Leavenworth.

For exercises, students were divided into small groups of five or six. They would then work against another student group—one was charged with the defensive plan while the other took the offensive. Sometimes the students would work against the instructors. There was a "school solution" to the problems, and all students would be graded on how their answers corresponded to the approved answers.

In addition, in the event he had forgotten since his cadet days, Harmon would be reacquainted with the intricacies of planning and leading infantry attacks, the placement of machine guns and small-caliber artillery, conducting reconnaissance, pursuing (on the ground of course) a retreating enemy, defending strong points, and moving troops by rail or motor vehicles.[25] Staff work was crucial to all of these activities. The World War had demonstrated that most Army officers were deficient in the necessary but often arcane aspects of staff work—especially for large units. That problem was vigorously addressed in the decades following the war. Army officers *would* know how to accomplish the paperwork required to manage a division at least and perhaps even a corps. World War II would indicate the emphasis placed on this skill was wise—the problems exhibited in 1917–18 were not usually repeated.[26]

Harmon had been performing as a staff officer for the previous decade, and doing so at the highest levels of the Air Service/Air Corps; his year at ACTS had served as a refresher. As a result, this part of the curriculum should have been easy for him. The numbing emphasis on infantry tactics was no doubt another matter. A mere seventeen hours were allotted to war planning during the second year, while more than three times that many were given to military geography and terrain exercises.[27] One study states that 54 percent of class time was spent on tactics; 24 percent went towards staff duties; 6 percent was devoted to military history; and the rest was scattered among a variety of other subjects including law, geography, and chemical warfare.[28] As for aviation, the instruction was minimal, and that presented focused on tactical aviation—discussions regarding strategic airpower, as Harmon had just experienced at Maxwell Field, were not entertained. This was deliberate. The Staff School official history admits that the Army was so fearful of an independent air force—a subject discussed with increasing frequency among airmen—that it refused to discuss strategic airpower lest it lead to "more independence and possible parity."[29] As an unfortunate result, the airpower concepts taught at Leavenworth as late as 1939 were the same as had been taught in 1923. For his major paper of the year, Harmon wrote on the subject of "A Balanced Air Force." Unfortunately, no copy of this paper exists; it would be interesting to know Harmon's thoughts on this subject at the time.[30]

The lack of emphasis on aviation was highlighted by the fact that only four of the School's seventy-one faculty members were airmen. These officers, led by Lieutenant Colonel George Brett and including Harmon's West Point classmates

Tom Hanley and George Stratemeyer—were limited in what they could teach, not only due to the strictures imposed by the Staff School administration, but also because of the paucity of modern aircraft on the post. Leavenworth graduates did not leave with a positive or realistic impression of the importance of airpower in modern war, and that failing would become painfully evident during World War II. One airman, Ennis Whitehead, spoke bluntly of his time at Leavenworth: "This school is as valuable to us as a course in advanced English literature would be. Nice to have, but of little practical value."[31]

Major Ira Eaker, Harmon's comrade from the Air Service staff days, arrived at Leavenworth in 1935 and wrote a humorous account of his tour in Kansas for the *Air Corps Newsletter*. Eaker, who had been to journalism school and had a flair for this sort of thing, noted that the Staff School was referred to by those on post as the "Little House" in order to distinguish it from the "Big House"—the Federal Penitentiary also on post. It was an old and venerable Army fort, and its facilities had seen better days. Most students—although not the Harmons—lived in an ancient and rambling converted barracks called the "bee hive" that was extremely hot and noisy. Eaker complained about the narrowly focused curriculum with its emphasis on tactics—although Eaker was a pursuit pilot even he thought this focus was a bit much. His advice to fellow airmen was blunt: they shouldn't waste their eyesight by attempting to accomplish all the assigned reading, much of which simply was not relevant. He also warned airmen not to "fight the course"; by that he meant, they should not attempt to disagree too strongly with the instructors over the "school solutions" being preached. The faculty had their collective mind already made up: it was not worth it to argue. Eaker was especially struck, negatively, by the amount of time all students were required to devote to equitation. To his mind, the large sign placed at the front gate said it all: "Horses have right of way."[32] It was not a favorable review of the Staff School or its curriculum.

Actually, Harmon probably enjoyed the equitation more than most—recall that he had owned two horses while stationed in Washington and rode each week with Rosa-Maye. Their daughter Eula also remembers the time at Leavenworth and especially the horses. The "equestrian culture" pervaded all: even the post children were encouraged to ride and participate in shows, hunts and rodeos.[33]

Perhaps in agreement with Eaker's later assessment, Harmon did not excel academically at Leavenworth. He graduated number 83 in a class of 118, but nonetheless worked far harder than he had at Maxwell—Rosa-Maye's diary often refers to his staying up late to work tactical problems. Harmon's effi-ciency report at the completion of his two years was unenthusiastic, concluding with a series of boilerplate terms: "dependable, hardworking, intelligent, ener-getic, thorough, level-headed, adaptable, self-reliant, of great ability."[34] That pretty much covers the waterfront. Rosa-Maye nonetheless remembered the two years at Leavenworth with pleasure. As usual, people made the difference. Five of Harmon's West Point classmates were there at the same time, including old friend Tom Hanley. In addition, there were a number of airmen who had already crossed paths with Harmon or who would soon do so: George Brett, Bill Streett, Willis Hale, Ken Walker, Don Wilson (these last two had been instruc-tors at the Tactical School), Oliver Echols, Delos Emmons, Idwal Edwards, and, of note, Robert Olds. Olds, a widower with a young son to raise, remarried while at Leavenworth to Nina Gore—the actress whose first marriage had been the occasion for Hubert and Rosa-Maye to meet in 1922.[35] Other Army officers at Leavenworth at the same time and who would later become famous included Matthew Ridgway, Maxwell Taylor, Mark Clark, Lucian Truscott and Al Wede-meyer. It was an impressive lineup. In fact, of the sixteen airmen who were in Harmon's class, ten would become generals.

Hubert Harmon had been at school for three years and away from opera-tional flying far longer than that—since 1918. It was time for him to put away the books and staff reports and reacquaint himself with the business end of airpower. In December he had heard a report that he would be posted to the Philippines, but in February that had changed to an assignment at March Field working for Hap Arnold. He thought that "too good to be true," but it was indeed to be his lot.[36] The Harmons left Leavenworth in the summer of 1935 and headed out to March Field in California, home of the 1st Wing of the new General Headquarters Air Force commanded by Brigadier General Frank Andrews. Also of great importance, the Harmons took with them a new addi-tion: Kendrick Harmon was born in Kansas City on October 26, 1934.

Operational Command

The ultimate goal of Billy Mitchell and like-minded airmen in the decade fol-lowing the World War was an independent Air Force. The Army and Navy were vehemently opposed to the idea, and the airmen's political support in Con-gress, although formidable, was still too weak to make independence a reality. Candidly, it is questionable whether the Air Service was ready for independent

*The Harmon family while stationed at
Fort Leavenworth in 1935.*

status in the early 1920s. Air leaders were young and inexperienced; their staff and administrative capabilities had been shown to be inadequate during the war, and the aircraft available—most of wartime vintage and increasingly obsolescent—were not up to the dreams that airmen conjured. Yet, changes had occurred.

The debilitating aspects of the Mitchell court-martial in 1925 were to an extent countered by the Air Corps Act of 1926, whose broad purpose was to create a combat unit of airmen within the Army analogous to the Marine Corps within the Navy. The name of the air arm was changed to the Air Corps to reflect its enhanced status, while also signaling recognition of its latent offensive and strategic potential. An additional assistant secretary of war—for air—was created to represent airmen in the War Department and Congress. The chief of the Air Corps would hold the rank of major general and would be given three assistants of brigadier general rank. The chief and two of his assistants were to be airmen. All flying units were to be commanded by aviators. Each of the War Department General Staff divisions would include an air section, headed by an Air Corps officer. Past promotion inequities between airmen and other Army officers were to be investigated and, if necessary, corrected. The Air Corps was to enjoy a five-year expansion program in both personnel and equipment.[37]

To many airmen, especially Billy Mitchell, these changes were too little and simply reflected another delaying tactic by the War Department. This attitude seemed confirmed when it became apparent that the expansion program would not take place as promised. Still, it was a start.

The next step was taken in the mid-1930s. Although the Air Corps was still under-funded and under-manned relative to the rest of the Army, its capabilities continued to increase, and this was apparent to observers. A key event occurred in 1934 when former Secretary of War Newton D. Baker convened a board to look into the role of airpower in national defense and its relation to civil aviation—the fifteenth such investigation since the end of the World War. The Board spent twenty-five days interviewing 105 witnesses and amassing over 4,000 pages of testimony. Its conclusions were a mixed bag. It rejected the notion of a Department of Defense with three branches for an Army, Navy and Air Force. It also dismissed the idea of a separate Air Force, noting that there were still serious limitations to military aviation. Even so, the increasing effectiveness and importance of airpower could not be denied, so the Board endorsed a further step towards air autonomy: it recommended the formation of a General Headquarters (GHQ) Air Force.[38]

The GHQ Air Force, which was formally established on March 1, 1935, took all of the combat aircraft of the Air Corps—except some observation units that remained attached to army corps—and grouped them under a single airman. Brigadier General Frank Andrews was the first commander of the GHQ Air Force, and during peacetime he reported directly to the Army chief of staff. In time of war, it was expected that the air force would deploy overseas as a combat unit, and Andrews would then report to the theater commander. The Army chief of staff, General Douglas MacArthur, was accurate and prescient when he stated: "The GHQ Air Force could be used as a great deciding factor in mass combat and for rapid reinforcement at distant threatened points, such as at outposts in Panama and Hawaii. It could be used on independent missions of destruction aimed at the vital arteries of a nation."[39]

The GHQ Air Force was organized into three combat wings. The 1st Wing, commanded by Brigadier General Hap Arnold, was headquartered at March Field, California; the 2nd Wing, commanded by Brigadier General Conger Pratt, was based at Langley Field in Virginia; and the 3rd Wing, led by Colonel Gerald C. Brant, was located at Barksdale Field, Louisiana. Initially, the GHQ Air Force was, like the Air Corps as a whole, under-manned and under-equipped, possessing only 40 percent of its authorized aircraft, 80 percent of its projected officers, and 40 percent of its enlisted complement. Nonetheless, the new organization—which possessed 60 bomber, 42 attack, 146 pursuit and 24 transport aircraft—generated enormous enthusiasm among airmen.[40] For the first time they had a vehicle to use for exercises, maneuvers and experimentation that would allow them to test seriously new ideas regarding the employment of airpower.

Lieutenant Colonel Hubert Harmon reported to March Field in August 1935 to become the executive and operations officer of the 1st Wing, which consisted of two bombardment groups, the 7th and 19th, and the 17th attack group; later it would also be assigned a reconnaissance squadron. Once again, he was working for Hap Arnold. This was the ideal position to make the best use of his finely-honed administrative skills. This had always been one of his strengths, but after three full years of school at Maxwell Field and Fort Leavenworth, he had become a consummate staff officer. These skills were certainly needed for such a new and in many ways revolutionary air unit. In October, the 19th Bomb Group, which had been based at Rockwell Field in San Diego, moved north to March. It was then performing highly important and secret tests on the new M1 bombsight—better known as the Norden.[41] In addition to its bombing mission, the 19th was also responsible for training all navigators for the Air Corps. In December, the GHQ Air Force held maneuvers to see how fast all units could gather in one place. The 1st Wing was given twenty-four hours to make it from California to Florida—Hap's boys made it in twenty-two.[42] This type of deployment was important, because normally units trained at their home stations, simply because the funds needed for traveling to maneuvers in other parts of the country were unavailable. At home, units also experimented with various organizational setups: maintenance units were integrated into flying units in some cases, while at other bases separate service squadrons were formed alongside the flying units.[43] It was an exciting and busy time.

Harmon was directly involved in all of these activities and was clearly an ideal officer for this type of work. His efficiency report from Arnold in January 1936 confirmed this appraisal. Arnold wrote that Harmon was "a very high grade officer who has a wide range of administrative experience. Is conscientious, reliable, and very thorough in all his work." Ominously, Arnold downgraded Harmon to "satisfactory" in the block labeled "Force."[44] This seemed a blunt announcement by Arnold that he believed Harmon was more suited to staff duties than he was for command. Arnold left for Washington soon after to become the deputy chief of the Air Corps, and his place was taken initially by Colonel Henry B. Clagett and then by Brigadier General Delos C. Emmons. The efficiency reports they signed were better, and in August 1936 Harmon was given command of the 19th Bomb Group. This was his first command in two decades—since his assignment in Texas in 1918—and his first of a non-training unit.[45]

Harmon relished the experience of command—although he still found time for golf. Indeed, one day young Kendrick was out in front of the house riding in his toy car when an officer stopped by and asked him where his daddy was. Kendrick's too candid reply: "he's at golfice."[46] It was not all fun. Around this time Harmon suffered a fairly serious foot injury. His medical records state: "wound, contused, moderately severe, dorsal surface, right foot; accidentally incurred while playing golf, when hit on foot by golf ball knocked by another player."[47] The price of freedom doesn't come cheap.

Harmon took command of the 19th Bomb Group as it transitioned from B-10s and B-12s to new Douglas B-18s. The "Bolo" was an unhappy design. Modeled after the DC-2 commercial airliner, the B-18 competed with the B-17 to be the Army's new heavy bomber in 1935. In a tragedy that reverberated through the Air Corps for years, the B-17 prototype crashed during the trials. Although the cause of the accident was pilot error—the crew had forgotten to disengage the elevator locks before initiating takeoff—the Army used the accident as an excuse to declare the far inferior B-18 the winner.[48] The Air Corps prepared detailed analyses showing that the B-18, although cheaper than the B-17, had a much smaller bomb load and also shorter range. The result: to deliver a similar bomb load over a given distance, it took far fewer B-17s, which in turn required 60 percent fewer officers. Furthermore, the excessive number of B-18s that would be required for such a hypothetical mission would use up almost the entire number of aircraft authorized for the Air Corps.[49] Army leaders were unmoved. To airmen, this foolish decision merely confirmed their suspicions that ground officers were deliberately attempting to throttle their growth and capability for their own parochial ends. Eventually, the Army hierarchy relented to the extent that it allowed the purchase of thirteen B-17s for experimental purposes.[50] When war broke out in Europe four years later, the Air Corps still possessed a mere twenty-six of the heavy bombers.[51] The B-18 was the standard bomber when the Japanese hit Pearl Harbor, but almost immediately all realized that the "Bolos" were nearly useless as combat aircraft. The hundreds of B-18s in the inventory were then relegated to training duty and coastal patrol.

Even so, for Harmon's men the new airplanes were most welcome. Training occupied most of the group's time, and Harmon insisted that all "aircraft commanders" be qualified as pilots, celestial navigators, bombardiers, and gunners. During his period in command, the 19th dropped over 8,000 bombs on the practice range at nearby Lake Muroc.[52] In addition, Colonel Clagett directed that all B-18 pilots be rigorously trained in over-water navigation, both day and night. If the mission of the 1st Wing was coast defense against an enemy fleet, then they had better know how to carry out that task. The 19th took Clagett's directive to heart and soon acquired the nickname of the "coastal cops" for the amount of time the group spent patrolling over the ocean.[53]

Harmon's group was able to put its rigorous training to the test when they were given the task of deploying "forward" to Lake Muroc (eighty miles north of March Field) and simulating a bare-base operation. From there, they loaded up with bombs and flew east 520 miles to bomb a simulated battleship in the Great Salt Lake. Flying at night and relying on celestial navigation, the 19th Group found the target and plastered it. The crews then landed in Salt Lake City to a heroes' welcome.

This exercise was part of major air maneuvers conducted on the West Coast in the spring of 1936. General Andrews came out to command the GHQ Air Force, and once again the idea was to concentrate a large force of combat air units from all over the US in one area—in this case at March and Hamilton Fields. Although none of the units were at full strength—an endemic problem—Andrews still assembled 260 airplanes and nearly 4,000 personnel for the maneuvers.

The 19th's attack on the Great Salt Lake was part of the offensive phase of this exercise. The defensive portion involved simulated attacks on March Field by units basing out of Hamilton. Of note, the defenders were aided by an innovative use of an early warning net manned by ground observers using telephones to call-in their sightings to a central intercept post. Due to manning problems, many of these defensive tasks were undertaken by civilian employees of California Edison Company. Overall, it was another very impressive showing.[54]

Upon completing eleven months in command, Harmon was returned to school yet again, this time to the Army War College located in Washington DC. His two years at March Field had been a tremendously valuable experience. He had put his staff skills to excellent use in helping to stand up the new GHQ Air Force—the forerunner of the independent service that would be born a decade later—and then commanded one of its premier combat units. After twenty-two years of commissioned service, Harmon had finally been intimately involved in air operations at the pointed end of the spear. It was a heady experience that he would seek to repeat in the years ahead. He performed well. His efficiency report for his year in command was solid, and in fact was upgraded signifi-cantly by Brigadier General Delos C. Emmons.[55]

In addition, Harmon had spent much time with men who would be key players in the war that was looming on the horizon: Hap Arnold, Carl Spaatz, Frank Andrews, Ira Eaker, Delos Emmons, Warner Robbins, Ennis Whitehead and others. In fact, at March Harmon began to play some serious poker, rejoin-ing the group he began with Eaker in the 1920s. One night he went off to play and did not return until after breakfast the following morning—Rosa-Maye was furious.[56] Hubert continued to play, but watched the clock more diligently. March Field had been an important tour.

The School for Senior Officers

Upon leaving California, the Harmons boarded the SS *Republic*—the same ship they had taken on their honeymoon cruise to England in 1927. The fam-ily sailed under the new Golden Gate Bridge and through the Panama Canal up the East Coast to New York. On board, young Kendrick managed to smack his mouth on a teeter totter, losing his front teeth in the process! From New York the Harmons took the train to Washington and moved into a house near the Naval Observatory. Hubert was slated to attend the Army War College located at what was then Washington Barracks (now Fort McNair). The War College was pitched at a higher plane than the Command and General Staff School. Officers were expected to know already the fundamentals of staffing and administration—it was a requirement that all attendees be graduates of Leavenworth. Now they would study broader topics of strategy, mobilization and logistics. They would devise war plans. The techniques they had learned at Leavenworth would be used to shed light on these higher-order problems, and they would use those same methodologies to present their findings and analy-ses in a common format that other Army officers could readily understand.

The goal of the War College was to produce staff officers for the War Department General Staff in Washington. At that time there was no Joint Staff, nor were there any theater staffs similar to the combatant commands during World War II and after. The result: although the Army benefited from this rich supply of top staff officers each year, it meant that the officers graduating from the War College would necessarily have a limited purview of joint and com-bined warfare—the employment of land, sea, and air forces as a unified whole or in conjunction with allies. This was first and foremost an *Army* school, and this deficiency in what would later be termed "jointness" would become glaringly apparent in World War II. Nonetheless, it would be unfair to criticize too severely the War College—and its Navy counterpart at Newport, Rhode Island, that suffered from the same myopia. The American experience in 1917–18 during the World War revealed major shortcomings in the rudiments of planning and staff duties for large military units. Those problems had been largely solved in the two decades afterwards. The educational deficiencies relative to joint and combined warfare would have to wait until after the conclusion of World War II.

The curriculum was divided into two main parts: the preparation for war and the conduct of war. Mobilization planning was a large part of this first phase, not only because of its intrinsic worth, but because the Army's own plans, devised during Douglas MacArthur's tenure as chief of staff (1930–1935), were outdated. America had a very small army in the early 1930s, the nation was in an isolationist mood, the international situation looked reasonably benign, and the mobilization base in the event of war was small and untapped. All of these conditions began to change dramatically as the decade of the 1930s advanced. The Army therefore expected the students and faculty at the War College to play a role in revamping the old plans.

Students were assigned to several committees to study specific issues. Each committee would prepare a report, which would then be briefed to the entire class with discussion following. All students would thus be able to delve into certain problems at great depth, while also being exposed to a wide range of other issues. Harmon, for example, was a member of two committees that worked on manpower issues, including the utilization of women in the armed forces. As we shall soon see, this foray into personnel issues would earmark him for similar staff duties in the years ahead.

The year at Washington Barracks began with a month-long course termed "Command" that dealt with large-unit operations at the field army or army-group level. This course was in some ways a refresher and overview of the Army as whole, discussing doctrine and organizational issues of all the branches; it also included an introduction to naval operations. Throughout this phase, and indeed during the entire year, the War College struggled to keep pace with the rapid changes taking place in technology. Airpower and mechanization, specifically, were revolutionizing warfare—facts that would soon become abundantly clear in the battlespaces of Europe and Asia.

The War College, frankly, was unable to keep up with many of these changes. For one thing, the move towards world war was apparent, and as had been the case two decades earlier in a similar situation, the faculty turnover accelerated as quality officers were needed to manage expansion and mobilization. For example, between the years 1935 and 1940 the War College had four different commandants. As a result of this personnel turmoil, the curriculum remained surprisingly static given the momentous events occurring around the world. As for new technologies, the Army expected the branch schools to deal with these issues. In the case of airpower, the Air Corps Tactical School certainly filled the bill—to a greater extent than many in the Army hierarchy wished—but in other areas, such as armored warfare, the branch schools were woefully deficient. The War College similarly did not address these changes: when George Patton attended, for example, an Air Corps officer proposed an airborne envelopment maneuver during one of the war games. The War College commandant promptly halted the exercise, declaring: "There will be no such nonsense."[57] As a consequence, the average Army officer entered the war a few years later with serious knowledge gaps, and only the harsh teacher of war itself would identify and correct those deficiencies.[58]

Because of the rapidly changing world situation, students were expected to keep up on events, but this proved difficult, partly because America's isolationist mood had the effect of making even officers at the War College introspective and conservative. This certainly was the case for Hubert Harmon. He was the chairman of a student committee tasked to study "A Current International Estimate." Harmon focused on the situation confronting the British Empire. Given his two tours in London, he was already well-versed in the subject. He began by noting the historical and geographical setting of Britain; essentially, its worldwide empire was so vast that it was dependent on its maritime lines of communication. A huge fleet of tankers and cargo vessels kept raw materials and goods traveling back and forth. This merchant fleet in turn required naval ports scattered about the earth not only for replenishment, but for major and minor repairs as well. This merchant fleet required protection; hence, the presence of the Royal Navy, but also far-flung garrisons that were needed to guard those overseas ports and basing facilities. As a maritime nation, Britain was acutely conscious of other countries that attempted to build a fleet that could grow into a rival. It was the determination of imperial Germany in the late nineteenth and early twentieth centuries to build a major fleet that so concerned London and was a factor leading to war in 1914. It was one thing for a mighty continental power to improve the size and quality of its land forces; when it ventured onto the sea as well, problems were inevitable.

Harmon then outlined the demographic situation in the British Empire, while also sketching out the size and quality of its military forces. He concluded by discussing Britain's strategic situation and her policies relative to other major nations: Italy, Germany, the Soviet Union, the United States, and Japan.

Frankly, Harmon's analysis was superficial and shed little light on the problems confronting Britain. To read this report, one would conclude that Britain was merely in a period of mild economic rivalry with neighbors. Although Italy was showing signs of territorial expansion, this was dismissed as being only temporary and a condition of Mousoulini's [sic] "personal ambitions." As for Germany, Harmon made no mention of either Nazi policies or Adolf Hitler; rather, he portrayed Germany as simply trying to redress the "excessive" restrictions placed upon her by the Versailles Treaty. Moscow was an enigma. British leaders viewed the United States as a social inferior that was not to be taken seriously. In Harmon's judgment, the true threat to Britain was Japan, and London must "view with increasing alarm Japan's naval expansion."[59] Given the date, mid-1938, and the facts that Germany had already occupied the Rhineland, united with Austria, and was threatening Czechoslovakia—all in violation of the Versailles Treaty—and that Japan was in a major war with China, this was a remarkably naïve survey. Harmon had fulfilled a class requirement, nothing more.

In the "conduct of war" phase, students looked closely at operational war plans while also conducting numerous map or terrain exercises.[60] Given the scarcity of funds for the military during the interwar period, large-scale maneuvers were rare. Instead, the students at the War College performed what were largely intellectual games, and although these played a useful roll, they were no substitute for actual exercises. Moreover, because of the nation's mood, even these games were largely of a defensive nature—it was assumed the United States would remain neutral during a war in Europe or the Pacific unless it was directly attacked. As a result, the map exercises focused on the defense of America's overseas possessions. Of significance for Harmon, one of these scenarios involved the threats facing the Panama Canal. Another exercise involved a war plan for a conflict in Europe that saw Germany, Italy and Austria-Hungary on one side, and France, Britain, and the Soviet Union on the other. Also, significantly, the students looked closely at War Plan Orange—an anticipated war with Japan.[61] The leadership at the War College had a fairly realistic view of the future; unfortunately, the nation's civilian leadership did not feel similarly. The year after Harmon's class graduated, the War College was forced to drop the exercises that involved Europe and Japan—US neutrality legislation prohibited such thinking. As a result, War College students in 1938 were forced back into a hemisphere-defense mindset—the major wargame that year would be against Mexico.[62]

The acquiescence to political guidance was a two-edged sword for the War College and the American military in general prior to World War II. Certainly, the essential primacy of civilian control over the military was indisputable. However, the military, which at some point becomes the implementer of government policy, needs to recognize its responsibilities in providing sound military advice to its civilian leaders. As the official historian of the Army War College aptly noted: "The War College saw its mission as preparing officers to carry out the policy despite all obstacles, not as encouraging or preparing officers to make recommendations that might lead to better policy."[63] The US Army in 1938 was not attempting to produce grand strategists; it was hoping to generate practitioners. There is razor-thin line here, and during World War II the question of military input to policy-making became a serious issue. It would not be the last time such tensions would arise.

Harmon undertook another noteworthy project during his year at the War College. Students were expected to write a paper on a topic that was not directly related to other course work. This "thesis" requirement was an individual project, and thus students did not form into groups and committees. Harmon decided to explore the issue of bombing accuracy—an interesting and important choice. He had heard a great deal about the subject in a theoretical sense during his year at the Air Corps Tactical School, but even more importantly, he had just come from an operational assignment with the 19th Bombardment Group. The issue of accuracy lay at the very core of all discussions regarding the efficacy of strategic bombing.

Unfortunately, Harmon's study was fairly pedestrian. He began by discussing the various forms used to record bombing scores at the unit level, but noted that there was no agency charged with an analysis of the results. Operational units were required to collect the data and then send it to the Air Corps Tactical School at Maxwell, believing that someone there would collate the data from all over the Air Corps, analyze it, and produce trends with any corrective actions that were then disseminated back to the operational units. Not true said Harmon: nobody at Maxwell actually performed these functions. His recommendation: someone should do so. He also called for the simplification and elimination of some of the forms used to collect bombing data.[64]

This was a useful start, but it betrayed a lack of understanding of the problems surrounding strategic bombing. In essence, there were three major questions that airmen needed to answer regarding the effectiveness and utility of their chosen weapon: could they hit their assigned targets; could they damage those targets if they were hit; and, most importantly, even if the answer to the first two questions was "yes," did it make any difference in the conduct of the war? These three fundamental problems would plague airmen throughout most of World War II. Harmon was certainly correct in identifying the first hurdle—could airmen find and hit their assigned targets. Experience early in the war would conclusively indicate that the answer was a resounding "no"—although accuracy improved significantly as the war progressed. Worse, the second and third questions were far more difficult to answer. For airmen, the issues of bomb damage assessment and the quantification of strategic-level effects would prove to be enormous challenges.[65] Harmon was not alone in failing to grasp the complexity of the problem, but it is notable that he at least identified the first step in this crucial shortcoming in airpower doctrine before the war.

As at Fort Leavenworth, there were airmen on the faculty at the War College, and it was their duty to explain the role of airpower to the student body. Also as at the Staff School, however, this was difficult given the small size of the air contingent, the lack of adequate aircraft to demonstrate air capabilities, and the institutional resistance of the Army as a whole to progressive ideas on the subject. Moreover, a classmate of Harmon's that year, who would then remain on the faculty, wrote in his memoirs that the senior airman on the faculty at the War College was "opinionated" and "dogmatic." This was precisely the wrong approach to take with such a volatile topic.[66]

Overall, this was another important year in Hubert Harmon's intellectual development. The War College was the fifth school he had attended since graduating from West Point in 1915, and it was obvious that he enjoyed the stimulation of the classroom—even if he was not always a top student. In fact, Rosa-Maye would later comment that the "pace of instruction was leisurely"—unlike at other Army schools, War College students were not graded or ranked—and Hubert enjoyed himself the entire year. There was much time for golf. This was certainly reflected in his efficiency report in which it was noted he had a "cheerful even disposition with a sense of humor and an engaging personality." There was no reference to academic brilliance.[67] The entire low-key approach taken by the War College was partly due to the fact that the faculty played a somewhat passive role. Students and faculty members mingled freely and were considered equals. In the seminars and map exercises the instructors made it a point to remain in the background—the students were to teach themselves and learn from each other. Given the personnel turmoil at the time as the nation began a buildup for war, this academic practice was questionable but also understandable. Fortunately, the quality of the officers chosen to attend the War College meant that the level of student discourse was quite high. Of the 305 general officers who would serve in World War II, 260 attended the Army War College. Hubert Harmon and many of his classmates would be among them.[68]

When Harmon and his colleagues graduated from the War College in June 1938, Nazi Germany was poised to move into the Czechoslovakian Sudetenland (it would occur in October), finally ending all delusions as to their true intentions. As expected, Harmon would stay in Washington and be posted to the War Department General Staff in the Munitions Building; specifically, he would be the chief of the operations branch of the Army G-1—the Personnel Division.

G-1 was one of five divisions on the General Staff.[69] At the time of Harmon's arrival, there were eighteen officers in G-1; that number would grow slightly to twenty-four by the time he departed in the late summer of 1940. By regulation, G-1 was charged to prepare plans and policies and to supervise activities concerning the procurement, classification, assignment, promotion, transfer, retirement, and discharge of all personnel in the Army—to include the Reserves and National Guard.[70]

The basic staff work Harmon performed was similar to that he had done while on the Air Staff in the previous decade, although obviously the work was more focused, and, more importantly, the pace of the activity was far greater as the nation edged closer to war. The acting deputy chief of staff stated clearly the duties of officers like Harmon. Brigadier General Lorenzo D. Gasser said that the duty of the staff officer was to be an extension of the commander. But, he was "no dweller in monastic solitude. His telephone is always ringing, his colleagues are demanding his help." He spends much of his time in the offices of other staff officers, solving problems. He was a "pick-and-shovel man" and no "dawdler in the dugout." His business was to find the facts and to draw sound conclusions, irrespective of his personal feelings or service branch. He was charged with doing what was best for the entire Army.[71] Although a bit melodramatic, this summary was accurate, and, it must be admitted, generally applies to all staff officers of any service in any time period.

These were hectic times, and Harmon would be tasked to prepare the groundwork for a massive expansion of the Army, not only in personnel, but in facilities as well. Over the next two years he would spend a great deal of time on the road, selecting sites for new airbases that were necessary to the ever-expanding air arm.[72] Originally, the sites for new airfields were chosen by Congress, but the Wilcox Act of 1935 placed this responsibility in the hands of the War Department. This act, designed to remove some of the political pressures involved in such important decisions, meant that the General Staff selected the best site based strictly on military considerations; Congress would then pass legislation to buy the land and build the facilities. Between 1938 and 1940 several major airbases were established: Westover, MacDill, Hill, and McChord.[73] This experience would prove extremely useful to Harmon, not only when he led the Personnel Distribution Command later in the war, but also when seeking a site for the Air Force Academy in the years thereafter.

The casual, almost lethargic pace of the Army for the two decades following the World War was at an end.

A Return to the Air

Increasing tensions in Europe and in the Pacific during the late 1930s led to a dramatic expansion of the Air Corps. Not only were tens of thousands of more aircraft needed, but so were a corresponding number of pilots, navigators, gunners and ground crew necessary as well. One could date this vast expansion to the White House meeting of November 14, 1938, when President Franklin Roosevelt called for the production of 10,000 new aircraft per year. Hap Arnold, the Air Corps chief, referred to this directive as the "Magna Carta of airpower."[74]

Reorganization for the training of the multitudes needed to fly these aircraft began on January 20, 1939, when Arnold created the Training Group, later called the Flying Training Command, to consolidate all training activities then spread throughout the Air Corps. In July 1940, three centers were established to handle the ever-expanding training plans of the Air Staff in Washington. These new Air Corps Training Centers would be the Gulf Coast Training Center with headquarters at Randolph Field in Texas, the West Coast Training Center commanded from Moffett Field, California, and the Southeast Training Center based at Maxwell Field in Alabama.[75]

Between the wars the Air Corps had turned out an average of 500 pilots per year. In June 1940, Congress funded the expansion of training facilities to generate 9,000 pilots per year, enough to populate 54 combat groups. Soon after, the number of pilots required jumped again, to 12,000. In March 1941, the Air Corps was directed to expand to 84 combat groups—the number of pilots required leapt to a staggering 30,000 per year.[76] Pilot training was to become a production line.

Hubert Harmon was to spend two years in Texas as part of the Gulf Coast Training Center, so we will focus on that organization, which was typical of the other two training centers.

The Gulf Coast Training Center (GCTC) initially controlled not only Randolph Field, but also Brooks and Kelly Fields as well—all three were located in San Antonio. The number of new fields grew rapidly and dramatically. By May 1942 the Air Corps expansion plans required forty-five new airfields nationwide; the GCTC would get nineteen of them, but it was just the beginning.[77]

Up to 1939 the general qualifications for officer flying duty stated that the candidate had to have a high school education (or an equivalency test in some cases), be unmarried, a US citizen, between the ages of 20 and 26, physically and mentally "normal," and of sound character. Applicants first took an academic test administered in or near their hometowns. Those who passed then took physical exams. In these initial screenings, nearly three-quarters of all applicants were rejected, usually for academic deficiencies, eyesight, or heart problems.[78]

The expansion of training after 1939 meant that qualifications were loosened. The maximum age was raised to 28, medical waivers more easily granted, academic standards lowered, and easier entrance examinations devised. The result was a drop in the rejection rate from 73.2 percent in 1939 to 25 percent in 1943.[79]

Applicants were then sent to boot camp as "aviation students." From there, they often attended special programs at civilian colleges where they underwent intensive education in all subjects. Aviators later referred to this phase in the College Training Detachments—which lasted three to four months—as an attempt to cram several years of college into several months. During this phase, aviation students were also given orientation flights in light, single-engine Piper "Cubs" to see if they had an innate fear of flying that would preclude their movement on to flight training. After this, there were more tests at "classification centers" where the men learned if they were qualified to attend flight school and become aircrew members.

Candidates for aircrew training then attended Preflight School: for the GCTC this was located at Kelly Field for pilots and at Ellington Field near Houston for navigators and bombardiers. The nine-week course was broken into three main areas: the academic portion, which was the largest segment and involved classes in air, ground and naval forces, math, physics, etc. The second portion was basic military instruction, and it included drill, pistol firing and guard duty. The third segment was physical education. Instruction was conducted mostly by "militarized" civilians who had been given commissions as lieutenants. The GCTC pioneered in this innovative program to bring these civilians teachers, most of who came from colleges and universities, into military service.[80] Elimination rates in the Preflight phase ran as high as 15 percent.[81]

Flying actually began in the next phase, Primary, where the weeding-out began of those who simply did not have the aptitude or stomach to fly. Early-on it was realized that this initial phase could not be effectively or efficiently handled

Brigadier General Millard F. Harmon, Jr. congratulating Colonel Hubert R. Harmon on his assumption of command at Kelly Field in September 1940.

by the Air Corps. Since 1919, pilot training had taken place at Randolph Field, but the expansion for World War II demanded a large number of instructors, and military pilots, and they were simply too scarce to be used for this phase.[82]

The story is told that Arnold went to a small group of aviators who ran civilian flying schools around the country. He wanted them to expand their facilities to train a hundred times their current number. He told them that funding was not yet authorized, but asked if they would go ahead and start anyway. The operators said they would.[83] The reality was not quite that dramatic, but it was close. Civilian flying schools employing civilian instructors—and lots of them—were needed, and Arnold used his great force and charm to cajole the flying schools around the country to expand quickly to meet the need. Once established, these Primary schools lasted ten weeks, giving around seventy hours of flying time in open-cockpit biplanes, usually the PT-17 "Stearman." Flight training was rudimentary—students soloed, usually after six to eight hours, but the emphasis throughout was on getting up and down safely.

From there, cadets attended Basic flying school, like that at Randolph Field. This too was a ten-week course involving about seventy hours of flying time, usually in the BT-9 or the BT-13. In this phase the aviation cadets were introduced to aerobatics, instrument flying, cross-country, and formation flying.

After this came Advanced training, and for the GCTC this was conducted at several airfields, including Kelly. Again, this course lasted about ten weeks with cadets receiving seventy flying hours while also spending about the same amount of time in the classroom. For those slated to become single-engine pilots, the main aircraft used in this phase was the AT-6 "Texan," one of the finest training aircraft in the world. (Later, more promising students would transition into battle-weary P-40s for the second half of their Advanced training.) For those slated to fly multi-engine aircraft—bombers or cargo planes—training was conducted in AT-24s or AT-17s located at Ellington Field. Upon completion of this phase, cadets were given the gold bars of a second lieutenant and the silver wings of a pilot. In the GCTC, this event occurred to nearly 12,000 men each year during the war.

Bombardiers and navigators had separate training facilities at Ellington; as with the pilots, the total time spent in training was around nine months initially. In May 1940, as the threat of war increased, the courses for all aircrew members were cut to seven months. The GCTC produced nearly 6,000 bombardiers and navigators per year.[84] Although the task of the Gulf Coast Training

Center was now completed, it would still be several months before all these officers would be combat-ready, but this specialized training in specific combat aircraft was conducted elsewhere.

Colonel Harmon arrived at Kelly Field in September 1940, dual-hatted as the base commander and commander of the Advanced Flying School located there. His superior was the GCTC commander—initially that was Brigadier General Millard Harmon. For six weeks Hubert served under his older brother, who judged him as "an active, energetic officer who bases prompt and sound decisions on thorough analysis and pertinent facts." He also wrote that Hubert's leadership engendered a high morale and that he had "superior qualifications" for either a high command or staff position. His next commander, Brigadier General G.C. Brant, was similarly pleased with Hubert's overall performance. Like Miff, Brant thought Hubert a "superior" officer as a commander. He compared Harmon to all other officers of his rank and experience and placed him in the top third.[85]

Based on his superior performance, Harmon was promoted to brigadier general and designated to take Brant's place as commander of the GCTC.[86] Almost immediately after taking command, however, Harmon was forced to endure what must have been an irritant if not an insult. In October 1941, Brigadier General Frank Lahm—the Army's first pilot—was brought out of retirement at age 64 and promoted to major general at the personal intervention of President Roosevelt. For his final tour Lahm was sent to Randolph to take command of the GCTC—for five weeks before his final retirement. During that period Harmon moved down the hall at headquarters and became the chief of staff.[87] The work was onerous. Harmon wrote his mother-in-law: "I used to think I was busy at Kelly but as things are going now, that was a vacation." He noted that everyone respected General Lahm, but "his coming here made it just about twice as strenuous as it might otherwise have been." He continued that "it will be a tremendous relief when his tour of duty is completed."[88] Touchingly, when Lahm retired he gave Hubert his major general stars—they would soon be needed.[89]

When Harmon resumed command in November his territory was enormous, encompassing several states containing dozens of airfields, including seventeen civilian Primary flying schools, six Basic schools, and ten Advanced flying schools. His duties kept him busy. As he wrote to his aunt and uncle, he was working eighteen hours a day due to "the dear old American policy of too little and too late, all over again."[90]

Harmon's main duties were of course administrative, and most of his problems centered on the shortage of planes and pilots. He wrote Washington, but was told to wait his turn—all units were under-manned and under-equipped. To compensate, Harmon put his command on a seven-day work week. When he was confronted with a serious shortage of pilots to fly the navigation training planes, he directed the use of newly graduated pilots from Kelly to move to Ellington for a month to fly the naviga-tion sorties.[91] Hap Arnold offered some help, suggesting that the Army Service Command could take over the adminis-

Brigadier General Hubert Harmon upon taking command of the Gulf Coast Training Center in November 1941.

trative and personnel functions of the GCTC, but Harmon responded with a spirited "NO." It had taken the Air Corps years to break away from ground-officer dominance; he had no desire to go back to those days.[92]

Harmon traveled frequently to oversee his sprawling command, often giving speeches and "pep talks" to military, civilian, and industrial groups. He would generally thank them for their support in the mobilization for war, while exhorting them to even greater efforts; he occasionally provided his audiences a primer on airpower's role in modern war. In a speech to the American Legion in Austin on the Fourth of July, he drew on the Gettysburg Address to talk of great hardships in a noble cause. He warned his listeners of the difficult road ahead, but to think of the alternative to sacrifice and suffering—Texas under Nazi rule with Heinrich Himmler as governor! At an aircraft factory he thanked the audience for what they had already accom-plished, and, as was typical, interjected a bit of wry humor. He remembered meeting a rural Texan before the war and in the course of the conversation asked the man if he thought they would soon be at war. The old Texan replied that he reckoned the US would eventually be dragged into a fight, and if that were the case, he allowed that Texas would probably join in too. And of course, that was indeed the case: there was hardly a town in Texas that was not somehow involved in the war effort. At one graduation of a navigator class

Harmon congratulating Captain Elliott Roosevelt, the son of the president, on his graduation from navigator training in December 1942.

he recalled the words of his football coach twenty-seven years earlier: carry the fight to your opponent; if things break badly, fight all the harder; and the team that makes the fewest mistakes wins.

Perhaps his most interesting talk was at a Primary flying school located in Uvalde, Texas. He told the student pilots and their instructors that they were embarking upon a tremendous career, a career that put them at the heart of airpower, the force that was becoming the dominant factor in war. He said that if General Douglas MacArthur had possessed an adequate air force, the Japanese would not have been able to overrun the Philippines. The same was true of the British defeat at Singapore. In fact, said Harmon, the entire situation in the East Indies was one in which airpower played the dominant role: "unfortunately, that dominant role is all in the hands of the Japanese and *not* with the United Nations." Adding a lighter touch, he noted the famous incident in which an airman in the Philippines wrote a letter to the president pleading, "Could you please send us another P-40; the one we have has holes in it."

Harmon concluded by explaining his role in all of this, and by extension, theirs as well. He said that the mission of the GCTC was to train a portion of those combat crews to become members of "the largest and finest air force ever conceived—an air force which we believe within another year will make Hitler's gigantic machine seem weak and antiquated." Current expansion plans called for the production of 30,000 pilots per year and an equal number of other crew members. They were all to be small parts of that "finest air force." In another talk he quoted US Ambassador Joseph Kennedy who had commented two years earlier during the Battle of Britain that "Nothing stands between the

British Empire and destruction but 500 tough guys of the Royal Air Force." Harmon's job was to produce thousands of such tough guys.[93]

Another of his tasks was entertaining the steady stream of visitors who came to San Antonio to view the expansion of the Army Air Forces and see their tax dollars at work. Others came to entertain the flying students and encourage their efforts. During his year as commander of the GCTC, Harmon escorted or hosted government luminaries including War Secretary Henry Stimson, Treasury Secretary Henry Morgenthau, the Army chief of staff, George Marshall, and the commanding general of the Army Air Forces, Hap Arnold. Foreign guests included Prince Bernhard of the Netherlands. More enjoyable perhaps were the visits of the *Folies Bergère*, the cast of *I Wanted Wings*—a popular propaganda movie detailing events at Kelly Field—and circus tall man Jack Earle who stood 8'6".[94] In addition, Harmon gained some notoriety for pinning navigator wings on Captain Elliott Roosevelt, the son of the president. In his graduation speech, Harmon referred to Captain Roosevelt noting that this was "democracy in action." The captain came to navigator school expecting no special consideration nor wishing any: "He got none. I single him out simply as a symbol of Democracy versus Dictatorship. In the United States, the President's son is one of us." The key to American success was and would continue to be selfless teamwork.[95]

Because he was often shown in the local newspapers escorting famous dignitaries, one newspaper had an artist draw a charcoal sketch of Harmon that they it ran whenever his name was mentioned thereafter. It was not an altogether flattering portrait, and when Rosa-Maye pressed him to buy the original he responded, "If I looked as ugly as this, I wouldn't want to be reminded of it."

In February 1942 Harmon received the second star of a major general—the same list included classmates Omar Bradley, Sammy Cousins and George Stratemeyer. Harmon was also awarded the Legion of Merit—the second highest non-combat decoration then available. His efficiency report for that year at Randolph Field, signed by Major General Barton K. Yount, the commander of the Flying Training Command, noted that Harmon's performance as commander of the GCTC was "Superior." As for the future, Yount noted that "the greatest part of his service in the higher grades has been in staff and training duties." It was time for an operational command. In November, Major General Harmon was named commander of the Sixth Air Force based in the Panama Canal Zone.[96]

CHAPTER 5

The War Years

*A*s the US entered the twentieth century it simultaneously began to depart from its traditional stance of isolation. The Spanish-American War presented the country with an empire of sorts—as well as typical imperial problems of policing and defending a far-flung perimeter. From this point on, the US had three overseas areas that required major and continuous attention: the Philippine Islands, the Hawaiian Islands, and the Caribbean basin—especially the Panama Canal.

The Canal, completed in 1914, cut through the Isthmus of Panama. The Panamanians sold the rights to it and a five-mile swath of land on either side to the US "in perpetuity" for an initial sum of $10 million, followed by additional annual "annuities." The Canal was a significant strategic asset that permitted US Navy combatants and support vessels, as well as oil tankers, freighters and a host of other ships, to pass to and from the Atlantic and Pacific Oceans far more quickly and safely than if those vessels had to make the long and arduous journey around South America's Cape Horn—a distance of 8,000 nautical miles.

With this great asset came great liability. A farsighted airman in 1911 noted that the Canal would be extremely vulnerable to enemy air attack. The locks themselves were surprisingly fragile, and the Panama coast at both ends of the Canal was largely defenseless.[1] When war broke out in 1914—the same month the Canal opened—the US attempted to remain neutral. Over the next three years that policy became increasingly difficult as both the *Entente* and the Central Powers challenged American interests and rights on the high seas.

As the country drifted towards war in 1917, the Army dispatched its first air unit to the Canal Zone. The 7th Aero Squadron arrived in March 1917 with its commander, Captain Henry H. Arnold. Upon his arrival in Panama, Hap

immediately became embroiled in arguments over the location of a new airfield. His commander told him the only recourse was to return to Washington
and see the chief of staff to resolve the issue. While on a boat en route home,
Congress declared war on Germany. Deciding that Arnold was of greater value
in Washington overseeing the expansion of the Air Service for movement to
France, the Army changed his orders so that he would remain in the capital; the
7th Aero Squadron was given a new commander.[2]

The war ended in November 1918 with no hostile activity in the Canal area,
although the Air Service did fly daily patrols, weather permitting, on the Atlantic
side of the Isthmus. More importantly, the principle that the Canal was of great
value was established, and both the US Navy and Army began increasing—albeit
slowly—their commitment to this aspect of hemisphere defense.

Until the late 1920s the threat to the Canal largely focused on a hostile
surface fleet. Naval exercises in 1923 and 1924 demonstrated that naval gunfire could easily render the Canal's locks inoperable for an extended period of
time.[3] By the end of that decade, however, it was becoming apparent that not
just naval gunfire would be a threat. Long-range bombers could carry more
than enough tonnage to disable the locks. Although some discounted this
possibility—where would such
bombers come from?—the growing capability of carrier-based
aircraft was a menace that could
not be ignored. Tests in 1929 demonstrated that a single, well-placed
bomb could disable the Canal.

And yet, given the stringent
military budgets of the 1930s as
the world struggled through the
Great Depression, the Canal's
defense forces were habitually
under-strength and under-funded.
The Air Corps, for example, was
unable to keep its units in the
Canal Zone at full strength. In
1935, airmen in Panama pushed
hard for more aircraft in the Zone,

*A proud Madelin Harmon stands with two of
her sons, Major Generals Millard and Hubert
Harmon, 1942.*

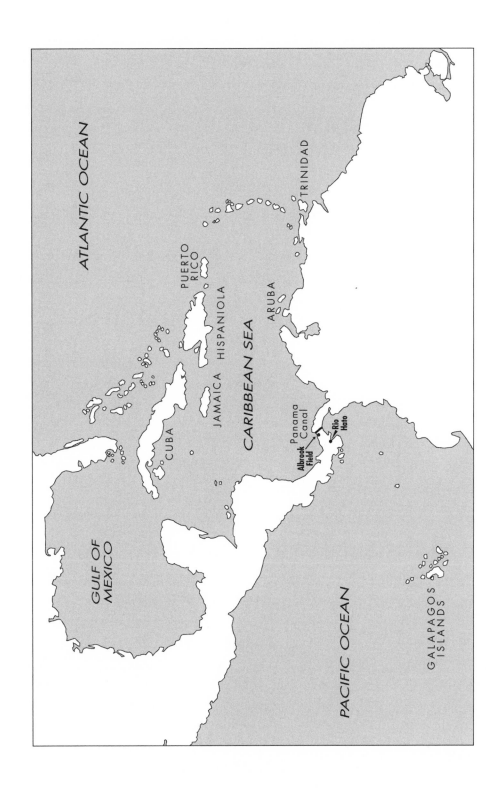

but they were ignored. Two years later, the air commander in Panama, Lieutenant Colonel George H. Brett, wrote Washington that unless air strength was greatly increased, an enemy air attack would be devastating: "the Air Force would be neutralized and we would play golf the balance of the war."[4] The Air Corps chief, Major General Oscar Westover, visited the Zone soon after to see for himself and agreed with Brett. Even so, when war broke out in Europe in September 1939, the Air Corps had barely 100 aircraft dedicated to the Canal's defense, all obsolescent. Of the fifty-odd fighters available, twenty-four were Boeing P-26 "Peashooters." In fact, this aircraft was an improvement. Not until January 1939 were the last of the Boeing P-12Es—open-cockpit biplanes from the 1920s—finally phased out in Panama.[5] Worse, fuel shortages due to budget restrictions meant that pilots averaged a scant ten hours of flying time each month—not nearly enough to remain combat-ready. The year after becoming Air Corps chief, Arnold visited the Canal Zone, saw the state of affairs, and promptly arranged for 600 more airmen to be moved south, but that would not be nearly enough.[6]

The Air Corps would need four types of modern aircraft to defend the Canal adequately. Observation planes were required to patrol both of the ocean approaches to warn of an advancing enemy fleet. Once a hostile fleet was located, bombers with sufficient range and payload were necessary to attack that fleet and either sink it or drive it off before its guns could come within range of the Canal. If the enemy fleet contained aircraft carriers, then the defense forces needed fighter planes to intercept and shoot down the attacking planes before they could fly over the vulnerable locks and unload their bombs. In addition, for reasons we shall soon see, long-range patrol aircraft—larger and with greater payloads than mere observation aircraft—would also be needed. In addition to more aircraft and personnel, more bases were essential. Other than the airfields in the Canal Zone itself, airfields were also needed in the Antilles—the island chain to the east of Panama—and also to the west, on the Pacific side. Bases were quickly built, leased, or improved throughout the region—including airfields in Puerto Rico, Trinidad, Aruba, and Jamaica. In the west, the Galapagos Islands, belonging to Ecuador, were the obvious location for the outer perimeter defenses and warning pickets.[7] Even so, construction teams and reinforcements were slow to arrive.

In 1941 the War Department finally decided the threat to the Panama Canal was serious. Japan, which had invaded Manchuria in 1937, was continuing to show aggressive signs throughout the Pacific. Germany had already overrun much of Europe, and it had been making diplomatic overtures and inroads in Central and South America for some time. In Panama, for example, Arnulfo Arias had assumed the presidency in 1940 and was viewed by the US as pro-Axis. The American ambassador cabled Washington: "What has developed in Panama is about as near an approach to Hitlerism as the characteristics of Latin Americans and the peculiar circumstances affecting Panama could be expected to permit."[8] Arias resisted all attempts by the US to increase its military presence in Panama. In fact, upon his inauguration in October 1940 he received a congratulatory telegram from Hitler who wrote that he hoped cordial relations between their two countries could "progress." Arias shared such sentiments, and the following year he threatened to grant concessions to "other powerful countries that would have the material force to defend" the Canal.[9] This was going too far. In October 1941, Arias was ousted in a bloodless coup with US approval. His successor, Ricardo Adolfo de la Guardia, was decidedly pro-American. Even so, questions of basing rights in Panama would remain a contentious issue throughout the war.

In a somewhat belated recognition of these varied and serious threats, the Caribbean Defense Command (CDC) was formed in February 1941 and Lieutenant General Frank Andrews was chosen to run its air forces. Andrews, along with Hap Arnold, was the most senior and well-respected airman in the Army. He had the confidence of General George Marshall, the Army chief of staff, who had appointed him as his G-3 (deputy chief of staff for operations)—the first airman to hold such a key position. Upon sending Andrews to the Canal Zone, Marshall wrote to the CDC commander, Lieutenant General Daniel Van Voorhis, that coordinating air activities in the area was "exceedingly important" and required "very special treatment." He therefore wanted Andrews, "a very competent man," to straighten things out.[10]

Marshall was hinting here at the problems of interservice rivalry. Simply, the Navy had no intention of placing its assets under a soldier—and especially not an Army airman. Although the defense of the Canal had been made the responsibility of the Army commander on the scene by executive order of the president, the Navy nonetheless resisted. Van Voorhis complained to Marshall that whenever he attempted to exert the authority given him by the president the local admirals replied tartly that "he was not in their chain of command."[11] Marshall went to Admiral Harold R. Stark, the chief of naval operations, and complained, grumping that the Panama Canal could not be defended by a "debating society."[12] In July 1941, Andrews moved up to take command of the Caribbean—at least the Army's portion of it; he was the first American airman to hold a theater command. This appointment signaled the realization that the main defense of the Canal would be through airpower. Even so, the difficulties of unity of command in the Caribbean would linger.

The attack on Pearl Harbor resulted in an inevitable frenzy of activity as commanders worldwide screamed for more assets to ready themselves for war. The War Department feared that an attack by Japanese carriers on the Panama Canal was possible, so eighty more aircraft were immediately sent south along with four more radar sets. In truth, the chances of a Japanese attack by carrier-based aircraft were remote. The distance from Hawaii to Panama was greater than that from Japan to Hawaii. The obstacles involved in attempting to project power that far across the ocean without logistics bases already in place were insurmountable. But such realities were obvious only in hindsight—the shock of 7 December was too awful for any American commander to take chances. Indeed, Secretary of War Henry Stimson opined that it would be worth it to the Japanese to lose four carriers if they could achieve the Canal's destruction.[13] Fortunately, they never tried.

Even so, it did not take long for the threat to the Panama Canal to change focus, dramatically. Within two months of US entry into the war, German submarines, or U-boats, began active operations in the Gulf of Mexico, around Cuba, and, ominously, in the eastern approaches to the Canal. The first sinking, an oil tanker, went down by torpedo on 19 February 1942. This was just the beginning. The following month there were six German subs in the Caribbean, each patrolling for up to six weeks before returning to France. The problem was obvious: if the U-boats could disrupt the sea lanes in the Caribbean so as to dramatically lower the volume of traffic transiting the Canal, it would be tantamount to attacking the Canal itself. Unfortunately, the mission of defense against the submarine was one for which the US was unprepared.[14] In February and March, thirty-one ships were sunk by U-boats; in April and May, forty-one more went down; a further forty-two became victims in June and July. During June, German submarines had sunk more shipping in the Gulf of Mexico and Caribbean than they had sunk the world over during any month previous.[15]

It was clear that the primary response to this threat, not only in the Caribbean but in the Atlantic, was airpower. Air patrols were necessary to spot the submarines when they surfaced to recharge their electric batteries or to travel more quickly.

The military soon formed the Anti-Submarine Command that combined Navy and AAF efforts, and by the summer of 1942 the worst was already over.[16] By September, long-range patrols by Navy and AAF aircraft were in place, as were the extensive use of convoys. Thereafter the U-boats seldom ventured near the Canal. Patrols continued to drive the subs eastward, and by late fall 1942 the main threat centered on the area near Trinidad.

As the anti-submarine campaign turned decisively in the US favor, Major General Hubert Harmon left San Antonio to take command of the Sixth Air Force based at Albrook Field in the Canal Zone. On 26 November he wrote Rosa-Maye, who had remained with the children in San Antonio, that he had arrived in "fine shape and had a wonderful welcome." He expected his new job to be "extremely interesting" and that he would be kept busy. He noted, however, that the command and control arrangements were "exceedingly complicated"—a reference to problems with the Navy.[17]

Although Harmon told his wife that he would try to write her at least a note every day, his duties prevented it. Over the following months he would generally write once or twice each week, usually beginning with an apology that he had meant to write earlier but had been too busy. Even so, his letters home were warm and detailed, asking about the children while also giving financial and parenting advice. When Eula had trouble in school and in making friends, for example, "Daddy"—as he signed most letters—wrote that this was "terribly distressing." He knew Eula was "highly intelligent, logical, versatile, practical and full of initiative—all in all exceedingly interesting." As for Kendrick, father warned Rosa-Maye that she must be "extremely vigilant re. matters of sex." Kendrick was at that age when he would begin to hear things from friends and at school and this would confuse him. He thought the solution was simply to stay that much closer to him, become his best friend, so that he would naturally turn to the family for help and advice.[18] Clearly, Harmon missed his family greatly, asking frequently for pictures, news and letters.

He stayed busy. His "realm," as he termed it in one letter home, was huge— the size of the continental US—requiring frequent travel to keep informed about all of it. His daily routine was routine—up at 0630, work till 1800 with short breaks for breakfast and lunch, dinner, socializing with other members of the staff and the frequent visitors that came through Albrook, and to bed "well before" official lights out (due to the black out to help protect against enemy attacks) at 2300. Occasionally he could get off on a Sunday afternoon for a round of golf. Because of his location, there was a steady stream of visitors from the US, as well as Central and South America. Always affable, Harmon was a gracious host but this too took a toll on his energy and health. He came down with malaria and dysentery in March and spent several days in bed.[19]

Harmon was also frustrated and restless, and these problems were job-related. Soon after his arrival in Panama, Harmon began pestering the Air Staff for more aircraft, specifically AT-6 "Texans." A somewhat surprising request, Harmon explained that he needed eight-to-twelve of the advanced trainers to keep his pilots instrument and aerobatic qualified. He followed up with a letter to Arnold, complaining that although he was told no "Texans" were available, he knew that several had been shipped to Venezuela to be cannibalized for spare parts![20] Arnold was unmoved, responding that at times political considerations took precedence over operational needs. Arnold had already run into problems with President Roosevelt regarding the necessity of supplying aircraft to allies. In his memoirs, Arnold related that his continual objections to the diversion of aircraft from the AAF earned him a pointed warning from the president that officers refusing to be team players ended up in places like Guam.[21]

Instead, the Sixth Air Force was sent BT-13s. The "Vibrator" was a serviceable workhorse basic trainer, but it was far too underpowered and rudimentary to provide the training needed to keep combat pilots fit. Harmon was also offered gliders for his command's use. Gliders? He responded acidly that he needed *real* airplanes and had no interest in having things "dumped" on him.[22] Still, the aircraft he received were of a bewildering variety: P-26s, P-36s, P-39Ds and Ks, P-40Bs, Cs and Es, B-17Bs, Ds and Es, A-17s, A-18s, A-19s, and a host of other bomber, liaison, observation and transport aircraft. Indeed, two one-of-a-kind aircraft under Harmon's command were the enormous XB-15—now converted to a transport and designated the XC-105—and an "impressed" German JU-52, re-designated a C-79. This wide variety of aircraft further complicated maintenance, logistics, and aircrew training.[23]

As the months passed, Harmon became increasingly restive. The war had moved eastward, near Trinidad, and there was little activity left near the Canal itself. Records show that from November 14, 1942—the date Harmon took command—until the following September, Sixth Air Force pilots sighted enemy submarines on only eighteen occasions; attacked them eleven times; and were attacked by the U-boats on twelve instances![24] Of course, as Harmon well knew, the reason the U-boats left the area was precisely because the defenses forged near the Canal and in the western Caribbean were so strong. The submarines needed to look elsewhere for easier pickings. In order to maintain pressure on the enemy and push them even farther out to sea, more and better aircraft were needed. In July 1943 Harmon wrote Arnold an impassioned letter citing the importance of his mission and the problems of the great distances involved that necessitated more capable aircraft:[25]

> In view of the importance of the mission assigned, the small number of aircraft available, the improbability of timely reinforcements in the event of an attack, the probability of strong fighter resistance, the small time available for strike on a carrier force, and the distances involved, it is imperative that all aircraft assigned to this Air Force be completely capable of performing all functions of modern heavy bombardment aircraft.

> In view of the great distances over which this Air Force may be required to operate, the lack of numerous aerodromes, the difficulties involved in transporting large replacement parts for four-engined bombers, and the shortages of available spare parts, it is almost equally important that all assigned heavy bombardment airplanes be of the same type.

At the same time, more B-24s were needed, although no longer was their prime duty to sink an enemy fleet. It was now recognized that the B-24s were the best aircraft available to patrol for long periods in search of U-boats. Their microwave radar was far superior to that of the "meter wave" radar used in the B-17s. This was crucial because studies showed that 67 percent of all submarine sightings were the result of radar.[26]

There was no positive response to these pleas, and in his letters home, Harmon vented his frustration. In March he wrote Rosa-Maye that interservice squabbling—beginning at the Admiral King-General Marshall level and trickling down to him—"has [meant] a rather long, tedious and at times a rather discouraging task." He continued pointedly, "of course, if we were a really active theater with honest-to-goodness fighting to do, we would not so gravely concern ourselves with such matters." He lamented that the "powers that be" regarded his command as of secondary importance, "and the inclination to short change us on personnel and equipment is becoming more pronounced each month." He wrote that he would "most sincerely" prefer to be transferred to an active theater, commenting "I would like for my children to be able to say that their daddy *fought* in World War II."[27] One week later he confided to his wife that he had written "Strat" (George Stratemeyer—his West Point classmate who was leaving his job as Arnold's chief of staff for an assignment to China) stating that *he* should be the one sent to China to work for General Joe Stilwell.[28]

He was not, however, totally inactive. Late on the afternoon of April 4, 1943, Harmon was with Brigadier General Russell Randall, his head of VI Fighter Command. A P-40 pilot had just bailed out over the ocean near Rio Hato on the Pacific side of the Canal. There was no air-sea rescue service at the time, and given the lateness of the day, Harmon suggested to Randall that they take their amphibian aircraft (probably the Grumman OA-9 assigned to headquarters) and go look for the pilot themselves. With Harmon in the copilot seat and Randall at the controls, the aircraft headed out to the area where the pilot radioed he was bailing out. They were unable to spot anything from the air, so decided to land in the ocean thinking it would thus be easier to see someone bobbing on the waves. They then shut down their engines so they could hear the pilot if he was trying to hail them. They would drift on the water, watching and listening for any sign of the downed airman. Eventually, Randall suggested it was time to leave—the waves and water were getting higher and it was getting dark. Harmon insisted they start their engines, taxi back a ways, and then shut down and drift through the area one more time. As soon as they cut their engines they heard a cry. They swung the plane around, turned on the landing lights, and saw him. Second Lieutenant Clarice B. Rumpf of Brownsville, Texas, was saved. Harmon, Randall and the other crewmembers aboard the OA-9 received Air Medals for their actions.[29]

This incident was illustrative. During Harmon's year in Panama his total strength fluctuated between 550 and 600 aircraft. During that same period, 147 aircraft were lost in the Sixth Air Force, most of them fighters. Of these 147 planes, *none* were lost due to enemy action.[30]

In July 1943 more bad news arrived. Harmon and others had been complaining of command and control problems repeatedly. Washington finally acted by splitting Harmon's command in two—he would remain in Panama with the Sixth Air Force, but a new command was now formed—the Antilles Air Command based in Puerto Rico—that would conduct anti-submarine operations closer to the scene of enemy activity. By this time the U-boats had been driven to beyond Trinidad—too far away it was argued—to control them effectively from Albrook Field 1,200 miles distant. Overnight Harmon's forces were cut by sixty-five planes. In one sense, he was not sorry to see some of the personnel leave. Many of these men had been "inherited" when he took command. They were set in their ways and were too smug to realize their deficiencies or to take guidance "from poor ignorant people like Tommy and me." He wrote that "our friend who went to Puerto Rico" was no help, and he expected his command would run more smoothly without him and his cronies.[31] This was perhaps a bit of rationalization to hide the disappointment at this latest blow to his command authority.

He did, however, get on well with his superior, Lieutenant General George H. Brett, the man who had replaced Andrews at CDC. Brett, also an airman, was a seasoned and respected officer whom Harmon had known for years—Brett was an instructor at Leavenworth when Harmon attended the Command and General Staff School. Brett had, however, fallen on hard times. He had gone to the Pacific early in 1942 to take command of Douglas MacArthur's air forces, but the two men never hit it off. MacArthur, perhaps smarting from his own rough handling in the Philippines, thought Brett disorganized and ineffective. In July 1942 Brett was relieved.[32] Arriving in Panama the same month as Harmon, the two men got along well—often playing poker together. Brett respected Harmon's leadership and organizational capabilities. On his efficiency report in June 1943, Brett ranked him twenty-fifth on a list of ninety-two general officers. Harmon's overall performance was rated as "Superior Plus."[33]

Harmon may have performed well, but he was still unhappy. In August he received a letter from a colleague in Personnel at AAF Headquarters hinting that Harmon might be in line for a tour in Washington as the Director of War Requirements—a grand-sounding title that meant he would be the assistant chief of staff to Arnold. He wrote Rosa-Maye that a staff tour was not his choice, but it was perhaps a stepping stone to a combat command. He noted dryly that "it does not take a master strategist to see that the importance of this place is going down and *down*." He also commented that as long as he was "tied to Brett" he would "never get anywhere with Arnold." Apparently, Harmon reasoned that Brett's problems with MacArthur were still fresh in Arnold's mind, and now he was tainted as well.[34] If that was his concern, it was unfounded, for a week later he was called to Brett's office to view a wire from Arnold: "Harmon is needed for a *vital* assignment in United States." Harmon was elated and wrote happily to Rosa-Maye that "you may see me soon."[35] The assignment fell through. A few days later Harmon wrote: "Disgust! Several times over—Disgust! Am I disappointed. All bubbles bursted. I was so sure that I was on my way that I had already started to pack."[36] The intended assignment was commander of Second Air Force—a training unit in the US—so Harmon was not terribly disappointed when things went awry, and he discovered the nature of the intended job. Still, he mused that it may have gotten him closer to Europe or the Pacific.

In October good news finally arrived. He had orders—he was going to the South Pacific. His boss would be Miff, the Army commander in the South Pacific under Vice Admiral "Bull" Halsey.

Combat Command

When the Japanese struck Pearl Harbor on December 7th and disabled the US fleet, it was only the opening gambit of their offensive strategy. In quick succession, Wake Island fell, followed by Guam and then Hong Kong. On 10 December the British capital ships *Prince of Wales* and *Repulse* were foolish enough to venture into the open sea without air cover: Japanese aircraft quickly sank both of them, proving once and for all that Billy Mitchell was correct when stating that ships, regardless of their size, were highly vulnerable to air attack. Japanese forces invested the British bastion of Singapore—it fell in February. The day after Pearl Harbor, Japan invaded the Philippines. General Douglas MacArthur, who had been recalled to active duty and put in charge of US and Filipino forces in the Islands, retreated into the Bataan Peninsula and declared Manila an open city. US and Filipino forces were gradually pushed back but eventually surrendered or fled over the water to Corregidor, the island fortress off the tip of Bataan. It fell in May. In January, the Japanese had swept through Burma, scattering the weak Chinese and other Allied forces under General Joe Stilwell, leaving but a small enclave unoccupied along the western

Harmon with Lieutenant General George Brett in the Panama Canal Zone, 1942.

border. China itself was virtually prostrate, although she still fought back from the sanctuary of her vast size. French Indochina and Korea had fallen to Japan prior to Pearl Harbor, but not the Dutch East Indies. That colony, centered on Java, fell in March 1942. The vital strongholds of Australia and India were now the front lines, looking ripe and vulnerable.

Finally, in April 1942 the US received a brief but welcome breath of good news: sixteen B-25s under the command of Lieutenant Colonel Jimmy Doolittle struck Tokyo. Tactically, these "thirty seconds" were a disaster—no serious damage was done to Japanese industry and all aircraft were either lost or crash-landed on the Asian coast. Strategically, however, the air strikes not only gave the Allies a much needed morale boost, but also induced the Japanese into a huge blunder. Emperor Hirohito was troubled by the attack on his capital city, and his military commanders were in turn humiliated. They therefore decided to push out their defense perimeter farther than planned; they decided to capture Midway Island. The resulting air battle at Midway is now generally termed the turning point of the Pacific War. Making excellent use of intelligence sources—the US had broken the Japanese secret codes—American forces were waiting for the attackers in early June 1942. When it was over, the Japanese had lost four aircraft carriers and a heavy cruiser, all to air attack, as well as 275 planes and 3,500 men. The US lost one carrier—crippled by Japanese aircraft and later sunk, along with its destroyer escort, by a submarine while being towed to Hawaii—132 planes, and around 300 men dead.[37] The tide had turned, although few as yet knew that.

The same month that Doolittle and his colleagues were bombing Tokyo, the Combined Chiefs of Staff were planning to take the offensive in the South Pacific. This area was chosen as the most logical place to hit Japan's overextended supply lines, while also helping to relieve pressure on Australia and US lines of communication to that country. The specific location for this first offensive was determined in part by the Japanese landings in the lower Solomon Islands on Tulagi and Guadalcanal. These obscure dots of land in the ocean were dangerously close to Australia and its supply link; they were thus the logical locus for the Allied counteroffensive. On 7 August 1942, American forces landed on both islands, and the long slog northwest towards the Japanese Home Islands began.[38]

The South Pacific was a most unusual place to fight a war. It was huge, but at the same time, it was a very primitive area. There were no cities, no

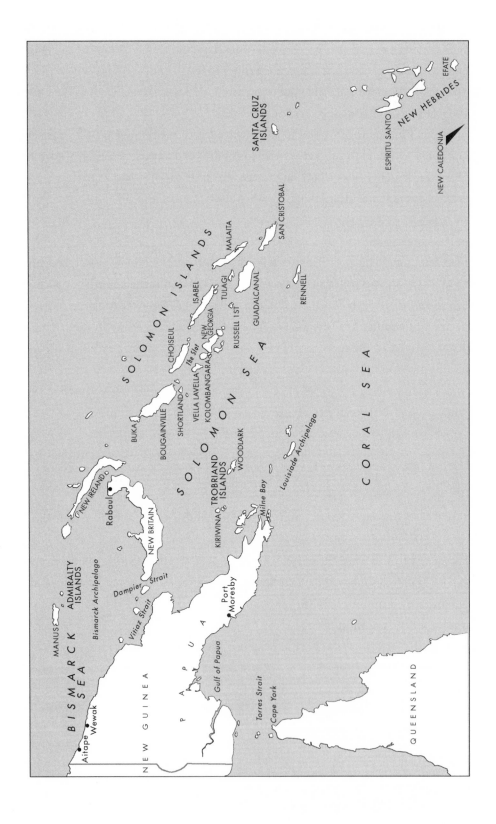

industry and no factories. There were no raw materials like oil, tin, copper or rice. The populations of the various islands were composed almost exclusively of illiterate natives who had never used or maintained sophisticated technology. These natives were largely apolitical and cared little for either side during the war. The islands themselves were dominated by rugged, mountainous terrain, jungles, insects, disease and heat. Few were actually occupied—by either side—in the traditional sense of the word. To do so was neither necessary nor desirable. In short, the South Pacific's true strategic value was not what it contained but where it lay—astride the lines of communication stretching between Australia and the United States. In addition, air bases in this area also enabled long-range bombers to strike at either Australia to the south—in the case of the Japanese—or the Dutch East Indies to the north—for the Allies. Both of these areas, of course, had enormous strategic potential due to the abundant natural resources and relatively large populations; they required protection.

Thus, the key to controlling the South Pacific—which in turn dominated Australia and the Indies—was the airbase. As phrased by one historian: "in terms of sorties flown, aircraft shot down, bombs dropped—indeed by any reasonable measure—the air war in the South Pacific was fought, won, and lost by land-based air forces."[39]

The necessity of land airbases was learned early in the war. The US Navy's carriers were too few and their aircraft often could not carry the payload necessary to provide air support for amphibious operations. Moreover, the paucity of the carriers meant their use was heavily constrained by the need to keep them out of harm's way. In one of the defining moments of the Guadalcanal campaign in 1942, the carriers supporting the marines ashore were ordered to withdraw—leaving the leathernecks exposed on the beachhead—for fear the carriers would be sunk by enemy aircraft. As one naval historian put it, naval commanders "were not about to expose these ships to the confined waters of the Solomon Sea where carriers would be sitting ducks for Japanese land-based air and submarines."[40] The only solution was the employment of land-based air-power provided by the marines and the AAF, and it was this need that dominated strategic operations. Planners would thus determine the next objective in the drive northwest—one that had an airfield nearby or a place to build one—and the AAF's long-range bombers would then begin pounding the enemy airfields on that island and those within supporting distance on nearby islands. Of note, these bombers required fighter escort—as was the case in Europe. As a result, the combat radius of Allied fighters—usually around 200-250 miles—determined the distance to the next objective. Once air superiority was imposed over the intended landing area, Army or Marine Corps troops would land. Invariably, one of their first priorities was to secure and if necessary lengthen the runway so that Allied cargo planes could begin bringing in reinforcements and supplies, and fighter aircraft could come in to provide air support. Eventually, the bombers would also move into the captured or newly-built airfield, and the planners would begin looking for their next objective.

Initial operations at Guadalcanal, the largest island in the lower Solomons, were conducted with only token AAF units present. A buildup soon began as Henderson Field was secured and enlarged; by November, B-17s began deploying into the field. By the end of 1942, P-38 and P-40 units were also based on Guadalcanal, as was a troop carrier squadron. In January 1943, the Thirteenth Air Force was activated under the command of Major General Nathan F. Twining and its headquarters soon placed on the island of Espiritu Santo, south of the Solomons.

The command and control arrangements in the vast Pacific area were a bit unusual. There were essentially two major theaters: the Southwest Pacific Area with General Douglas MacArthur as the commander in chief, and the Pacific Ocean Areas under Admiral Chester Nimitz. Under Nimitz were sub-theaters, one of which was the South Pacific, commanded initially by Vice Admiral Robert Ghormley and later by Vice Admiral "Bull" Halsey. Because of the vast distances involved, and because the major combatant assets at his disposal were land-based and sea-based aircraft, Halsey organized his command functionally. The land-based air assets of the AAF, Navy, Marine Corps and those of New Zealand, were all grouped under a single commander—COMAIRSOPAC, or Commander of Aircraft, South Pacific. By 1943 this commander was Vice Admiral Aubrey Fitch, but his responsibilities were largely administrative. He established a forward or tactical commander early-on for the Guadalcanal campaign. This individual, Commander, Aircraft Solomons, or COMAIRSOLS, was the actual combat commander who controlled the Allied air assets in the battle against the Japanese in that theater. Twining, as commander of the Thirteenth Air Force, thus had little control over his own forces; rather, he simply provided those assets to COMAIRSOLS for employment.

This farsighted functional organization—which later became standard US joint doctrine—combined diverse air assets into one unit under a single air commander to ensure unity of command for more efficient and more effective air operations. Indeed, two later observers would state that this air arrangement was "the high water mark of jointness and unity of effort in air operations until the Persian Gulf War of 1991."[41]

COMAIRSOLS itself had four functional sub-commands: a Fighter Command handled air defense and was composed of fighters from all the services; Bomber Command, consisting mostly of Thirteenth Air Force assets (B-24s and B-25s), was used for long-range strikes against enemy airfields and positions. Strike Command (mostly Navy and Marine Corps dive bombers) was used for low-level attacks on enemy positions; and Search Command, which was employed as a wide-ranging reconnaissance and rescue service. By late 1943, COMAIRSOLS had around 725 aircraft at his disposal, mostly US.[42] The COMAIRSOLS position rotated between the services, and the first man to hold the post was Rear Admiral Charles P. Mason. He gave way two months later to Rear Admiral Marc A. Mitscher, and he in turn to Twining.[43]

The Army commander for the entire South Pacific under Halsey was Lieutenant General Millard Harmon. Although he had no command authority over the individual tactical units, because of his position as the senior-ranking Army officer in the South Pacific he had great prestige and influence, not only with Nimitz and Halsey, but also with George Marshall and Hap Arnold back in Washington.[44]

About the time the Thirteenth Air Force arrived in the Solomons, the battle for Guadalcanal was largely over and the fighting had shifted to the northern islands in the chain, especially New Georgia and Bougainville. Throughout early and mid-1943 while Hubert Harmon was still in Panama, the Thirteenth Air Force was engaged in the campaign to secure the Solomons, while also chipping away at the major Japanese air and naval base at Rabaul on the island of New Britain, just northwest of the Solomons.

On November 16, 1943, Major General Hubert Harmon was on a B-17 en route to his new assignment and wrote Rosa-Maye of how wonderful it had been to see her and the children, if only briefly. He said that "there would be no such thing as real happiness until the war is over." He concluded by noting that it was customary to cross the ocean at night so as to arrive at their destination just after daybreak. That way, he commented in a vein that hardly could have lifted his wife's spirits, if the aircraft went down there would still be plenty of daylight left to search for the wreckage![45]

He arrived in New Caledonia at Miff's house in the midst of a party. He remained with his brother for six days, being briefed on the situation, reading reports, studying the intelligence, poring over future plans and orders, and generally getting acquainted with the combat environment. Here he also learned from Miff that he would initially serve as the deputy commander of aircraft South Pacific under Admiral Fitch while he came up to speed on his new duties. He told Rosa-Maye that he could not divulge details, but he was certain that his new job would be "exceedingly interesting" and would be "rich in future prospects." He also wrote of his admiration for Miff, who was "beloved" by everyone in the command. He realized that comparisons between him and his brother were inevitable, and that it was "a tough precedent to live up to—will do my best." On the other hand, in an attempt to put her mind at rest, he confided that it was against the rules for "old fossils like me" to fly combat missions, so he would be "as safe as I was in Panama." He concluded with a note of melancholy that there would be "no heroic feats with which to regale Eula and Kendrick. Alas!"[46]

Harmon arrived in the Solomons just as landings were taking place at Empress Augusta Bay on Bougainville, 200 miles northwest of AAF airfields on New Georgia, which in turn were 200 miles northwest of Henderson Field on Guadalcanal. It should be noted that these 200 mile leaps—the standard range of fighter aircraft—were obvious to the Japanese as well. Their own operations were just as dependent on these airfields. The Marine Corps official history noted this when discussing the Bougainville operation: "of paramount importance in selection of a target area was the availability of local cover in the form of air and sea support. Cape Torokina [the prominent terrain feature where the Allies actually landed on Bougainville] was found to be within range of fighters based at Munda and bombers based at Guadalcanal."[47]

The South Pacific was dotted with thousands of islands; as a consequence, whoever dominated the air above them also dominated the seas around them. Once air superiority was obtained over an island, the enemy garrison on it was essentially cut off from re-supply and would slowly but inexorably begin to die. Given the critical importance of air superiority, the air battles preceding every operation were fierce and bloody. Harmon acknowledged this accurately when he wrote that airpower was "the key to the situation" and that "nothing can move safely in the forward areas without air cover."[48] It is noteworthy that the top two air aces in US history were both AAF pilots flying P-38s in the Pacific

during World War II—
Dick Bong (forty victo-
ries) and Tommy McGuire
(thirty-eight victories).[49]

As soon as he
became established in his
new job as Fitch's deputy,
Harmon began looking
at the lot of the common
airmen, soldiers, sailors
and marines under his

Harmon's living quarters on the Guadalcanal beach in 1944.

command. Typically, he worried about their conditions, and complained to
Fitch that too much of what was being shipped in for the Navy consisted of
non-essential luxury items used for the construction and improvement of officer facilities that were not justified. These materials, and the personnel being
used to build these unneeded facilities, would be far better employed on food,
housing and medical care for the troops. Moreover, this "diversion" of resources
was promoting a "slow-moving complacency about the war" that he thought
dangerous.[50]

When Twining departed for Europe, Harmon took his place as commander of the Thirteenth Air Force on January 5, 1944. This was what he had
been waiting for. His command was strewn over an enormous area, and his
aircraft, usually around 220 assigned, were housed on airfields at Guadalcanal,
Fiji, Munda, Sterling, Ondonga, Espiritu Santo, Torokina, and elsewhere.[51] At
that point the battle for Bougainville and its airfields had passed its climax.
As operations were consolidated for the next move—the neutralization of
Rabaul—Harmon moved his headquarters to Guadalcanal so as to be closer
to the fighting front. He wrote Eula that his new quarters—he drew a detailed
diagram of his Quonset hut—was on the beach, and he would be only six miles
from Uncle Millard—who had also deployed forward. He wrote to both Eula
and Rosa-Maye that he thought quite highly of the Navy men he worked with,
especially Admirals Fitch and Halsey, calling the former "a peach" and, with
respect to the latter, stating that you could search a lifetime and not find "a
finer trio then he, Miff and Admiral H[alsey]."[52] Such comments were not just
cant. One of Harmon's great strengths throughout his career was his ability
to get along with just about everyone. He did not make enemies, and most of

his colleagues—both superiors and subordinates—found him to be delight-ful company. He had strong opinions about war strategy and the role of airpower in that strategy, but he refused to let those opinions hamper his relations with officers of the other services. In an efficiency report written later, Hap Arnold would comment on Harmon's ability to "get along" with the Navy—to Arnold that was high praise and one of the strongest compli-ments he could pay one of his subordinates.[53]

Although the Solomons were clear, Rabaul remained the key to Japa-nese defenses in the Southwest Pacific. Approximately 400,000 tons of shipping passed through its harbor in December 1943 alone. It was guarded by a large force of over 350 aircraft that was constantly being reinforced to ensure the gar-rison's full strength. As the campaign in the northern Solomons wound down in early 1944, attention turned increasingly to Rabaul, which was pounded almost daily by Thirteenth Air Force aircraft. For the Japanese it was a losing proposition, and by the end of February 1944 most of the aircraft remaining at Rabaul were transferred to Truk Atoll where they were deemed to be safer. Dur-ing the air battle over Rabaul, the Allies claimed 705 enemy aircraft destroyed, 266 of which were downed by the Thirteenth.[54]

As noted, COMAIRSOLS was a position that rotated between the services. It was, in essence, Fitch's forward headquarters in direct control of tactical air operations. The other air commanders took a back seat in this set up, although as Harmon noted, if a commander believed the performance of his units in the forward areas was not what it should be, he could always exercise his preroga-tive to go there and "use his influence" to shake things up, "provided he does not interfere with active operations." Harmon conceded, however, that when not serving as COMAIRSOLS the air commanders were largely rele-gated to administrative and supply issues.[55]

When taking over as COMAIRSOLS on 15 March, Har-mon moved up to Bougainville where isolated packets of Japanese were still "fighting ferociously" on the island. Tommy Musgrave, who had worked for him in both Texas

Harmon while commander of the Thirteenth Air Force in 1944.

and Panama, joined him and proved to be of great help, as did Colonel Earl Naiden, a West Point classmate who served as his chief of staff. Another individual, who would become very important to Harmon a decade later when establishing the Air Force Academy, was Dr. Robert L. Stearns, his director of operations analysis. Stearns held an important position. He and his team completed a number of studies for Harmon on such topics as training effectiveness, tactics, air-sea rescue operations, and bomb fuzes.[56]

Still, he missed Miff who was temporarily in Washington. One complaint was that the Thirteenth Air Force seldom got the publicity he thought it deserved. Harmon attributed this to the massive propaganda machine at MacArthur's headquarters in the Southwest Pacific Area. As a result, the American public, when they heard anything about Pacific air operations at all, heard about the exploits of George Kenney's Fifth Air Force. For example, he wrote Rosa-Maye disgustedly that *Time* magazine reported a large and effective air strike on the Japanese positions at Truk as being accomplished by the Fifth when it was actually the Thirteenth's aircrews that flew the mission.[57]

With Rabaul effectively neutralized by late February 1944, attention turned towards the Japanese bastion at Truk in the Caroline Islands. The air campaign to soften Truk and adjacent airfields on Palau and Yap occupied most of Harmon's efforts when he was COMAIRSOLS. Over the two-day period of 29-30 March, for example, the Thirteenth Air Force destroyed 130 Japanese aircraft at Truk in a surprise strike that entailed a 2,000 mile roundtrip, thirteen-hour combat mission for B-24s stationed on Guadalcanal.[58] It was this mission that *Time* mistakenly gave credit to the Fifth Air Force for flying, so irritating Harmon. After less than two weeks of continual pounding the air defenses at Truk were largely eliminated, so the bombers of the Thirteenth moved north again, to Los Negros in the Admiralty Islands. From this position they dominated the Bismarck Sea, the approaches to Rabaul, and the northern coast of New Guinea—the scene of MacArthur's continuing offensive. Harmon relinquished his duties as COMAIRSOLS on 20 April, just as his joint air forces plastered all the remaining Japanese airfields on New Guinea in preparation for the landings at Hollandia and Aitape two days later.[59] All told, during his tenure the Thirteenth had flown nearly 15,000 combat sorties, shot down or otherwise destroyed 250 enemy aircraft (for a loss of 55 in combat and another 29 in "operations"), and dropped over 12,000 tons of bombs on Japanese positions, mostly airfields.[60] It was a powerful showing, and prompted a message from General Marshall to Admiral

Halsey: "The close fighting on Bougainville coupled with that on New Britain and Manus Island and the naval and air strikes on Truk, Rabaul, Wewak, Hollandia and finally Palau and Woleai, present a picture of catastrophe for the Japanese high command."[61]

As the tide continued to turn against the Japanese—"the Japs have got tired (not to speak of 'dead') banging their heads against this place"—Harmon basked in the satisfaction of a job well and successfully done. As his tour at COMAIRSOLS drew to a close he summed up his tenure to Rosa-Maye in self-congratulatory terms: "All I can say is that because of disposition, temperament, inefficiency or whatnot, I find that I do a great deal more detailed work than do any officers I know who are in a corresponding position." As he packed his things for the return to Guadalcanal, Harmon found four cans of beer on his shelf. It would not do to waste them. Unfortunately, he decided to write his bride while finishing them off; the result was obvious not only in what he wrote but also in his rapidly failing penmanship. Rosa-Maye was not amused, prompting Hubert to retort: "You have no sense of humor. I wrote you a screamingly funny letter which I might have sold to the *Saturday Evening Post* and all I get is a bawling out for being drunk." His mood was also down because the future of the Thirteenth Air Force—and therefore his own—was obscure.[62]

The problem was one of success: the South Pacific command had achieved its strategic goals. Harmon conceded as much on 25 February when he wrote that "the Nips are pretty well beat down in this particular part of the world just now and our operations from now on appear to involve continuous repressive measures rather than the give-and-take slugging fest of the past two months."[63] The Thirteenth's history echoed those sentiments, stating bluntly: "When General Harmon became Commander, Aircraft Solomons, 15 March, the only task that remained in the New Britain and New Ireland area was to keep the airfields of the enemy neutralized, and to conduct an air blockade against his shipping lanes."[64] The war was now shifting westwards towards MacArthur's theater as he drove up New Guinea towards the Philippines, and also to the north where Admiral Chester Nimitz drove across the central Pacific towards the Marianas. It was apparent that the Thirteenth Air Force would soon be attached to MacArthur. In such a case, Kenney would become the commander of a new Far East Air Forces that would comprise the Fifth Air Force under Ennis Whitehead and the Thirteenth Air Force. But would Harmon remain its commander?

Throughout April and May 1944 Hubert caught signs that his position was insecure. In the hope of securing a place in the new setup, Harmon penned Kenney: "I am writing, so to speak, to report to you for duty." He continued that he was "anxious to remain over-seas, anxious to fight, anxious to help win the war." Harmon did not want to be "thrust upon" Kenney simply because he was Miff's brother, but hoped that he would be moved west to work in any capacity, although he would certainly prefer to remain commander of the Thirteenth.[65]

While awaiting a response, he wrote Rosa-Maye that if he was sent home it would mean he was "not wanted, and that certainly would take all the conceit out of me." He blamed part of his plight on poor publicity. Not only were MacArthur and Kenney to blame, but the entire Marine Corps as well—its propaganda machine was bigger and more active than anyone's! To his mind, "if they were half as good as they say they are they would be pretty hot." But such was not the case. They had no "staying power" and in their "scientific use of artillery they are amateurs." He noted that he and Miff had discussed this and concluded that the marines were simply too light and this forced them always to keep "one eye on the beach," meaning they were always waiting for the Army to come and relieve them so they could "return to a life of ease in the rear areas." Nor could they hold a position in the face of a determined counterattack. In Harmon's view, it was the Army that took Guadalcanal.[66] The point of this ranting apparently was to grouse that MacArthur, Kenney, and the marines were sucking up all the press coverage, leaving none for him. This in turn meant that he was not getting sufficient recognition as a top-flight combat leader.

These thoughts seem incongruous given earlier arguments that Harmon was an excellent joint officer, but his uncharacteristic grumbling was colored by his profound disappointment. On 14 May, Miff had received a wire from Arnold stating that "H.R. Harmon's services desired in U.S. for important assignment." This was not what Hubert wanted to hear. The main villain in his mind was Kenney: "He is rather fanatical about *not* accepting people who rank him in peace time and I am one of those." It was also possible, he continued, that Kenney simply did not have a high regard for his capabilities, or perhaps, mused Harmon, he had *too* much rank and prestige—"he does not wish to share his glory with anyone big enough to lay claim to any part of it."[67]

In truth, this was all simply anger and frustration bubbling over into his letters. The state of affairs was obviously bothering Harmon greatly. He was hurt, disappointed and embarrassed. Miff tried to put a brighter face on things, telling his brother that he had heard rumors of a B-29 assignment in the works—Miff had just returned from Washington where the new Twentieth Air Force was much discussed. Such a plum job was not to be: the B-29s scheduled to arrive in the Pacific theater in a few month's time were to be headed initially by Ken Wolfe and "Possum" Hansell—later they would be consolidated under Curt LeMay. Still, Harmon hoped that Arnold had something sufficiently important in mind "to satisfy my vanity."[68]

On 20 May word came through that Harmon was being relieved. The Thirteenth Air Force would indeed move west under Kenney, but the commander would be Major General St. Clair Streett. "Bill" Streett, who was already working for Kenney and who had been on the Air Staff in Washington before that, told Harmon that the decision for his relief was made between Kenney and Arnold. He also told him that he thought Harmon would be returning to a job in personnel.[69] Harmon wrote home that he was so excited about seeing his family the "disappointment, chagrin and pique at my removal from the theater and combat are pushed way back." Actually, they were not that far back. In the same letter he returned to his situation, arguing that he felt he had done "a damn good job," and that he had demonstrated his ability "not only to command an Army Air Force from the administrative side, but to successfully conduct combat operations with a *large* air force made up of four different components. Frankly, and regardless of what Kenney may think, I have no feelings of failure or inadequacy." He continued in this vein, grumbling that he knew he could do a better job than the guy currently handling Kenney's combat ops—Whitehead. Harmon concluded this gloomy letter stating that "it will of course be impossible to explain to our friends (outside of the family) so we will just not try."[70]

Hubert Harmon's relief from command of the Thirteenth Air Force after only five months was his greatest disappointment. Despite the fact that almost his entire career up to that point has seen him in staff or training positions—exceptions had been his command of the 19th Bombardment Group before the war and the Sixth Air Force in Panama—he firmly believed that he had the stuff to be an outstanding *combat* leader. While in San Antonio and again in Panama he had repeatedly pestered Arnold for such an assignment. Finally, in 1943, he had been given that shot. He believed in his heart that he had succeeded, but lesser men who were jealous of his seniority and capabilities had him pushed aside.

At this distance it is difficult to agree. Although Harmon's performance in the Solomons was solid, it was also nonetheless true that by the time he arrived the heavy fighting had already ended. As with his arrival in the Panama Canal Zone just as the German U-boats were defeated and driven eastward, so too his arrival in the Pacific coincided with the shifting focus of the war elsewhere. Harmon suffered from bad timing. His efficiency reports echo this assessment. Admiral Fitch, although only having Harmon under his direct supervision for one month, wrote that his physical activity and endurance were "normal"—hardly a ringing endorsement. As for recommended positions, Fitch suggested he would be suitable for command of an Air Task Group or Area Tactical Commander—these were *not* the same as a numbered air force.[71] Arnold's evaluation was even more compelling. He rated Harmon's physical activity and endurance as "excellent," not "superior," and recommended him for a "very high *administrative* command." He also fixed him as number sixty on a list of 175 general officers under his command in the AAF. When it is realized that there were perhaps no more than a score of top combat commands worldwide in the AAF, such a rating was a clear indication that Arnold did not think Harmon was among that elite category.[72] Significantly, and almost sadly, the best rating came from Miff. He judged him worthy for command of a numbered air force, his performance was "superior," and he rated him third on a list of forty-five generals he knew.[73]

In a personal letter to Arnold, Miff expanded on his views regarding his brother. After opening that "in some ways it is no doubt a mistake for brothers … to serve too closely together," he went on to extol the virtues of his brother nonetheless. Miff wrote that Hubert used his brain as well as his background of experience "to correct deficiencies in the South Pacific air organization." He was particularly successful in integrating air operations with air logistics, and, despite initial resistance, was able to convince Navy and Marine Corps commanders of its importance. Miff also noted his brother's "inquisitiveness" that resulted in noticeable improvement in the "tone, bearing, and discipline of the Thirteenth Air Force." Miff also lauded Hubert's "smooth efficiency and effectiveness" as COMAIRSOLS during the Bougainville operation. He concluded by recommending his brother for "any high command or staff assignment in the Air Force."[74] It was a terrific letter.

There were some good memories from his tour, and those mostly dealt with people. He was genuinely fond of Admirals Fitch and Halsey; he had old friends Tommy Musgrave and Earl Naiden working for him; his brother was nearby; and he thought the world of his aide, Major Bob Westbrook. "Westy" had fifteen victories as a P-38 ace when he came to Harmon's headquarters. He was tall, handsome, affable and modest. Harmon had mentioned him several times in his letters home, once commenting that his tales of dogfights would leave Kendrick "goggle-eyed." Harmon viewed Westbrook in a fatherly way, wanting him to rest and recharge his batteries at headquarters before returning to combat. As an aide, he was great fun, although like "others in his generation" a bit forgetful. Still, his "Aw, General" responses to Harmon's corrections were "sufficiently pathetic to melt a stone."[75] It was a great blow to Harmon when "Westy" was killed in action on 22 November 1944. He had twenty victories at the time, making him the Thirteenth Air Force's top ace of the war.

Perhaps most enjoyable of all his experiences in the Pacific was the chance to serve with Miff. Throughout his life Hubert idolized his older brother, and never more so than when seeing him in action in the South Pacific. As he phrased it: "Miff is all they say of him as a commander and leader—I don't think there is a better in the U.S. Army. He has developed into a big man."[76] At his going-away party, the Big Man composed a poem for his little brother.[77]

> To: Two Star –
>> *Now you will be sorry as you*
>>> *never were before*
>> *To have told me of your Eastbound*
>>> *jaunt by B-24.*
>> *So list' you Bonnie Paidie to the*
>>> *things you'll have to do*
>> *You, your Vulcan's Lady and your*
>>> *private crew.*
>> *Just park 'er on the tarmac, swing*
>>> *the waist gun windows wide,*
>> *And start to throw the following*
>>> *from the out to her inside:*
>> *Those twin ship's lamps from*
>>> *Guadal and the spears that are there too,*
>> *And that Maori box from Zealand*
>>> *that by Lake Tampo grew.*

Then the medal for the DFC that
  Berta Harmon wants,
The necklace made of bats' teeth
  from Rennell's dismal haunts.
There are lances, bows and arrows and
  a small pagoda bug,
And other things without a name
  that you will have to lug.
There are trays and trays of butterflies,
  whose beauty you can feel
That epitomize the ethnic
  interests of Central Bougainville.
So take them home you
  little runt and mind your
  manners too,
God's guiding on your
journey and to hell with you!

The Personnel Expert

The rumor passed by Bill Streett that Harmon would be returning to Washington for a job in personnel (A-1 in the nomenclature used by the AAF) proved accurate. Specifically, Hap Arnold wanted him to take over a new organization called the Personnel Distribution Command (PDC). The genesis of the PDC occurred in late 1943 when it was realized that up until then all efforts had been to train men and send them overseas. In mid-1944, however, those men would soon be coming home—in large numbers. The PDC's purpose, therefore, was to "receive and disperse" all personnel returning from overseas theaters, while also "receiving" incompetent or mal-assigned officers on duty in the US and then determine whether they should be reassigned, retrained, demoted or separated from the service.[78] This was a mammoth task that was to get even bigger as victory became increasingly apparent. At that point, PDC's mission would begin increasingly to shift towards demobilization of the millions of airmen being sent back from overseas. Originally, this organization was termed the Redistribution Center and was placed under the A-1. In June 1944 it was renamed and made separate from the Personnel Division. Harmon's headquarters was in Atlantic City, New Jersey.[79]

Harmon, ever optimistic and upbeat, quickly overcame the depression of his relief as commander of the Thirteenth Air Force, and wrote Rosa-Maye that he was much looking forward to this new challenge, which he thought would give him the opportunity to apply once again his well-honed organizational and administrative skills.[80] The truth was, and at some level he must have realized it himself, Harmon's forte was precisely in these areas, more so than in operational command.

The entire issue of handling AAF personnel was something Arnold had been sparring with the General Staff over for years. He wanted his airmen handled by other airmen who understood the unique needs of the air service, not by soldiers who would treat his personnel as infantrymen. The problem was a welter of conflicting and confusing regulations, policies, and directives that seemed to be ever-changing, but never changing fast enough to keep up with the ebb and flow of operational air requirements in the combat theaters. One of the main problems was dealing with officers and enlisted men who were simply substandard—who did not want to be in the AAF and whose performance was so poor that their commanders did not want them in their units—but who had done nothing bad enough to warrant a court-martial. By the middle of 1944 the manning situation was such that there was no longer any need to keep such malcontents in uniform. Arnold told Harmon that he wanted not one man extra in the service than was needed for the war effort. Harmon initially responded cautiously, arguing that the worldwide number of excess officers, over 31,000, was not a "surplus"; rather, it constituted a "reserve."[81] As the combat situation continued to improve, however, such a rationale, although clever, was overtaken by events. Harmon's job was to get rid of this excess, but to do so with fairness.

The problem of excess personnel was closely related to that of determining the best course of action for combat personnel returning to the States on temporary leave. The plan devised by Harmon was first to have PDC personnel at Debarkation Points on the coasts meet those returning from the combat theaters. They were given a quick screening to determine which were casualties (sent to convalescent hospitals) and which were "casuals." Initially, the casuals were put up in the best hotels where they were given thorough medical exams, their uniforms squared away, and personnel records updated. Most then went home on furlough for twenty days. Afterwards, they returned to the Redistribution Stations for another interview. If all was well, the men would be sent to a new assignment—or back to their old one. If problems were detected, the individuals were sent to rest camps or convalescent hospitals until they were ready to return to duty.[82]

As the war in Europe began to approach a climax in late 1944, this issue took on increasing significance. Harmon realized that how this situation was handled would serve as a model for the future. As men came home from combat tours in Europe, how would they be processed and sent to the Pacific to finish the war there? Which returnees would be sent to Stateside training units, and which would be discharged? Harmon's thinking on this crucial issue was revealed in a series of letters to Bill Streett, the man who had succeeded him at Thirteenth Air Force.

Streett had written Harmon with suggestions regarding procedures to send tired combat veterans home for a month to relax and regain their strength before returning to the Pacific. Harmon responded that Streett's proposal was essentially "unsound." (In his typical way of softening such messages, Harmon wrote that the suggestion's main problem was that "we aim to be allergic to new and good ideas.") Experience with European combat veterans had shown that when men came home for a rest, they quickly got used to it and had no desire to return to combat—even if their initial intention had been to do precisely that. Instead, they began to get anxious as their time for going back to the war approached. This apprehension soon gave way to anger as they saw thousands of men in training units who had not yet been overseas. Why should they serve in combat twice when others had not gone even once?[83]

Major General Harmon giving a radio address while commander of the Personnel Distribution Command in 1945.

Military efficiency was at odds with human nature, which in turn impacted military effectiveness. In other words, operational commanders like Streett recognized that their best personnel needed a break from combat to recover their vigor and nerve, but they also needed those men back— their expertise gained by many hours in combat was not easily replaced. Yet, Harmon realized that once these combat veterans came home, the feelings of injustice noted above began to set in. If forced to return to their former units, these men often displayed physical and psychological problems that greatly reduced their effectiveness while also resulting in disciplinary problems.[84] In short, attempting to solve the problem of retaining experienced and capable combat crewmembers, in turn created alienation among those very same crewmembers. It was a thorny problem. Harmon's solution was to bring men home on leave; then send them to training units where they could recover, while also imparting the skills they had learned against the enemy to their students. Their places overseas would then be taken by those already in training units who had not yet been to combat. These men would undergo enhanced operational refresher training—which, argued Harmon, was far superior to that given in the past. The result would be fresh crewmembers sent overseas who had extensive flying experience, combined with more realistic combat crew training. Although their actual operational skills might be a bit less than those sent back for recuperation, rehabilitation, and recovery, they would be fresh and eager to prove their mettle.[85] To help in the recovery of those returning from combat, more than a dozen convalescent centers were established around the country, and these centers ministered to both the physical and psychological needs of the veterans.

Once again, however, this issue, although serious in the fall and winter of 1944-45, was quickly overshadowed by that of demobilization. All talk of "excess" or "reserve" forces became meaningless when it became obvious that Nazi Germany was about to collapse. Although Harmon's command was charged with working out a system whereby many of those in Europe would be transferred to combat units in the Pacific—the Eighth Air Force, for example, would re-deploy to Okinawa after transitioning to B-29s—the cries to discharge as many airmen as possible soon became deafening. From the AAF's standpoint, the easiest and most efficient procedure would be simply to demobilize entire units. Harmon and others realized, however, that this would never pass muster with the American people. "Individual discharges" would have to be done, and the procedures for doing that were contentious.[86]

Eventually, a system was devised that allotted points for various categories such as length of service, combat time, overseas time, age, rank, marital status, and job specialty. When a certain number of points were attained—that total varied—the individual was eligible for discharge. Unfortunately, the exact criteria and the weights assigned to these factors changed constantly. Beyond that, there were operational considerations that could trump other factors. What if, for example, following the point system would result in the majority of enlisted radar operators being discharged at one time, thus rendering a night fighter interceptor squadron non-combat ready? In April 1945 it became AAF policy that "military necessity" would take precedence over all other considerations.[87] Soon, lists of indispensable job specialties were established—and these lists changed on a bewilderingly rapid basis—that extended individuals with a designated expertise for an automatic six months.[88] In addition, there was a finite number of ships and aircraft available to transport back to the States those who did meet all the criteria. With the surrender of Japan, this entire process became a severe headache—not least for those sitting in tents on Pacific islands waiting to go home. When all was said and done, America, as it had in the past, simply ignored all talk of military necessity and operational requirements—it wanted its fathers and sons home. In a very real sense, America's military did not demobilize, it disintegrated. The number of AAF combat-ready groups fell from 218 to 2 by December 1946.[89]

Through all of this turmoil, Harmon retained his balance. His schedule was a killer, and he seemed to be traveling constantly—visiting the dozens of PDC facilities and hospitals across the country, while also searching for desirable sites to locate the additional installations necessary for the flood of personnel returning from overseas. He once wrote that as commander of the PDC he "owned and operated" nearly all the hotels in Miami, Atlantic City, and Santa Monica.[90]

When the war in Europe ended and then in the Pacific as well, the inevitable swamping of his many centers soon gave way to an ebb, and it became necessary to shut down facilities no longer required. Initially, his office was in Atlantic City, New Jersey, but in February 1945 Harmon moved back to Washington where he was elevated to the position of A-1—now he was in charge of *all* AAF personnel matters, not just those of the PDC. Here he was even more deeply involved in redeployment and demobilization issues. More specifically, his job description read that he was in charge of military and civilian personnel, plus ground safety, the chaplaincy, the Women's Air Corps, personal affairs, the Air Provost Marshal, the various Air Boards, and all matters dealing with awards, decorations, and promotions.[91] It was a full plate. Typically, Harmon warmed to it immediately: "in spite of myself I find the job engrossing. By that I mean taking all hours of the day and night."[92]

During this time his family remained in San Antonio where they had been since 1940. As always, he missed his wife and children tremendously and wrote all of them frequently. Being forced to work at a distance from his loved

The Phoenix Bird, *Harmon's converted B-24, which he used until his retirement in 1956.*

ones was always bittersweet for Harmon. He wanted to be home, but at the same time his loneliness compelled him to spend most of his waking hours at work, thus increasing his productivity and making him look even more indispensable. It was not an uncommon problem with those of his makeup.

All of this took its toll on his health. In September 1944 he came down, again, with severe bronchitis. Earlier, he had injured his shoulder, somewhat embarrassingly, in a volleyball game on Guadalcanal. He had tried to ignore it, but the problem grew worse and eventually resulted in a two-month hospital stay and operation, followed by daily physical therapy. In January 1945 an emotional blow fell when he learned that his beloved aide, Bob Westbrook, had gone down in combat. A far heavier blow fell the following month when Miff's aircraft was lost on a flight en route to Hawaii. He was on his way to meet briefly with Nimitz, and then the two of them would fly to Washington for an important conference. Miff's plane took off from Kwajalein on time, but after a position report sent an hour later, nothing else was heard. There was no wreckage. Hubert assumed that the plane had exploded in mid-air due to an electrical malfunction touching off the fuel tanks.[93] This loss hit very hard. Because of his own age and that of his two older brothers, Hubert had always been closer to Millard than to Kenneth. Moreover, because the latter had remained in the Ordnance Corps, they were never stationed together; whereas, he and Miff had crossed paths frequently in the Air Corps and AAF. He loved, respected, and admired Miff.

CHAPTER 6

Transitioning to Peace
and then to Cold War

Despite the turmoil and frustration in Harmon's life, aggravated by the loss of his brother, he remained ambitious and had not given up hope of returning to the Pacific for a combat assignment.[1] When this idea was squashed, he began to fret about his fate when the war was over. In March 1945 he wrote Rosa-Maye that he had seen a list prepared by top AAF leaders that rank-ordered all the major generals in the AAF. Harmon was sixth on the list: "While this is not very flattering from my viewpoint, it (if the same general standing continues) assures me a place in the first 15 of the Air Corps." He noted that "strangely enough I got my best rating from Kenney, my worst from Spaatz and Eaker."[2] Actually, those rankings were not all that surprising. The future of the AAF—and by extension the independent Air Force that would follow the war—was then being contested between the European and Pacific factions. In the event, the Europeanists won handily. The leaders of the postwar Air Force would be those who had commanded in Europe—Carl Spaatz, Ira Eaker, Hoyt Vandenberg, Larry Norstad, Nate Twining and Curt LeMay. Airmen from the Pacific—Kenney, Ennis White-head, Bill Streett and Claire Chennault—would be quickly pushed aside.[3] Perhaps sensing this, Harmon began to talk of retirement. On 17 March he wrote: "All of this leads to a pretty definite intention to retire as soon after this war as it becomes apparent that my prospects are as I conceive them to be."[4] The following week he wrote similarly, and on the 27th revisited the issue once more, noting that he was not interested in "a subordinate position in a *stagnated* Air Force."[5] The following month he had a lengthy talk with Ira Eaker, Arnold's deputy.[6]

Eaker told him what he had already suspected: Arnold, Spaatz and he (Eaker) had held long discussions about the postwar situation, and they were determined that the old men should retire and give way to the "young guys." Given that Harmon was of the same generation as Spaatz and Eaker, the implication was clear. Yet, Eaker also told him that Arnold still held him in "high (if not the highest) regard." Harmon was further told that if he wanted an assignment to England it could be arranged—obviously as part of an occupation force, the role he had played in 1919. If, on the other hand, he wished to stay in Washington, he could do that as well. Harmon's diplomatic reply was "If Arnold wants me to go, I will go."[7]

Throughout the summer Harmon continued to wrestle with his future. He repeatedly discussed retirement, but clearly this was a last resort. He would retire if it became obvious that he was to be forced out or sent to a do-nothing job. As long as he felt he had a future in the service, he would remain in uniform. As a consequence, in June he heard rumors that he would be sent back to Panama, only this time as the theater commander to replace George Brett. This appealed to him because it would give him an independent command, as opposed to putting him in a senior staff position—the likelihood if he went to Europe. Panama fell through for the simple reason that Brett did not want to retire yet and no one was willing to force him! Would Harmon care to go down there to become Brett's chief of staff?[8] No, he did not.

In the meantime, Fred Anderson, who had been the director of operations of the Eighth Air Force under Jimmy Doolittle during the last year of the war, arrived in Washington to understudy Harmon at A-1. Harmon needed to find a job. In July, he heard that he might be going to Alaska; or perhaps it would be back to Panama, only as commander of Sixth Air Force again; or maybe he'd get Third Air Force in the US. It was even hinted he would stay in Washington as Eaker's assistant. He did not know. Rosa-Maye was against the European assignment, simply because she feared it would mean she and the kids would have to remain behind. As she wrote her mother: "I don't know what on earth we'd do if H left us again!!"[9] While all this was going on, he wrote a poignant letter to his wife apologizing—they had had a midnight heart-to-heart phone call a few days previously and it was clear that Hubert had been ignoring the concerns of his family. He had been so caught up in worrying about his career and his future, he had forgotten their needs. He promised to be less self-centered.[10]

Less than a week later he was back in the dumps, grousing that "when one becomes characterized as a leper few are those willing to risk life or reputation by offering a hand."[11] All of the job possibilities noted had fallen through; instead, Harmon was to be sent back to the Personnel Distribution Command, now headquartered in Louisville, Kentucky. As always, given a lemon, he made some lemonade, commenting: "I rather like the idea as the work is interesting and along my line. After the war we will get out and go fishing."[12] Characteristically, he was much concerned about how Ralph Royce, the man who had succeeded him at PDC and was now being replaced by him, would take the news. Harmon had just made an inspection trip to the new PDC headquarters in Louisville, and feared that Royce would suspect that he had just been stabbed in the back when the inspector showed up a week later to move into his office. Harmon begged Eaker to deal directly with Royce and explain things.[13]

Harmon did not retire when the war ended the following month. Rather, he moved to Louisville where his family was finally able to join him. First to arrive was Eula, who came early to begin school. Dad and daughter spent a wonderful month alone together getting reacquainted. Soon, Rosa-Maye and Kendrick arrived. The Harmons lived in a spacious brick house on Bowman Field in Louisville. Though now reunited with his family, the move back to the PDC was a surprising turn of events. Clearly, this was a step down from his position as A-1. One must therefore conclude that other factors were at play, and one of those must have been word from Eaker to sit tight because better things were coming. This seemed confirmed in October when Harmon was in Washington for a personnel conference. While there, Arnold pinned the Distinguished Service Medal on his chest that he had won in the Pacific. Afterwards, the two sat down over a private lunch. This one-on-one time with Hap was the tonic Harmon needed. To him, the chat was like old times, and he wrote Rosa-Maye: "I got the impression that Arnold was more favorably inclined in his attitude towards me than at any time since the early 1920s. Perhaps it was my imagination. I have a dream that something will come of it."[14] He would be correct. In January 1946 Hubert wrote to Rosa-Maye to pack her bathing suit; it appeared they would be heading south after all.

Harmon left the PDC in February 1946, and at the same time received his second Distinguished Service Medal. The citation noted that he had "pioneered the conception, development and effective operation of the Redistribution Stations, Convalescent Centers and Overseas Replacement Depots."

The citation also lauded his shrewd selection of suitable installations and how he had obtained the best possible personnel to man the AAF. He had done an outstanding job as an organizer and administrator.[15] Before leaving Louisville, however, Harmon had one more important task remaining.

In a lengthy and strongly-worded letter to Arnold, Harmon expressed his concern over current AAF personnel policies. He began by stating that AAF manpower accessions had peaked two years earlier, which meant there were few young airmen still entering the service. Because surveys indicated that only 4 percent of the enlisted force intended to remain in uniform after the war ended, this translated into a serious manning problem down the road. The reason for the low regard that enlisted men held for the AAF was, he feared, policies that showed "a lack of concern for individual welfare and unnecessary subjugation of individual dignity." Airmen did not feel they were being treated fairly and equitably in regard to rank, pay, and advancement. Needed was a "well considered policy backed by a scientific personnel administration."

Harmon stressed the need for strong recruiting devices, followed by a battery of aptitude tests to ensure airmen were channeled into the appropriate job specialties. A clear and logical career path should be established for all fields that would nurture and groom individuals for increased responsibility and competence. Productivity in the AAF, which was then only half that in civilian industry, had to be dramatically improved. An adequate Reserve force, which had not been taken seriously before the war, must be a prime objective *after* the war. Finally, he argued that the personnel function was too big and too complex to be run by the Air Staff; some type of separate Personnel Center needed to be established.[16]

This was an insightful and common-sense letter that identified the AAF's personnel problems and proposed practical solutions. The key step—the establishment of a Personnel Center—did in fact occur. This did not ensure all other difficulties noted would be solved, but it was an essential first step towards their solution.

Harmon's final efficiency report at PDC was signed by Carl Spaatz, who had just replaced Arnold as commanding general of the AAF. Spaatz wrote that Harmon was qualified for "any Air Force major command or any staff duty requiring a major general."[17] Harmon would get a command.

A Return to the Tropics

The new assignment was actually an old one—Harmon was returning to Panama, only this time, happily, his family would be going with him. The downside of this duty was that it entailed only the command of the Sixth Air Force—the same unit he had led three years previously. The name had changed—it was now termed the Caribbean Air Command—but its size, scope, and mission were even less vital than before—and now there was no war to generate interest, resources, or focus. Harmon had hoped he would replace George Brett as the theater commander, but instead that post went to Army Lieutenant General Willis D. Crittenberger.[18]

Harmon flew on to Panama alone, while Rosa-Maye and the children left Louisville by car and stopped through San Antonio to see friends and arrange storage for their household goods. From there, they went on to New Orleans where they caught a ship to rejoin "daddy."

Harmon believed that the importance of Panama would continue to grow in the years ahead, while that of Europe would decrease.[19] The opposite was the case, and it soon became apparent that the duties in Panama were even less demanding than at first anticipated. Recall that the Canal had never been seriously threatened during World War II. Rather, the main action in the Caribbean Theater had been stamping out the German submarine threat. In the war's aftermath, the strategic value of the Canal decreased even further. First, the US Navy had grown so large during the war that it had easily been able to build two fleets—one for the Atlantic Ocean and another for the Pacific. It was no longer necessary to worry about shuttling ships back and forth through the Panama Canal in order to contend with unexpected emergencies. Moreover, combat ships had grown so large that most of the Navy's battleships and aircraft carriers were too wide to get through the Canal's locks. As for threats, the only possible concern on the horizon was ally-turned-adversary the Soviet Union, but she possessed only a tiny fleet. It was expected, however, that the Soviets would soon develop atomic weapons—her first atomic test would occur in August 1949—and a means to deliver them, which meant long-range bombers. Ironically and paradoxically, however, this eventuality would lower the Canal's defense priority further—even a near miss with an atomic bomb would destroy the Canal.[20]

Crittenberger and Harmon nonetheless went about their duties diligently; pressing Washington for more resources to defend the Canal, which, they argued, was still of vital importance to American security. In a speech in August 1946, Harmon called for a defensive zone of 1,000 miles in radius to keep Soviet aircraft at bay.[21] The Joint Chiefs of Staff agreed with the commanders in Panama, but a problem soon presented itself—the leases for the scores of military facilities built and occupied in Panamanian territory during the war (as opposed to those in the Canal Zone itself) were due to expire. In the past, this would not have been a concern, and the Panamanian government would have deferred to its northern neighbor and simply renewed the leases with little fanfare. By 1946, conditions had changed.

There had been nationalistic elements in Panama that resented American dominance ever since the Canal was built. During the war, the strategic significance of the Canal was such that these nationalistic elements were held in check. As the war wore on, however, the era of good will began to ebb, largely because of the steep decline in revenue earned by the Canal: traffic was down by 75 percent over prewar figures, and this meant a recession for Panama's fragile economy.[22] In addition, the sheer size of the American presence (67,000 personnel), combined with the large number of US military facilities throughout Panama, began to cause increasing resentment. As unrest simmered following the end of the war, the Panamanian government reacted by hiring more police to keep a lid on things. By mid-1946 there were more police per capita in Panama than in any other country in Latin America.[23]

Things came to a boil in early 1947 over the subject of lease renewal. In 1942 the US had leased over 100 sites in Panama for the duration of the war plus one year. To the Panamanians, the clock began ticking on VJ-Day. Crittenberger and Harmon convinced the State Department to negotiate for the leasing of 134 separate sites throughout Panama. The largest and most important of these was the big airbase at Rio Hato, home to a squadron of B-17s.

It soon became obvious that this large number of sites and installations

Major General Harmon at the time he took over the Caribbean Air Command in February 1946.

would never be approved given the political climate in Panama. The list was therefore progressively trimmed down to Rio Hato plus thirteen one-acre sites. The US position was to lease Rio Hato for ten years with an option for ten more, while the other sites would be on five-year leases.[24] Even this was too much. When news of the proposed treaty was made public in December 1947, thousands of Panamanians took to the streets protesting the "gringos" who were threatening their national sovereignty and pride. The National Assembly, in fear for their lives, voted 51–0 to reject the treaty. The US would need to move out, quickly.

Within three months the US had evacuated all 134 sites in Panama, including Rio Hato. The withdrawal hurt the country's weakened economy even more, as thousands of US military personnel—and their paychecks— precipitously withdrew. Regrettably, this economic downturn led to greater unrest, which in turn meant the hiring of more police. It was a vicious cycle that eventually led to a series of military juntas that dominated Panama for four decades. Ironically, the last, led by Colonel Manuel Noriega, was brought to an end by US intervention in December 1989.

Harmon missed the climactic events of December 1947; he and his family had left Panama two months earlier. Even so, he had seen the direction that events were headed. When Harmon had written of his command in an article for the *Army and Navy Journal* in December 1946, he had stressed the importance of defending the Canal, but, as noted, there were few threats around to cause worry. As a result, in his article Harmon dealt mostly with personnel issues, especially the quality of life for the military people stationed in his command. This was a serious concern. The Caribbean Air Command, like so many others worldwide, had been "crippled by the reduction in military personnel following demobilization."[25] As was the case during Harmon's first tour in Panama, Europe was getting all the attention in Washington—and the resources. As a result, Harmon spent a great deal of his time on the mundane but essential tasks of working on small but numerous problems to improve morale and keep everyone on task. Once again, Harmon's extensive background in personnel and his innate belief in the importance of taking care of his people were obvious.

The Caribbean Air Command's monthly history from this period invariably mentions the subject of morale. It was generally down due to several recurring factors: lack of suitable housing for dependents; a perception of

Hubert and Rosa-Maye attend one of the many functions they hosted at the Caribbean Air Command.

inequality in promotions; under-manning that led to more work for those remaining; and boredom. The result of this malaise was an increasing disciplinary problem combined with a sky-rocketing venereal disease (VD) rate. There were other problems. The history notes ominously that "on 20 February 1947 an unknown amount of liquor was discovered in possession of military personnel stationed at Galapagos Islands. Several of the enlisted men were known to be under the influence of liquor."[26]

Harmon's response was to improve housing facilities so as to allow families to join their military spouses—a huge morale boost; better educational opportunities on base; improved athletic facilities; better clubs; and a ruling that allowed personnel to wear civilian clothes off base. This last was a two-edged sword. Airmen were delighted to shed their uniforms for mufti, but this in turn led to an even higher VD rate—military police were now less able to spot airmen frequenting off-limits establishments![27]

In addition to problems, there were the usual time-consuming visits of dignitaries from Washington, Latin America, and even Europe. There were also welcome guests, such as the new Army chief of staff, classmate and old friend Dwight Eisenhower and his wife, who visited in August 1946. Typical of his personality and style, Harmon entertained Ike at a stag party in quarters, while Mamie was hosted at a wives' luncheon in the Officers' Club. As Eula remembered the former event:[28]

> When dad was head of Sixth Air Force [sic], Eisenhower visited the
> Canal Zone. He came through in uniform with his cadre of men. When
> they arrived at our quarters, they were ushered in and presented with a

Hawaiian shirt and given the opportunity to change into it. Mind you, there's no air conditioning. Then they were served, not rubber chicken, but a meal that had been concocted between Dad and our little Jamaican cook, which consisted of cheese soufflé, green salad and lemon meringue pie. Everything was on that completely drop-the-official, informal basis. Have a good time.

Other special guests were the Duchess of Gloucester, Admirals Bull Halsey and William Leahy, and actors Tyrone Power and Cesar Romero. For these visits, Rosa-Maye was usually on-hand to run things, which had not been the case during the war. The presence of children was also a boon, and in fact, Harmon "hired" Eula to run the household so as to take some pressure off her mother.[29] In August 1947 Harmon arranged the first annual "Air Force Frolics," a musical comedy to raise funds for the Air Force Aid Society that saw the general dress up in a silly costume and a fake mustache. More to his liking, the fact that his command was, frankly, a bit of a backwater, allowed much time for golf and deep-sea fishing. In fact, in August 1947 Harmon flew back to Fort Benning, Georgia, to participate in the "Worldwide Service Golf Tournament." He competed in the senior tourney.[30]

The worst part of his tour was undoubtedly the fact that his beloved mother died in July 1947. When Hubert got word from Kenneth and hurried back to Washington to be by her side, she was already in a coma; he did not get to say goodbye.[31]

In October, Harmon and family—minus Eula who had left earlier to attend Madeira School in Washington—boarded a ship to head back to the States. The eighteen months in Panama had been enjoyable and relaxing if not particularly stressful or even challenging. As usual, however, Harmon's gracious personality and affability were noted. Later, he would

Harmon enjoying one of the welcome fringe benefits of his Caribbean command.

receive news that if he retired from the Air Force he would be a strong candidate for US ambassador. The Panamanians thought highly of Harmon and wanted him for the post.[32] In the event, the president would have other plans.

As for his military career, Harmon continued to fret. Although wearing the stars of a major general, he was still only a permanent colonel. This meant that if he were to retire—or more of a fear, if he were *forced* to retire—his retirement pay would be at the lower rate. As we saw earlier, these issues worried him continuously, and this speaks to a character trait that was quite commendable. Hubert Harmon saw it as his responsibility, and his alone, to take care of his family. Yes, his wife came from a wealthy family, and, indeed, Rosa-Maye had a significant income—she had inherited from her father a large number of cattle on the ranches in Wyoming that produced a sizeable annual revenue.[33] Harmon, however, refused to fall back on this money. As a result, throughout the war financial matters gnawed at him. The issue of retirement, and more specifically, at what rank, was therefore frequently on his mind. In July 1946 a permanent brigadier general's list was released, but Harmon was not on it. That night he and Rosa-Maye sat down to talk about their future: "it was a disappointment to both of us and left us wondering what had been the use of the years of effort and study."[34] Old colleagues who were on the list—and which apparently irritated Harmon—

Harmon receiving a box of cigars from an aide while in Panama.

included George Stratemeyer and Bill Streett. This disgruntlement and frustration were aggravated when another promotion list appeared in February 1947, and again Harmon was not on it. He and Rosa-Maye were "staggered" by the omission.[35]

It was a relief, therefore, when he hosted Tooey Spaatz for several days in June. Spaatz had been the senior combat air commander during the war, and a close friend and confidant of Hap Arnold; he took Arnold's place as commanding general of the AAF in 1946. When Spaatz visited Panama he told Harmon confidentially that he would be on the next permanent brigadier general's list, and then would also appear on the permanent major general's list to be published shortly thereafter. This was good news. He immediately sat down to write Rosa-Maye, who was visiting her ailing mother in Wyoming. He told his wife that the news from Tooey was "gratifying as it gives me an opportunity to compete again on equal terms with the dumb clucks who have passed me by during this last year or so." He wrote that Tooey, who had graduated the year before him at West Point, showed "real friendship and affection" towards him. He was told "he was one of the gang."[36] He was elated.

Harmon's new position would take him to New York City for duty with the United Nations. Soon after, he would receive the third star of a lieutenant general.[37]

The Sinecure, not the Cynosure

Harmon was on his way to New York City to replace West Point classmate Joe McNarney as the US Air Force representative to the United Nations. Harmon's abilities as a diplomat and his personality were important factors in his selection for this assignment. Indeed, one officer told Eula that her father got the job partly due to Rosa-Maye and her social upbringing: "she was practically reared in the atmosphere of national and international politics."[38] The Harmons moved into quarters at Fort Totten in Queens where their active social life required the services of four enlisted personnel to act as maids and cooks. His aide was Major Tom Hanley, Jr., the son of his old friend and classmate. At first, this appeared to be an important and highly visible assignment, but it would not turn out that way. Harmon would say later: "I thought I was going to be a cynosure but instead was sent to a sinecure."[39]

The United Nations was an effort to foster world peace. Such an idea was not new. For over a century peace groups had sprung up seeking to limit if not eliminate war's devastation and suffering. After World War I the League of Nations had been formed to accomplish this purpose, but it had systemic problems that spelled its doom. The US, due partly to internal domestic political battles but also due to a century-old strand of isolationism, refused to join. When Japan and Italy broke the peace in the 1930s (by invading China and Ethiopia), the League was unable to take effective action to punish the aggressors. When civil war broke out in Spain and several foreign powers intervened, the League once again stood aside. As a result, the League was ignored and became irrelevant.[40]

In August 1941, several months before Pearl Harbor, Britain and the United States signed the Atlantic Charter, pledging the two countries to strive for world peace—once the war was over. A few years later, the Soviet Union and China joined in agreeing to the same basic goal. The payoff came when these countries, plus several dozen others, met in San Francisco between April and June 1945 to hammer out a charter for a new United Nations. The representatives of fifty countries signed the UN Charter in October 1945, and all ratified it by the end of the year.

There were six major organs of the new United Nations: the Security Council, General Assembly, International Court of Justice, Secretariat, Economic and Social Council, and the Trusteeship Council. Arguably, the most important of these bodies was the Security Council. It consisted of eleven members: six countries elected for two-year terms, and five permanent countries—the United States, Great Britain, France, China (then led by Chiang Kai-shek), and the Soviet Union. The "big five" were, essentially, the victorious powers of World War II. These five permanent members had veto power over resolutions proposed by the Council.[41]

In an attempt to redress the greatest deficiency of the old League, the UN Charter included Article 43, stipulating that arrangements should be negotiated that would make available armed forces, as well as their facilities and support units, to the Security Council for the purposes of maintaining international peace and security. The wording of Article 43 was, however, vague, probably deliberately so, in order to ensure ratification. Implementation of this article, which required specifics, would prove to be impossible. An agency under the Security Council was the Military Staff Committee (MSC), composed of military representatives from the five permanent members. The purpose of the MSC was to advise the Security Council on military matters and to direct the armed forces placed at the Council's disposal—when such forces were constituted. On April 30, 1947 a special staff committee report, consisting of forty-one articles, addressed how these proposed armed forces would be raised and governed. Problems surfaced almost immediately.

Four MSC members came to agreement quickly on all forty-one articles of the staff report. The Soviet Union, however, disagreed with the others on sixteen of these articles, and maintained that all decisions must be agreed to unanimously. In effect, the Soviet position meant that failure to agree on one article meant failure to agree on any.

One contentious issue concerned military forces that were to be supplied by member states. To ensure this force would be able to deter potential aggressors, it would have to be substantial. The majority argued that the forces needed to be large, balanced, well-equipped, forward-deployed, and in a state of constant readiness. The US submitted its recommendations on the size of this contingent in June 1947. It called for a UN force of 3,800 aircraft, 20 ground divisions, and a naval force of 24 major surface vessels, plus 84 destroyers, 90 submarines, and a sufficient number of landing craft to transport six divisions.[42] This was a substantial force indeed.

The Soviet Union insisted that such a large military was unnecessary. After all, with Germany and Japan defeated, who could it possibly be used against? The Soviets proposed a force about half the size suggested by the US. Significantly, it would contain neither capital ships nor landing craft. Thus, its ability to project power would be sharply limited. To the US, this was a crucial point. The US representative, Herschel V. Johnson, argued that history showed repeatedly that it was far easier to deter a potential aggressor by acting quickly to deploy military forces to a crisis area, than it was to wait until occupation of territory had already occurred and then attempt to push the aggressor out. The absence of a quick-strike force would render the UN's military arm essentially useless.[43]

There were other thorny issues. Where would these UN forces be based? The Soviets refused to allow bases on their territory or to allow other member nations the right of transit. As for the length of time UN forces would be deployed, four nations stated that they should stay for as long as necessary to accomplish their mission. The Soviets argued for a limit of thirty to ninety days.[44] And so it went. As one historian summed the problem: "disagreements resulted primarily from a lack of confidence between the Soviet Union and the United States in each other's good faith and intentions."[45] This was an understatement.

Harmon arrived at the UN for his duties on the MSC just as the difficulties in reaching unanimous agreement by the five permanent members were becoming obvious. It did not take long for frustration to set in. In a speech on December 20, 1947—the month after he arrived—Harmon stated that his main job was to advise the Security Council on military matters, and to exercise "strategic direction" of the armed forces placed at the disposal of the Security Council—should such forces ever be constituted. Because he was the Air Force representative, he admitted that there could be disagreement among the US services as to the appropriate position. In such cases the US representatives would discuss matters among themselves but always present a unified front; differences of opinion were resolved in private, by the Joint Chiefs of Staff in Washington if necessary.

According to Harmon, the problem was not in securing agreement among the US services, but gaining unanimous agreement by the five permanent MSC members. Referring to the report of April that contained forty-one articles, Harmon noted there was agreement on twenty-five; however, these articles were "completely innocuous and did little more than paraphrase the Charter." On the other sixteen articles, Harmon was blunt: "I am violating no confidence when I say that the area of disagreement is such as to retard the establishment, restrict the employment, and render less effective the United Nations' security forces."[46]

Regarding the disagreements over the composition of the military forces, Harmon opined that the Soviet Union's insistence on "equality of contribution" to a UN military force was a calculated attempt to render that force useless. Because most nations did not have large air or sea arms, they would be unable to contribute; since there would be no equality, there could be thus be no air or sea forces. Given the Soviet Union's huge army, her intentions of dominating the UN military force seemed clear.[47]

Harmon saw little hope for agreement. Since the staff report had been submitted in April, there had been twelve meetings of the Security Council and there had been no agreement reached on any issue concerning the UN military force. Even so, Harmon finished on a more hopeful note: the situation was discouraging but not hopeless. He noted that "only one nation stands out as an obstructionist." He hoped that freedom-loving people around the world would unite to oppose hatred and propaganda and insist that the new United Nations insist on agreement to provide for global peace. In response to a question afterwards, however, Harmon bluntly labeled the Soviets a "lustful, greedy minority" who should be ostracized by the rest of the world and perhaps even thrown out of the United Nations. This last comment earned a sharp rebuke from the UN assistant secretary general, also present at the meeting, who stated that expelling the Soviet Union was unthinkable and that "we might just as well close our doors" if that were to occur.[48]

In March 1949, nearly eighteen months after arriving in New York, little had changed. In that month Harmon flew to the Air War College at Maxwell AFB to give a speech detailing the duties of the Military Staff Committee. He began by covering the administrative and organizational aspects of the matter.

He listed the members of the Committee from the five member nations, and said they met at least every fourteen days, usually on Thursday mornings, at their offices in Manhattan. They sat at a semi-circular table—the chairman's position rotated between the nations—and each spoke in their own language. Translators then retransmitted the comments. It was a long and tedious process. In the eighteen months he had been on the MSC, very little had been accomplished.[49] The US Army representative, Major General Matthew Ridgway, later put the problem cleverly: "Very little is known of the MSC because it did practically nothing under conditions of absolute secrecy."[50]

To the audience at Maxwell, Harmon again summarized the staff report of April 1947 that saw the Soviets disagreeing with sixteen articles. Unfortunately, "these disputed articles covered matters of more vital importance than all the others put together." The five key issues that Harmon said had become insoluble included: 1) "equal" as opposed to "comparable" contributions of armed forces; 2) positioning of forces; 3) status and location of forces; 4) withdrawal of forces within a fixed time limit; and 5) the degree of readiness for the military forces, especially air forces. To Harmon this last was particularly crucial because he knew that a quick response from the UN to potential aggression would require air strikes; these air forces would in turn need to be kept at constant readiness. The Soviets saw no such urgency.[51] The thrust of the Soviet position, in Harmon's view, was to ensure the UN military forces would be small, weak, unbalanced, not forward deployed, and slow to react. In short, they would be useless.

The following year Harmon returned to the Air War College with an update. Conditions had worsened, due largely to the outbreak of the Korean War. Now, the Soviets refused even to discuss subjects unless the other four permanent members agreed in principle beforehand to the Soviet position.[52] Harmon was rapidly becoming a Cold Warrior as a result of his contact with the former wartime ally. In stark terms he told his audience: "The Soviets do not speak the same language as the rest of us … What we know as honesty, integrity, personal and national honor do not appear in their vocabulary. At every meeting they hammer away at the same set of lies … They twist and distort facts and couple them with falsehoods." It was clear to Harmon that the former allies in the fight against Hitler had now become implacable adversaries and were bent on world domination.[53] Later, he would tell cadets at the Air Force Academy that in his view the Soviets had no intention of making any concessions to the Free World. Yet, he also noted that his tour at the UN convinced him that Air Force officers needed to be able to express their ideas clearly and forcibly so that they could hold their own with representatives of other nations and other military services.[54]

This was an extremely frustrating period for Harmon. All his gifts of human diplomacy and interpersonal skills were useless in the face of such intransigence. Worse, it was obvious that his job had become meaningless. Harmon was a lieutenant general with thirty-five years of service, and he was accomplishing virtually nothing. He labored to find other tasks to keep busy. He attended the almost-daily General Assembly sessions and was frequently called upon to offer military advice to the US ambassador. He also worked with the United Nations Atomic Energy Commission on the issue of world disarmament of atomic weapons. Even so, he was restless and bored. As his son later phrased it: he was a born project officer who found himself without a project. He went to the Joint Chiefs in Washington and asked for more gainful employment. He was given a task that was more than he had bargained for.

Unification and Disunity

The drive for Air Force independence had never gone unchallenged. Both the Army and Navy had fought this development for decades. World War II demonstrated, however, that the time had come. Global war against powerful enemies had resulted in unified theater commanders, like Eisenhower, Nimitz and MacArthur, who had controlled the forces of all the services, plus those of allies, within their respective theaters. Individual service parochialism would no longer be acceptable. Moreover, airpower had shown itself to be critical to victory in all theaters, culminating with the atomic strikes on Japan that had brought surrender without the necessity of a bloody ground invasion of the Home Islands. The war seemed to indicate that a unified defense department consisting of coequal branches for land, sea and air was in the offing.

Even so, peace did not bring harmony among the services. Various studies were conducted to determine the postwar defense setup, but unanimity was not reached. Essentially, the Army was reconciled to releasing the AAF to become an independent service, but the Navy was not. Nor did the Navy want a defense department, which it feared would limit its influence with Congress and the president. Finally, under pressure from the White House, compromise was reached, and with the passage of the National Security Act, the Air Force was established in September 1947.[55]

This was only a first step. The next problem to arise was determining roles and functions within and among the services. Much of the rationale behind the concept of "unification"—as the grouping of three services under a new Department of Defense was termed—was to eliminate waste and duplication. The resultant debate over these roles and functions was a bitterly contested list of tasks that were doled out to the services. The idea was that a single service would be given primary responsibility for a certain function, although other services might receive a secondary responsibility for that same function. The services, however, fiercely resisted limitations on their responsibilities and traditional prerogatives. For example, a major bone of contention to come out of these agreements, reached at Key West, Florida in 1948, concerned strategic air warfare. The Air Force was assigned it as a primary function, but the Navy received it as a secondary function. This meant that the Navy could assist in the conduct of a strategic air campaign, but only after it had sufficiently covered all of its primary functions and even then only under the direction of the Air Force.[56] Although this guidance seemed reasonably clear, many in both services continued to disagree. While the Air Force pushed to procure large numbers of heavy bombers, the Navy also moved to build large aircraft carriers that could house multi-engine bombers. The Navy wanted to move into strategic bombing in a big way, ignoring—as least as far as the Air Force was concerned—its primary function of sea control.

Dwight Eisenhower, then chairman of the Joint Chiefs of Staff, summed up the problem so succinctly in his diary that it deserves to be quoted here in full.

The Air says:

(a) The job of operating against an enemy country by bombing belongs to the Air, exclusively.

(b) The latest type of bombers now assure a technical practicability of operating against targets 3,800 miles removed from the base. Thus, from several points within our possession we can easily reach vital Russian targets.

(c) These planes fly so high, so rapidly and by such diverse routes that interception will be difficult—so difficult that our losses will be easily supportable!

(d) The Navy refuses to accept the agreed principle that its primary role is control of the seas; it is encroaching on the Air Force job in order to provide an excuse for greater size & power and is doing it by means of the expensive "carrier"—especially the super-carrier, which can have no other mission than that of participating in great bombing operations against land targets.

(e) The Navy is conducting a relentless propaganda campaign, regardless of approved decisions of the JCS, to delude Congress and the people into building up a useless & expensive Navy—thereby depriving the Air of what it needs.

The Navy says:

(a) The big bomber can never again operate against a well prepared, alert defense. The Navy (Radford) calls the new Bomber a "sitting duck."

(b) Because of this all appropriations for big bombers is sheer and stupid waste.

(c) To bomb an enemy successfully the bombing plane must be accompanied by fighters.

(d) Only the movable base can provide this support. Fixed bases will be knocked out.

(e) Ergo—the bombing must be done by Navy from huge carriers

(f) Therefore the Navy should have more money—the Air Force far less.

Eisenhower went on to note that the fight had become personal.[57] It had indeed.

In early 1949 rumors were leaked that corruption was involved in the contract for the new Air Force bomber, the B-36. Specifically, it was alleged that Air Force Secretary Stuart Symington and the Air Force chief of staff, General Hoyt Vandenberg, had accepted bribes from Consolidated-Vultee, builder of the B-36. The rumors became loud enough to prompt the House of Representatives to hold hearings on the subject. In the course of these hearings it became known that the source of the rumors was a civilian official in the secretary of the Navy's office, who received help from high-ranking naval officers. Officials and admirals were fired, while Congress found "not one iota of evidence" to substantiate the allegations against the Air Force and its leaders.[58]

The fires were not extinguished. The Navy still believed it was being short-changed in the new national defense setup and the B-36—and the Air

Force—was being oversold. More hearings were held on these broader issues of national strategy and the defense structure with mixed results. In essence, Congress felt the Navy's pain, but could not or would not do anything to change things where it counted—in the budget.[59]

In the midst of all this, questions regarding the fundamental thrust of the US warplan—then codenamed TROJAN—and the roles and capabilities of the Air Force and Navy in that warplan were constantly being raised. Could the Air Force carry out its pivotal role in the execution of TROJAN by successfully completing its atomic bombing offensive against the Soviet Union?

In February 1949 the Joint Chiefs appointed a board of senior officers to examine that question. They chose Lieutenant General Hubert R. Harmon to chair the board—he had been looking for something to do. Other members were Brigadier General J.K. Rice and Colonel H. McK. Roper of the Army, and Rear Admiral T.B. Hill and Captain G.W. Anderson of the Navy.

In gathering facts and data, Harmon and his team paid a visit to Strategic Air Command headquarters in Omaha, headed by Lieutenant General Curtis LeMay. Harmon pointedly asked LeMay for briefings on targeting plans, aircraft availability, crew training, and performance. LeMay was irritated by this intrusiveness, and called the Pentagon to complain that he did not like the depth and specific nature of Harmon's questions. Vandenberg responded firmly that he expected LeMay's unqualified support to be given Harmon and his team, writing: "We cannot afford to be hypersensitive when we are questioned about our capabilities."[60]

LeMay was sensitive for good reason. On May 12, 1949, the Harmon Board submitted its report, "Evaluation of Effect on Soviet War Effort Resulting from the Strategic Air Offensive." The report was not a ringing endorsement of airpower.

It began by making two critical assumptions: first, the Air Force could implement TROJAN as directed; i.e., it could fly all its missions and deliver atomic weapons on the designated targets. Second, the accuracy figures specified in TROJAN would be achieved.[61] These were not trivial assumptions, because they ignored the effectiveness of Soviet air defenses—which were unknown—while also granting accuracy in delivering atomic weapons that had not yet been demonstrated in practice. Nonetheless, the Board saw its task as evaluating whether or not the strategic air offensive—if conducted as planned—would bring about the defeat of the Soviet Union.

Harmon and his colleagues concluded that the atomic offensive "would probably affect the war effort, and produce psychological effects upon the Soviet will to wage war." For air advocates, this was an unusually weak beginning. Although the effects on the Soviet war effort that the Board predicted appeared significant—30 to 40 percent of Soviet industrial production would be neutralized—this loss would not be permanent. The length of time industrial capacity was reduced would be dependent upon Soviet recuperative powers (which were unknown), and the ability of the US to follow up with more airstrikes, both atomic and conventional. The Board did note, however, that certain key industries, like petroleum, would be particularly hard hit.[62]

Soviet casualties would amount to 2.7 million dead and another 4 million wounded, "depending upon the effectiveness of Soviet passive defense measures." Physical destruction would be massive in the targeted cities, and living conditions for survivors would be "vastly complicated." Considering that the Soviet Union had suffered over twenty million deaths in World War II and had gone on to victory, the statistics regarding an atomic air offensive were not remarkable.

Another disappointment for Air Force expectations came in the section dealing with psychological effects. The Board maintained that the atomic offensive "would not, per se, bring about capitulation, destroy the roots of

Harmon welcomes his West Point classmate, General James Van Fleet, to the United Nations in March 1953. Also in the photo are the Navy representative to the Military Staff Committee, Vice Admiral Arthur D. Struble (far left), and the US Army representative, Lt Gen Withers A. Buress, (far right).

Communism, or critically weaken the power of Soviet leadership to dominate the people." Indeed: "atomic bombing would validate Soviet propaganda
against foreign powers, stimulate resentment against the United States, unify
these people, and increase their will to fight." Regarding the effect of atomic
strikes on the Soviet military forces, the Air Force was given more bad news.
The Board asserted that despite the air offensive, Soviet forces would still overrun most of Europe, the Middle East and the Far East. However—a glimmer of
optimism here—the Soviet offensive would gradually run out of steam due to
the severe disruption of the industry—especially petroleum—to their rear.[63]

   This was a serious body blow to the Air Force and the foundation upon
which its doctrine and force structure were based. Vandenberg was livid. He protested the report's findings and submitted several changes to correct what he said
were its "unwarranted conclusions." For example, he wanted to add that "Soviet
recuperability would be vastly complicated by the great extent of the damage
obtained within such a short time and by the destruction of industrial capacity vital to recuperation efforts." He also wanted to strengthen the paragraphs
concerning the psychological effects on the Soviet population.[64] Admiral Louis
Denfeld, the chief of naval operations, would have none of it. He was delighted
with the Harmon Board's conclusions and thought they were quite logical and
fair—after all, the chairman was a senior Air Force officer. In the end, the report
was submitted with only minor changes made by the Joint Chiefs. Vandenberg
submitted a dissenting opinion to the secretary of defense.

   Omar Bradley, who was the Army chief of staff at the time—and Harmon's West Point classmate and teammate—wrote in his memoirs: "The
air-power zealots were shocked and stunned by the report and felt betrayed by
their own, Hubert Harmon. Van mounted a vigorous effort to have the report
suppressed or altered to eliminate its pessimistic tone. Denfeld gleefully seized
upon the report."[65] The *New York Times*' Hanson Baldwin, a Naval Academy
graduate, wrote that "considerable pressure" had been put on Harmon to
change his views, but he had refused.[66] Harmon vehemently denied this, stating that "whoever said that, lied." He went on that "at no time, before, during or
after the preparation of the committee's report did any officer or civilian of the
Air Force in any degree, however slight, attempt to guide, direct or influence
me in any approach to, or solution of, the problem before the committee."[67]
This situation actually said a great deal about the integrity of Harmon and the
Air Force leadership.

In truth, the Harmon Report, like the Congressional hearings then on-going, had little effect on US defense posture. President Harry Truman and Congress had already turned their attention to rebuilding the domestic economy in the wake of the Great Depression and World War II. They did not wish to be distracted by a budget fight between the military services. More to the point, the Korean War, which erupted the following year, threw all assumptions and plans to the wind. Ironically, in the aftermath of the Korean War it was a soldier-president, Eisenhower, and an admiral serving as JCS chairman, Arthur Radford, who devised the national strategy of Massive Retaliation, a strategy that relied almost exclusively on the Air Force and its nuclear strike capability.

As for the Harmon Board's disappointing report and its outspoken chairman, Hoyt Vandenberg would not forget.

In December 1949, five months later, the issue of an air academy, which had never been far from airmen's thoughts, finally appeared to be nearing a reality. The Air Force was independent, and all logic pointed to the need for a separate academy, similar to West Point and Annapolis, to provide the requisite number of commissioned regular officers for the Air Force. Congress seemed favorable to the idea and ready to move on the appropriate legislation and funding. Even so, standing up a new military academy would be a difficult and challenging task. To shepherd the concept through Congress, to select a site, to design a curriculum, to choose a faculty and senior staff, and then actually to construct the new institution would require a senior officer of strength and resolve. It would require someone who knew the problems of building an organization from the ground up, and who could do so without alienating the many people and organizations that would be needed to see such an enterprise through to completion. Furthermore, the task of establishing an air academy required an officer of unquestioned integrity—a straight-shooter who would not be afraid to tell the truth as he saw it and to do what he believed was right, regardless of the effect his decisions would have on vested interests who wanted different answers.

Vandenberg turned to Hubert Harmon, the man who had defied him several months earlier and had voted with his conscience.

CHAPTER 7

The Man and the Idea
Hubert Harmon and the Academy Dream

*I*n December 1949 Lieutenant General Hubert R. Harmon had already served a full and distinguished career. Since his commissioning from West Point in 1915, he had spent nearly thirty-five years in uniform, almost all of them in the air arm. His career had been defined largely by his abilities as a staff officer and administrator. At the same time, he was extremely well liked by all those who served with him, regardless of rank or specialty. His personality was one of his strongest assets. [1]

In stature, Harmon remained slight, around 5'8" and 135 pounds. He had hazel eyes, which had been a hawkish 20/15 as a young pilot, but which by middle age had "deteriorated" to 20/20. His hair, never thick, was now decidedly thinning and moving from brown to gray. He smiled often, although after having his teeth replaced by dentures in 1936, his smile was not as wide and beaming as it had been in his youth. His overall health remained good but not excellent. As a child he had experienced pneumonia and dysentery; he had nearly died of influenza and pneumonia in 1918; lost his tonsils in 1924; suffered from shingles in 1947; and came down several times each year with serious coughs and colds. But in 1949 there were no heart problems that troubled him and nothing serious was yet on the horizon.

He continued to smoke prodigiously, usually *Camels* or *Chesterfields*. Rosa-Maye had been trying to break him of this habit since before they were married, but she was unsuccessful. Even after being diagnosed with the lung cancer in 1956 that would soon result in his death, Harmon was unable to stop smoking. His long-time driver, Master Sergeant Frank Wall, later related that he too would badger his boss about his smoking, to no avail. Harmon would direct Wall to stop at a store off-base where he could buy cigarettes—Rosa-Maye was not to be told.

Harmon also enjoyed a scotch and water before dinner (*Glenlivet*), and liked a good wine with the dinner itself. He drank an occasional beer, but generally reserved that for afternoons—after a round of golf or while watching a football game. He was never known to drink in excess or embarrass himself. Given his size, he obviously was not a large eater, but he did enjoy a good meal. For breakfast he generally had a soft-boiled egg and toast. His favorite desserts were lemon meringue pie or Lady Baltimore cakes.

Rosa-Maye was the only woman in his life. Throughout their marriage he remained devoted to her, and those feelings were returned. His lifetime partner, she remained a combination of dreamer and realist. She set high standards for herself, her children, and even her husband. Raised in near-isolation on a cattle ranch, she grew up a voracious reader of Victorian romantic literature and poetry, which she had learned at her mother's knee. Yet, life on the ranch was hard and parlous. A bad blizzard could decimate a herd of cows, and crippling accidents were not uncommon. This environment probably accounted for Rosa-Maye's stoic and practical nature. But she also kept a deep love for cultural events, perhaps stimulated by the efforts of her mother and her female friends to soften and elevate the culture they found around them on the frontier, and also heightened by her years in Washington working for her father, who she adored. She was always more serious than her husband, but they seemed to fill each other's gaps. Rosa-Maye and Hubert remained each other's best friend throughout life. Their personalities were wonderfully complementary.

As a father, Hubert remained attentive and affectionate. He loved to play outside with the children, take them to the park, talk to them, and read to them at night. He taught Kendrick to play chess, which they did together often. In fact, he seemed to love all children, and spent many Saturday mornings outside inventing games for the kids down the block to play. Eula was always his princess, and he harbored enormous affection for her throughout his life. Many of his letters to Rosa-Maye finished with "hugs to Eula." Rosa-Maye recounted in one letter to her mother, when Eula was three, that daddy was rushing off to work when his daughter shouted: "Stop! Haven't you forgotten something, Daddy?" The something was of course a kiss goodbye.[2] Harmon was also very pleased when his son Kendrick applied to West Point, although surprisingly and somewhat bluntly, he advised him not to apply for the new Air Force Academy.

Harmon expected the first few classes to be composed of high caliber men, some of whom had been waiting two or three years for the Academy to open, and who therefore often had a few years of college under their belts. In the event, the Air Force Academy did not open as early as planned, so Kendrick went on to West Point, graduating in 1957.

Harmon was enormously proud of his son's attendance at West Point. In one letter, he wrote: "What the blankety-blank goes on up there? What do you mean getting on the Dean's List without warning us? Mom swooned, Eula fell flat on the floor, and I passed out cold!"[3] Another letter from father to son speaks to Hubert's wonderful sense of humor and ability to communicate. Kendrick was a plebe and obviously a very busy young man. Yet, mom and dad wanted to be kept informed. It is probable that the general used his contacts at West Point to keep tabs on his son, but he wanted more direct information. Kendrick therefore received a letter with a series of questions; Cadet Fourth Class Harmon merely needed to check the required blocks and, if necessary, add commentary. Below is a shortened rendition of the letter with Kendrick's (Kindrik to his father) responses in italics:[4]

Kindrik—

Fill out and return following questionnaire, PRONTO:

How many room-mates have you? *2*

Have you been to call on Col. And Mrs. Beukema? *NO!*

Why not? *No Excuse sir!*

Is your watch performing OK? *No. It stops frequently*

What do you want with money at West Point?

1. Boodle. 2. Buying things I need at the Cadet Store, so as to keep out of debt and build up a reserve. After I have obtained a backlog of about $25, this reason will no longer be valid. Also I am planning to drag one of these weekends [get a date], and me and she will have to eat. The last batch lasted for 2 months, so you see there isn't a great need.

How much do you really need? *$10.00*

Daddy

Harmon's warmth, which was genuine and obvious, came from his family. Eula and Kendrick remember Banny Harmon, their grandmother, as a loving and demonstrable woman who always came equipped with long and close hugs. She was incapable of disciplining her grandchildren, and Hubert inherited this trait: he too found it almost impossible to be hard on his kids, especially if it involved spanking. At the same time, he was devoted to his mother and his mother-in-law. Both visited frequently, sometimes at the same time and were always given a joyous welcome. When Harmon received his first star and moved into larger quarters at Randolph Field in 1941, he wrote "Muvver" (Eula Kendrick) that she must come to visit soon: "we especially need you to lend poise and dignity to the household. Bring your pearl necklace as our living room needs something like that to set it off."[5]

He remained a devoted Army football fan, but his great love was golf. He was good but not outstanding, and his ease at finding partners no doubt had more to do with his position and personality than his prowess with a club. To even the playing field, he invented what he called "the Harmon method" that allowed players with a wide range of abilities to play together. Each player vied against himself—predicting his performance on a given hole or round and being docked on how far off he was on the prediction. He had tried to hit the links at least once each week throughout his career. Rosa-Maye understood this addiction and tolerated it, attempting to see it in a lighter vein: "H stayed home ostensibly to study for a speech he is making on Tues. However, he punctuated it with frequent practice periods on the lawn with a 5-iron."[6] While Academy superintendent he golfed with Ben Hogan, Omar Bradley, Governor Dan Thornton, Secretary Talbott, President Eisenhower and many others. In a 1954 letter, Harmon noted that he had played golf with Ike several times during the past few months, noting that "he usually beats the tar out of me. A few days before he left Colorado he had a 77 on a real tough course."[7] To be Harmon's aide, an officer had to be an accomplished golfer and card player.

Horseback riding had largely been forgotten. Indeed, Rosa-Maye contended that their rides together around Washington DC during their courtship had largely been a ploy: once they were married she was seldom able to get him back on a horse. She, however, continued to ride. At West Point, for example, she took extensive lessons and became an accomplished jumper. Rosa-Maye passed on this affection to Eula, who had her own horse. There was usually a cat or dog around the Harmon household, and when the family moved to Colorado in 1955 they brought with them a poodle named *Airlift*. Another favorite was a dachshund named *Blitz*. Harmon used to play with him in the house, having him chase a ball tossed into the next room. The family had long taken a fancy to oriental rugs, and these were spread around the floors; *Blitz* would often slide into them and knock them askew. Hubert taught him how to fetch the ball, and then go back to straighten the rugs.

Harmon remained addicted to games—especially crossword and mathematical puzzles, chess, and card games. While in the hospital during his last illness he was in the midst of a chess match via correspondence. He designed a wargame using a world map as the "board," tokens for units, and a complete set of rules. His favorite card games were poker, bridge, and gin rummy. He was a good poker player and sometimes played for high stakes. During one session at the Army-Navy Club in Washington he won enough to buy a new Cadillac.

He liked to read and respected those who could add literary allusions to a conversation. Rosa-Maye later recalled that Hubert was raised with four books at his side: the Bible, a dictionary, an encyclopedia, and a thesaurus: "During my married life I sometimes sighed to think no meal seemed to get eaten in our house without the Dictionary. I have known it to be brought out even when we had guests, if a question of a word's meaning or usage arose." He was also well-grounded in geography and loved atlases of all types. When Eula was three years old, she received a globe from her father as a birthday present![8] Even so, when in his spare time he wanted to pick up a book to relax, Hubert tended towards lighter material: Mark Twain, Rudyard Kipling or Jack London. He enjoyed happy movies, especially when they starred classy ladies. One of his favorites was Greer Garson. As for music, he still enjoyed classical, a taste he had acquired in his youth.

Hubert's most enjoyable and rewarding hobby was carpentry, which he had been pursuing since he was a teenager. In 1906, at age 14, he wrote his father that he had just made a glove box for "momma" with an inlaid top—a technique he had mastered while suffering through chicken pox. He had also made an oak chair with no nails used, just mortises and tenons. His next project was to lower the head of momma's bed by two feet because she thought it was too high.[9] He continued this activity for decades thereafter and throughout his career he had been able to maintain a workshop in his quarters that was well stocked with tools and wood. In this sense, he took after his oldest brother Kenneth—Miff had been an outdoorsman. Rosa-Maye's diaries over the years noted that many evenings were spent with her at a desk writing, and Hubert tinkering in his workshop. He much enjoyed making a chair, table or towel rack for friends and family. On one occasion, while staying with friends he noticed that the stone walls in their bathroom did not permit the attachment of a toilet paper holder, so he designed and built an ornately carved and finished toilet paper stand that complemented their décor.[10] In addition, he continued to doodle, and his many drawings, often humorous, are scattered throughout his papers and letters.

He remained a plain-spoken man. He was honest, forthright, and candid. He was a man of rigid integrity—he did not even cheat on his golf scores! If you asked him for his opinion, you would get it, unvarnished. Yet, it was this simplicity of spirit that was so appealing. As Kendrick phrased it: "He was not a politician; he was not a diplomat; he was not a schemer. He was not ambitious in a calculating way. He was ambitious because things came to him spontaneously and generally because he was exceedingly popular. My dad was loved and gave love back." He was the life of any party he attended, and would often be near a piano singing lustily with a group of young officers and their wives clustered around him.

In his correspondence, which was usually personalized to make the respondent feel that Harmon had just pushed everything aside to write them a note, he invariably blamed any misunderstanding or difficulty on himself. His sense of humor is easily illustrated by the letter written to an old friend:[11]

> Dear Mr. Bryan:
>
> As you see (if you consult your calendar) I am a poor man who has to work on Saturdays and none of the stenographers will help me because it is a long Labor Day week-end and they have dates and are not interested in my problems which include not having a typewriter like you do along with why the Air Force Academy should or should not have been located at Bryan simply on account of poker and choral extra curricular activities for such nuts as Howard Davidson who makes boats in the basement and then can't get them out through the narrow door which reminds me to thank you for mentioning without derogation my appointment as Superintendent and to say that I am very happy and hope you are the same.

As a boss, he was a dream. Sergeant Wall commented, "I didn't work for him. He treated me like one of the family." He never yelled and seldom even got angry. One of his aides later recalled that when Harmon first sat down with him he made it clear that he did not want him going around saying "General Harmon wants so and so." There were very few occasions when he was authorized to use his name. Nor did he want the traditional "honors" when flying into a base—customs that generally included being met by the base commander or his staff. Yet, these directives made little difference because everyone liked him so much they would do anything for him: "I always felt," wrote one aide, "that he could do anything, and the reason he could do it was that people worked *for* him and didn't work because they were scared of him."[12] On those occasions when it was necessary to discipline a subordinate he would seek humorous ways to soften a blow or do so in a way that brought a smile. Sergeant Frank Wall gave several examples of this trait. For example, Wall told how another of Harmon's aides, Captain Tom Curtis, was a good fighter pilot, but a poor organizer. On one occasion the two were headed for the flight line to catch a plane to Washington and Harmon asked: "Tommy, did you get the flight lunches." "Oh geez, general, I forgot!" Harmon then reached behind the seat and brought out the boxes, showed them to Curtiss, and said: "Tommy, I'm the best aide you've ever had." On another occasion, Wall related:

> He had a sly sense of humor. You had to listen. They were coming back from Washington one time, and Captain Tom Curtis was the aide. They got in the airplane, and he [General Harmon] said, "Oh, Tommy, by the way, I got a new pair of shoes. Those shoes are really going to take a couple of strokes off my handicap." He kept alluding to the shoes, alluding to the shoes. Curtis is trying to figure, "What's he trying to tell me?" He [General Harmon] said, "Did you see the new shoes when you were in the Army-Navy Club?" He [Curtis] said, "Yes, sir. The last I saw of them they were on the shelf in the closet." General Harmon said, "Yes, and they're still there. They're still there, Tommy."

Wall stated that his General was simply a kind and good man who was loved by everyone—military and civilians—because he treated everyone as an equal. Wall remembered another incident when Harmon was at the United Nations. Harmon's US Navy counterpart was a bit of a blowhard. For example, when getting on the elevator he would tell the operator (all elevators had manual operators in those days) to go directly to the eighteenth floor. He was in a hurry. Wall noted that the operator seldom did so, simply out of spite, because he did not like being told what to do. But when Harmon came on, he invariably said hello to the operator, asked him how he was doing, and got to know him. Soon, whenever he boarded, the operator took him directly to whichever floor he wanted, simply because Harmon would not ask for such favoritism. And yet, he had a colder side. When this same admiral tried to call him Doodle, Harmon made it clear that nickname was reserved for his friends.

He had always possessed an active mind and enjoyed the arts and a good discussion. Rosa-Maye's literary bent was inclined in these directions as well, and the two continued to attend the theater, concerts and political events. Politically, Hubert and Rosa-Maye began as Democrats, largely as a consequence of Senator John Kendrick's long career, but as the years passed they switched to the Republican Party. Despite the politically fascinating environment, Harmon did not enjoy his job at the United Nations from 1947 to 1953; even so, the expo-

Harmon demonstrating that his drive is ready for the PGA tour.

sure to world and national political activities was stimulating and reinforced his long-held beliefs that military officers must know and understand the world about them.

The Quest for an Air Academy

The idea for an air academy was voiced at least as early as 1918. In November of that year—as World War I was ending—Lieutenant Colonel A.J. Hanlon wrote a memo to his superior stating: "As the Military and Naval Academies are the backbone of the Army and Navy, so must the Aeronautical Academy be the backbone of the Air Service."[13] There were numerous other suggestions regarding an air academy—by Billy Mitchell, Mason Patrick, Bert Dargue, Bart Yount and others—but nothing ever came of these proposals. It would take nearly five decades for Hanlon's vision to become a reality.

The main reason for this slow progression was the bureaucratic situation the air arm found itself in during that period. In essence, airmen first had to justify to the War Department, Congress, the president, and the American people of the need for a separate Air Force, equal in importance and political power to the Army and Navy. To accomplish this feat, airmen had to prove they could perform a unique mission of strategic importance that would justify independence.

Once those arguments were compelling enough to create a separate Air Force, it would then be possible to use the same rationale to explain the need to train and educate officers possessing unique qualities and abilities to populate that Air Force. In short, until airpower could prove its importance to national security to such an extent as to warrant independence, officers trained at West Point, Annapolis, ROTC and other commissioning sources were adequate.[14]

As we have seen, this move towards a separate Air Force was slow but inexorable. As aircraft became ever more capable in the years following World War I, more and more observers in and out of uniform pushed for greater autonomy for the air arm. In 1921 the Air Service was officially established within the Army as a combat branch. In 1926 the Air Corps Act gave the air arm greater authority to run its own affairs as well as an increased budget. The GHQ Air Force of 1935 was a further step toward independence. War brought the Army Air Forces, commanded by a five-star airman, and virtual autonomy.

The AAF began planning for independence, as well as an air academy, during the war. In July 1945 the Air Staff Personnel Division (A-1) prepared a preliminary study on the academy issue. It concluded that a four-year school, similar to that of West Point, was far superior to the idea of a "National Combined Academy" that would educate officer trainees for all the services—an idea going the rounds at the time. A-1 thought the combined plan inadvisable because such a degree of integration in joint warfare was not necessary for junior officers: it was more important for them to know their own service and its capabilities first. The Military and Naval Academies were adamant that the nature of war operations on land and sea were so fundamentally different from each other as to require separate educational systems. Similarly, air operations were also unique, so the same logic dictated a separate air academy. Moreover, although West Point and Annapolis could supply the AAF with some of its graduates, those quotas would not be enough. More to the point, such a scheme would not resolve the problem of ensuring that officers were trained first and foremost as airmen.

The study continued that the air academy should procure its students using the same procedures as did West Point. The curriculum should offer a bachelor of science degree with a specialty in aeronautical engineering. The school should incorporate all "character-molding features basic to academy training—military discipline and direction to build character, honor and leadership." As for flying training, the study recommended familiarization training only—perhaps twenty-five flying hours.

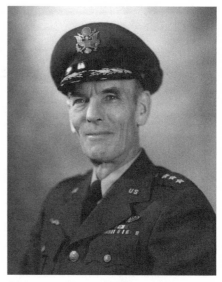

The Personnel Division's study concluded that the "Army Air Forces should announce a policy that a separate Air Academy, covering a four-year course of instruction, is necessary to provide the type of Academy training needed to commission regular officers for the AAF."[15]

In broad terms, this was to be the rationale and outline used by the Air Force to push for an air academy over the next decade. The head of the Personnel Division who approved and

Lieutenant General Hubert R. Harmon.

forwarded this study was Major General Hubert R. Harmon. It was neither his first nor certainly his last in-depth thinking on an air academy.

World War II made clear to all but the most inveterate opponents of change that airpower had earned its place as a coequal branch of the armed services. The Air Force became a reality on September 17, 1947. Step one achieved.

The following month, Congressman Paul J. Kilday from Texas acted on the second step, introducing legislation to establish an air academy, to be located at Randolph Field. The following month Texas Senator Thomas Connally introduced a companion bill. A flurry of similar bills followed, introduced by congressmen and senators from all over the country—most stipulating that the new air academy be located in their state or district.[16] Air Force leaders were ambivalent about these legislative efforts. There were a host of critical issues that needed to be addressed by the new service; an air academy was but one of many. In fact, even within the realm of education the Air Force was more concerned with establishing the Air War College and the Air Command and Staff College than they were an air academy.[17] In addition, Air Force Secretary Stuart Symington, a bit distressingly, informed Defense Secretary James Forrestal and Representative Kilday that if the Army and Navy would allocate one-third of their academy graduating classes each year to the Air Force, a new air academy might not even be necessary! Finally, the Air Force was reluctant to embrace any bill that tied an academy to a specific site. The exact location and even purpose of an air academy—notably, should it include flight training—were not yet obvious, so Symington thought it was premature to commit to specifics.[18] Obviously, the Air Force did not yet know what it wanted.

It was also clear, however, that such positive impulses from Congress should not be ignored. In early 1948, Symington directed the deputy chief of staff for personnel, Lieutenant General Idwal H. Edwards, to prepare legislative language that more clearly defined Air Force requirements. The resulting proposal called for a four-year program, located at Randolph, which would award an accredited baccalaureate degree. There was no mention of flight training.[19] At the same time, Symington directed Air Training Command (ATC) to prepare a study on the structure of an air academy. This study, submitted in April 1948, assumed that the new institution would be part of ATC, would be located at Randolph Field, and *would* include flight training in its curriculum.[20] On 1 June the Air Force forwarded its hastily prepared legislative language to the Bureau of the Budget for review, approval, and forwarding to Congress. The director, Frank Pace, declined to forward the proposal, stating that it was incomplete. Pace instead called for a "thorough study to be made of the functions which such an Academy is expected to perform … and of the organization, size, and type of training required." In addition, the director noted that there was a wealth of existing legislation already on the books regarding West Point and Annapolis. The Air Force must also ensure its proposed legislation would parallel and be consistent with those existing laws.[21]

Pace's dash of cold water contained wisdom. Despite its eagerness to move forward on an academy, the fact was, Symington's musings made clear the Air Force had not really thought the matter through. Decisions regarding the size, function, duration and mission of an air academy were not obvious, and several suggestions had been made over the years. Hap Arnold, for example, had called for a joint, two-year school that would inculcate basic ideas on scholarship, discipline, common military customs and courtesies—the "National Combined Academy" already mentioned. He saw this period as useful at instilling a sense of teamwork and helping to combat the debilitating interservice parochialism he had so often witnessed. Students would then separate and attend service-specific academies for two more years to learn the details of their profession. All would graduate with diplomas and commissions.[22]

Other senior airmen had different ideas. General Carl Spaatz, Arnold's successor, thought that prospective officers should first attend two years at a civilian university. An air academy would then serve as a two-year finishing school that would award a commission. Major General Hugh Knerr, an Annapolis graduate who had transferred to the Air Service many years before, rejected the entire idea of service academies, believing that ROTC units around the country would prove more than adequate. Major General Frederick Anderson, Hubert Harmon's successor at A-1, wanted a four-year military school like West Point.[23]

To clear the air, the Air Force chief of staff, General Hoyt Vandenberg, convened a board at Air University chaired by his vice chief of staff, General Muir Fairchild. This Fairchild Board was composed of several high-ranking Air Force generals, but also included the superintendent of West Point, Major General Maxwell Taylor. The Board was directed to address two fundamental questions: first, should an air academy include flight training in its curriculum. Second, should the air academy be a four-year military school like West Point and Annapolis, or should it be a composite school that entailed two years at a civilian university followed by two or three years at a military school.[24] Both of these were important questions that inspired debate.

For six hours on 9 August 1948 the Board discussed these two questions and concluded that flight training should not be included, but, in an eight-to-five vote, stated that the Air Force should adopt a composite plan for its academy. Maxwell Taylor immediately wrote Vandenberg, warning him of the Board's vote regarding a composite plan. Taylor thought this would be a "serious mistake" and urged Vandenberg to think this matter through carefully and to consider the long-range implications on all of the service academies.[25] Vandenberg did think it through, and on 1 September wrote that he concurred with the recommendation for no flight training because of the severe negative impact it would have on the academic program. A full-up flight training program was simply too intense and time-consuming to allow for a quality baccalaureate degree. On the other hand, Vandenberg rejected the proposal for a composite academic scheme. He stated that the plans for establishing an Air Force Academy would be based upon a four-year course of instruction "generally along the lines of the present service academies."[26] Vandenberg's insistence on a four-year curriculum patterned on West Point is interesting and deserves some explanation.

Vandenberg was a West Point graduate, class of 1923. His cadet experience was marked by turmoil. During World War I the demand for Army officers had caused West Point to graduate and commission cadets after only two or three years of school. When the war ended, Congress, seeing the possibilities of saving money with seemingly little downside, passed legislation making West Point a three-year school. The new Military Academy superintendent, Brigadier General Douglas MacArthur, objected strenuously to this decision and lobbied to have the program restored to a full four years. He was successful, and Congress eventually reversed itself. However, because three classes of cadets had already entered West Point expecting to graduate in three years, Congress decreed that all cadets then enrolled would have a choice: graduate after three years as planned or remain for a fourth. Vandenberg opted for a full four years. Considering that he was a mediocre cadet both academically and militarily, this was a surprising decision. One can only conclude that West Point had a deep and powerful hold on him.[27] Twenty-five years later it apparently still did. Vandenberg insisted that an air academy be a full four years and that it be patterned on his alma mater.

Vandenberg then directed Air University to follow up and establish the Air Force Academy Planning Board to thoroughly study the entire question of an academy. The results of this effort were impressive.

The Planning Board's project officer was Lieutenant Colonel Arthur E. Boudreau, a man who would remain associated with air academy matters for the next several years. The Board consisted of four groups that examined specific issues: site and building construction, legislative affairs and the matter of an interim academy, administration and organization, and, most importantly, curriculum. The standing members of these groups were officers, but they were assisted by a large group of very distinguished civilians and military advisors. The thirty-nine civilians included a number of university chancellors, presidents, deans, and professors, and the military consultants included two generals, three lieutenant generals, and a number of lesser lights. In this group were Major General Taylor from the Military Academy and Colonel Herman Beukema, the head of West Point's Social Science Department. No Navy officers were invited to participate.[28]

The Board's report, published in January 1949, stated the problem clearly. During the late war the officer corps of the AAF had grown from 1,600 to over 385,000. Many of those commissioned were not college graduates, and the result was "an increasing number of officers who do not measure up to the standards of education required for the execution of their duties at the highest peak of efficiency." In late 1948 only 41 percent of regular Air Force officers were college graduates, compared to 72 percent in the Army and 75 percent in the Navy. Moreover, only 10 percent of Air Force officers were Academy graduates, compared to 30 percent in the Army and 38 percent in the Navy. The solution was to have more college, and preferably Academy, graduates. Although West Point and Annapolis were willing to provide a percentage of their own off-spring for the Air Force—40 and 7 percent respectively whose education would be paid for by the Air Force—this number, around 250 officers per year, was not enough.[29] The Board argued that the Air Force needed an influx of 1,000 officers each year; half could come from ROTC, the Aviation Cadet Program, or Officer Candidate School, but the other half needed to be academy graduates—the same percentage that was the goal of the other services. West Point and Annapolis could not provide this number for the Air Force. Although both schools were making plans to expand their facilities so as to accommodate larger student bodies, these additional graduates were earmarked for the Army and Navy. It would be impracticable, said the Planning Board, for West Point and Annapolis to physically expand to such an extent that they could accommodate their own service needs plus those of the Air Force.[30] In addition, and this was crucial, Air Force officers needed to be educated and trained as *airmen*, not as transplanted soldiers or sailors. In other words, if the entire rationale for separate schools for the Army and Navy was that their unique operating mediums required unique expertise for their officer corps—the point made by Harmon in 1945—than those same arguments provided the justification for specially-educated airmen.[31] The only solution was an Air Force Academy to provide the required number of regular air officers.

The Board gave the mission of the new air academy as being threefold: to provide an assured and constant source of regular officers to the Air Force; to provide men with the requisite educational background essential to career officers; and to provide an adequate officer corps that could be augmented in time of war or national emergency. This mission statement was then expanded to include other goals: a thorough grounding in Air Force principles; a broad-based education; and the inculcation of loyalty, duty, and service.[32] To achieve these varied objectives, the academy would consist of three main pillars: the academic departments headed by a dean; military training under a commandant; and athletics under a director of athletics. The overall commander would be termed the superintendent—in keeping with the practice at the other two service academies.

Of these three divisions, the academic portion was the most important. Indeed, the entire second volume of the Board's report was devoted to an extremely detailed description of what this curriculum would look like. It would be "student-centered" and would foster creative thought; there would be little emphasis on "rote" learning. Classes would average twenty students, with an overall student-to-faculty ratio of ten-to-one. The faculty would consist of both military officers and civilians. Although not wanting to pin itself down on exactly what the mix of civilians versus military officers would be, the Board opined that of the 260 faculty members envisioned, 74 should have doctorates, 111 a master's degree, and the remaining should have bachelor's degrees.[33]

Significantly, the Board then confessed that it could not ascertain how many Air Force officers were qualified to teach at an academy. It therefore recommended that the Air Staff institute procedures to collect detailed information on the educational qualifications of its officer corps for future use. Further, it recommended that the Air Force begin an "upgrading program" that would send selected officers to civilian universities to obtain advanced degrees. This would begin to form a pool of qualified officers who could be tapped for academy teaching assignments at a later date.[34]

The curriculum was detailed at length. The faculty would be divided into three divisions: humanities, sciences, and military studies. The Board listed every course to be taught, the course objectives of each, the method of instruction and grading practices, and even suggested textbooks. It was a very thorough job.[35]

The Planning Board also covered such issues as entrance requirements, pay for cadets ($78 per month), intercollegiate athletics, intramurals, the cadet uniform (an officer uniform with distinctive cadet insignia), and the disciplinary system. There would be an Honor Code.[36]

It is difficult to underestimate the importance of the Planning Board Study. The rationale used for the formation of an air academy, to include the necessity for a cadre of officers specially educated with an air-focused viewpoint, combined with the argument as to why continuing the practice of siphoning off a percentage of West Point and Annapolis graduates each year would not be satisfactory, were to become standard Air Force talking points for the next several years. In addition, the call for a quality faculty and a plan for how to assure it for the long term, as well as the detailed examination of a notional curriculum for a four-year academy, were seminal. It is no exaggeration to say that these proposals would become the focus of the extended debate over an Air Force Academy for the next decade.

At the same time, it should also be noted how conservative these proposals were. The Planning Board looked to the West Point model and used it extensively. It recommended that the curriculum was still to be fixed for all cadets regardless of ability or prior college experience. As at West Point, disparities in student knowledge and abilities would be addressed by "sectioning": brighter cadets would be grouped into higher class sections, and less gifted cadets would be gathered in the lower sections. The better instructors would be assigned to the lower sections where their expertise was most needed.[37] As at West Point, there would be no electives and no academic majors. There was, seemingly, a bit more emphasis given to the humanities and social sciences in this proposal, but not enough to shift the overall preponderance of academic focus from mathematics, science, and engineering—39 percent of the curriculum would be mathematics/science based, and 34 percent would cover humanities and social sciences. The remainder would be military studies. To indicate a modicum of change, courses in aerodynamics would be substituted for "bridge-building." [38]

As for other aspects of cadet life, once again the similarities to West Point were more remarkable than the differences. Classes would be conducted six days per week; athletics, drill, and tactical training would occupy a cadet's after-class time. Commissioned officers, termed tactical officers as at West Point, would be assigned to each air cadet squadron. An Honor Code would be imposed on cadets to inculcate the proper aspects of ethical conduct.

Given these similarities between the proposed air academy and West Point—and note that Annapolis was consciously ignored—it could be argued that the Planning Board's members were distressingly unimaginative, or that they truly admired the West Point system and what it had achieved over the previous decades.[39] Regardless, the report was definitive enough that Vandenberg declared in a speech soon after its release: "I think you will agree with me that the Air Force need is definite, and that now is the time, after years of discussion on this matter, to start building an Air Academy."[40]

Not just an air academy was at stake. There were on-going discussions of service academy education in general, prompting Defense Secretary James

Forrestal to solicit ideas for a service academy board to study the issue. Retired
General Dwight Eisenhower, then president of Columbia University, responded
with a detailed letter endorsing such a study and recommending two possible
civilian university presidents to chair the board, as well as suggestions on the
military members. He even provided Forrestal with a draft "terms of reference"
for the board.[41] Forrestal liked this proposal, and in March 1949 announced the
formation of the Service Academy Board. In his guidance to the Board, Forrestal noted that the world had changed dramatically as a result of the world war
recently ended, and this meant a heightened need for officers, in all the services,
who had a broad understanding of political and economic, as well as military,
affairs. Moreover, these officers must be imbued with knowledge of the current
military establishment that emphasized integrated, joint warfare. Now there
were movements afoot to establish an air academy alongside the two older
institutions. Forrestal wanted the Board to recommend "that general system of
basic education which it believes is best adapted to provide all three Services
with a sufficient number of young men qualified to meet the needs of the regular armed services." Although recognizing the "fine traditions and splendid
contributions" of West Point and Annapolis, Forrestal wanted the Board to feel
at liberty to recommend changes to their roles if logic so dictated.[42]

To chair this Board, Forrestal appointed Dr. Robert L. Stearns, the president of the University of Colorado—the same Robert Stearns who had been
Hubert Harmon's director of systems analysis at Thirteenth Air Force in 1944.
For vice chairman, Forrestal named Eisenhower. Stearns and Eisenhower were
to be assisted by a small group of five civilians and three military officers—the
superintendents of West Point and Annapolis, and Major General David M.
Schlatter, who was slated to be the first Air Force Academy superintendent.[43]

The Stearns-Eisenhower Board's report began by emphasizing the need
for the service academies. The nation needed "a highly trained, intensely loyal
corps of professional officers," and the academies should produce the nucleus
of these officers.[44] After noting that officers required the qualities of leadership, mental alertness, good health, a broad base of knowledge "comparable
to that possessed by graduates of our leading universities," the Board recognized that few men possessed the desire for a military career upon entering
an academy. Rather, this motivation for a military career was instilled during
their undergraduate years at the academies.[45] This last was a key point that
would underpin all arguments regarding the utility and indeed necessity of

the military academies to the present day. Certainly, there was any number of civilian universities that could produce men who were healthy, alert and learned, but it was only a military academy that could instill in them a vocation for a military career.

The Board then considered—and rejected—various plans calling for a single joint academy or a composite scheme whereby students would attend civilian institutions initially and then transfer to the service academy of their choice. No. The Board wanted each service to have its own academy. In unusually common-sense terms it wrote: "The young man does not enter military life as a whole. He chooses West Point because he likes the military life; he chooses Annapolis because he is attracted by life on the sea; he will want to enter an Air Force Academy because of his interest in flying." It concluded that "an Air Force Academy should be established without delay."[46] Significantly, this last recommendation was not what the Board members had originally believed. General Schlatter later commented that most members, military and civilian, were skeptical of the need for an air academy. As the discussions proceeded, however, its necessity became patently obvious to everyone.[47]

The Stearns-Eisenhower Report offered many recommendations: there should be three service academies; they should be undergraduate in nature and of four years duration; they should lead to a baccalaureate degree; and they should produce, during peacetime, not less than 50 percent of the regular officers for each service.[48] After that, the Board's findings were unexceptional. It confirmed the idea of a set curriculum with "sectioning" to somehow accommodate brighter students, and that the "recitation" method should be continued as a method of class instruction. There was no mention of electives or academic majors.

Once again this was an unusually bland report that served to support the status quo. Its one major breakthrough was its insistence on the need for a separate Air Force Academy to be established "without delay." At the same time, the Board's rejection of all other service academy schemes involving joint or composite programs was emphatic. Because of the prestige enjoyed by Stearns and Eisenhower, and given their unequivocal statement regarding the necessity of three service academies to function in the traditional manner, this report would be cited repeatedly by military academy advocates—of all the services— in the years ahead.

Congress and the Special Assistant

It was certainly useful and important that boards were established and reports written to clarify Air Force thinking on the need for an academy and the form that it should take. In reality, however, nothing could actually be done about establishing an academy until Congress passed the required legislation and appropriated the necessary funds. Congressional action proved to be an enormous hurdle.

Various congressmen had been proposing legislation to establish an air academy since the 1920s, but nothing had come of these efforts. As the air arm moved towards an independent status during and after World War II, the number of legislative proposals regarding an air academy increased. The dam burst with an independent Air Force in September 1947.[49] Still, because most proposals were tied to specific sites, the Air Force was reluctant to support any of them. At one point the Air Force attempted to write a bill on its own, but Representative Carl Vinson, chairman of the powerful House Armed Services Committee, told Air Force leaders that his staff would do it instead. This task became far more difficult than it first appeared.[50]

At the same time, Frank Pace, director of the Bureau of the Budget, was still not satisfied that the Air Force had done all its homework regarding an academy proposal. Although the Planning Board Study had clarified a number of key issues, Pace wrote that the Air Force plan "will raise questions as to location, cost, size of cadet corps, curriculum and its relationship to curriculum of the other academies which cannot be answered in enough detail to insure favorable consideration by this Congress."[51] How much would the academy cost? The Air Force had come up with several estimates over the previous two years. In March 1948, Lieutenant General Joe Cannon, commander of ATC, advised Secretary Symington that the academy could be built at Randolph Field for around $70 million.[52] The following week, Symington informed Congressman W.G. Andrews that an academy would cost $90 million.[53] At the same time, however, General Spaatz told Symington that the academy would run $82 million if built at Randolph.[54] In May, Symington wrote the secretary of the navy that an academy built at Randolph Field would cost $65 million, but if located somewhere else it would run either $90 or $95 million.[55] Of note, two years later, Brigadier General James B. Newman did an in-depth cost analysis and came up with a total expense of a whopping $153,272,390. Although this figured appeared quite scientific, it should be noted that Newman based this figure on "a site yet to be selected."[56]

These cost estimates are important because the Air Force's strategy was to argue that a new air academy would be cheaper than expanding the size of West Point and Annapolis so they could provide the required number of officers to the Air Force. In February 1948, Lieutenant General Lauris Norstad had written Secretary Symington that the cost for expanding West Point and Annapolis to generate annually 605 officers for the Air Force would be $179 million—far higher than all the estimates for a new air academy.[57] In sum, besides theoretical arguments regarding the need for officers educated to think like airmen, the Air Force was trying to convince Congress that such a school would also be more economical.

In addition to cost estimates, Pace made it clear in his letter that location was also a critical issue. How could he, or Congress, agree to legislation for an Air Force Academy when the Air Force had not yet decided where it would be located? He had a point.

The Air Force had given some thought to the issue; in fact, the Air University Planning Board had looked specifically at Randolph Field as the academy's location. The Board examined four sites in the vicinity of the base, the most desirable being three miles northwest of the main gate.[58] This was a useful practice run, but it was only that. Was Randolph the *best* site for an academy? That was a different question.

On December 31, 1948, Brigadier General Newman, the head of the Planning Board's site committee, sent a letter to the Air Staff regarding procedures for site selection. He recommended a site board headed by a senior officer, staffed with "professional and technical experts," who would visit sites already vetted by US Army District Engineers. He included procedures for dealing with local officials and urged that there be a comprehensive report written afterwards that described all advantages and disadvantages of proposed sites. This was useful advice, and it would be followed.[59]

The on-going difficulties with Congress and the need to focus on air academy matters prompted General Vandenberg to take two important steps. First, he appointed a Site Selection Board on November 25, 1949. The president of the board would be retired General Carl Spaatz. Other members included Major General Schlatter, Lieutenant General Hubert Harmon, and Dr. Bruce Hopper from Harvard University—a wartime colleague of Spaatz and a man Harmon had known since World War I. Lieutenant Colonel Boudreau would be the Board's recorder. Schlatter quickly dropped off the Board due to other responsibilities. His place was initially taken by Major General Laurence Craigie, but he too soon left for another assignment. Finally, retired Brigadier General Harold L. Clark, an engineer, was added to round out the group. Additional specialists, mostly engineers or architects, were to be called upon for their expertise.

Vandenberg's second appointment was of even greater significance.

After the completion of the Planning Board Study in mid 1948, the responsibility for matters dealing with the air academy was shifted from Maxwell AFB to Washington; specifically, it was given to the deputy chief of staff for personnel, Lieutenant General Idwal Edwards. He in turn delegated academy responsibilities to Major General Richard Nugent, his director of personnel planning. Nugent, however, was snowed under with a host of other duties resulting from Air Force independence, such as the Pay Act then before Congress. Nugent asked Edwards for relief from academy responsibilities stating: "I can't give it all the personal attention it needs." He suggested someone of "stature, background and experience."

Soon after, Harmon walked into Edwards' office and related the problems regarding his do-nothing job at the United Nations. He told Edwards, who had been with him at both Leavenworth and the War College and been part of the poker group: "I'll be very glad to do any chores or any special jobs that you want to throw my way." Edwards immediately realized that Harmon would be the ideal man to take on the academy responsibilities: "He was a graduate of the Military Academy—he was very much of a forward thinker—he had lots of energy and enthusiasm, and so I thought I would discuss with General Vandenberg whether we could not give this planning job to General Harmon."[60] Harmon was "extremely enthusiastic" about the proposal. Edwards then discussed the matter with Vandenberg who agreed to the appointment. Given the flap over Harmon's role as chairman of the board that examined the Air Force's ability to carry out the atomic war plan a few months earlier, Vandenberg must have had some reservations. It would seem that the chief's desire to have an officer with a reputation for integrity, who was also respected as a top-notch organizer and administrator, and who had a facility for working well with politicians, were qualities that outweighed any lingering irritation he may have had over the earlier incident. Harmon was offered the job as Special Assistant for Air Academy Matters in a meeting with Vandenberg on 29 November. He was told, however, that this was *not* a commitment that he would be the academy's first superintendent. That would be a separate decision made later.[61] When that "later" date arrived, Vandenberg asked Harmon if he would like to be the first superintendent: Harmon replied, "I certainly would." Vandenberg warned that the superintendents at both West Point and Annapolis wore only two stars; if Harmon took the job it would probably be necessary for him to drop back to that rank. Was that acceptable? Harmon replied without hesitation: "I don't care. To be the first Superintendent, I'd take it if I have to go back and be a colonel." A reduction in rank would not prove necessary.[62]

What is most interesting about this turn of events is that Harmon had already given considerable thought to an Air Force academy. As noted, he had supervised a study on the subject in 1945 when he was the AAF personnel chief. In addition, in August 1948 he had responded to a request from General Edwards with a lengthy and detailed letter discussing a wide range of subjects relative to an air academy.

Harmon began by stating that planning and decisions for an academy should be sufficiently developed prior to Congressional action to preclude lengthy delays. Any resulting proposal should be as broad and general as possible to allow flexibility down the road. Legislation governing West Point and Annapolis should be studied closely to determine the good points and the bad and incorporate the good into the legislation for an air academy. He wrote that the fundamental decision to be made concerned the mission of the institution: "upon this all other plans and decisions depend." The articulation of this mission statement should then clarify such other key questions as size, entrance requirements, academic instruction, physical plant, and climate. Regarding location, he argued that the academy should probably not be on the East Coast—where the other academies were located—so as to show recognition "of the full development of the entire continental area of the United States."

Harmon engaged in his favorite pastime.

Regarding the specific site for the new academy, he noted several factors that needed to be considered: accessibility, cultural and social advantages of the community, existing facilities, prevailing construction costs in the area, size of the site, availability of utilities, availability of household services, and the nature of the terrain. Concerning the last, Harmon emphasized that "beauty and variety should contribute to culture, character, and recreation."

Harmon then stressed to Edwards the importance of the selection process for cadets, the doctrine they would be taught, the organization of the academy, cadet pay, uniforms, and other matters. Regarding the school's initial operations, he suggested starting from scratch with freshmen from civilian life and then bringing in junior officers to train them; alternatively, upperclassmen could be transferred from West Point and Annapolis to train the first class.

Finally, Harmon suggested that there should be appointed a "Project Director," a senior individual who would be responsible for setting up committees for site selection, construction, academics, military training, athletics, flying training, legal affairs, and administration. Regarding the site committee, he warned Edwards that it should be composed of the most senior people available because of the importance of the task and the pressures that would probably be applied to them by Congress, politicians, and local business leaders.[63]

This was a remarkable letter. Fully seventeen months before he was appointed the Special Assistant for Air Academy Matters, and before the Fairchild Board, Air University Planning Board or Stearns-Eisenhower Board had even met, Harmon had presaged their findings in most areas. The agenda that he laid out—and the pitfalls to be wary of—were to be the blueprint followed for the next six years. To be sure, even Harmon underestimated the problems with Congress, but in other areas he was prophetic.

CHAPTER 8

Frustration and Triumph

*H*armon kept his responsibilities at the United Nations, but after December 1949 when he became the Special Assistant, his primary focus would be the academy. He established an office in the Pentagon where he and four others were assigned: Lieutenant Colonel Arthur Boudreau, Lieutenant Colonel Arthur Easton, Major Thomas Sheldrake, and a secretary, Virginia Cupina. Harmon himself operated largely from his office in New York and came to Washington weekly. Colonel William S. Stone, an Air Force officer who was on the faculty at West Point working for Herman Beukema, was a part-time assistant. Stone would focus on curriculum issues and would remain associated with the academy project for many years to come, working out of a satellite office at Bolling AFB.[1] For the next five years, these small offices would be the focus of all air academy planning. By necessity and temperament, Harmon was intimately involved with all aspects of the academy issue. Besides tenacity, Harmon would display a flexibility of mind that caused him to entertain countless ideas, some of them fairly radical, in a quest to push the required legislation through Congress. He never wavered from the goal—to gain an Air Force academy—but the paths to that objective could be many and varied. He never gave up. The struggle for legislation to provide an academy was long and frustrating, but in the end, Harmon and his service prevailed—on 1 April 1954, President Dwight D. Eisenhower signed the bill establishing the United States Air Force academy.

Harmon and his team got right to work. One month after his appointment as Special Assistant, he sent a memo to General Vandenberg outlining his plans. At this point, Harmon, like many others in the Air Force, erroneously assumed that Congress would act quickly. He thought an academy would be authorized prior to June 1950, with an interim site opening the following summer. He proposed that the academy should begin with all four classes in place: the freshmen would be 200 civilians selected by the process specified in the enabling legislation. The sophomore and junior classes would be composed of equal numbers of West Point cadets and Annapolis midshipmen who would voluntarily transfer to the new air academy. The senior class would consist of 100 West Point cadets who would be "loaned" to the new academy. They would return to the Military Academy for their graduation exercises, but could certainly be commissioned into the Air Force if they so desired. The total number of air cadets at the interim site at any one time would be approximately 800.[2]

The question of who would comprise the initial upper classes of a new air academy would be hotly debated over the next five years. Over time, Harmon would change his mind on this issue—returning to his suggestion of 1945 regarding the use of junior Air Force officers brought in to serve as "surrogate upperclassmen."

The matter of class makeup, however, quickly took a back seat to two major issues: the attempt to get appropriate legislation through a recalcitrant Congress, and the selection of the academy site. It was apparent that the two were tied together, but site selection would almost certainly have to precede enabling legislation.

The first meeting of the Site Selection Board had been held in Washington on November 28, 1949. General Newman, the head of the Planning Board's site committee, attended and summarized the advice he had given the previous year regarding criteria and procedures to be used for choosing a location. His advice was taken with some modifications, and the Board soon after sent letters to Congress and local communities all over the country advertising the fact that they were seeking recommendations for the site of a future air academy. The Board's letter began by stating that "the site selected must permit of proper aesthetic development and should contain natural beauty befitting an institution of national importance." It then listed the following specific considerations that needed to be addressed by prospective applicants:

1. Location of site relative to population centers
2. Transportation facilities (rail, air, highway)
3. Availability of power
4. Availability of water

5. Sewerage facilities on site

6. Drainage in area

7. Engineering difficulties such as grading

8. Labor and materials available in vicinity

9. Climatic conditions—rainfall, temperature, humidity, etc.

10. Availability of land (approximately 9,000 acres)

11. Cost of land

12. Cost of preparation of land

13. Obstructions such as farms, etc. that must be removed from the site

14. Location of nearest airfield at which the Air Force could acquire immediate landing rights

15. Availability of housing, cultural, recreational, educational and other facilities in nearby population centers.[3]

As a result of the public announcement, 221 sites had been proposed by January 13, 1950. This date had originally been listed as the deadline for submissions, but the response from around the country was so heavy the Board ignored it. By August 1950, 354 sites had been received and surveyed.

Winnowing the large number of sites proposed was to follow a multi-step process. First, the Army's Corps of Engineers would screen the sites and eliminate those obviously unsuitable. Next, architectural engineers would survey the remaining locations. It was hoped that these preliminary inspections would be completed by the spring of 1950, narrowing the list to ten sites. The Board would then visit those ten sites and submit a final recommendation by mid-May. The surprisingly enthusiastic response from around the country made it clear fairly quickly that the May deadline was overly optimistic. On 5 April the schedule was dealt a fatal blow when Secretary Symington told the Board that flight training *should* be included in the air academy curriculum. This new criterion, which had profound implications for the size, location, weather and topographical features of a proposed site, meant that the Board would need to start over.[4]

The question of whether to include flying in the curriculum had been batted back and forth for years. During the war, West Point had actually been designated as an AAF flying school. Cadets took flight lessons at Stewart Field—the same airfield Harmon had surveyed and recommended before the war—and upon graduation, which occurred after only three years due to the war, they received a diploma, commission, and wings all on the same day.

This was a controversial program. Military Academy officials were reluctant to accept the turmoil that flight training would produce on the cadet curriculum and training program. The Army chief of staff, George Marshall, was not a West Point graduate, so he deferred to Hap Arnold on the issue. Arnold was adamant. He thought the program important enough that a certain amount of disruption was acceptable. Even so, the small number of cadets who received flight training, 657 of the 193,443 who won wings during the war, made the program expendable. It was terminated when the war ended.[5]

As we have seen, however, Air Force leaders remained ambivalent. In April 1948, Secretary Symington had stated that flying would be included at an air academy. The Air Training Command had then argued that Randolph Field, "The West Point of the Air," should become precisely that and a new air academy should be located there, and it should include flying. The Fairchild Board recommended otherwise, and General Vandenberg seconded this view. Symington then changed his mind.

In March 1950, however, Representative Vinson made it clear to the Air Force that he was opposed to an air academy that simply gave students a general education. He wanted flight training back in the program.[6] It was this unexpected blast from Vinson that prompted the Site Selection Board to change its plans, pushing back its schedule by six months.[7]

Spaatz intended that the Corps of Engineers and the architects would narrow the list of finalists to ten sites, which would then be visited by all the Board members. Harmon, who by this time had also been named as the Special Assistant for Air Academy Matters, disagreed, telling Spaatz that it would be "politically expedient" for the Board to visit at least one site in each state.[8] Although his suggestion was not followed, it signaled Harmon's awareness of the importance of political influence on the selection of a site for the air academy.

Other factors soon intruded to make even these revised plans unworkable. First, it became clear that legislative action was going nowhere that year. In April, Harmon wrote General Vandenberg in obvious frustration that Congress had wanted the Air Force to conduct a thorough planning study: it did. Congress wanted the Defense Department also to study the matter: it did. Congress wanted a board to look at suitable locations for an academy; such a board had been formed. The Air Force, he told Vandenberg, had presented a bill before Congress; if it was unsuitable in some particulars, he would readily submit amendments.[9] It was time to get moving!

Harmon was whistling in the wind. Congress was not budging; indeed, it was obvious that nothing would happen until after the elections in November. As a further complication, Spaatz announced that he would be leaving the Board after the first of the year to attend to other matters. Worse, at the end of June 1950 the Korean War broke out—a totally unexpected event that further distracted Congress, the Air Force, and Harmon from academy concerns.[10]

Despite the increasing tempo of his air academy responsibilities, Harmon still spent much time and effort in New York working at the United Nations: he would not relinquish those duties until his first retirement in February 1953. The war in Korea was of enormous importance of course, and Harmon's thoughts would often dwell on the situation there—his duties as a military diplomat forced him to do so. The result was a growing maturity in him of the world beyond the military and of the critical importance of a nation's leadership having the ability to wield all the levers of power at its disposal.

In August 1952 he prepared a confidential letter to the US ambassador to the UN giving his thoughts not only on Korea, but the Asian situation in general. His opening comments were stark and insightful:[11]

> In order to bring to an early conclusion the debacle now confronting us in Korea, I think very serious consideration should be given to the idea of recognizing Communist China, and giving her a seat in the U.N., in exchange for agreement, under adequate guarantees, for a free, independent, united Korea.

> Our intervention in Korea is costing us five billion a year. It is accomplishing nothing (unless it be the destruction of Korea), and forces Communist China into the Soviet camp. We should do everything we can to split the two apart. They are natural enemies.

Regarding China specifically, Harmon argued that both Chinas—the Communist mainland and Formosa (now called Taiwan)—should be represented in the UN, although neither should be on the Security Council. Indeed, he was much discouraged by the lack of aggressiveness shown by the Council and thought it should be abandoned in favor of the General Assembly. To Harmon, the Security Council was created at a specific point in history following the war—conditions had changed dramatically since then, but the Security Council was frozen in time and would remain so.

In his letter, Harmon also commented on a hot topic at the time—atomic disarmament. He believed that elimination of such weapons, while desirable, would not be sufficient and would, in any case, be impossible to verify. Instead, Harmon called for massive, mutual disarmament of all weapons of war except hand-carried weapons. Gone would be all artillery, aerial bombs, submarines and guided missiles. Only purely defensive weapons would remain. This was a stunning proposal for a military officer—not unlike the ideas that surfaced between the world wars at various disarmament conferences. But it was certainly not in keeping with Air Force thinking much less US military policy. Once again, as in the Harmon Report of 1949 regarding the atomic war plan, the general was showing his independence of thought.

He concluded his comments to the ambassador by stressing the moral high ground that America enjoyed: "We should be very sure that our ideas on self-determination and anti-colonialism are sound, consistent and practical."[12] Clearly, he was already foreseeing the collapse of the old European colonial empires and was strongly urging that the US not be trapped into propping them up.

Undoubtedly, his years at the United Nations gave Harmon an appreciation of the need for military officers with a broad and global outlook.

But first things first. Despite the war and roadblocks in Congress, the Site Selection Board pressed on. The Corps of Engineers and architects continued with their tasks of drawing down the list of possibilities. One method was to assign point values to such categories as "health," "cost," and "community," with a total of 100 points possible. When Symington added the criterion of flying, points had to be reallocated and the list redone. Harmon then disagreed with the point values assigned to some categories and rearranged them, revealing that the decision process was a bit more subjective than the Board might care to admit.[13]

In August 1950, the Board came up with a list of forty-eight potential sites. This was too many for them to visit by the end of the year. (The new schedule was to arrive at the top four choices by January, thus allowing the engineers and architects to revisit these sites for an extensive survey, followed by the announcement of a final selection in February.) In October, Harmon wrote Vandenberg with an update, giving him details on the process, including the disagreement over point values assigned. The list of possibilities had been whittled down to twenty-nine sites.[14]

On July 22, the Board had met with Vandenberg and the new Air Force secretary, Thomas Finletter, to discuss academy affairs. Vandenberg was blunt, stating that Congress might consider the Air Force was "playing a game" if it moved too quickly on the academy while the country was at war and men were dying. He told Spaatz and Harmon to "sit tight."[15]

The Board sat until November, although Harmon remained active behind the scenes regarding possible legislative developments. As will be discussed below, this issue was the thorniest problem of all, and Congress would simply not be rushed, nor would it agree to anything until it had a chance to study it thoroughly.

As a result, not until November 17—after the elections—did the Board release its list of twenty-nine possible sites for the air academy. The plan was to visit the eastern sites between 20–29 November, and those in the western US between 3–20 December. The first trip would visit eleven sites in eight states:[16]

Georgia	Atlanta–Duluth
	Atlanta–Griffin
Indiana	Madison
Louisiana	New Orleans–Hammond
Michigan	Detroit–Kensington
	Detroit–Waterloo
Missouri	St Louis–Weldon Springs
	Kansas City–Sedalia
Illinois	Alton
Pennsylvania	Harrisburg–Mechanicsburg
Wisconsin	Milwaukee–Kenosha (Lake Geneva)

The western trip would entail:

California	San Francisco–Santa Rosa
	San Francisco–Napa
	Los Angeles–Riverside (March Field)
	Sacramento–Mather Field
	Sacramento–Marysville (Camp Beale)
Colorado	Denver–Buckley Field
	Denver–Cherry Creek
	Denver–Westminster
	Colorado Springs–North Site
	Colorado Springs–South Site
North Carolina	Charlotte–Huntersville

Oregon	Portland–Canby
Texas	San Antonio–Randolph Field
	San Marcos–Wren Ranch
	San Marcos–Pilot Knob
	Dallas-Fort Worth–Grapevine
Washington	Seattle–McChord Field
	Seattle–Lake Sawyer[17]

The Board began this whirlwind tour of prospective sites, meeting local officials, walking the ground, and receiving detailed briefings from local experts. Although Harmon confided to Rosa-Maye in one letter that he was most fond of the Atlanta sites, neither was included in the Board's final recommendations.

Regarding the Colorado Springs north site, Colonel Boudreau later stated that one Sunday while out driving, he noticed some particularly desirable land to the north of town and west of the major highway connecting the Springs to Denver. The northern site suggested by local officials had been east of that highway. The next day Boudreau took the entire Board out to the area and all were impressed. The Board then asked the Colorado Springs municipal officials if they could make available the land they had just viewed. The following April city officials agreed. The Air Force Academy was eventually built on this site.[18]

Just as the Site Selection Board was going through its deliberations to come up with a shortlist of finalists, Harmon received bad news from Congress.

In late December, Vinson made it clear to the Air Force that no funds would be made available in 1951 for an air academy. The reason for this decision centered on Korea. Elation over General MacArthur's success at Inchon turned to despair two months later when the Chinese Communist Army attacked in force, driving United Nations' forces south of Seoul—again. This was a "totally new war," and President Truman declared a state of national emergency. The result: Vinson's committee deferred all "unessential projects"—a category into which the academy fell—until defense emergency measures were dealt with first.[19]

On 21 December the Site Selection Board met with Finletter and Vandenberg to discuss options. It was decided that the secretary and the chief would go to Chairman Vinson personally and attempt to change his mind. In their view, the academy *was* an essential element in national defense. The war had increased dramatically the need for Air Force officers. It had also, of course, increased the need for officers in the Army and Navy as well. The other services were therefore increasingly reluctant to supply the Air Force with Academy graduates that they themselves desperately required. Until the Air Force had its own academy and its own guaranteed supply of regular officers, the service would find itself constrained in attempting to accomplish its mission. The Air Force needed a bill pushed through Congress.

Vinson was unmoved, repeating to Finletter and Vandenberg that any attempt to force him or Congress into funding an academy during such perilous times was "inappropriate." Regarding the proposed site of an air academy, Vinson advised the Air Force to "drag its feet" and not release its findings in February as planned.[20]

Harmon sat down and thought things through. Perhaps there were other paths to his goal. Several months before he had surfaced the idea of bypassing Vinson's committee and having legislation introduced by an Air Force friend in Congress. Indeed, was Congressional approval even necessary? Perhaps the Air Force should just open an academy on its own. This was a risky strategy that would no doubt alienate the powerful Vinson. But would it work? Harmon talked to Major General Tommy White, his old friend who was now the Air Force's legislative liaison. He also met with Eugene Zuckert, the Air Force assistant secretary for management, and Air Force lawyers. For their part, the lawyers responded like lawyers, stating that there was, technically, nothing in the law that would prevent the Air Force from opening an academy without Congressional authorization. After all, the Air Force was already permitted to establish schools to train its personnel, and there was nothing in the applicable laws that stated how long such schools could run—four years in this case. However, it was not certain the academy could be academically accredited. When the Military Academy went through the accreditation process it first obtained Congressional approval—a precedent. Plus, and here was the rub, once the academy was up and running, the Air Force would still need to go to Congress each year to ask for funds to operate it. The members would no doubt remember the slight of having been bypassed in the academy's foundation. Foiled. Harmon wrote on the lawyers' response: "We can let this rest until the prospects of an AF Academy are definite, one way or the other."[21]

The consensus was clear: going it alone was risky and a last-ditch option. To confuse matters further, Defense Secretary Louis Johnson, who had been an

academy supporter, was fired—things were not going well in Korea and someone had to go. His replacement was the now-retired General George Marshall.
Any end-run around Vinson would require Marshall's support, but it was not
known where he stood on such matters or even what his thoughts were on an
air academy.[22] To help educate Marshall, Harmon prepared a memo outlining
the reasons for a new academy, its cost, and its organization. He concluded: "I
hope you will agree that the time is very ripe."[23] Marshall expressed his support
for an air academy two days later, but gave no indication he would support a
plan to bypass Congress.

Resigned to delay, Harmon nonetheless continued to push the rock uphill.
The year 1950 ended with much hard work performed, but little accomplished.
The legislation in Congress was stalled, and the Site Selection Board was "drag-
ging its feet" as directed. Perhaps 1951 would prove more successful.

Stagnation in Congress

Legislation desired by the Air Force followed a well-defined path. Understanding this time-honored but cumbersome process helps to explain why Congress
took so long to approve an air academy.

Legislation proposed by the Air Force first had to be approved by the
Department of Defense. If the secretary gave his concurrence (and this meant
it had been coordinated with the other two services to obtain their acquiescence), then DoD would send the bill to the Bureau of the Budget, who would
have to approve it for the administration. The Bureau would look closely at
the cost and direction of the bill: was it in accord with the president's wishes?
Assuming it was, the Bureau would then send the bill to the Speaker of the
House—this was in effect stating it had been approved by the Air Force, the
DoD, and the administration. The Speaker would then refer the bill to the
appropriate committee—in the case of Air Force Academy legislation that
would be the House Armed Services Committee. If the chairman of that committee was in accord—from 1948 to 1952 that was Carl Vinson—he would
still need to hold hearings on the subject and put the bill to a vote before his
committee and then the entire House. Of course, even if the House approved,
the bill would still need Senate approval; and then the president would have to
sign the bill into law.

Although the Army and Navy were not necessarily all that eager to assist
the Air Force, they did agree that an air academy was a good idea simply because

it relieved the pressure on them to provide a quota of their own officers to the Air Force. Yet, there was always a lingering suspicion that the Navy would quietly oppose what the Air Force wanted. Recall that the "Revolt of the Admirals" and the debate over the B-36 versus the "super carrier" were only recently in the past. Interservice relations were strained. Nonetheless, successive secretaries of defense—James Forrestal, Louis Johnson and George Marshall—approved the air academy plan, and their pressure on the services was important. Unfortunately, President Truman never put his weight behind an air academy bill. If he had done so, it would have greased the process in the Budget Bureau, and—assuming the House was controlled by the same party—would probably also have ensured a favorable reception by the committee chairman and the House as a whole. Because Truman never committed himself to an air academy, the required legislation was always in an uphill battle.

On 24 January 1951 Secretary Finletter visited Chairman Vinson once again in an attempt to convince him to move forward on legislation. Vinson remained committed to the notion of handling war matters first, but was willing to allow the Site Selection Board to complete its work; he even expressed willingness to at least address the air academy bill.[24]

The day following Finletter's visit to Vinson, Harmon went to see Budget Bureau officials, who were also attempting to write air academy legislation. There were problems. The Budget Bureau decided to write a bill that would not only include an air academy, but would also clean up inconsistencies and other irregularities in the various pieces of legislation relating to West Point and Annapolis that had accumulated, almost willy-nilly, over the decades. It insisted on the need and desirability for omnibus legislation, believing an Air Force-only bill—the direction of Vinson's effort—would tend to complicate matters down the road. The Bureau's reasoning was that omnibus legislation was necessary to simplify and standardize; it wanted one bill governing all the academies that would then permit the repeal of all other existing legislation on the matter. Although assuming this would be a fairly simple task, the Bureau ran into unexpected difficulties. For his part, Harmon remained skeptical the Army or Navy would ever agree or compromise. They liked the way legislation was written governing their academies, and they had no desire to change anything.[25] He was correct. One Bureau staffer whose job it was to help write the omnibus bill later stated: "We had very little cooperation in getting revisions to the service academy legislation because of rejections from vested interests."

Harmon thought this intransigent stance was deliberate and an attempt to block the foundation of an air academy: "The Air Force should not be penalized by the inertia of the Department of the Navy which is dragging its feet on the omnibus bill." He thought this conduct "unconscionable." He became so frustrated that he exclaimed: "Let's just go out and rent some girls' school that is not being used, any place, just to get this thing going."[26]

Harmon's reference was not totally frivolous. He had already suggested the idea of going around Congress. In addition, the concept of an interim site for an air academy had been floating around for some time. Even when Congress finally passed legislation and appropriated funds, it would be several years before actual construction could be completed on a permanent academy. The Air Force, understandably, did not want to sit by idly for those years— Congress might change its mind. The solution was to open a temporary air academy at an interim site once enabling legislation was passed. This would allow a chance to start quickly, but also slowly—there would be a smaller cadet class and a smaller staff. The emphasis would be on quality not quantity. This would allow bugs to be worked out while the permanent site was being prepared. Harmon's contact at the Budget Bureau urged him to examine this path, although it too was fraught with danger. Harmon and others realized that once an academy was opened, despite its "temporary" designation, there was a danger Congress would decide its job was done and move on to other matters. In other words, the interim academy would quickly become permanent—at the wrong site and on a much smaller scale than desired.

And yet, starting small was better than nothing—which is what the Air Force was left with at that time. In a clever move, Harmon and his team therefore considered interim sites that they deemed would be unlikely choices for a permanent location. Because West Point and Annapolis were both located in the East, it was thought Congress would object to an air academy located there as well. So that is precisely where Harmon looked. More specifically, to ensure even less chance of the interim site becoming permanent, he focused on the states of New York and Maryland—homes to the other academies. The two sites considered were Mitchel Field on Long Island and Bainbridge, Maryland.[27]

Mitchel Field was then home to the Continental Air Command (CONAC), but that organization was considering a move to Kansas. Long Island was becoming increasingly congested and CONAC needed more room. The base's small size was no deterrent to a new, *temporary*, air academy.

The site at Bainbridge, owned by the Navy, had originally been a prep school, Tome Institute, which had closed. Nonetheless, several fine buildings, including a barracks and dining hall overlooking the Susquehanna River, still stood. The Navy decided the facility was surplus and was willing to make it available to the Air Force.[28] Randolph Field also remained in the running. Even so, Harmon still worried that advocating an interim site was risky. He therefore intended to announce a permanent site first, to preclude that possibility. On February 2, 1951, Harmon sent a memo to Vandenberg with his recommendations on the way ahead:

- Press for the establishment of an academy, on a small scale, as soon as possible
- Allow the Spaatz Board to finish its work and determine a permanent site
- Move forward on an Air Force-only bill (vice the omnibus bill)
- Lobby Congress to enact legislation to name the permanent site, but authorize the opening—on a "small scale"—of an interim site
- Refrain from starting construction on a permanent site until the war in Korea was over
- Start operations at the interim site (he now recommended Randolph Field simply because it would be the easiest and cheapest to permit rapid implementation): "This school is intended not only for benefit of selected enlisted candidates but to provide a vehicle for the testing and development of academic administration and procedures."

Harmon's logic was that "the sooner we get started, the better off we will be. By starting at once on a small scale, we can proceed with the development and perfection of curriculum, organization, and administration procedures."[29] Clearly, he was not overly optimistic about the prospects for a full-up academy anytime soon.

At the same time, by early 1952 Harmon was honing his arguments regarding the need for an air academy. In February he sent a draft of his proposed Congressional testimony on the subject to an old friend, Ben Wood at Columbia University. Harmon's arguments now included a heavy dose of Cold War rhetoric—obviously his experience at the United Nations had left him profoundly suspicious of and disgusted with the Soviets.

He began by noting that there was "no longer any mystery about the purposes and motivations of the aggressors who threaten to plunge the world into the universal holocaust of atomic and biologic war." When stripped of its camouflage, it could be seen that "the Kremlin imperialism clearly is another stage of the age-old conflict between tyranny and freedom, between cruelty and charity, between a monstrous dictatorship that deifies itself, and 'government of the people, by the people, and for the people,' which seeks to develop the brotherhood of man under the Fatherhood of God."

This was a heady start to his proposed testimony that displayed a histrionics that although out of place today, was common fare at the time. The opening years of the Cold War were seen by many, including Harmon, as an almost Manichean struggle between good and evil. Although a later generation would reject such a notion, for those who had fought a world war against the horrors of Nazism and its death camps, the revelation that its erstwhile ally was little different was a rude shock.

For Harmon, this painful history meant there was a critical need for academy graduates "who are educated citizens as well as effective military officers." The air academy's curriculum would provide a good general education in the humanities and social sciences—history, philosophy and psychology classes that were as essential for the future air officer as for the future citizen. But even if the Soviet empire were to collapse quickly, problems would still abound: "I do not believe that any nation—not even ours if we had an atomic monopoly—can be morally healthy or militarily secure so long as half the world's population is suffering from the physical, moral, and spiritual degradations that are the inevitable concomitants of perennial hunger and periodic mass starvations." The problems were huge, and that was why "you cannot produce air officers by merely 'training' boys to fly and shoot: we need educated officers who can help prevent war, as well as to insure winning a war after shooting begins."[30]

Harmon was pushing for air officers who were broadly educated and who understood what was going on around the world. As we have seen, he had held such beliefs for decades. Indeed, one could argue that his initial tour in Europe during World War I, followed by his introduction to the vivacious and politically aware Rosa-Maye Kendrick, had set him down this road. His perspective was in turn reinforced by another tour in Europe and his professional military education experiences during the interwar period. World War II, followed by the debilitating assignment at the United Nations, only solidified his long-held opinions on the need for air officers with a broad education who were politically attuned to their environment.

Harmon concluded his spirited discourse in a stirring fashion: "Thus they [air academy graduates] will go forth on their missions, in peace as well as in war, armed not only with the best tactical training and strategic education, but also armed, and invulnerably armored, with that moral authority which is the best ultimate justification of our way of life."[31]

Overall, this proposed testimony, which was not used, showed the depth of Harmon's passionate belief in his country, his service, and the need for an academy to produce outstanding airmen. Moreover, Harmon always viewed the military academies as democratizing institutions. They were not for the elite or moneyed classes; they were for all Americans: "There must be no opportunity to apply the term 'rich man's son's school' to the service academies. It must be possible for the young potential leader who has intelligence and ambition to enter the service academies directly from the nation's secondary schools."[32] Harmon's father had been a perfect example of this ideal.

Finalizing the Initial Site and Generating Momentum
On another front, the Site Selection Board publicly announced its seven finalists for a permanent location on 1 March 1951:

> Madison, IN
> Colorado Springs, CO
> Grayson County, TX
> Grapevine Lake, TX
> Randolph AFB, TX
> Charlotte, NC
> Camp Beale, CA

The engineers and architects then visited these locations once more and concluded, anti-climactically, that none of them fulfilled all the requirements for an air academy![33]

Nonetheless, the Board visited all seven locations in April and then sat down on 7 May to discuss its findings. At first there was no agreement, but after three days all were of one mind—the winner was to be Colorado Springs—the site Boudreau had "discovered" the year before. Even so, the Board made clear that at least four other sites would be suitable—only Charlotte and Camp Beale were not—thus giving Secretary Finletter some latitude to make a final decision.

Because the legislative imbroglio had still not been resolved, no announcement was made. Harmon took the Board's final report and locked it in his safe. It would remain there for the next three years.[34]

The next problem to surface, the one that caused Harmon to stick the Spaatz Board's report in the safe, came from the Bureau of the Budget. Despite Harmon's visits, the Bureau announced on 27 March that it would definitely *not* approve the Air Force-only bill. It also rejected the proposal for a temporary school—although it had previously pushed Harmon in that direction. Instead, the Bureau advised that all the services should agree to an omnibus bill.

Harmon's patience was wearing thin—not for the first or the last time. Again he thought it might be time for an end-run, although this time the target was the Budget Bureau. He proposed to Secretary Finletter that the Air Force undertake a campaign to convince Chairman Vinson. If he could be moved to propose concrete legislation, than the Budget Bureau's approval would perhaps not be necessary. Finletter agreed and the effort began.

Vinson seemed open to the idea as well. On 21 May he requested specific information from the Air Force regarding the justification for an academy, a revised Air Force-only bill, and a comparison of the bill to existing laws relating to West Point. The changes insisted upon by Vinson were that flight training be included in the curriculum and that the cadet selection process be the same as that at West Point. If the Air Force agreed to these changes, Vinson said he would introduce the bill in Congress.[35] At the same time, Vinson wrote an article for the *New York Times Magazine* calling for an Air Force Academy—the former chairman of the House Naval Affairs Committee had become a staunch Air Force ally.[36]

On a parallel front, the Defense Department entered the fray. Daniel Edwards, the assistant secretary of defense for legal and legislative affairs, told the services to re-engage on the omnibus bill and to redouble their efforts to come to an agreement. The Army and Navy replied they would need at least six weeks "to complete required work on repealers and to effect coordination among their various activities." While the services continued to work this issue, Edwards then suggested that a separate bill, a "brief bill" be prepared to get an air academy up and running—something along the lines that Harmon had suggested earlier. Given the pressure from DoD, the Budget Bureau agreed.[37]

Harmon got busy on another bill to fulfill the requirements of Edwards and the Budget Bureau. This new enabling legislation would simply allow the

Air Force to establish an academy, authorize operations at an interim site, and grant a limited amount of money for construction. In this plan, no mention would be made of a permanent site.[38] This was hardly the desired solution, but if it got the ball rolling, Harmon would try it.

On 20 June, Assistant Secretary Edwards sent a letter to Sam Rayburn, Speaker of the House, proposing the new bill. It called for an academy to provide undergraduate instruction and training comparable to that supplied by West Point and Annapolis. The secretary of the Air Force would determine the permanent site. The Air Force could acquire land for this installation and make plans to build on it. A temporary site could also be obtained to begin early operations. A sum of $10 million would be provided for this purpose. Edwards then gave the now standard reasons why an air academy was necessary and desirable.[39]

Two days later Secretary Finletter took the new bill over to Vinson who "indicated enthusiastically" that he would get behind it. Vinson indeed introduced the bill, H.R. 4574, the next day.[40]

Things looked promising, and Harmon quickly set to work. He hoped that an academy could be opened as early as July 1952. One of the key issues to be resolved was how big the initial class of cadets would be and where they would come from. It was initially thought the first group of cadets would be transplanted from West Point and Annapolis. After considerable reflection, Harmon rejected this idea. He wanted civilians in the first class, men who wanted to be airmen and who would be trained as airmen from the first day. He would hold to this belief for the next several years. As for location, Randolph and Mitchel were the top choices, although Selfridge AFB north of Detroit was another possibility.[41]

Nothing happened. Congress was behind in its work, and several important bills were ahead of the academy legislation in the queue.[42] Worse, in August a huge cheating scandal was uncovered at West Point, leading to the expulsion of ninety cadets. The timing did not seem propitious for Congress to begin discussing the need for another academy. Congress recessed on 1 October. After discussions with Vinson, Air Force officials still hoped that the logjam could be broken when Congress reconvened in January. Vandenberg was especially optimistic, and directed the Air Staff to get ready to move quickly on an air academy to be opened the following summer.[43]

It was not to be. Things continued to move slowly. The administration's plans to enact universal military training met with hostility in the House. And it was an election year. All of these factors led Vinson to believe that an academy bill would stand little chance of success. Rather than have the bill defeated, he elected not to bring it up for a vote. There would be no air academy in 1952. In a letter to Bruce Hopper at Harvard, (he had been a member of the Spaatz Board), Finletter summed the situation:

> I had hoped that it would open at its tentative location by July of this year, but we ran into a Congress that is in no mood to pass even our basic appropriations, let alone the Air Academy. So, on the advice of that good friend of the Air Force—Vinson—I have held up.[44]

If there was any bright news, it was that the Academies Omnibus Bill, as it was now called, seemed finally to have passed muster with the other services. That later proved not to be the case, but at the time it appeared that the bill could be introduced early in 1953.[45]

In December, Secretary Finletter, James T. Hill (the assistant secretary), and Harmon called on Vinson. The Republicans had won the 1952 elections, and Vinson would be turning over the gavel to Congressman Dewey Short. Vinson thought Short would make a fine chairman, but he still promised to do everything he could to help push the academy legislation through in the coming year. He cautioned, however, that the new team coming in would probably need to be educated on the issues. Ominously, he also reminded them that the new administration was committed to cutting taxes—and a new air academy would not be cheap.[46]

The same month, Harmon went before the Air Force Council and briefed it on where matters stood in his planning efforts for the academy. It was assumed that 1953 would be a good year legislatively. In such case, an interim academy would be established, probably at Mitchel AFB—CONAC was moving so the timing was right. The organization of the air academy would be similar to that of West Point—a superintendent overseeing a dean, commandant, athletic director, and air base group commander. Many West Point customs and doctrines would be adopted for the air academy. Only one class would be enrolled initially, and "surrogate upperclassmen"—lieutenants termed tactical officers—would be brought in to help train the new cadets. There would be one tactical officer for every ten cadets. The interim site would be in operation for four years; at that point the organization would move to the permanent site (which had never been announced). The design of the cadet uniforms, to include the decision as to whether cadets would carry rifles or swords, would be deferred. Flying training "to the greatest degree practicable" would be included in the curriculum. The Council rejected Harmon's plan to have one (1) elective taught during a cadet's senior year. Instead, that gaping hole in uniformity would be plugged by a mandatory class in either aeronautical engineering or a foreign language.[47]

The New Year dawned with a degree of optimism. There would be a new Congress, eager to tackle problems and get things done. More importantly, there would be a new president—Dwight Eisenhower.

Despite the hopes of a few months earlier, the Academies Omnibus Bill was not agreed—the Navy continued to object; indeed, the bill was never passed. Harmon gave up on it and recommended going forward solely with the Air Force bill in 1953. In the meantime, Harmon briefed the new Air Force secretary, Harold Talbott, on the entire air academy situation. Talbott was "enthusiastically in support" of the project and agreed that Harmon should brief the new Defense secretary, Charles Wilson, to gain his support as well.[48]

Ever optimistic, the following month Harmon sent another memo to Vandenberg with a list of recommendations. Assuming speedy Congressional action would allow an academy to open that summer, he suggested the site to be at Randolph AFB. He hoped that such an already-established location would persuade Congress to expedite enabling legislation. Harmon proposed that the academy would begin operating on 1 September. Existing facilities at Randolph would be used for staff offices, classrooms, cadet barracks, a mess hall, and a gymnasium. More permanent buildings would be built, to be completed within two years.

Harmon's decision to opt for Randolph was interesting. He argued that this airbase had been one of the finalists in the sealed report of the Spaatz Board, while also noting that the Board had not found any of the locations to be completely suitable. Although admitting Randolph had not been the Board's first choice—he declined to reveal what was—if the academy was to have a vigorous flying training component after all, then Randolph was the obvious choice. He concluded, in some frustration: "We have experienced all along a great difficulty in finding a suitable interim site. [Recall the debates over Mitchel AFB, Selfridge AFB and Bainbridge.] Why not take the bull by the horns, forget about an interim site and put the Academy once and for all at Randolph."[49] Harmon's frustration was understandable, but prompt action was still not in the offing.

In early March, Harmon gave a speech to an Air Force personnel conference where he recounted the travails of the previous four years. He began by reminding all of the old story about the horse being led to water, but in the academy's case, things were different: "we have gone to the trough many times only to have the water turned off just as we were about to dip in." They had been thwarted by the Korean War and by the West Point honor scandal. There were financial concerns, from not only Congress but the Bureau of the Budget. There was ignorance and prejudice regarding the need for an air academy—even among some airmen. The location of the academy was also problematic—those states and districts that believed they had little chance to land the academy had "no burning enthusiasm" to support the new school. Indeed, Harmon lamented that people seemed far more concerned with where the academy went than they were with what would be taught there. Nonetheless, his team had worked tirelessly and had developed a highly integrated curriculum. Whenever Congress was finally ready to act, his office would be well prepared.[50]

Harmon was pleased that Secretary Talbott was on-board so quickly, but he felt it necessary to throttle back Talbott's enthusiasm. In a memo to the vice chief, Nate Twining, Harmon wrote that he had informed the secretary of the Spaatz Board's first choice—Colorado Springs—and that Talbott was "enthusiastic about this site." Indeed, Talbott then suggested they obtain a grant from the Ford Foundation with which to make a preliminary architectural-engineering survey of the site and begin making building plans. Harmon warned Talbott that would be unwise—Congress should not be told of the Site Selection Board's decision until legislation was enacted. There was no need to make enemies of the losers.

Harmon had told Talbott that the key to the academy process now rested with the president. Although several appointments had been made to brief President Eisenhower, all were cancelled. Deferentially noting that he was not a policy maker in the Air Force, Harmon suggested that he (Talbott) get together with Defense Secretary Charles Wilson and the new Budget director, Joseph Dodge, and the three of them secure Eisenhower's support. If that were done, he felt confident Congress would move smartly.[51]

Harmon would be proven only partially correct.

On 5 January 1953, the assistant secretary of defense for legal and legislative affairs, Roger Kent, had sent a letter to the new House Speaker, Joseph W. Martin, introducing a bill "to provide for the establishment of a United States Air Force Academy."[52] Chairman Short submitted the bill, H.R. 2328, on the 28th. Yet, Congress did not move. As Harmon suspected, because the president had not expressed his opinion on the question of an air academy—at least not since taking office—the House would not act. Word from the White House was necessary.[53]

It should be mentioned here that the relationship between Harmon and Eisenhower was a warm one that dated back decades. This is indicated by a letter from Eisenhower—who was then the Supreme Allied Commander Europe, to Harmon in April 1952.[54]

> Dear Doodle
>
> I cannot tell you how good you made me feel by writing such a letter as you did. It breathes selflessness as well as dedication to our country. Moreover, it goes without saying that I would far rather have the good opinion of one valued friend who has known me for forty years than the uninformed publicity-spurred opinion of thousands. While in these days it is frequently difficult for a man to know exactly where the path of duty leads, yet he can scarcely go far wrong if he has the support—and particularly the counsel—of such as you.
>
> With all the best,
>
> As Ever
>
> [Ike]

This is an unusually warm letter, probably referring to Eisenhower's decision to run for the presidency later that year. It is obvious that the future president thought highly of his old teammate. Did this affection carry over to the subject of an air academy?

In a response to a question at a press conference on 19 March, Eisenhower responded: "I think we ought to have an Air Academy. I was on a board some years ago, and I thought it was all settled that we were to have an Air Academy. I think we should."[55]

Harmon and the Air Force went forth with new hope. This appeared to be the decisive signal that would finally set wheels in motion on the Hill. Meanwhile, however, Harmon's time was running out. In September he had written to Lieutenant General Larry Kuter, the new personnel chief on the Air Staff, that he was due for mandatory retirement in February 1953. As a result, someone should be appointed soon to take his place, both at the United Nations and as the Special Assistant. He then raised an interesting issue: "I am most emphatically not seeking to have my retirement postponed. I raise the issue only in the interests of appropriate preplanning." Because of his deep interest in the academy and his loyalty to the Air Force, however, he would be willing to either remain on active duty or be retired and then recalled to active duty. He then concluded: "However, I would not desire to be held over except with the understanding that, in the event the Academy is opened during 1953, I would have the privilege of establishing the Academy and of serving for at least one year as Superintendent."[56]

Vandenberg approved the plan, and to his mother-in-law Harmon confided that he would retire on 28 February, but would be recalled to active duty the following day and serve for an additional four months. He hoped that during those months the academy legislation would be approved. If passed by 1 April, then an interim academy would be opened in July. He would then be extended for another year to serve as the first superintendent. If legislation was not passed by 1 April, he would retire permanently.[57] He, Rosa-Maye, and the children would move to San Antonio.

That is in fact what would happen, because if Harmon and Air Force leaders thought the support of the president and the Republican-controlled House would break the logjam, they were sadly mistaken. For nearly one month the proposed legislation remained bottled up in the Pentagon. The green eyeshade folks there were still troubled by cost estimates. The latest figure supplied by the Air Force, $148 million, was viewed as a "foot in the door" ploy. Indeed, the new leadership at Defense—in several different offices—felt compelled to review the entire issue of an academy from top to bottom. The assistant secretary for manpower and personnel, for example, stated his opinion that "now is not the time for this legislation." As a result, the Air Force's legislative liaison officer advised Talbott that unless he moved forward quickly and took "a very strong position" with those in DoD on the floor below him, the academy would be dead for at least another year.[58]

A pensive Harmon ponders the way ahead.

Talbott acted. Upon reviewing the proposed legislation he was concerned that Congress would balk at the proposed $20 million just to establish an interim academy. He now thought that perhaps the whole idea of an interim academy should be jettisoned. Instead, the secretary proposed that *he* would select around 600 cadets then-enrolled in Air Force ROTC programs and have them sent to as many as ten civilian universities. At the same time the Air Force would go ahead with the site selection, design, and actual building of the permanent academy. Talbott assumed all of this could be done in two years; then those 600 cadets in the civilian schools would be transferred to the new academy to complete their education.[59] Talbott even went so far as to issue a press release stating that since everyone seemed to be in agreement (?), "Congress will be asked" to pass legislation.[60] Clearly, Talbott was energized, believing that Eisenhower's support would push a reluctant Defense Department and Congress to take immediate action.[61] He was wrong.

Nothing happened: Congress was too busy with items of a higher priority. Consequently, on 30 June Harmon reverted to retirement status once again. On the following day he wrote Lieutenant General "Rosie" O'Donnell, Kuter's replacement at personnel, that he was in the final stages of packing up for the move to Texas and clearing out his office. He therefore attached the copy of the Spaatz Board site selection report that had been locked in his safe for the previous three years. He also advised O'Donnell that the chief should immediately appoint someone to take his place as Special Assistant for Air Academy Matters. Although the situation was in another stage of interminable delay, it was still necessary to keep a senior officer manning the desk. That person should also be the academy superintendent-designate. He recommended Major General Roscoe Wilson for the job. He did, however, note that he would still be available to assist if called upon.[62]

The Harmons bought a large house on Westover Road in San Antonio and moved in. His retirement ceremony was memorable. Five other generals retired at the same time, and a joint ceremony and parade were held at Bolling AFB with General Nate Twining officiating. At a party afterwards, Harmon received a cherished present: a bound leather volume containing letters of thanks and congratulations from President Eisenhower, Generals Marshall, Bradley, Spaatz, Vandenberg, Twining and LeMay; Secretary Finletter, Governor Dewey of New York, and Admiral Nimitz among others.[63] With his military career at an end, it was time to sharpen his golf game. After thirty-eight years in uniform, Harmon was finished. Or so he thought.

Soon after, Nate Twining—who had replaced Vandenberg as chief of staff in June 1953—wrote Secretary Talbott that it appeared things were indeed finally coming to a head regarding the air academy. Congress seemed

ready to act decisively. The president gave it a push, telling Chairman Dewey
Short to make the air academy a priority in the New Year.[64] In fact, Chairman
Short issued a press release on 1 August 1953 stating that academy legislation
would be "the first order of business" when Congress reconvened in January
1954.[65] As a consequence, Twining urged that a knowledgeable Special Assistant be appointed immediately. The position had been empty since Harmon's
retirement, perhaps because Twining anticipated bringing him back yet again.
Indeed, in late summer Twining suggested to Talbott precisely that: in the event
Congress appeared ready to move at long last, Harmon should be brought out
of retirement for a second time to occupy his old position. He wrote: "General
Harmon having served four years as Special Assistant for Air Academy Matters
and as a member of the Site Selection Board, is the only senior officer thoroughly familiar with the Academy planning."[66]

On another front, Larry Kuter, who had left his post as personnel chief to
become the Air University commander in July 1953, wrote the new vice chief,
Tommy White, that because there was no longer a Special Assistant in Washington, he would be prepared to assume those duties from Maxwell.[67] Washington
demurred: academy affairs would not move to Alabama, and a new Special Assistant would not be named; instead, Harmon would serve as an unofficial advisor
to the Air Staff. Kuter repeated his readiness to take over academy responsibilities in October. Once more he was told no, and O'Donnell informed him the
secretary had decided that Harmon would be called to duty for a third time.
Even so, Kuter continued to angle for the academy job, even announcing to the
press that same month that there was a possibility an "experimental Air Academy" would be opened at Air University. The Air Staff quickly repudiated that
statement, while also directing Kuter to hold his tongue regarding academy matters.[68] Harmon tried to mend fences with his friends at Maxwell, and wrote them
with some feeling that they probably thought he was "suffering from some sort
of possessive pride about this Academy project and that I am part of a conspiracy
to muzzle you enthusiasts down there at Maxwell. Nothing could be further from
the truth."[69] They were all on the same team and had the same goal.

On 7 August, Harmon sent the Air Staff proposed Congressional statements for Secretary Talbott and himself, although he noted that someone else
might actually deliver his own statement. At a meeting in Washington in late
October, Harmon met with Talbott and other staff members to discuss the
academy. In a memorandum for record, Harmon noted that Talbott continued

to be an "enthusiastic supporter of the Academy idea," despite the fact that he did not know many of the details surrounding the project. Nonetheless, Harmon suggested that Talbott should be the main witness at the upcoming hearings. Talbott said he was willing to do so, but Harmon later heard from members of the secretary's staff that he was actually uncomfortable with such an idea: he would prefer to give a short introduction to Congress, but then leave detailed testimony to an expert. Harmon should carry the ball.

When discussing the particulars, Talbott told Harmon that the proposed cost of the new academy—$175 million was the latest estimate—seemed far too high and "would likely kill the project before it was born." He therefore listed a number of buildings—the library, museum, hospital, field house and stadium, that he thought could be built from private funds—contributions from wealthy citizens—and this might drive the price down considerably, to perhaps $100 million. Harmon then suggested that perhaps the architectural plans, which at the time called for a design resembling West Point—could be reduced considerably by using a "cheaper type of architecture." Talbott rejected this idea, stating that he wanted "only the best"; they would save money by eliminating "non-essentials."

As for flying training, Talbott also noted concerns. Current plans called for a fleet of fifty Convair T-29s for navigator training and a further thirty-five T-34s for pilot training. These aircraft would cost $25 million to buy and an additional $10 million annually to operate and maintain. He felt this was "extravagant."

On the question of a permanent site, Talbott indicated he would appoint a new Site Selection Commission to study the problem anew. He appreciated the fine work done by the Spaatz Board three years previously, but he thought it had given insufficient consideration to the "community factor." He noted that Eisenhower had told him the permanent site should be near civilian educational facilities. It appears Eisenhower wanted to avoid the new air academy becoming isolated and monastic like his alma mater.

Regarding timing: Talbott assumed that favorable legislation would be passed in early 1954. If so, construction could begin at the permanent site in January 1955 to be completed in two years. In the meantime, the first 1,000 cadets would complete their first two years of education at an unnamed interim site, and in 1957 would move to the new permanent site.[70]

As events would show, this was overly optimistic. Nonetheless, after five years of dashed hopes and faulty estimates, dreams of an Air Force Academy finally moved beyond wishful thinking. To cement this feeling of momentum and to ensure there would be no missteps in the Air Force's presentations to Congress, Acting Air Force Secretary James Douglas wrote the president requesting that he recall Harmon to duty as a lieutenant general to resume his position as Special Assistant for Air Academy Matters.[71] On 8 November Hubert Harmon was recalled to active duty for a third time; in this case, by President Eisenhower himself.

It is difficult to exaggerate the importance of this move. The fact that the president intervened personally to appoint Harmon to the position of superintendent presumptive sent a strong and unmistakable signal to Congress. Eisenhower wanted an air academy, and he wanted it now.

"Enthusiasm, Gloom and Despair—but Never Lethargy"

As promised, soon after the first of the year Chairman Short announced hearings in his Military Affairs Committee for mid-January 1954 on H.R. 5337. On the appointed day, brief statements were made by representatives from DoD and the other services, all stating that they supported the new academy. The assistant secretary of defense for manpower and personnel, John Hannah, proved an impressive figure. Before his appointment he had been the president of Michigan State University. He told the Committee that, frankly, he had thought another academy unnecessary. His long career in education led him to believe that civilian institutions could do the job just as well, at lower cost. Since arriving at the Pentagon, however, his daily contact with outstanding generals and admirals, who were Academy graduates, and his own visits to West Point and Annapolis had convinced him to change his mind. He now believed the academies were necessary, and that an Air Force Academy was essential. The academies, said Hannah: "instill in their students and in their graduates a loyalty to the service, a loyalty to the Government, and appreciation for ethics and integrity, to a degree beyond what we do in our civilian universities." It was a powerful presentation.[72]

Secretary Talbott then gave a justification for the need for an air academy. General Twining did not appear, but his statement reiterating such a need was submitted for the record. Hubert Harmon followed Talbott on 14 January.

Gone was the Cold War rhetoric that had characterized earlier drafts in years previous. Instead, Harmon launched into a discussion of the new academy itself. He began by noting that in their plans—which had been on-going for six years—the Air Force looked "quite naturally" to the other service academies, but especially to West Point. As a result, the laws pertaining to the Military Academy were seen as most applicable to the air academy. He also made clear, however, that the air academy would be unique: "we have been hampered by no established customs or traditions, no preconceived ideas, no vested interests." The new school would be four years in duration and offer a baccalaureate degree. It would be commanded by a superintendent, whose two main assistants would be a dean of faculty and a commandant of cadets. Pay and allowances for air cadets would be the same as those for West Point cadets and Annapolis midshipmen. Harmon's vision for this new academy was austere yet elegant: "we propose to establish and enforce the highest standards of loyalty, integrity, and patriotism, and to motivate our cadets to a lifetime of service in the Armed Forces."[73]

Although the model used was West Point, the air academy would not be a carbon copy. There would be "considerably less" emphasis on infantry drill, for instance; instead: "Our mission is to train for the Air Force." Harmon wanted his air cadets to be "air-faring men in the fullest sense; air-minded and thoroughly indoctrinated in all aspects of air operations." To help ensure this result, cadets would work in and around aircraft, spend their time in actual hangars and shops, and, of course, they would fly during all four years.[74]

The flying training program outlined by Harmon was substantial. During the first two months at the academy, new cadets would be given a parachute and instructed in its use. They would be taken on local orientation flights. When not in the air they would spend time on the "flying line" and be taught how to clean and service aircraft and how to move them about on the ground. In the second phase, cadets would take an aircraft observer's course—a phase to last for three years and involve 355 hours of ground school and instruction and a further 171 hours of flying. On completion, all cadets would be fully qualified in aerial navigation and aerial bombing. In their senior year, cadets would be given preliminary training as pilots—50 hours in the air and a further 150 on the ground. Those who showed the requisite aptitude would, upon graduation, be sent to regular Air Force flying schools to win their wings.[75]

Turning to the academic program, Harmon stated that the current curriculum had been first laid out in 1948 (the Planning Board Study), but had been constantly revised and adjusted. It provided for a broad education that stressed both the social sciences and the technical sciences—like the curriculum at West Point. The advanced technical courses would, however, emphasize aviation matters: thermodynamics, jet propulsion, aerodynamics, and aircraft design. Harmon continued that the academy did not intend to produce aeronautical engineers, but he believed that the grounding received by cadets would allow them later to earn a master's degree in aeronautical engineering at a civilian university.[76]

As to timing, Harmon told the Committee that assuming the legislation was soon passed, the first class of around 300 cadets would enter the academy in July 1955, with the next class of perhaps 324 entering the following summer. Both of these classes would be taught at the as-yet-unnamed interim site. He hoped that the permanent site, also unnamed, would be ready in the summer of 1957 and would then house the first three classes of cadets. Who would instruct them in military affairs and leadership? All talk of importing upper-classmen from West Point and Annapolis went over the side: Air Force officers, fresh out of flying school, would serve as surrogate upperclassmen.[77] Not only did Harmon want cadets to be trained as airmen, but he also frankly admitted that to borrow upperclassmen would require a full, four-year curriculum in place on the day the academy opened—that was not possible.

The selection process for cadets proposed by Harmon was controversial. For West Point and Annapolis, each senator and congressman nominated one primary candidate for each academy each year, along with two or three alternates. If the primary candidate passed both the written and physical examinations, he was offered an appointment. Harmon wanted a different procedure at the Air Force Academy for the first six years. Each senator and congressman would nominate ten young men each year, but the academy would decide, based on test scores, who would be the primary appointee.[78] Harmon wanted to do this to ensure the highest quality cadets were selected during the academy's formative years, and thus avoid the possibility of patronage concerns supplanting the standards of quality. Patronage was, however, a time-honored aspect of the academy appointment system, and politicians were leery of surrendering their prerogatives. Under Harmon's system, there was no guarantee congressmen would be able to place any of their nominees into the first several classes—they would be too small. Moreover, as we shall soon see, questions of quality were often much in the eye of the beholder—test scores were not necessarily the best determinant in selecting the top candidates: grade point average in high school, and the size and quality of that high school were also valid criteria. In addition, assuming the Air Force wanted well-rounded young men who were also physically fit and with demonstrated leadership potential, how did one weigh athletic participation and prowess, as well as other activities such as holding class office, or extracurricular activities such as debating teams or scouting, in the overall evaluation process? There were differing ideas on this.

In any event, most questions from the Committee centered on the permanent site to be selected and the flying program. The legislation stated that the Air Force secretary would appoint a committee to select a site; if its recommendation was unanimous, that would be the winner. If there was a split decision, the final determination would be made by the secretary. The congressmen questioned Talbott and Harmon closely on this issue—hoping for hints as to where the academy would be sited—but the two men refused to say anything about the results of the previous Spaatz Board other than to note the identity of the finalists—which was already a matter of public record.

When the hearings ended, Chairman Short came up to the table where Talbott and Harmon were sitting and said: "Mr. Secretary, I think you have the right officer in the right place. He has wrapped up the package. It is a masterful presentation. I appreciate it very much."[79] The Committee voted 26-0 in favor of the bill for the Air Force Academy. The full House debate the following week did not result in any amendments to the bill, and H.R. 5337 was approved on 21 January by a vote of 331 to 36 with 67 members not voting.

Harmon and others met with the Senate Armed Services Committee staff the following month. There were no major problems noted or anticipated, and on February 18, the Senate hearings began. Assistant Secretary Hannah led-off this time, giving another powerful statement. Army and Navy statements were read into the record, and Secretary Talbott gave his testimony—largely the same as he had given before the House. Harmon then offered a prepared statement to be entered into the record, similar to his House testimony but containing more information on the selection process—a touchy point for the legislators. Questions centered on this, and the permanent site to be determined—another key subject. Indeed, Senator Lyndon B. Johnson of Texas grilled Talbott extensively on this issue. Harmon's reception was more friendly.[80]

The Senate passed its version on 8 March, but insisted that the revised cadet selection procedure that put the Academy in charge be cut from six years to four. At the end of the month the House and Senate staff members met to reconcile their minor differences—the House agreed to the change to four years.[81] The House re-voted and passed the bill on 25 March; the Senate voted "yea" four days later. On 1 April 1954, President Dwight Eisenhower signed the bill, now Public Law 325. The Air Force Academy was a reality. The next day

Talbott wrote Harmon: "We all believe that the authorization for the Academy is due to the untiring efforts you applied, particularly your forceful presentations to the Congress."[82] His performances in the House and Senate hearings were among Harmon's greatest moments. He was prepared, professional, articulate, calm, and in command of all the details.

It was an important day that had been a long time coming. For decades the Academy had been a dream, and for over six years, since Air Force independence, it had been an eagerly sought and fought for goal. This extended battle was well summed by the Academy's official history, which characterized this period as one of "enthusiasm, gloom and despair—but never lethargy."[83]

Now the hard work would actually begin.

President Eisenhower signs the law authorizing the Air Force Academy on April 1, 1954. From left to right: Air Force Secretary Harold Talbott, Congressman Carl Vinson, General Nate Twining the Air Force chief of staff, House Military Affairs Chairman Dewey Short, Air Force Assistant Secretary James Douglas, and Harmon.

CHAPTER 9

Preparing the Academy Home

*A*lmost as soon as President Eisenhower signed the Air Force Academy bill into law, Secretary Talbott moved to nail down the school's permanent site. Although he had expressed enthusiasm when Harmon had confided to him that Colorado Springs had been the Spaatz Board's first choice, Talbott testified before Congress that he did not know of the Board's findings. Senator Lyndon Johnson of Texas pressed him on the subject, hoping to ensure the site decision was still wide open. (Recall that three of the Spaatz Board's finalists had been in Texas.) Johnson asked Talbott if he would oppose an amendment stating that the president, rather than he, should have the final say. The secretary replied that he had already discussed that matter with Eisenhower who told him: "Not on your life. This is your baby and you settle it."[1]

Nonetheless, given the obvious sensitivity on this subject, Talbott acted quickly to start the site selection process over.

Legislation called for the secretary to appoint a five-person commission for that purpose, and Talbott had already given thought to its membership. He proposed as chairman the former Air Force secretary, Thomas Finletter. Other members would include Generals Spaatz and Harmon, Merrill C. Meigs, the vice president of Hearst Publications, and Dr. Virgil Hancher, the president of the University of Iowa. When Finletter declined the invitation due to other duties, Talbott asked Charles Lindbergh, the legendary aviator who had recently been promoted to brigadier general in the Air Force Reserve, to the Commission. Colonel Arthur Boudreau, who had been part of the Academy team since 1948, was appointed as the Commission's non-voting secretary.

The group met in Talbott's office on April 5, 1954. The Commission members declined to appoint a chairman and instead insisted on working together as equals—"five old mules that can't get together" as Spaatz phrased it. After breaking so that the members could attend the funeral of Hoyt Vandenberg, who had died of cancer the week prior, Talbott discussed the criteria for the permanent site, which were similar to those identified by the original Board, but that also stressed the suitability for flight training. The nine specific criteria that were to guide the Commission included:[2]

- *Acreage*: approximately 15,000 acres would be needed
- *Topography*: the site must possess "natural beauty" and be able to accommodate an airfield
- *Community Aspects*: proximity to educational, religious, cultural and recreational facilities was necessary
- *Climate*: the area should enjoy a four-season climate without extremes of heat or cold
- *Water Supply*: three million gallons per day would be needed
- *Utilities*: electric power and natural gas were required
- *Transportation*: the site should be convenient for rail, airline and highway access
- *Cost*: not just of the land itself, but for the removal of existing buildings and the construction of access roads
- *Flying Training*: large enough to accommodate flight training at the site.

This list of criteria was released to the public the following day. Admiral Hall, the superintendent of the Coast Guard Academy, then wrote Harmon suggesting another criterion: the new Academy should be located next to an existing girl's school. He cited three practical reasons for such a location: it would keep the cadets at home; it would cut down on the number of traffic accidents on the weekends; and it would encourage the cadets to court "high-class brides leading to future marital success."[3] Co-location of the all-male Academy with a school for young women would stand in sharp contrast to the monastic setting of West Point!

With respect to the actual site, it appears that Colorado Springs was still favored by Talbott, because the Commission spent two days in his office reviewing the information regarding that location. A major concern was the requirement for flying training—would the high altitude at Colorado Springs be a problem? Meigs talked to the head of the Civil Aviation Authority on 6 April and the response was pessimistic: a runway altitude of 3,000-5,000 feet was tolerable, but could possibly lead to a higher accident rate. An altitude of over 5,000 would render a proposed flying school airfield "distinctly undesirable."[4] The elevation at the Colorado Springs site most likely to house an airfield was over 6,000 feet.

The following day the Commission discussed the matter of health. Harmon expressed reservations on it earlier and therefore had requested the Air Force surgeon general, Major General H.G. Armstrong, to look into it. On 7 April Armstrong responded that the area was known for its unusually high incidence of rheumatic fever—the rate in Colorado Springs was nearly twice the national average, and Denver was twelve times higher. The area also had unusually high occurrences of flu, streptococcus, and other respiratory ailments. Why this was the case was not clear.[5] When Armstrong contacted the American Public Health Association, it concluded that "the Rocky Mountain area was not recommended for the Air Academy."

Despite these seemingly significant difficulties, the Commission decided that Colorado Springs was still a highly viable candidate.

The Site Selection Commission in front of its aircraft. From left to right: Virgil Hancher, Harmon, Charles Lindbergh, Merrill Meigs and Carl Spaatz. On the far right is General Curtis LeMay.

There were many sites to visit. Boudreau was told to compile a list of locations from the 1951 Spaatz Board and add those resulting from the new announcement. On 9 April the Commission members flew to Florida to begin inspections. Their routine was to not announce a visit until the day before arrival. They would meet with local officials to review the specifics of the site. They would avoid luncheons or dinners set up by the city; instead, they would eat lunch on their plane and dinner at the Air Force base where they would spend the night. Meigs, because of his newspaper background, would handle all contact with the press. No other Commission members would grant interviews. Photographers were warned to keep their distance, especially regarding Lindbergh.[6] These stringent rules were designed to eliminate political or economic pressure being applied to the commissioners. Harmon had reckoned in 1948 that lobbying by local politicians and businessmen could be intense. The members, therefore, had to be beyond intimidation and blandishment. Given the characters of the five men chosen, this was quickly established to be the case. When Spaatz was later asked if the pressures on him had been a problem, he responded that no, the members had simply refused to allow themselves to be lobbied or pushed.[7] When Lindbergh was asked if there had been special agendas or influences at work within the band, he responded: "Within the Commission itself there was no political activity. I have never taken part in a group of this kind that was freer of politics."[8]

The Commission relied heavily on the work done by the Spaatz Board, using all the data it had gathered, including the brochures provided by the local communities bidding for the site. Over the next month the Commission flew around the country visiting dozens of sites. Altogether, there were 580 proposed locations, 354 of which had been considered by the Spaatz Board. Using the winnowing methods employed earlier—comparing the data provided by the local officials to the established criteria and then relying on local Corps of Engineers personnel—the Commission quickly narrowed the list to sixty-seven possibilities. Of these, thirty-four sites in twenty-one states would be inspected on the ground, the remaining thirty-three sites in seventeen states were to be seen only from the air.

The Commission was busy but efficient. A typical day was that of 9 April. At 0900 the Commission members boarded their aircraft, a C-121 "Constellation," at National Airport (now Reagan National Airport) and flew to Orlando, Florida, arriving at 1300. En route they overflew and viewed the sites at Charleston, SC, and at Fernandina Beach, Palatka, Gainesville and Ocala, all in Florida. While in Orlando they met with local officials and then drove out to the site, ten miles north of the city, and walked the ground. They took off at 1535 and flew to MacDill AFB where they received a call from Secretary Talbott directing them to fly to Maxwell AFB. The Commission headed back west and along the way viewed Pinecastle AFB, Lakeland, three sites in the Tampa area, and then Cross City, Tallahassee, and Marianna, Florida. They spent the night at Maxwell. Usually, all members would get together over dinner and for a few hours thereafter and discuss what they had seen that day.[9]

It was apparent that Colorado, either the Colorado Springs or Denver sites, was high on the Commission's list. Knowing this, officials in Colorado Springs began urging the state legislature to allocate funds to buy land for an Academy site. On 12 April the Commission met in Denver with Governor Dan Thornton, Denver Mayor Quigg Newton, Robert Stearns, and others. The area's health environment was raised again, and Dr. Ward Darley, president of the University of Colorado and a physician, stated that his school (located in Boulder, north of Denver) had experienced no such health problems. He suggested that medical advances since World War II (when the high rates of rheumatic fever had been registered) had largely eliminated the threat.[10]

The Commission then drove to Colorado Springs to meet with local officials. General Benjamin Chidlaw, commander of Air Defense Command headquartered in Colorado Springs, was on hand to assure the Commission that the high altitude did not negatively impact the flight operations of his command.

After all travel was done, the Commission gathered in Washington on 6 May to confer with Secretary Talbott, General Twining, and other members of the Air Staff. Colorado Springs was discussed, including the altitude and its effect on flying operations. The consensus was that although the ground elevation's impact on flight training was an important consideration, "when it is considered along with other important factors which are advantageous to such location, I don't think that it should override or preclude the selection."[11] Moreover, Charles Lindbergh, who had flown over the area personally during the 1920s as a barnstormer, noted that four civilian flying schools in the Denver area had no difficulty handling the thinner air, and their accident rates were no higher than that of flying schools at lower elevations. Finally, the commander of Air Training Command, in a letter written shortly after the meeting, indicated that he too considered the elevation at Colorado Springs to be of minor significance. Even so, Harmon thought it necessary to get a formal reading from General Twining. The chief responded on 26 May: "Elevations of approximately 3,000-6,500 feet should be no bar to selection of a site for the Air Force Academy."[12]

The next day the commissioners reviewed their notes. Initially, the members were all over the map: Spaatz liked Battle Creek, Michigan; Lindbergh liked Hamilton AFB in California; and Harmon was partial to Colorado Springs. By the end of the day, however, they had arrived at five finalists: Alton, Illinois; Lake Geneva, Wisconsin; Madison, Indiana; San Francisco, California; and Colorado Springs. They eliminated Madison due to topography and weather and Hamilton because of crowding. Three of the Commission members, Spaatz, Lindbergh and Harmon, favored the Springs, but because they wanted to make a unanimous choice, Meigs and Hancher—who favored Alton—stated they would re-visit Colorado. As a result, two reports were drafted: the first listed Colorado Springs as the unanimous choice; the other simply named the three finalists—in no order of preference. Hancher and Meigs then stated they flew to Colorado—Lindbergh went along—to examine the area north of the city once again.

Upon arrival, Lindbergh entered the Pine Valley airfield, a small gravel strip located on the site, to rent an aircraft. Meigs related that the old codger behind the desk said he could rent them a plane, but he'd need to see a flying license from somebody to show they knew how to fly. Lindbergh then produced a dozen or so different pilot licenses from around the world, prompting the man to exclaim: "You ain't Charlie Lindbergh, be you? " He got the plane and proceeded to fly Meigs and Hancher around at low altitude. Lindbergh later noted that his passengers were heavy, the plane was small, and when he said low altitude, he meant it. The plane could not even get safely over the top of Cathedral Rock—a large limestone formation that rose over 100 feet above the ground, or about 7,300 feet above sea level.[13] Still, the three men flew over the area repeatedly. Having promised Harmon an answer quickly, Hancher phoned him on 28 May to say that he would agree to vote for the Springs. Meigs, however, remained "very negative" about the site, largely due to its relative isolation. Recall that criterion number three required that the Academy be near other educational and cultural facilities. President Eisenhower had highlighted this consideration as well. The Colorado Springs site was, however, eight miles north of town center. Phone conversations between Meigs and both Spaatz and Harmon failed to change his mind, so the second report—listing three finalists—was forwarded to Secretary Talbott on 3 June. This list was released to the public the same day.[14]

The decision was now up to Secretary Talbott. For his part, Spaatz was not at all displeased, thinking that a single site would have caused real estate prices to soar and community interest to lag.[15] The report submitted to the secretary noted that the final three choices were well balanced. In fact, the report concluded—as had the Spaatz Board three years earlier—that no single site was superior in all respects.

Talbott decided to visit all three sites personally during the month of June. What he encountered surprised him. Quite simply, both at Alton and Lake Geneva there were large segments of the populace and local leadership that were not pleased the Air Force Academy might be headed their way. For example, the board of supervisors for Jersey County, the area that contained the Alton site, stated that it "violently objected" to the Academy. Although this stance was disputed by both the Alton and St Louis chambers of commerce, the negative element gave Talbott pause. When the secretary arrived in Lake Geneva, the response was even colder. It was judged that 90 percent of the landowners in the area opposed having the Academy in their county. In fact, the Geneva Lake Civic Association sent Talbott a telegram stating that it wished to "vigorously protest" the arrival of the Academy. The telegram stated that Lake Geneva "has been a quiet peaceful resort" and the Academy would do "untold harm to the community." A letter to President Eisenhower from an irate farm owner near Lake Geneva was even more exercised about the thought of the government stealing her land; this is not democracy at work! Both missives suggested that the Air Force should find a location where the populace actually wanted the Academy.[16] In addition to this lack of enthusiasm, the two Midwestern locations also sought a great deal of money for their land: Alton said the required acreage would cost $18.75 million; Lake Geneva wanted $12.28 million.[17]

In contrast, city officials, business leaders, and residents in Colorado Springs welcomed Talbott and the Academy with open arms. They had already raised funds from private sources and lobbied the state legislature with the result that the 17,500 acre site to the north of the city could be had for a mere $2.15 million. The stark differences between the cost and enthusiasm of the three sites were compelling.

On 22 June Talbott departed Colorado Springs for Washington. Two days later he called a meeting in his office with General Twining and others, and they reviewed the results of his own trip, those of the Commission, and those

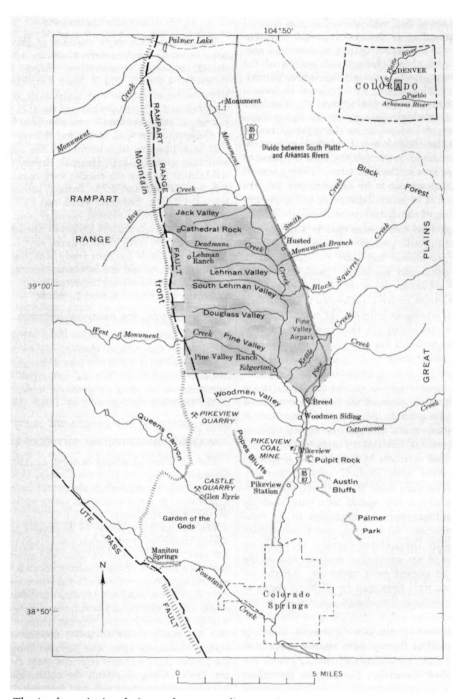

The Academy site in relation to the surrounding area in 1954.

of the survey teams that had been sent out to all three locations. That afternoon the secretary called a press conference and announced Colorado Springs as the winner. The interim location for the Academy while the permanent site was under construction would be in Denver.

It would appear that the enthusiastic support of Colorado Springs civic leaders and politicians was the key factor in Talbot's decision. Other factors were cost and the natural beauty of the site. Colorado Springs, then a city of 75,000, also had a decades-long reputation as an Air Force-friendly town. And finally, connections to the president—his wife was from Colorado, his mother-in-law still lived in Denver, and he himself visited the state frequently on fishing trips—probably sealed the choice. Indeed, in a conversation with Talbott on 19 June, Eisenhower said "two or three times" that the Academy should not be located in the Middle West. Eisenhower liked Fort Logan in Denver—where he and Mamie had spent their honeymoon—but he was not at all displeased with the Colorado Springs site.[18] Harmon himself was happy with the decision. Later that month he wrote a candid letter to fellow Commission member Virgil Hancher on his feelings:[19]

> Having spent three days exploring the Colorado Springs site by jeep, foot and horseback I am convinced that its final selection was sound and proper. No one knows better than we members of the Commission that it is not perfect but I feel myself that the grandeur of the setting is so inspiring as to off-set any disadvantages. I was also impressed anew with the wide open spaces and the opportunities for adventure. Most of the other sites left me with a feeling of being fenced in. At the Colorado site, backed up against a huge forest reserve our boys can climb mountains, get lost in the woods and otherwise commune with nature.

There were protests over the decision, but they faded quickly. Those in Alton were most disappointed, but they accepted the outcome with grace. The citizens of Lake Geneva were relieved.

This critical issue decided, there were a number of other matters to be addressed.

The question of an interim site for the Academy had taken up a great deal of Harmon's time and efforts over the previous several years, but now that decision became relatively simple. Before, the interim site had always been contrasted against an undetermined permanent location, but with the permanent site selected, it seemed logical to establish the temporary Academy somewhere nearby. Public Law 325 had specified that the interim site be located either on an existing military facility or at an established civilian university.

On 10 July Harmon flew to Denver to examine three sites: Denver University, Fort Logan—one of Harmon's PDC facilities during World War II that was no longer in use—and Lowry AFB. Although the president of Denver University was eager to help, it was obvious that the facilities on campus were inadequate. Fort Logan had deteriorated to such an extent that the cost to rehabilitate and renovate it would be prohibitive. Lowry, on the east side of the city, was the obvious choice. That it was being run by Air Training Command was a significant bonus.[20]

On 19 July, Secretary Talbott took Harmon's recommendation and announced Lowry AFB as the interim site.[21]

A Site of Grandeur

There is no more dramatic joining of plains with steep mountains in the continental United States than along the front range of the Rocky Mountains. After passing through endless miles of flatland prairies and wheat fields, a traveler from the east suddenly encounters the awe-inspiring sight of the Rampart Range jutting abruptly and vertically from the plains, with the 14,000 foot Pike's Peak, snow-covered nearly year round, towering above all.

The 17,500 acre, 27-square mile Academy site stretched from eight miles north of Colorado Springs for another six miles to just beyond Cathedral Rock—a large limestone formation. The western boundary was the Rampart Range and Pike National Forest. From there, the land ran nearly five miles east to Monument Creek, railroad lines, and Highway 85/87, which connected Colorado Springs to Denver. The Air Force insisted, however, that a 500 foot-wide strip of land east of the highway also be included so as to prevent "development blight" from lining the edge of the road and spoiling the view.

Ranches, homes, a tavern, several motels, and a railroad station already existed on the Academy site; most of these would go, although the three largest houses would ultimately be remodeled as quarters for the superintendent, commandant and dean.[22] The land itself was extremely hilly and dominated by a series of ridges that extended eastwards from the mountains, with these ridges tapering and flattening as they reached the highway. The difference in elevation from the high point to the low was around 1,600 feet. The valleys between these ridges—Pine, Monument, Douglas, Lehman and Jack—were to provide settings for many Academy facilities and activities. The largest and flat-test ridge, Lehman to the north, would become the site for the Cadet Area.[23]

The issue of who would design and build the Academy on this impressive site was hotly contested. The Academy was one of the largest and most presti-gious construction projects of the postwar era, and many architects were eager to display their talents and explore new ideas and new materials. The Academy would be one of the largest and newest military facilities in the country—the selection of its designer and builder would generate great interest.

In 1952, Harmon had met with noted architect Eero Saarinen to discuss ideas, but no designs resulted. Secretary Talbott then commissioned New York architect Ellery Husted and his firm to prepare some preliminary designs for a generic location—the permanent site had not yet been selected.[24] The Hus-ted firm's concept resembled that of Randolph AFB—a circular plan with the Cadet Area in the center, faculty housing on the rim, and the airfield off to the side. This was a useful exercise. It confirmed for Harmon that the Cadet Area should be clustered in one location—this would become a dominant design consideration. Harmon argued that cadets would be very busy, so he wanted to ensure they could move between the dormitory, academic building, dining hall, and gym within ten minutes.

Realizing that architectural design for a large university was something Air Force leadership knew little about, Harmon and others decided to fly to Mexico City where a new campus had recently been built for the University of Mexico. The team was impressed. Two of the more interesting features of the design were the heavy use of mosaic tiles on the building facades, and place-ment of the buildings themselves atop large pillars. This latter feature meant that an individual standing at ground level could look through to the horizon in all directions: the buildings appeared to float or fly above them. These were ideas Harmon would remember.[25]

In anticipation of Academy legislation being passed, the Air Force estab-lished a project office in Washington to plan for construction and supervise the operation—to the chagrin of the Corps of Engineers that usually handled such things.[26] The Air Force planned to solicit bids for the design and building of the entire Academy facility, review them, and select a winner. One idea called for a consortium of several large firms to carry out the project. Harmon rejected this approach: "The Air Force if it did this, would be responsible for any lack of har-mony among the group or for any inadequacies on the part of any member."[27]

Harmon wanted an architectural advisory board composed of senior military officers to review the designs, but was talked out of this idea: there would be an advisory board, but it would consist of noted civilian architects who reported directly to the Air Force secretary.[28]

As proposals began to flood in to the Academy project office, political pressure accompanied them. Senator Sam Irwin wrote Talbott suggesting the new Academy be built of North Carolina granite—quarried from his state. Senator John Kennedy wrote that he thought Massachusetts granite would be more appropriate.[29] Such special pleadings were largely ignored, and the selection process moved quickly. Talbott appointed a board of civilians and general officers to study the proposals; within a month the 300-plus applicants were narrowed to six finalists and soon after to just two. Skidmore, Owings and Merrill (SOM) was a Chicago-based firm whose major claim to fame was the erecting, from scratch, of an entire town. Oak Ridge, Tennessee, was constructed during World War II to house the top-secret uranium-separating facility that was needed for the first atomic bomb. As the town swelled from 3,000 to 75,000 people during the war, so did the need for homes, schools, stores and hospitals. SOM had other military experience, having also built the Navy's Postgraduate School in Monterey, California. In addition, there were a number of impressive new commercial buildings on its resume. The other finalist was Kittyhawk Associates, a group of firms put together by a Cleveland architectural company. It had what at first appeared a key advantage—its chief designer would be the legendary Frank Lloyd Wright.

Both firms were invited to Washington to brief their proposals to a group of Air Force officials. Wright balked. He stated imperiously that "The world knows what I can do in architecture. If officials of the Air Force have missed this, I can do no more than feel sorry for what both have lost."[30] He refused to travel to Washington, and that put Kittyhawk in a bit of a bind during their presentation, making the final decision easy. After only a few hours of deliberation, Talbott announced on July 23, 1954 that the winner was Skidmore, Owings, and Merrill. Later, the secretary admitted that his wife had been a major influence in his decision: SOM had built the New York Infirmary, of which she was chairman of the board, and both greatly admired the building.[31] The company also promised to have the Academy finished in time for the graduation of the first class—June 1959. In the days before extensive and time-consuming environmental impact statements and other such permits, this was a fairly reasonable promise—and it would be met. Soon after, an advisory board was established consisting of three noted architects: Pietro Belluschi, Welton Becket and Eero Saarinen.[32]

The first question to resolve was the location of the various facilities on the extensive Academy site. The most important of these decisions concerned the location of the Cadet Area. Harmon initially argued for this crucial section to be located in one of the valleys, hidden away in Shangri-la fashion; he thought the Lehman ridge venue—the largest and highest ridge on the northern side of the reservation—would be "overly dramatic." He was also concerned that the ridge would be too narrow to accommodate future expansion and that its 7,250' altitude might have an adverse effect on personnel living and working there. The architects convinced him that when you are blessed with a mountain site, "it was foolish to cower down in the valley."[33] The Cadet Area would be built on Lehman Ridge, but, as Harmon noted, it would need to be significantly enlarged to accommodate the academic building, library, dormitory, dining hall, administration building, social center, planetarium, and chapel. Still, it was an outstanding site. To the north, in Jack's Valley, would be firing ranges and a maneuver area for cadet training. Faculty and staff housing would be built in Douglas and Pine Valleys; the community center and hospital would go on ridges. Later, the officers' club and alumni center would also be situated along a ridge. The service and supply area, as well as the football stadium, would be built on flat land at the eastern edge of the ridges. The airfield would have to be located on the eastern rim of the reservation—the only level area large enough to accommodate it. Even then, the Highway-85/87 would have to be diverted to the east because of wind patterns and runway orientation.[34]

Harmon had strong feelings about other aspects of the architects' master plan. He wanted a wildlife zone on the reservation's north side where deer, fox, coyote and other animals could roam freely. He objected to any road built on the western edge of the property; rather, "it should be kept as nearly as possible in its natural state." He desired two or three lakes to be created on the grounds for beauty, but also for canoeing. He insisted that throughout the planning and construction process "emphasis should be placed on the preservation of trees." Finally, it was Harmon who pushed for the Academy reservation to include the east side of Highway 85/87 so as "to prevent honky-tonks, motels, etc." These were admirable ideas, largely followed.[35]

The design for the buildings would be far more contentious. Several styles would be considered. At one point Harmon had favored the Collegiate

Gothic style of West Point. On another occasion he leaned towards the Spanish Colonial or hacienda style used at Randolph AFB. Frank Lloyd Wright later stated that he would have used sandstone for his design. Harmon seemed to like that idea too, but when he asked Nathaniel Owings about it, the reply was simple: "would the Air Force build an airplane out of sandstone?"[36] Eventually, Harmon would come to favor the design that SOM was offering, a modernistic scheme of rectilinear buildings made of aluminum, glass, marble, and mosaic glass tiles. It was a striking concept that contrasted sharply with the rugged mountains. The architects had no intention of blending their design with nature; they envisioned an Academy that stood apart from its majestic surroundings and was sharply different from them. A Collegiate Gothic style of granite would have been imposing, but immediately forgettable. As one SOM designer argued: the Academy should be uniquely of the West. They were not building in Vermont or attempting to replicate the other two military academies back East. They were out to create something "new, tough, large-scaled, with awe-inspiring vistas."[37] They delivered. Over the next several months, Harmon and his staff worked closely with SOM, exchanging ideas and requirements and reviewing design proposals. Eventually, they together hammered out a master plan and architectural concept that specified where each building would be located, where connecting roads and walkways would be placed, and, most importantly, how the buildings would look inside and out.[38]

The model of the future Air Force Academy prepared by Skidmore, Owings and Merrill in 1954.

Harmon's public affairs officer set up a major display at the Colorado Springs Fine Arts Center. It contained a large model of the planned Academy, plus dozens of photographs of the site. The news release stated: "The concept is designed to take advantage of a site which architects consider to be as thrilling as the Acropolis of Athens."[39] When Skidmore, Owings, and Merrill unveiled its plans to Congress and the public on May 15, 1954, some observers were, however, less than thrilled. In fact, the design

The Cadet Chapel under construction.

created a firestorm. Senator John Stennis disliked the entire scheme, thinking it too modern. Representative John Fogarty stated it was "not American in conception and is unworthy of the traditions of this nation." Fogarty, former president of the Rhode Island bricklayers union, wanted the Academy built out of bricks, not aluminum. Frank Lloyd Wright—still miffed that the Air Force had not bowed to his greatness—weighed in with an announcement that the SOM design was "shocking … a fiasco … a glassified box on stilts" and that it "lacked a soul." He did, however, write Nate Owings noting that because his firm had no real talent to speak of, he would be willing to take over their design function. SOM politely declined.[40]

The Cadet Chapel received the sharpest barbs. The modernistic tetrahedron design with its seventeen spires rubbed many the wrong way. One commentator stated that it looked like a group of fighter planes—or wheelbarrows—stacked on end; another scoffed that it resembled a row of teepees or a "tin tent."[41] Senator A. Willis Robertson muttered that "he did not hear the rustle of angels' wings" when gazing at the model. Others objected to the fact that three denominations would occupy the building: the Protestants on the main floor with the Catholics and Jews "in the basement."[42] Originally, Harmon had wanted three separate chapels, but the high cost made this impossible. He then suggested a cruciform design, like that used in the great cathedrals of Europe. Jewish groups quickly protested, saying they could not worship in a structure built in the shape of a cross.[43]

Fogarty, who chaired the House Appropriations Committee, suspended funding for construction to show his displeasure. This in turn led the Air Force to protest that this would cause excessive delay, which would in turn drive up the cost.

Skidmore, Owings and Merrill did a redesign, but it actually changed very little. Eventually, a backlash set in as architects began protesting that Congress was no judge of design; the professionals should be allowed to get on with the job. (Wright's negative comments were dismissed: "His massive contempt for literally all save his own efforts is one of his best known and least noble traits."[44]) In truth, Harmon admitted that "any style of architecture proposed for the Air Force Academy will be resented by some element of the American people."[45] One newspaper captured this sentiment when it editorialized that "No greater calamity could befall the air force than to have its long-needed academy involved in a congressional long-haired squabble over what is 'art,' over the merits of functional versus classical design, over the nuance of aesthetics."[46] The tide seemed to turn when Walter Gropius, an architect hardly less renowned than Wright, came down squarely in favor of the SOM plan:[47]

> At last we have found—away from weak imitation of borrowed styles of the past—a genuine architectural expression which vigorously characterizes the present American approach in science and industry. A proud example is the design of the Air Force Academy which shows progressive American leadership in architecture. I am confidant that its cultural merits will prevail against sentimentality and ignorance.

The firm's new design added a bit more masonry—beautiful marble slabs on the academic building and library facades—while reducing the amount of glass. Congress was placated: it restored funding on 26 July and moved on.

SOM got to work with a will. On the Cadet Area alone the company used fifty-two subcontractors employing six thousand workers. Many of the building materials used, such as tinted, mirrored glass, mosaic glass tiles from Italy, and anodized aluminum, were new or had not previously been used extensively. Walter Netsch, one of the firm's designers, later noted that the materials book used by all architects was four volumes long when the project started; by the time the Academy was finished the book had grown to seven volumes.[48]

The chapel was not alone in design innovations among the Academy's buildings. For example, the dining hall has no internal pillars for support but is large enough to seat the entire Cadet Wing at one time. Its two-acre roof was hoisted into position as a single piece to sit atop the side girders. So as not to have the structures dominate the individual, SOM designed some of the buildings to rest on the edge of the artificial mesa. This allowed half of the dormitory and academic building to be "below ground" with one side overlooking the valleys on either side of the mesa. The top two floors were set on large square pillars, thus allowing cadets a clear vista to the horizon. This entire effort required the moving of two and one-half million cubic yards of earth and the erecting of two miles of retaining walls.[49] Because the cadets needed to march and form up, a large terrazzo area was put in front of the dormitory, leading to the chapel, dining hall, and academic area. Originally, the southwestern side of the terrazzo, the area directly opposite the dormitory, was left open to allow a clear view towards Cheyenne Mountain. (Another dormitory was built on the south side of the terrazzo a decade later.) A thirty-acre parade field was also positioned east of the dormitory and academic building. In determining where to put the Academy's roads, the architects cleverly observed the cattle then grazing on the reservation. Cows always take the easiest route, so that is where the engineers laid the pavement.[50]

Harmon was intimately involved in all of this. He had been a frustrated architect most of his life and had told Rosa-Maye that he considered resigning from the Air Service in 1923 so he could go to architectural school. He did not of course, but it was obvious he still dreamed about such things. He made detailed, scaled drawings of every house in which the family lived. Having toured Europe he thought he had a good feel for classical architectural design, and, as a result, often made suggestions to the SOM architects about various aspects of the Academy's construction. Most of these ideas were not accepted. As noted, he toyed with the Collegiate Gothic style and favored the use of granite or sandstone. He wanted the Cadet Area tucked away in a valley rather than in a prominent place on a ridge. He liked the idea of having latrines in the basement of the "barracks"—as was the case at West Point for peculiar reasons of instilling discipline. (He insisted, however, that the latrines be equipped with stalls: "Man demands a greater dignity" than simply a row of open commodes.[51]) He suggested a cruciform plan for the Cadet Chapel. Most of these ideas were not employed in the Academy design. There were, however, other useful insights that Harmon provided. His trip to Mexico City had opened his eyes to the possibilities of a modernistic design, as

did his recollection of the El Panama Hotel in Panama City that he quite liked—
another modern design.[52] At the Academy, he questioned the idea of one large
barracks building, fearing that it would present major light and ventilation problems. He continued that "I, myself, like the idea of enclosed area or areas, i.e., one
or two large buildings, each in the form of a quadrangle with a large open 'patio'
in the middle."[53] He said such a plan reminded him of the Great Quadrangle of
Christ Church at Oxford that he had visited with Rosa-Maye. This design feature
was in fact used—although the grassy "patio areas" in the center of the dormitory
quadrangles were never as grand as he or the architects initially envisioned. He
also insisted that all of the cadet classrooms be wired for closed-circuit television,
at the time a farsighted idea.[54]

Harmon grew concerned about the design's relentless linearity: squares,
rectangles, triangles and tetrahedrons. He once turned to Netsch and asked
somewhat plaintively: "Walter, can't you do anything round?" As a concession,
the designers included a beautiful and technically impressive spiral staircase in
the library.[55] Harmon also wanted the library to be a separate structure from
the classroom building and to include fireplaces—he wanted it to be a place of
refuge where cadets could relax while studying. The library was made separate,
but it did not include fireplaces.[56]

SOM also had plans for faculty and staff housing, to be located in Douglas
and Pine Valleys. Harmon did not like the design proposed for the superintendent's quarters. Then one day he visited the Carlton House, the large, Spanish
hacienda-style house in Pine Valley. He said instantly "that's where it's going!"
SOM's concept for the other 1,200 base housing units was rejected outright. As
one officer put it: the cadets can live in something that looks futuristic, but we
want to live in base housing that looks like basing housing anywhere else in the
world.[57] Unfortunately, they got their wish.

In addition to the buildings, there were a myriad of other, more detailed
matters, which also had to be addressed. For example, the cadet rooms and
their furniture had to be designed to be durable ("to last fifty years"), functional, and in keeping with the overall design. New aluminum furniture was
designed—and it did last for fifty years. Harmon insisted that the cadets be
kept together in their squadrons—a squadron would not be divided by being
on separate floors or in different quadrangles. The classrooms were also to be
unique. Harmon wanted rooms with wall-to-wall blackboards—he envisioned
the type of daily recitation and board work still being used at West Point. This

necessitated clusters of small classrooms, with no windows, that could each seat perhaps twenty cadets. The windows would be in the hallways, giving cadets a view of the mountains as they proceeded to and from their classes.[58]

Besides the buildings and their contents, Harmon also wanted the cadet uniforms to be distinctive as well, but most designs envisioned a standard Air Force uniform with unique cadet insignia. It was too late to fashion totally new uniforms for the first class, but he hoped they could have something special in a year or two. When he and Colonel Stillman took some ideas to Talbott, the secretary stormed: "You two don't know a damn thing about uniforms. I know even less than both of you. What we need is some real imagination."[59] Talbott then contacted an old friend, film producer Cecil B. DeMille of Paramount Studios, the creator of numerous classic Hollywood extravaganzas— *Samson and Delilah*, *The Greatest Show on Earth*, and *The Ten Commandments.*

The Cadet Area under construction looking north. In the foreground is the aeronautics laboratory; behind it to the left with its roof already in place is Mitchell Hall (the cadet dining hall), and to the right is the academic building, Fairchild Hall. The flat building in the rear center is the dormitory, Vandenberg Hall. At the extreme left is the Academy headquarters building, later named for Harmon. The gymnasium can be seen in the rear right. Cathedral Rock is in the far distance.

DeMille's associates urged him to decline the invitation, but he was intrigued by the challenge. In addition, DeMille always had a soft spot in his heart for aviation: he had begun taking flying lessons with the Air Service during World War I, but the conflict had ended before he had won his wings and his commission. Afterwards, he started his own aviation company. Because of all this, DeMille decided to get involved: he took some of his best costume designers off their current project—*The Ten Commandments*—and told them to come up with a cadet uniform ensemble. He wrote the superintendent: "It is our intention to be instrumental in equipping your cadets with the best looking family of uniforms of any Academy in the world."[60] The Western Costume Company made the specimen uniforms, and the results were spectacular. Stillman took the designs to the Pentagon and later wrote Harmon: "All the people who have seen the prototype are most enthusiastic and it will be a long time before I forget the pleased schoolboy grins on the faces of Generals Twining and White when they first saw the modeling of the complete wardrobe."[61] DeMille later recalled that when the uniforms were first shown to the cadets they actually cheered! "These are uniforms that cadets themselves will want to wear. If the man in the uniform is happy with them," he said, "that is the main thing. If his girl admires them that is even more important."[62] With but minor modifications, the De Mille uniforms are still in use today.

Construction, although not completely finished, was far enough along to allow the cadets to be bussed down from Denver in July 1958. They then marched from the highway to the Cadet Area and their new home. Many had been driving down on the weekends, when the workers were gone, to explore and get a feel for the site. They were both impressed and awed.

Terms often used to describe the Academy structures and their setting included: "a sense of grandeur," "awe-inspiring," "Olympian," and "magnificent." One observer referred to the "Air Acropolis" and another to the "Air Age Gothic" design. One, more artistically inclined, wrote: "Against the formidable background of the front range of the Rockies, the chapel registers a thinly, strident, silvery note amidst dark, massive harmonics."[63] Indeed, it is the Cadet Chapel that is the iconic image that has come to define the Air Force Academy in the eyes of millions. Few today see it as controversial: it is simply beautiful and instantly recognizable.[64] At the same time, it must also be noted that by the 1980s the rectilinear design and emphasis on glass and aluminum used in the chapel and other buildings was already seen as dated. Many structures employing these same materials around the United States did not hold up to the elements well and have been torn down. Not the Academy. It has expanded in size dramatically with the erection of a new dormitory and field house, along with major expansions to the library and academic building—although the museum envisioned by Harmon was never built—and all have employed the original pattern and similar materials. The structures have remained new and surprisingly modern looking. Part of this is due to an extremely rigorous maintenance program that keeps them looking fresh, with maintenance personnel acting quickly at the first sign of a crack or discoloring. The Academy's enduring, alluring appeal is also due to its incredible mountain setting.[65] Few are not moved by the windy and majestic Cadet Area, the rugged starkness of the mountains, the staggering sunsets, and the remarkable sil-

ver glow that often emanates over the Rampart Range at gloaming.

The Academy was not completed until after Hubert Harmon was gone; in fact, construction difficulties delayed its opening until the summer of 1958.[66] In his honor, the Academy administration building that houses the superintendent and his staff was named Harmon Hall. The building is on pillars so that approaching visitors can see through to the cadet campus area. In truth, Harmon probably would have preferred being memorialized with something more cadet-centric rather than an office building—perhaps the dormitory or social center. To Harmon, cadets *were* the Academy.

The winter (blue) and white (summer) parade uniforms were designed by Cecil B. DeMille. The blue uniform remains in use today with only minor alterations. The white uniform was used initially, but later modified: the white pants stayed but were mated with the blue jacket for use in the summer. Note: the gold sash on both is worn by first classmen.

Selecting the Team

While construction questions were being resolved, Harmon also needed to assemble a team to operate the Academy. He had worried about the matter for quite some time. In the fall of 1951, Harmon had written Vandenberg that he thought it appropriate to identify the dean of faculty and commandant of cadets so they could join his office, select their subordinates, and begin detailed planning. For dean, Harmon recommended four possibilities, all West Point graduates: Brigadier Generals Delmar T. Spivey, Ralph P. Swofford, Jr., and Matthew K. Deichelmann, and Colonel William S. Stone. Both Swofford and Stone had been West Point cadets when Harmon was assigned there as a tactical officer—and Stone had been a lieutenant in the 19th Bombardment Group when Harmon was its commander. Despite his junior rank, Stone was Harmon's first choice—in his letter to the chief he quoted his old friend Herman Beukema (head of the Social Science Department at West Point, in which Stone taught) as stating that Stone's "talents and performance have not been surpassed by those of any officer who has served in this department during my 20 years as head." Harmon placed him last only because he was still a colonel.[67]

For commandant, Harmon recommended in order of priority: Brigadier General Robert B. Landry, Colonel George F. Schlatter, Brigadier General Sydney D. Grubbs, Jr., and Colonel Harris E. Rogner. The first three had been cadets at West Point while Harmon was assigned there from 1929 to 1932. Harmon wanted the first dean and commandant to serve for three years; the commandant's position would then remain a three-year tour, but the dean's slot would become more permanent. Even so, the first dean would be assigned for a shorter period, presumably because Harmon thought a trial period was necessary before making a long-term commitment.[68] Colonel Stone was approved as dean and Brigadier General Thomas C. Musgrave, Harmon's old friend but not on his list, was designated the commandant. Because Academy legislation was going nowhere that year, Stone and Musgrave were released from these appointments.[69]

The following year, Harmon tried again, writing Lieutenant General Larry Kuter, the Air Force personnel chief, that he still wanted Stone for dean. Because Stone had recently been promoted to brigadier general and because a new Academy would initially consist of only one class, Kuter argued that colonels would be sufficient for the commandant and dean positions. For the former he suggested Colonel Jack G. Merrill, and for dean he recommended Colonel Dale O. Smith. Harmon agreed to both.[70] Smith was a West Point graduate, class of 1934, who flew thirty-one combat missions as a B-17 bomb group commander during the war, and had earned a doctorate in education at Stanford in 1951. In November 1952 he was the director of education at Air University.

Smith was a solid choice with excellent operational and academic credentials. He was enthusiastic about the idea of being the Academy's first dean, and from his office at Maxwell AFB where he kept his day job, he wrote long and philosophical letters to Harmon about the curriculum and faculty of the new institution. For his part, Harmon clearly enjoyed the exchanges with "Dean" Smith.[71]

In early 1954, however, Smith abruptly withdrew his name from consideration as dean. Later, he stated in an interview that he strongly objected to the role being played by Secretary Talbott: "The Secretary was treating the Air Force Academy as if it was his personal accomplishment." To Smith, the Academy was established in spite of, not because of, Talbott's actions. In addition, Smith believed that Talbott was opposed to flying at the Academy, a position at complete variance to his own. As we shall see, Smith thought flying training should be the core of the Academy experience. It also irritated Smith that Talbott alone chose the architectural firm that would build the Academy—without a nationwide competition. (This was not the case as we have seen.) Smith conceded that Harmon did much to "tone down thoughtless statements and to modify unilateral actions of the impetuous Secretary of the Air Force," but it was not enough. As a subordinate of Talbott, General Harmon could protest only so far.[72] Actually, Smith was not alone in resenting the heavy-handedness of the secretary. The first Academy chief of staff, Colonel Robert Gideon, later argued that construction was pushed too quickly: "Former Secretary Talbott's hand in this matter was one of a well-intentioned idiot's with a child's desire to run the show."[73] Harmon disagreed with these assessments and got on with Talbott quite well.

Because Smith had stepped aside, the Academy needed a new dean. In February 1954, Harmon asked once again for Stone, but by this point he was already on the major general's list, so the request was again denied. (Stone's wife later recalled that he wanted the job as the dean very badly, but General White, the vice chief, told him: "No, I won't send you out there as Dean. I'm going to send you out there as the Superintendent later." Stone thought that he was just being let down gently, but in actuality, White did indeed name Stone as superintendent in 1959.[74]) As a result of White's decision to hold back Stone, in July 1954 Brigadier General Don Z. Zimmerman was announced as the new dean.[75] It was an unusual choice. Zimmerman's name had surfaced earlier as a possible candidate, but he had not made Harmon's shortlist.[76] Nonetheless, on paper Zimmerman was a good choice. He was West Point class of 1929 and had done very well as a cadet, serving as a cadet captain and class president, while also distinguishing himself as an athlete—he was captain of the baseball team. Although a pilot, he had spent much of his career as a weatherman and had a master's degree in meteorology from Cal Tech. The Academy's official history states that Harmon requested Zimmerman on July 20, 1953, but another source argues that Harmon did not know Zimmerman, nor did his staff, and that he was appointed by the personnel chief, Lieutenant General Rosie O'Donnell, without Harmon's input.[77] The letter signed by Harmon to the chief of staff states that Zimmerman was selected "after a careful review of his records by the Deputy Chief of Staff, Personnel. He was considered outstanding for the job as Dean."[78] Given the wording used by Harmon, it appears that he was indeed left out of the decision process. Zimmerman himself maintained that he had no idea who requested him for the job, or why. The first he heard about it was when he received orders to report to Lowry.[79] In any event, it soon became apparent that it was an unhappy choice.

At a dinner that summer in the White House for the Class of 1915, hosted by its most illustrious graduate, Harmon pulled aside Herman Beukema and expressed his concerns regarding Zimmerman. Beukema opined that if Zimmerman was a weak link, then Harmon needed a strong vice dean to compensate. He mentioned a man from his Social Science Department, Colonel Robert F. McDermott.[80] "McD" was West Point, a graduate of the abbreviated class of December 1942. He had been one of those who had earned his wings while a cadet, and this experience may have contributed to his later lukewarm support for flying training at the Air Force Academy. Upon graduation, McDermott checked out in P-38s and flew combat over Germany. Following the war, he served in Washington. Significantly, his job on the Air Staff involved looking at civilian universities as possible locations to send Air Force officers for advanced degrees. In 1948, McDermott earned a master's degree in business administration from Harvard, and was then assigned to West Point. There he was not only an excellent teacher but also an indefatigable worker; hence, Beukema's recommendation to Harmon.

Although McDermott had applied for a position "on a career basis" on the Air Force Academy faculty in March 1954, he later enjoyed telling the story that he was a reluctant recruit and was caught by surprise by Harmon's job offer. According to this tale, McDermott said that he told Harmon he was pleased to be considered, but politely declined—he wanted to get back in the cockpit.

Besides, said McDermott, his orders were already cut and he was within thirty days of his port call for Japan. Harmon could not change things even if he tried. Clearly, the colonel did not know who he was dealing with. When Harmon wanted someone he was cleared to go directly to the chief. He did just that. The next day McDermott received a telegram canceling his orders and his "irrevo-cable" port call. He would be going instead to the Air Force Academy to become the vice dean and professor of economics.[81]

Others found it more difficult to say no—although the results were the same. Lieutenant Colonel Tom Corrigan, Harmon's first director of information services, knew that Harmon would ask him to come to the Academy, but he made up his mind to say no. But then, "I walked into his office and saluted. He said, 'Good morning Corrigan, how are you?' I said, 'Fine sir.' He said, 'How would you like to work for me?' I said, 'I'd love to!'"[82]

For assistant dean, Harmon chose Colonel Arthur Boudreau, the jack-of-all-trades who had been with him since 1949 and involved with Academy affairs since 1948 when he had headed the curriculum committee of the Planning Board.

The following month, September 1954, Harmon announced the appointment of the first commandant of cadets: Colonel Robert M. Stillman. "Moose" had been an All-American football player at West Point, class of 1935. Upon graduation he transferred to the Air Corps and won his wings. During the war he flew B-26s in Europe until shot down in May 1943. He spent the rest of the war in a German prisoner-of-war camp. In 1948 he had been a member of the Air University Academy Planning Board and afterwards he, like McDermott, had been assigned to the Personnel Division on the Air Staff. He was an outstanding choice to be the first commandant. Stillman was not, however, Harmon's first choice. In a letter to Rosa-Maye, who was still in San Antonio, he admitted that he had offered the job to his old friend Tommy Musgrave who had worked for him in Texas, Panama and the Solomons. But, wrote Harmon: "Since the great Tommy Musgrave was not interested we have selected 'Moose' Stillman—football player and a fine 'figger' of a man."[83]

When the Academy was officially established at Lowry on 14 August 1954, it was an under-whelming event. Only six people were present for duty: Harmon, Zimmerman, Lieutenant Colonel George C. Cooke, Major Arthur J. Witters, and Major Robert Hutto.[84] Zimmerman later recalled his experience: "I'll never forget the first time I walked into a building at Lowry where the temporary Air Force

Academy was located at that time, and the total property of the Air Force Academy was a room about 12 by 12 in size with one bare wooden table and one G.I. chair."[85] It might not have looked like much, but that would soon change.

The Academy's staff began to fill out. Lieutenant Colonel Cooke handled manpower, personnel, and administrative issues; Colonel Robert R. Gideon became Harmon's chief of staff; and Major Witters was assigned to facilities. Witters had been intensely interested in architectural plans for the Academy, and he would play a key role in that area over the next two years.[86] For operations chief, Harmon chose Colonel Thomas J. Hanley, Jr., his former aide and the son of his classmate. Hanley's assistant would be Captain John B. Wogan, also the son of a West Point classmate and old friend. Stillman was important in all of this, having worked in Air Force personnel as the chief of officer assignments prior to his appointment as commandant. In fact, one of his subordinates there was Colonel Robin Olds, the All-American football player from West Point and fighter ace who was the son of Robert Olds and the stepson of Nina Gore. Olds would later relate that he made a deliberate attempt to place as many athletes on the new Academy staff as possible. He defended this policy by stating simply that he believed collegiate athletics gave officers a sense of teamwork, discipline and aggressiveness that was unmatched. He thought it wise that the Air Force Academy benefit from such qualities.[87]

The commandant, Brigadier General Robert M. Stillman, receives his first star with the help of Harmon and Mrs. Stillman.

This was not a foolish idea. Harmon's thinking was not much different than this, and he once asked West Point if it had any data on how well athletes fared in their military careers. The results were surprising. The Military Academy responded that participation in athletics helped produce a "dynamic character" and that fully 63 percent of all graduates who became general officers had either lettered while at the Academy or at least participated in intercollegiate athletics.[88] In a letter to a friend, Harmon revealed

Superintendent Harmon signs the order formally standing up the Air Force Academy, August 14, 1954.

his strong views on this subject: "We are convinced from actual experience and rather exhaustive research that young men who are top-notch physical specimens, who have superior coordination, and who combine team play with a keen competitive spirit make the best combat fliers ... We welcome boys of this type. On the other hand, we are not remotely interested in athletes per se."[89] This last qualifying sentence was crucial. Later events would show that others did not have the same understanding.

Overall, it was an impressive and talented group; they were aggressive, opinionated, and self-confident. As a result, there were numerous disagreements among them, often heated. One of the principals later admitted that "the extremely high quality of the personnel assigned to the Academy led to sharp differences of opinion and to frequently expressed divergent views on organization, manning, faculty, and training problems."[90] The deputy commandant, Colonel Ben Cassiday, recalled the frequent arguments between McDermott and Stillman. Harmon would sit impassively and listen to both sides, never giving an indication of his thoughts until they were through. He would then simply say: "This is what we are going to do." Once Harmon had spoken, disagreement stopped.[91] Another member of this original cadre implied that the Academy staff was united in only one area—they all respected and admired Harmon. It was the common bond that kept them together and moving in the same direction.[92]

As the staff began to meet in their conference room at Lowry, it became standard procedure for all present, regardless of rank or position, to take part in discussions over all sorts of policies. Some of the faculty professors present suggested that they begin calling themselves the Academic Board—as was the practice at West Point. Stillman objected. Because they were dealing with broad matters far beyond the confines of curriculum concerns, he thought the group should be termed the Academy Board. It was a subtle but significant shift. Harmon agreed, and moved to formalize the body. Zimmerman drew up a proposal for a permanent membership that would include fourteen voting members, nine of whom would be from the faculty. When he took this proposal to Stillman, the commandant objected. One of the enduring problems at West Point was that faculty dominance of the Academic Board had thwarted all attempts at reform. Stillman did not want to replicate that problem by institutionalizing faculty hegemony at the Air Force Academy. Zimmerman withdrew his proposal. [93]

Harmon instead formed an Academy Board as of 1 August 1955 that had eleven voting members: himself, the dean plus five professors, and the commandant plus three of his directors. Under this scheme the faculty still maintained a majority—argued to be necessary for academic accreditation purposes—but it would not dominate.

For duties, Harmon approved a charter stating that the Academy Board would be responsible for the following:

- Screening nominees to enter the Academy and determining which to forward for presidential appointments
- Recommending cadets who should be disenrolled for academic, aptitude or conduct deficiencies
- Recommending qualified alternates to bring the Cadet Wing up to full strength
- Recommending which cadets, previously disenrolled, should be considered for reinstatement
- Performing other duties as directed by the superintendent. [94]

A discerning observer later raised an obvious question: why was the Academy Board not designated to review curriculum decisions or determine admission standards? [95] The answer is not clear, but perhaps Harmon wished to ensure that those key decisions remained his purview at this early stage.

Don't send my boy to West Point
The dying mother said
Don't send my boy to Annapolis
I'd rather see him dead

Don't send my boy to VMI
It's no better than the rest
But send my boy to AFA
And there he'll get the best![1]

CHAPTER 10

Finalizing the Program

In 1954, Lieutenant General Hubert Harmon commented to his wife: "I'm not an Educator, as you know, but I have an idea that by the time I finish this Air Force Academy assignment I may *be* one."[2] He was right.

We have seen that the Air University Academy Planning Board of 1948 had drafted a detailed curriculum for a proposed air academy. The Board had extensive help and advice from noted civilian educators, and foreign military schools (especially the Royal Air Force's Cranwell) were also studied for ideas on cadet education. This draft curriculum was a serious and solid effort and would remain the paradigm for the next seven years. Harmon's part-time curriculum advisor, Colonel William Stone, and his team at Bolling AFB consciously adapted the Board's report as the basis of their efforts. It would not be an exaggeration to state that the Planning Board curriculum would survive, with relatively minor tinkering, to become the Air Force Academy's actual starting point in 1955. In fact, Stone's major effort was to ensure each course recommended by the Planning Board would have an air-centric focus if at all possible. Back in 1951 when it appeared that air academy legislation would be quickly approved and the school would open within the year, some wanted simply to replicate the West Point curriculum and even import some of its faculty to teach it. As legislation stalled, that idea was dropped. Instead, Harmon's staff revised the Planning Board curriculum, while still holding firm to its basic thrust. There would be a total of 218 semester hours, 88 in the sciences (40.4 percent), 84 in the social sciences and humanities (38.5 percent), and 46 in military training (21.1 percent).[3] In comparison, the Planning Board had called for a curriculum of 39 percent science, 34 percent social sciences and humanities, and 27 percent military training.[4] Over the next four years, Harmon's curriculum advisors continued to refine the program, even drawing up detailed lesson plans and faculty notes for every course.[5] In addition, they received much help from Air University; numerous students at the Air War College wrote their theses on various aspects of the proposed air academy.[6]

Harmon remained an advocate of what he termed "a balanced curriculum." In October 1955, he argued that "Since modern air warfare touches all facets of national life, it is vital that air leaders possess also a sound knowledge of the political, economic and social factors. Thus, while the air officer must possess as a minimum a considerable technical skill in air matters, he must also be broadly educated in the social sciences and the humanities."[7] As with many other things, however, "balance" meant different things to different people.

By January 1954 the curriculum was ready to present to others. Harmon was proud of what his team had accomplished. That month he briefed his Senior Advisory Board—retired generals and old friends Tooey Spaatz, Bill Streett and Conger Pratt.[8] Harmon thought the proposed air academy curriculum was unique—no college or university in the country could boast of such a balance that emphasized both the sciences and humanities, while at the same time including a significant airmanship component. He was convinced that the new beginning to be offered by the Air Force Academy was a blessing, allowing the staff to start fresh without the crushing conformity of tradition, excessive political guidance, or instructor whims.

In 1954, however, voices at Air University began to complain that the curriculum was too social sciences and humanities oriented—there was not enough science and engineering. One claimed that the new Academy would be "70 percent cultural and 30 percent scientific."[9] Lieutenant General Larry Kuter, the Air University commander, argued that the Air Force was a far more technical service than were the Army and Navy, so it only made sense that the Air Force Academy should be more technically oriented than the other service academies.[10] He reminded Harmon that justifications for an Air Force Academy had continuously referred to the unique and highly technical nature of airpower—was it now appropriate to design a curriculum that emphasized the humanities?[11] Harmon disagreed with Kuter's criticisms. Citing the latest statistics, he noted that there were essentially two tracks: those cadets with an aptitude for foreign language would take extra language courses their senior year; other cadets would take more aeronautical courses. Language students would thus take 52.5 percent "cultural" courses and 47.5 percent technical. Other students would essentially reverse those percentages. Harmon also noted that the curriculum had been reviewed by academic experts at Purdue, Stanford, MIT and Columbia, and all had lauded the balance achieved. He concluded his response to Kuter by stating "all of the foregoing is by way of stating the facts; not an apology nor a justification."[12]

Nonetheless, in November 1954 Harmon formed an *ad hoc* committee to look at three specific areas: the freshman curriculum, the freshman schedule, and the four-year curriculum. The members of the board included Colonel Josephus A. Brown, professor of geography, McDermott, the vice dean and professor of economics, and Colonel Archie Higdon, professor of mathematics. Although the group appeared weighted in favor of "culture," the professors decreased the social sciences and humanities side by eighty-six class hours—cutting mostly from history and geography. The technical side went up seventy-one class hours, mostly in mathematics, chemistry and drawing. Overall, concerned that cadets would be overburdened, the group cut the entire curriculum by fifteen semester hours.[13]

The concern of overburdening would surface again, and for good reason. The Academy curriculum was an extremely heavy load. The average civilian university required 120-145 semester hours for graduation. The Academy plan called for an astounding 218 semester hours. Granted, some of those hours were for athletics, military training, and airmanship courses, but all those activities soaked up time.[14] And time would prove to be a commodity that cadets found in short supply.

But, as Harmon had noted, it would be impossible to please everyone. Colonel Peter R. Moody, the professor of English, was displeased with the recommendations of the *ad hoc* board, stating the change to the curriculum "veers at least thirty degrees off the previously planned course in the direction of Scientific Studies." He thought the mission of the Academy was to produce *leaders* not engineers.[15]

Harmon nonetheless accepted the recommendations of the *ad hoc* committee. Although he continued to advocate a "balanced" curriculum, strong forces pushed the course towards science. In fact, in January 1955 Brigadier General Zimmerman stated at Columbia University that the Air Force Academy would be "essentially an engineering college."[16] When some complained that he wanted the Air Force Academy to be no more than a carbon copy of West Point, the dean was unmoved. He stated that the Military Academy "had long experience in building their curriculum" and it had performed its mission of turning out qualified military officers with enormous success.[17] Zimmerman later maintained that he had attended the University of Oregon, American University, Cal Tech, the University of Hawaii, the Air Corps Tactical School, the Command and General Staff School, and the Imperial Defence College in London; yet, West Point was superior to all of them! He then visited several universities after he became dean, seeking ideas for the new Academy curriculum, but concluded they had little to offer over what West Point was doing. To him, the mission of the Air Force Academy was to produce second lieutenants; courses in foreign policy and international relations would do nothing to advance cadets towards that goal.[18] It was a stark view.

After all of these discussions, Harmon was becoming ambivalent on the curriculum's thrust. In a letter to Colonel George "Abe" Lincoln he wrote: "anyway you cut it, we are trying to build an Air Force version of West Point, and whatever success we have will be a tribute, directly or indirectly, to our dear old Alma Mater on the Hudson."[19] In other words, he appreciated the focus of the West Point curriculum, at least in some particulars; nonetheless, in March 1955 Harmon asked Zimmerman to study the idea of cadets choosing academic "concentrations." He suggested that cadets take additional courses in areas of specialization, so that if an officer later attended graduate school, he would need to take fewer prerequisites. This suggestion went nowhere at the time—Zimmerman was opposed to the notion—but clearly this was a precursor to the ideas that McDermott would push so effectively a few years later.[20]

The murmurings over the ideal curriculum were inevitable and, indeed, a positive occurrence in that they forced a continuing examination and debate among those responsible for making the Academy work. Harmon was not overly concerned by these disagreements. In February 1955, he wrote Bruce Hopper at Harvard: "Figuratively speaking, the hinges are nearly on, and given a little oiling our doors will open in July with, I hope, a minimum of squeaks and groans."[21] Note that although Harmon was pushing for "culture," he chose a mechanical metaphor to describe the state of affairs.

As a result of continual adjustments, the curriculum actually published in the first Air Force Academy catalog was not the same as that approved by Harmon on April 29, 1955—barely two months before the first class arrived. The actual curriculum, as the *ad hoc* committee had recommended and Harmon had agreed, decreased the freshman workload by over twelve semester hours.

To sum up this long and arduous journey: the Academy curriculum that greeted the first class of cadets in September 1955 was similar to that roughed out by the Air University Planning Board in 1948. It was a unique academic approach in that it contained a set curriculum fairly equally distributed between the sciences and engineering on one hand, and the social sciences and humanities on the other. The balance was slightly in favor of the former, and indeed, still is. It was a balance that had detractors on both sides—it is probable that Harmon would have preferred more emphasis on the humanities, but the weight given these subjects was far greater than at either West Point or Annapolis. In that sense, Harmon's long-held beliefs on the importance of a broad education were implemented at the Air Force Academy. On the other hand, the faculty was exclusively military and would largely remain so for the next four decades. Initially, this military faculty had modest academic credentials—although somewhat higher than those of the officers at either West Point or Annapolis. The Air Force Academy recognized this was a problem, however, and moved quickly to upgrade the credentials of its faculty by instituting a robust program that would send dozens of officers each year to civilian universities to obtain advanced degrees.

The most significant shortcoming in the academic program was its rigidity. As at West Point, there was no validation credit for entering cadets who had prior college. There were no electives, and there were no academic majors. To Harmon, this was a concern, but he could do little about it at this early stage. It would be left for the new superintendent and dean to rectify this deficiency.[22]

More contentious than the discussion of science versus culture was the debate over the role of flying training and how it would be integrated into the cadet schedule. This had been a controversial matter since World War II. In essence, the major question revolved around whether cadets would receive *pilot training*—and by this it was meant they would graduate from the Academy with pilot wings. Would they receive *flying training,* which implied a less intensive navigator program? Or would they simply receive *flying indoctrination*—cadets would fly as passengers in military jets on orientation rides, and perhaps also take light airplane lessons as first classmen? Early plans had called merely for flying indoctrination with thirty-five hours of flight time. That eventually changed. Although all involved with the issue wanted some type of flying program to distinguish the Academy from a civilian school, disagreements arose over how much flying cadets would receive, in what types of aircraft, and to what end. The answer to these questions in turn led to the considerations of time and cost.

Typically, undergraduate pilot training in the Air Force lasted a full year with each weekday filled with ground school or flying. Could that much time be carved out of the cadet schedule, even if over a four-year period? As we have seen, the cost of such a program was expensive: $25 million to buy the airplanes and another $10 million per year to operate and maintain them.

When Harmon asked Spaatz about the issue, the former chief was characteristically blunt: "every graduate ought to be able to fly a plane."[23] In the face of varied inputs, Harmon opted for a hybrid of sorts: all cadets would receive flight training and navigator wings upon graduation, but first classmen would also be given pilot indoctrination lessons. Harmon arrived at this decision because he realized that a robust flying program was essential—many high-ranking officers in the Air Force expected it, as did many members of Congress. In addition, to ignore flying would no doubt discourage prospective young men from applying to the Academy, would lower morale, and would leave graduates behind their ROTC contemporaries who *were* receiving flying training in their programs.[24] Yet, it was a full slate, and when Stillman first brought the complete four-year plan to him, Harmon was taken aback, asking "can you do it all?"[25] They would try.

Harmon cuts the cake prepared by his staff on the occasion of the Academy's first birthday.

The initial concern over how flying training would impact cadet study time for academic classes was temporarily muted by the fact that the dean-designate, Brigadier General Dale Smith, was a strong advocate of flying at the air academy. In fact, Smith wrote Harmon in December 1952 that flying "should be basic to our curriculum." He dismissed the notion that flying training would so occupy a cadet's time as to hurt his academic performance. Moreover, he objected to the opinion that academic courses should be primary while courses like flying, athletics, and military training were secondary and should be taught only after the academic day was complete. To Smith, the latter subjects were crucial to the mission of an air academy and did not belong in the "back seat." He disputed negative references to flying training at West Point during the war, arguing that cadets were then on a three-year program, so they could ill-afford the time for flying. Also, the weather in New York was dreadful in the winter, and Stewart Field was twelve miles from the cadet area, on the other side of Stormking Mountain. These conditions would not be present at a new Air Force Academy. [26]

When Smith decided not to become dean, the controversy over flying training rekindled. In January 1953, a board of general officers was convened by General Vandenberg at Harmon's request to review the question of flying training and its place in the curriculum. The board argued that the academy's academic program should lead to a bachelor of science degree—which necessitated a majority of the course work for all cadets to be in the scientific/technical fields. As for flying training, "global indoctrination" should be included in the curriculum—this meant essentially an air observer course combined with plans for cadets to travel extensively, not only around the US, but overseas as well. Finally, the generals stated that cadets should complete the equivalent of Phase I Primary Flying Training.[27] In short, the board concurred with Harmon's opinion.

The air observer course, which would lead to navigator wings, was taken seriously by the Air Staff. In June 1954, the chief of the Flying Training Division in personnel wrote bluntly that any cadet failing to complete that course should be eliminated from the Academy. He conceded, however, that if a graduate then failed to complete pilot training and win his wings, he would not lose his commission![28]

The first official catalog of the Academy, for 1954-55, took the approach that Harmon had outlined before Congress in January 1954: all cadets entering the Academy had to be physically qualified to become pilots—a fairly high physical requirement. Over four years a cadet would become a qualified navigator and receive wings. He would receive 171 hours of flight time and a further 385 hours on the ground.[29] The fact that the interim Academy would be located at Lowry AFB, an Air Training Command base, made such a heavy flying program feasible. What Academy officials seemed to ignore, however, was that the permanent site at Colorado Springs would be sixty miles from Lowry—a daily commute of that distance was totally impractical. Moreover, although a sizeable airfield would eventually be built on Academy grounds, physical constraints meant that neither large cargo aircraft nor jets could use it.

A Quality Faculty

Another question that caused considerable debate concerned faculty composition. Recall that when Harmon was a cadet—and when he returned as a tactical officer in 1929—the West Point faculty was almost exclusively military. Exceptions included three instructors in foreign languages, the bandmaster, dentist, and a few others. When the Department of History was formed as a separate entity in 1918, its first head was brought in from civilian life—and then promptly commissioned as a lieutenant colonel so he could wear a uniform in class. West Point believed that an all-military faculty was essential to instill a proper sense of discipline and professional motivation to cadets.

When serious discussions first began in 1948 regarding the curriculum and faculty for an air academy, the Planning Board favored a mixed faculty of military and civilian instructors. The Planning Board's argument seemed to make sense—a quality education demanded a quality faculty, and since the Air Force was not able to determine which officers were even qualified to teach at an academy, the use of civilian professors appeared essential.[30]

There the matter stood until March 1951 when Harmon's curriculum advisers looked at the issue anew. The fundamental question was what qualifications were necessary to teach at the academy? The response included three basic requirements: military experience, the "desirability" of a graduate degree, and enthusiasm. Previous teaching experience was not deemed necessary.[31] This was a steep fall from the idealistic words of the Planning Board. Indeed, as late as March 1953, Colonel Dale Smith wrote Harmon that the three criteria for faculty officers should be that they were "enthusiastic volunteers," know their subject thoroughly, and "be equipped with a broad general knowledge as demonstrated by seasoned argument and experience. This would normally involve at least a Bachelors Degree." Such weak criteria were hardly inspiring or conducive to fielding an outstanding faculty. Furthermore, Smith argued that "all faculty members will be in uniform." If it were absolutely necessary to hire civilians, they should immediately be commissioned into the Air Force.[32] Although Smith dropped out of the picture by the end of the year, his ideas lived on.

Harmon continued to lean towards a mixed faculty, long believing that West Point's curriculum was insufficiently broad and an all-military faculty would represent too narrow a viewpoint. In March 1952 he expressed his thoughts on the subject to Abe Lincoln, who would soon replace Herman Beukema as head of West Point's Social Science Department: "I personally do not have the horror of employing civilians that has prevailed and may still prevail at West Point ... As a matter of fact, we hope to set up some sort of system under which we could 'borrow' instructors for three or four years from the best universities. These could keep our faculty relatively youthful and insure the continued infusion of new blood."[33] It was an interesting idea, but it would soon be abandoned.

Harmon then wrote Beukema, pushing him on the issue as well. On 13 April he wrote his old friend: "The use of officer instructors in the Academic Departments is inefficient and extravagant. It is impossible to tell in advance whether or not a selected officer will prove to be an effective teacher. At best he is not trained in the art of teaching." He continued that "carefully selected civilian instructors, men who have already the necessary educational background *and* the demonstrated ability, should be able to do a far better job."[34] This is a remarkably candid letter, and far more emphatic on the issue of faculty composition than

Harmon and the first dean, Brigadier General Don Z. Zimmerman, discuss the curriculum.

anything else Harmon wrote. It is possible that he was deliberately overstating the case in order to provoke a spirited response from Beukema. He got just that.

Beukema shot back that he was in "complete and violent disagreement" with Harmon's argument. Essentially, he argued that a careful selection process would ensure quality officers were chosen as teachers and to attend graduate school. In addition, he warned: "don't conclude that by limiting your selection to civilian teachers you are going to have an assured safe ride to effective teaching." He went on to cite examples of poor-quality instruction at major universities.[35] It was a cogent and forceful letter and Harmon was receptive to its message.

When Harmon went before an Air Force-wide personnel conference that month, he said it was probable that military officers would teach the science courses, but the social sciences and humanities offerings could be taught by civilians. The four ranks within the faculty would be professor (of whom twenty-one would be "permanent" as at West Point), associate professor, assistant professor, and instructor.[36] As it turned out, however, the forces pushing for an all-military faculty were proving to be quite strong. Zimmerman wanted an all-military faculty, preferably all pilots, and his deputy, McDermott, was "vehemently opposed" to civilians on the faculty, using the standard argument that civilians merely taught the lesson, but officers also served as professional role models. He shrugged off questions of an all-military faculty lacking academic credentials, stating simply that the Air Force Academy's faculty would be better qualified than that of West Point.[37]

In August 1954, a member of Harmon's staff responded to an inquiry by stating that there would probably be no civilian faculty members at the Academy. Soon after, reservists were also nudged aside: the faculty would be staffed exclusively by Regular officers.[38] Although this strict policy was not carried out, it is apparent there were very strong feelings on this issue on Harmon's staff. The following month Harmon admitted to Virgil Hancher, who had helped him to screen faculty applicants, that the faculty would be all-military for at least the first year; "What we shall do later on, as to civilian faculty members, is a very big and difficult problem, yet to be resolved."[39]

In October 1954 the criteria for the Academy faculty was promulgated:[40]

- Professors were to select their instructors
- At least one-half of the faculty was to be rated (wear wings)
- If the professor was non-rated, his deputy should be rated
- Effectiveness reports for prospective instructors should have ratings of

no lower than "very fine" or "outstanding"

- Graduates of the two service academies and honor military colleges (such as Virginia Military Institute and the Citadel) should be well represented
- Selection would be Air-Force wide
- Whenever possible, the Academy should draw from the rosters of West Point and Air Force Institute of Technology graduates who had demonstrated high instructor potential
- Professional experience should be carefully considered in light of accrediting agency policies
- An effort should be made to secure individuals with outstanding war records or who had achieved national recognition
- At least one-half of the faculty should be Regular officers
- At least one-fourth should be graduates of the service academies.

Soon after the criteria had been announced, the process began for hiring the first fifty-seven instructors and assigning them to Lowry AFB so they could finalize the curriculum and prepare the course syllabi in anticipation of the arrival of cadets the following summer. (Although Harmon initially considered the idea of officers from other services, he ultimately rejected it—at least for the next two to three years.[41]) All fifty-seven were Air Force officers; the majority were Regulars, and over half were pilots. As for academic qualifications, eight held doctorates— although only one of these was a department head; nine had bachelor's degrees, and the bulk of the faculty, 67 percent, had a master's degree.[42]

In short, despite all the talk of a broad approach that would involve civilian instructors teaching at least the social sciences and humanities courses, the initial faculty would consist of military officers with modest academic credentials.

One year later, in July 1956, there were eighty instructors on board at Lowry—all military officers. Of those, twenty had doctorates, forty-six had a master's degree, and the remaining fourteen had only a bachelor's degree. At that time there was considerable talk of visiting professors being brought in—civilian professors from noteworthy colleges and universities to teach for several weeks. Yet, at the Board of Visitors meeting the following month (April 1956), Harmon conceded that he did not foresee hiring any civilians for at least three or four years: "We feel that in the formative years, at least, it is important to have instructors who are familiar with the organization, the problems, the

Brigadier General Robert M. Stillman, Harmon, and Colonel Robert F. McDermott stand in front of the Academy headquarters at Lowry AFB in 1956.

traditions, and the objectives of the Air Force."[43]

The Board received this news without enthusiasm. In fact, Dr. Virgil Hancher, Harmon's colleague on the Site Selection Commission and still president of the University of Iowa, stated bluntly that this all-military stance sounded like "academic interbreeding" and questioned the Academy's academic legitimacy.[44] Harmon held firm. Obviously, his staff had changed his mind on the matter. Harmon's replacement as superintendent also advocated an all-military faculty, later commenting that the civilian instructors at Annapolis "were mere castoffs from civilian colleges."[45] It would be decades before civilian professors became fixtures at the Air Force Academy.

A related question concerned who would train the new cadets in military matters. This too had been discussed for years. Harmon had come to believe it was best to have Air Force officers serve as surrogate upperclassmen for the initial classes. General Twining agreed, and in June 1954 suggested that bachelor officers be assigned as Air Training Officers (ATOs). They would supervise a Cadet Wing (formally established on 1 March 1955) that would eventually consist of six groups and twenty-four squadrons of 100 men each. In a letter to Air Training Command, General Stillman wrote that he wanted officers fresh out of pilot training. They should be "of the highest type obtainable, must be regular, or potential regular officers, have a good educational and military background and possess more than average qualities of leadership. Athletic proficiency is also highly desirable."[46]

Of the sixty-six ATOs in the initial cadre, eight were Annapolis graduates, eleven were West Point graduates, twenty-three had been commissioned from ROTC, and twenty-four had been through the Aviation Cadet program.[47] This was a gratifyingly wide and broad-based mix of officers. One of the more outstanding and well-remembered of this group was then-Second Lieutenant Jerry

O'Malley, who would later wear four stars. O'Malley was so highly regarded that when he initially expressed reluctance to take the job as ATO because he wanted to marry, Harmon promptly jettisoned the bachelor requirement. O'Malley, a West Point graduate, was appointed the first Cadet Wing commander.[48] Over each cadet squadron and the ATOs would be an air officer commanding (AOC), usually at the rank of captain. These officers would fulfill the functions of the tactical officers at West Point. In fact, that term had initially been proposed but Harmon did not like it—"they aren't doing anything tactical." Colonel Ben Cassiday (the vice commandant), who had served in Britain, suggested the term used by the RAF—air officer commanding. Harmon liked it.[49]

The Pace Quickens

On 27 July 1954, Harmon officially assumed command of the Air Force Academy at Lowry AFB and became the first superintendent. Colonel Robert L. Petit took over Harmon's former position as Special Assistant for Air Academy Matters with an office in the Pentagon. Petit's job was to be the focal point on the Air Staff for issues relating to the Academy—he would be a two-way communications conduit between Washington and Colorado. Significantly, the Academy was put into the same status as an Air Force major command (equivalent, for example, to Air Training Command), which reported directly to the chief of staff without an intervening organizational layer. Some, especially those at

The Air Force Academy compound at Lowry AFB in 1955.

Maxwell, thought the Academy should have been placed under the jurisdiction of the Air University commander.[50]

An area at Lowry AFB was assigned to the Academy, and in November 1954 contracts were let for the rehabilitation and modification of twenty-seven barracks. Congress had allocated $1 million for such projects, but it was soon realized this would not be enough. The Academy's installation chief, Major Arthur Witters, sat down with the Lowry civil engineers and suggested that "the Base submit some M&O [maintenance and operations] projects to pick up items which could not be identifiably tied to the Academy. Items such as curbs, sidewalks, and planting the big parade ground were submitted." This clever ploy saved $130,000.[51]

Even so, Academy personnel later complained that they received only lukewarm support from Lowry. Because funding was slow to come through the pipeline, much had to be begged and borrowed from the host base. The first Academy chief of staff, Colonel Robert Gideon, later wrote that the Lowry commander "had never operated a first-class establishment and could not understand, in fact he resented, problems associated with establishing one of the USAF's most important organizations, the Academy."[52] In July, Harmon wrote ATC that "we are still having troubles with the high command at Lowry AFB on the question of the suitability of quarters for bachelor officers"—and at that time there were seventy-two such officers, mostly ATOs.[53] One officer expressed his frustration regarding the lack of cooperation in a memo: "Notwithstanding the lack of logic, common ordinary Western hospitality, precedent and *authority*, I am firmly convinced that Wing Headquarters of Lowry AFB intends to proceed merrily on the way in continuing to review all purchase documents covering this Headquarters, regardless of the fact that the documents cite USAF Academy funds."[54] Fortunately, the Pentagon and ATC were responsive and supportive, largely because Secretary Talbott was a strong advocate. Such friction was probably inevitable; after all, Lowry AFB was a major ATC base and the Academy—its people seen as prima donnas by base personnel—was merely a temporary tenant. Nonetheless, most of the work was completed by Dedication Day the following July.

Harmon's plan for selecting cadets was a variation of the West Point and Annapolis systems. Instead of senators and representatives appointing primary and alternate candidates, Harmon received an exception for the Academy's first four years that called for each member to nominate ten men: the Academy would then select the most qualified. For the first class, Harmon wanted 300 cadets. Ideally, these would be "Rhodes Scholar" types. To one interviewer he stated:

> We want in this Academy boys who are intelligent, of course, but we want to get the emphasis on leadership. We want young men who want to fight, young men who want to fight in the air for their country. We want courageous fellows, youths who want to take a challenge and meet it. We want the venturesome type, the pioneer lad. We'll give him plenty of opportunities to exploit these traits.[55]

Lieutenant General Rosie O'Donnell was equally pithy. He wanted "the kind of man with good appetites and the ability to control them; men with zip, interest, dedication, and inquisitive minds—the kind of fellows you'd want your daughter to marry."[56] Well, that would be a bit difficult to ensure.

Harmon intended that the Academy grow to its authorized strength of 2,496 over a period of several years. Based on the West Point attrition rate of 22.8 percent, an incoming class would eventually average 775 cadets, and the Academy would build to that number by 1965. The Air Staff, including Talbott, thought that progression a bit slow. Instead, it was agreed that the first class would be 300, followed by 400, then 625; the number of 775 entering cadets would be achieved in 1962.[57] To ensure a healthy pool of applicants, Harmon wanted officers to spread out all over the country as "talent scouts" to find and encourage prospective cadets. He himself gave dozens of talks all over the nation. His public affairs officer later stated that Harmon never turned down a speaking engagement.[58] It was a grueling schedule, but the efforts paid off. One particularly memorable event was Harmon giving his pitch for the Academy on television to Edgar Bergen and his dummy, Charlie McCarthy. Bergen, an outstanding ventriloquist, was so convincing that Harmon found himself mesmerized: "I honestly talked to that dummy, Charlie! I talked to *Charlie* because I had the feeling it was Charlie talking to me, not Edgar."[59] The show was nominated for a Peabody Award.

By April 1955 over 6,000 applications had been received for the Class of 1959—twice the number applying to either West Point or Annapolis.[60] The eligibility criteria for the first class were as follows:

- Be at least 17 years of age
- Must not have reached age 22 by 1 July 1955
- Be a male citizen of the United States
- Be of good moral character

- Be unmarried and must never have been married
- Be a resident of the state or district from which nominated
- Stand between 5'4" and 6'4" and be within designated weight limits
- Be medically qualified for flying[61]

All prospective cadets were required to take a special Air Force Pilot Aptitude Test, the College Entrance Examination Board Test, and a physical.

Everyone recognized that these should not be the only standards for entrance. Harmon therefore appointed the Admissions Criteria Committee to develop a suitable formula for selecting cadets. Basically, points were allocated for high school grades and standing, athletics, extracurricular activities, and even work outside of school. If an applicant was in a leadership position in any of these areas—class officer or team captain for example—he received additional points.[62] Part of the reason for this scheme was Harmon's concern that sons of military personnel would be at a disadvantage compared to civilian students because they had moved around so much during their school years. They would also probably not, therefore, have had the opportunity to become class officers or team captains. Other activities, like "delivering papers" or other similar endeavors, could therefore demonstrate leadership potential. Using this "whole man" system, a board of senior officers then reviewed the file on each applicant, quickly eliminating 1,500. It seemed like a reasonable system—until it was necessary to narrow the numbers to 300 new cadets.

At a climactic meeting on May 2, 1955, key Academy officials met to select the first class. Problems surfaced quickly when it was realized that the agreed-upon formula meant that twenty-one of the forty-four athletes that Colonel Robert V. Whitlow, the athletic director, had recruited for the Academy would not be chosen. Whitlow therefore pushed for what he termed a "J Factor"—the Academy should use "judgment" to give recruited athletes—most of them football players—an added boost to get them within the acceptable point range. McDermott, the vice dean, strenuously objected, arguing that this "J Factor skewed the entire selection process." After hours of fruitless debate, Zimmerman told McDermott to go back to his office; the Committee would handle matters without him. McDermott was outraged but there was nothing he could do. In his absence, the process moved on without further hitches—and Whitlow got his athletes. Harmon tried to soften the blow by telling McDermott: "I may be dumb, but I am honest, and I will assure you that nothing dishonest will be done.

The solution may not be the one your committee recommended, but it will be an honest solution to the problem." [63] Eventually, the Board settled on 306 prospective cadets; they would report to Lowry AFB on 11 July 1955.

It was an impressive group of young men. Of these 306, 57 had been members of their high school student councils; 67 had been class officers; 77 had won scholastic awards; 24 were athletic team captains, and 36 had been members of the Civil Air Patrol. One cadet was the son of a Medal of Honor recipient ("Pappy" Boyington, the Marine Corps fighter ace in the Pacific during World War II), and 44 others were the sons of military fathers, including five wearing stars. The average cadet was 5'10" and weighed 165 lbs., was 18 years old, and had an I.Q. of 125.5.[64] Even so, it soon became apparent that high school achievement did not automatically translate into success as a cadet. Motivation—would a cadet *want* to be at the Academy and be willing to pay the price necessary to excel—was the key factor, and it was not predictive. As the Academy registrar noted: "As yet, we have not found a test that will properly measure motivation and eliminate such cases prior to their arrival at the Academy."[65] Looking ahead, 207 of these men would graduate and 206 of the 306 who entered the Academy would receive commissions—a 32 percent attrition rate.[66] One would be a Rhodes Scholar—Bradley Hosmer, who would finish his career as the Academy superintendent and a lieutenant general. Three others would eventually become full generals: Michael Carns, Hansford T. Johnson, and Robert Oaks. Overall, nineteen of the first class would become generals. Brock Strom, the football team's captain, would be named an All American.[67] Yes, it was an impressive group indeed.

At the end of June, Harmon traveled to Washington to give one last briefing to the Air Force Council before the first class was due to arrive. The briefing was well received. General Twining commented that when all was said and done, the Academy's success would be determined by the type of leaders it produced. He emphasized the importance of toughness, discipline, and thoroughness. To him, inculcating these qualities was even more important than academics and athletics. In an interesting comment, Twining also stated that athletics should not be over-emphasized. The teams should be built up slowly, with primary emphasis on "building outstanding leaders." The chief was, however, still undecided on the nature of the Academy's flying program. He suggested that the entire matter of airfield construction at the permanent site be deferred.[68]

The stage was set. Dedication Day was to be a long-remembered and historic occasion. The young men arrived at Lowry AFB from all over the country and were issued cadet uniforms—their sizes had been obtained in advance—given haircuts, sworn in, and then quickly given the rudiments of marching in formation. Around 3,000 dignitaries and guests arrived that afternoon to watch the opening ceremonies, among them the Air Force secretary and chief of staff, members of Congress, foreign diplomats, family and friends, and cadet/midshipman contingents from West Point and Annapolis. The president had wanted to attend but was ailing. Special guests included aviation pioneers Generals Benjamin Foulois and Frank Lahm. The event was televised and narrated by Walter Cronkite. Guests could visit the barracks and classrooms and see the architectural models for the permanent site.

At 1500 the band began to play, and the West Point cadets and Annapolis midshipmen marched onto the field followed by the new Air Force Academy cadets. Formations of bombers and fighters roared overhead. The "Thunderbirds," the Air Force aerial demonstration team, also performed. Close observers would have noted, however, that one of the planes usually involved in the aerobatic maneuvers was absent. It seems that the evening before, one pilot had gotten into a scrape with the Denver police. Strong drink was involved. Lieutenant Colonel

The first cadet class arrives at Lowry AFB in July 1955.

Gordon Culver, the Academy protocol officer, recalled hearing of this incident late on the night of 10 July. He hurried down to the police station to see if he could talk the police into releasing the star of the morrow's airshow. They were reluctant, but repeated cajoling and promises of endless good will finally caused them to relent—until the drunken fighter pilot, known to generations of cadets only as "Black Bart," walked out of his cell and promptly punched another cop in the nose. Back in the slammer he went and no amount of talking would

In a sketch by Henry Koehler, Secretary Talbott speaks on Dedication Day, July 11, 1955.

bust him loose. Culver was, however, able to kill the story of the incident that the *Rocky Mountain News* was planning to run the next day.[69]

No matter. Secretary Talbott gave a speech that outlined the dangerous world situation dominated by atomic weapons and hostile enemies. The Academy was brought into existence to produce officers with the discipline and leadership to keep the peace in a troubled world.[70]

General Harmon followed. He began with a statement elegant in its simplicity: "Future air commanders are gathering at the new Air Force Academy." The cadets assembled before him represented a "new breed of pioneer" dedicated to their country and intent on an endless search for a solution to the nation's problems. He wished these young men congratulations, encouragement, and "God Speed" in their adventure.[71]

Overall, it was a memorable ceremony. One attendee later wrote to Harmon: "As to the dedication ceremony, it will always remain a high vivid thing in my memory. It was appropriate, military, spine-tingling, short, to-the-point, like a dramatic story that leaves the reader with a lump in his throat looking with awe and hope at the future."[72]

CHAPTER 11

"Instruction, Experience, and Motivation"

The mission of the United States Air Force Academy is to provide instruction, experience, and motivation to each cadet so that he will graduate with the qualities of leadership and knowledge required of an officer in the United States Air Force, and with a basis for continued development throughout a lifetime of service to his country, leading to readiness for responsibilities as a future air commander.

S uch was the mission statement devised for the new Air Force Academy in 1955. Harmon had argued in 1948 that getting the mission statement "right" was key, simply because all else would flow from it. The accuracy and applicability of that premise is as true today as it was then. Any organization, of any type, must first begin with the basics: it must define what it is and what it is about. The Air Force Academy mission statement would be a matter of continued debate. The vision noted above stated that the goal of the Academy was to produce future air commanders; payoff was something that would occur only far down the road. The Academy planted seeds, which, hopefully, would one day bear fruit. The opposite thrust of such a mission statement would be a more short-range focus—to produce qualified second lieutenants who could, soon after commissioning, become quality officers and make an impact—an impact greater than that provided by ROTC or OCS graduates who obtained their commissions at far less cost to the taxpayer. As we saw, this was the belief held by General Zimmerman. The tension between short and long-term goals was inherent in the Academy's mission. How to manage this tension, which is critical to the successful functioning of any service academy, has been a subject of debate for fifty years.

★ ★ ★

The glow from the stirring Dedication Ceremony on 11 July 1955 ended quickly. Upon returning to the barracks after the festivities, the new "Doolies," as they were soon called—from "doolus" meaning "slave"—were set upon by the ATOs. These young officers in their distinctive uniforms would become the new cadets' constant companions and would remain so for the first two years of Academy operation and the third summer training period. A number of them would be in the barracks twenty-four hours a day. They were the officers who cadets dealt with most closely on a daily basis, soon inspiring a not untypical love/hate relationship. As one cadet ditty phrased it, "and when you go below, you'll find the devil is an ATO."[1] Yet, in later years the cadets and ATOs became fast friends, and all mingled at future Academy reunions. Harmon had counseled the ATOs carefully about how to fulfill their duties as role models and training instructors. He told them that they must act like officers. Rather than screaming at the new cadets, they should say something along the lines of "I do not believe, Mr. Malanaphy, that you are making a sufficient effort to stand up like an airman. Raise your chest."[2] One unusual self-appointed task of the ATOs was to teach cadets about suitable pranks. Thus, it was the ATOs who painted a Navy plane on the flight line with "Beat Navy" signs before the first athletic contest with the sister academy.[3] Of interest, most of the ATOs were fighter pilots—Stillman wanted them because of their dash and aggressiveness—and this fact much irritated General LeMay at SAC.[4] One should also note that flying was still a precarious occupation in those days—four ATOs were killed in plane crashes during their tours at Lowry.

Over six weeks in the summer of 1955, the ATOs and other members of the commandant's staff administered 270 hours of military instruction, 30 of flying training, and another 72 of physical education. The basic military training was typical: military introduction, drill, rifle manual, marching, sentry duties, an introduction to the Air Force and its heritage, and an introduction to an Honor Code.[5] On the last, more later.

It was a busy schedule: up at 0550, breakfast, drill and physical training until lunch; then more drill, marching, and rifle manual until dinner; that was followed by lectures and then time to clean rooms and uniforms, and to write letters. For field training, the cadets marched fifteen miles out to the Lowry bombing range where they learned small unit tactics, individual combat, ground warfare, field fortifications, and map reading. There was a great deal of this, far more than some thought necessary for future airmen. McDermott, upon seeing cadets engaging in bayonet practice, derisively referred to the encampment as "Fort Stillman." After field training, the basic cadets returned to their barracks at Lowry and became fourth classmen.

Classes were to begin on 7 September 1955. The situation on the faculty was frenetic. One professor later recalled that there were at least thirty different class schedules generated, studied, and rejected in the months preceding the start of academics.[6] Instructors had been brought to Lowry several months before classes were scheduled to begin. For the most part, the first officers assigned to the Academy were those slotted to teach freshman courses. Those expected to teach sophomore classes would be in place no later than the summer of 1956. Harmon had initially hoped that all new instructors would have attended a civilian university for a "refresher course" and also have completed the Academic Instructor's Course at Air University. Time constraints put these ideas on hold. Most new officers arrived expecting a three-year tour, which could be extended to four years. Under unusual circumstances a fifth year could be added with Headquarters USAF approval.[7] Harmon thought this relatively stable rotation system was a positive factor: "We have a continuing advantage in our system of selection and rotation of instructors which will tend to preclude stagnation in our teaching methods and curriculum development."[8]

Harmon was referring to plans to continually upgrade the faculty by sending selected officers back to school for advanced degrees. This was needed to bring the academic quality of the Academy faculty up to acceptable levels. In practice, department heads would select officers, who were then approved by the dean and superintendent. Once approved, the departments would work with the Air Force Institute of Technology (the descendent of the Engineering School that Harmon had attended in 1925) to identify the appropriate graduate schools.[9]

The air at Lowry crackled with enthusiasm and expectation. The young instructors, and even their more experienced seniors, saw it as an exciting time. They were starting fresh, with a blank slate. It was impossible to ignore the shadow of West Point traditions and routines, but there was a chance here to shake loose from them—to create a curriculum for an institution established to fulfill a new and unique mission.[10] It was a heady time to be at Lowry AFB.

Many Academy organizations, such as the Library and the Athletic Department, had to begin from scratch. For the Library this meant not only hiring a large and knowledgeable staff, but also finding and purchasing the tens of thousands of books and articles needed to support cadet and faculty research.[11] The Athletic Department was equally busy, hiring physical education instructors and coaches, building a swimming pool and baseball diamonds, and buying hundreds of pieces of athletic equipment. Little thought had been given to this function in previous Academy studies. Since military regulations prohibited the use of appropriated funds for intercollegiate athletics, the Air Force Academy Athletic Association was formed to raise money to fund the many Academy teams. The Association soon provided the cash "to buy everything from jock straps to blocking machines."[12]

There were a host of things that the faculty members had to get straight—one of these was textbooks. If the faculty truly wished to make each course air-centric, then existing textbooks were inadequate. The average mathematics, mechanics or physics text, to say nothing of those for English and foreign languages, did not have a military—much less an aviation—audience in mind. As a result, as at West Point, instructors at Lowry scrambled to write their own textbooks. The Chemistry and Law departments took the lead in this area.[13]

Similarly, the engineering and science departments needed to design and build laboratories for their courses. How could these facilities be designed with airmen in mind? In the case of aeronautics and aerodynamics courses this would not be a problem. With the other disciplines, however, such unique designs would be problematic.[14] Moreover, how much would such labs cost? No one knew, so the budget officers were flying blind for much of this early period.[15]

As a way of highlighting the issue of an air-centric curriculum, General Zimmerman told his faculty that he thought nuclear warfare ought to be a main underpinning of the Academy's academic program. In other words, political science, international relations, and history courses should emphasize nuclear

Harmon on his way to work at the Academy in 1955.

diplomacy and world disarmament issues. Science and engineering courses should study nuclear technology. The faculty balked at this notion, arguing that it smacked of tampering for the sake of contemporary concerns. Would such a focus be relevant a decade hence? Zimmerman was warned that such a direction could set a precedent that would ring a discordant tone when accreditation agencies came to call. One historian has written that this incident demonstrated that Zimmerman was not cut out for the job of dean. Simply, he did not know the difference between training and education.[16]

It was becoming increasingly clear through the summer and fall of 1955 that General Zimmerman was having difficulties as dean. McDermott later said that Zimmerman "was not prepared. He wasn't a teacher, had no natural talents there."[17] Colonel George Fagan, the head of the Academy Library, noted that although Zimmerman "looked like a Dean," he was "fuzzy." Fagan remembered that the dean "didn't have answers, he didn't know, he was puzzled about the core curriculum."[18] A more stark assessment came from Harmon's chief of staff, Colonel Robert Gideon: Zimmerman was "rather neurotic" and "an intellectual nut." Gideon argued that "as he became more and more unreasonable and impossible, stories from Air Force generals trickled down to the effect that they believed his assignment was a gross mistake in the first place. Unfortunately, because of General Harmon's health, heavy schedule and kind nature, General Zimmerman was allowed to screw up Academy affairs for too long a period before he was fired."[19]

Harmon finally acted. In March 1955 he had flown to Washington to discuss the Zimmerman problem with General O'Donnell. Even so, it was not until November that he finally summoned the dean to his office. As Zimmerman remembered it: "General Harmon called me in and made these allegations of things that seemed to be wrong with what I had been doing. I vehemently protested every one of them." When later asked what Harmon's complaints were, Zimmerman could only recall being accused of trying to "throttle or control the departments and not give them a free voice." The entire encounter hit him like "a complete thunderbolt."[20] On 1 December 1955, Zimmerman was relieved. Surprisingly, however, Harmon then elected to assume the duties of dean himself. McDermott remained the vice dean and Boudreau moved over to become the director of admissions. It is likely that Harmon took this unusual step because he was reluctant to commit to a new dean. He wanted to watch his faculty longer before he made a decision. McDermott later claimed, however, that he was offered the job at that time but declined because of his relative youth and short time in grade.[21] Zimmerman's problems were widely known outside the Academy. At West Point, Herman Beukema wrote Abe Lincoln: "I can conceive of situations where his flights of ideas, and scorn for those of other people, could have made continuance in the Dean's spot impossible."[22] It is illustrative of this whole sequence of events that one professor commented: "I don't think they ever made a formal announcement. I think he just disappeared."[23]

Discipline and Cadet Activities

Stillman's office was responsible for all military and physical training, as well as housing, feeding and equipping the cadets. He was also charged with finding appropriate off-duty activities for them.

The leadership and discipline systems were much like those at West Point. Cadets were given military grades each semester that were a combination of the input from the AOC—which was influenced by the comments of ATOs and faculty members—and peer ratings from other cadets. Based on these military rankings, cadet leaders were chosen. There was a strong intent that cadets would govern themselves: "all cadets, regardless of rank, were to use their influence to maintain the discipline, standards and traditions of the Air Force Academy and the Air Force."[24]

Cadets who transgressed were generally given a Form 10—the document used to record infractions of regulations. The AOC could assess demerits and confinements, the numbers depending on the nature of the offense: a disorderly desk was worth three demerits; failure to prepare for an inspection earned seven demerits. A cadet was permitted a maximum of twenty-three demerits per month—any more than that had to be marched off as "tours"—one hour of marching outside with a rifle, usually on the weekends. More serious offenses—failure to follow orders, insubordination, sleeping in class, or "embracing a young lady"—would generally be referred to a Group Board, similar to the Battalion Board that Harmon had chaired from 1929 to 1932. Class III offenses were those thought serious enough to meet a Commandant's Board. A violation such as sneaking off base (OTF or "over the fence" in cadet parlance), could garner fifteen demerits, twenty-five tours, and thirty days on restriction. "Capital crimes"—being drunk or using narcotics—were severe Class III offenses that could lead to dismissal.[25] As with academic grades, all military grades and punishments were posted on squadron bulletin boards. Cadets could protest a decision if they thought their "award" excessive.

During this first year a host of seemingly trivial but nonetheless essential tasks had to be accomplished. The Academy needed its own flag and seal—something original and appropriate, but that had to pass muster in Washington. The Academy also needed a mascot, a requirement that came to the fore as the freshman football team readied for its first game. As usual, Harmon did not want to push the cadets too hard on such matters; he wanted them to make up their own collective mind on the subject.[26] A canvass of the Cadet Wing produced three possibilities for a mascot: a tiger, an eagle, and a falcon. A local falconer, Harold M. Webster, sent a letter to Harmon explaining the customs and practices of falconry, and asked if the general would care to view a demonstration. Harmon agreed and scheduled the event to ensure the cadets were present as well. Webster later recalled that he brought a large Peale peregrine falcon to Lowry and released it in front of the assembled cadets. The raptor flew up several hundred feet and began to circle. Webster then released a pigeon. The falcon immediately went into a screeching dive and nailed the pigeon in midair. The cadets were impressed, and on 25 September the Wing voted that the falcon would be the Academy mascot.[27] Soon after, a peregrine falcon was donated to the cadets, followed by a magnificent white gyrfalcon caught in Greenland by an airman stationed there. Prairie falcons were often caught by the cadets themselves near Cathedral Rock. Soon, several falcons were trained, and the impressive birds began performing during halftime at football games—a custom still practiced today.

Other activities were needed to keep cadets busy on the weekends and during free time. Again, Harmon was reluctant to dictate, so he advised Stillman to wait and see which activities the cadets themselves wished to generate. Clubs formed quickly, and within several months included: debate, radio, chess, the cadet magazine (*The Talon*), ski, judo, fishing, riding, choir, photography, model airplane, and more. As for traditions, Harmon specifically stated that he did not want to replicate such antics as "throwing pennies at the feet of Tecumseh" or "dropping class rings in the waters of the seven seas"—customs then prevalent at West Point and Annapolis. Rather, he advised Stillman that he wanted the cadets to discover their own traditions.[28]

At the same time, in order to ensure that the future officers would have appropriate social graces, an Academy hostess was hired to work with cadets and their guests on proper etiquette. Gail McComas, the widow of a World War II fighter pilot, was hired for this position in April 1955.[29] Cadets were given dancing lessons, and dances were held periodically in the cadet social center, with women from the local area flocking to Lowry for these events. Indeed, one source noted that the parking area between Arnold Hall and the Base Exchange had become a "veritable den of iniquity" on the weekends, requiring a regular patrol by the Officer in Charge.[30]

There were other matters, of a more local interest, which Harmon needed to address. As construction began at the permanent site, Colorado Springs school officials grew concerned because a large number of workers had moved into trailers near the site and brought their families, including hundreds of children, with them. How would these children be educated and who would pay for it? In addition, because school districts received funding from the Federal Government based on tax revenues in the local area, city officials were concerned that because the government had purchased 17,500 acres for the Academy, there would hence-forth be no tax revenue from this vast area—this in turn would negatively impact the local school districts. Harmon directed his legal office to work with the locals on the problem, and the solution would eventually include schools on Academy grounds, paid for by the Federal Government.[31]

Another concern involved Protestant chapel services. The majority of cadets categorized themselves as Christian, but from a wide variety of denom-inations—twenty to be exact. The Sunday services for these cadets therefore had to be non-denominational. In August 1955 a local Episcopalian minister wrote Harmon asking if he could give a service for Episcopal cadets one Sunday per month. Harmon responded that, regretfully, it would not be possible. Cit-ing the large number of denominations represented in the Cadet Wing, such permission would mean all other local ministers would request similar treat-ment—that would be totally impractical.[32] In short, establishing the Academy involved a welter of tasks involving a wide range of expertise and experience.

Among the wide variety of start-up challenges facing Academy officials during the first year, the airmanship program, one of the Academy's seemingly most crucial facets, proved especially problematic. It was expensive and time consuming. The end product, navigator wings, was of marginal utility to new lieutenants on their way to pilot school. Moreover, the training itself was tedious and uninspiring. Colonel Gideon, the Academy chief of staff, believed that the entire program was a mistake: "the cadets don't like to ride in the back of an airplane, it makes them sick and de-motivates rather than motivates ... This is the greatest weakness of our program."[33] Others agreed. Cadet airsickness was a problem on these flights; worse, the commandant's office decreed that any cadet becoming airsick on three flights would be dropped from the program—in other words, airmanship training became punitive for those unfortunate cadets with a weak stomach.[34] There were also scheduling concerns. Stillman suggested that all academic classes be scheduled in the mornings so that afternoons could be reserved for flying training to increase efficiency on the flightline. The dean thought such a scheme inadvisable: with one class following another all morning every day the cadets would be "too packed," with no time for decompression and reflection.[35]

The air observer program was soon jettisoned. Upon the move to the permanent site in 1958 it became impractical. The airfield on the Academy itself was not built, largely for financial reasons. The intent had been to construct a "first-class airfield" with an 8,000' runway that could accommodate all cadet training aircraft, plus cargo planes to transport staff members, faculty, and the Cadet Wing.[36] It would be another decade before the Academy was able to buy a number of Cessna T-41C light trainers to give senior cadets pilot indoctrination training. Even then, the aircraft were initially based at Peterson AFB on the east side of Colorado Springs. Cadets were bussed to and from their flying lessons. It would be 1975 before the Academy airstrip was enlarged to house the flying training squadron and its aircraft.

There were many highlights during that first academic year, and one of the brightest occurred in September when President Eisenhower visited. He had been unable to attend the Dedication Ceremony in July, so instead flew into Lowry one week after classes began. He toured the Academy compound, spoke to cadets, attended chapel services, and, in an old tradition that *did* transfer from West Point, granted amnesty to cadets then serving punishments. Afterwards, he wrote Harmon: "I congratulate you on the staff you have gotten together, and on their general appearance of keenness and competence. Results of this work show also in the smartness of yesterday's morning parade. To have done that much in two months is in itself quite an achievement." The president then closed with a suggestion. Both the Military and Naval Academies were known by geographic place names—West Point and Annapolis—should not the Air Force Academy be named something appropriate as well, perhaps "Manitou"? That did not happen.[37]

"We Will Not Lie ..."

An Honor Code had always been part of the plan for the Air Force Academy. The Air University Planning Board of 1948 had called for one, based on the Code at West Point. Many of those associated with the new Air Force Academy were West Point graduates, but in some cases, like that of Hubert Harmon, the Code they remembered had evolved considerably since their cadet days.

The Honor Code at West Point had been largely informal for its first century. Cadets were expected to act honorably. If a man did not, a group of cadets, a "Vigilance Committee," would confront the alleged offender and question him. If the Vigilance Committee determined the cadet had indeed acted dishonorably, he would be encouraged to leave. Sometimes, the encouragement involved force. Harmon later recalled an incident that occurred while he was a cadet: "we took up a collection, $100, gave it to the guy and told him to beat it."[38]

Such was the system that Hubert Harmon lived under as a cadet. The decade after his graduation in 1915, however, the Code was formalized. Brigadier General Douglas MacArthur, a graduate of 1903, became the Academy superintendent in 1919, and resolved to do away with the Vigilance Committees—which smacked to him of vigilante committees— and instead form an Honor

President Eisenhower visits the new Academy in September 1955.

Committee run by cadets. A chairman was duly elected, but the transition was not as easy as anticipated.

In 1921 a cadet was accused of an honor violation and found guilty; he was told to resign. He refused to do so. The Honor Committee then decreed that he should be silenced—no cadet was allowed to speak to him or interact with him again, except in the line of duty. The cadet would room and eat alone for the remainder of his time at the Academy. In most cases this punishment was so unnerving that the cadet ultimately resigned. However, in this case, the accused's classmates refused to go along with the orders of the Honor Committee. The first classmen running the Committee resolved to take strong action against this mutiny. MacArthur found out about all of this and told the cadet First Captain, who was also the chairman of the Honor Committee *and* the class president, to do nothing. MacArthur held him personally accountable for the safety and well-being of the accused cadet. Less than a week later, however, this cadet was rousted in the middle of the night, stripped of his uniform, given civilian clothes and $20, and put on a train headed west. When MacArthur heard of this the next day, he was livid. He immediately summoned the First Captain and busted him to cadet private and required him to walk tours until his graduation day nearly a year later.[39] MacArthur wanted cadets to take more responsibility for running the Corps, but he also insisted that they do so within strict guidelines that ensured both legality and ethical conduct. The narrow ground fulfilling these criteria was to be an issue at all the service academies in the decades ahead.

When Harmon arrived as a tactical officer in 1929, this new system was firmly in place. Another new wrinkle that had been added since his graduation concerned the offense of stealing. Heretofore, the Honor Code had dealt only with lying and cheating: stealing was handled as a criminal offense and punished accordingly under the Uniform Code of Military Justice. In the 1920s, stealing—but of a nature less than criminal activity—also became a violation of the Honor Code.

One other aspect of the West Point Honor Code that would become a controversial issue at the Air Force Academy was "discretion." Two of the main philosophical and ethical questions surrounding the Honor Code concerned the severity of an offense and the severity of the resulting punishment. Most ethical, criminal or religious codes distinguish between felonies and misdemeanors or between mortal and venial sins. The Honor Code did not: all lies, cheats and steals were of equal weight. Similarly, the punishment for all such transgressions was the same—disenrollment. Thus, a black-and-white standard was superimposed on a decidedly gray world. West Point eventually came to believe that this was out of balance, and increasingly during the 1940s and 1950s cadets administering the Honor Code began to take into consideration such mitigating factors as age and experience of the violator, severity of the offense, and whether the offense was self-reported. In some cases, the Honor Committee would decide that the violator should be given a second chance—he would be given "discretion." This policy was formalized at West Point in 1959. It would provoke controversy and vigorous debate at the Air Force Academy as well.

Given this background, in 1954 Harmon formed a group headed by Colonel Ben Cassiday to study the honor codes of West Point and Annapolis, as well as those of several other schools. After reviewing the results, Harmon decided on the wording of the proposed Code: "We will not lie, cheat or steal, nor tolerate among us anyone who lies, cheats or steals." Harmon did not, however, want to impose the new Code upon the cadets; rather, he hoped that after receiving instruction on the concepts of honor and integrity and how they relate to an Air Force career, the cadets would accept it voluntarily.[40] As he wrote to a friend: "We do not feel that we can literally transplant the West Point system to our new Academy. It is something we will have to develop as best we can within our own walls."[41]

The first step was to educate the faculty and staff, many of whom were not service academy graduates and were thus unfamiliar with such stringent honor standards. Similarly, the ATOs, who would be responsible for indoctrinating the new cadets, would need to internalize the Code as well. Many unusual issues arose; for example, the faculty was urged to trust the cadets: thus, they should *not* give different exams on different days. Such a practice would indicate a lack of trust in the cadets: virtue untested was not virtue at all.[42] The "toleration clause" also rubbed many the wrong way, and it was suspected that it would trouble new cadets as well. Many youngsters were raised on the principle that they should not tattle or "rat-out" their friends or siblings—loyalty was an important virtue—but the toleration clause required cadets to do precisely that: to inform on friends they saw committing an honor violation. Many faculty members and ATOs questioned whether such a principle was viable. Proponents cited the experience of West Point, which had a toleration clause. Opponents cited Annapolis, which did not.

To Harmon, the toleration clause was the heart of the Honor Code. It made the Code self-policing and served to remove the "us versus them" syndrome—officers as enforcers attempting to identify transgressors among the cadets who would then close ranks and protect each other. Harmon and others recognized this would be the most difficult idea for cadets to grasp, and would probably be the one most violated. The first officer-in-charge of the Honor Committee, Major William B. Yancey, later admitted that even selling the idea to the ATOs was difficult: "we actually [had] to eliminate one or two officers who had trouble complying."[43]

Harmon intended to introduce the Honor Code to the new cadets during their basic training in the summer of 1955. Officers from the commandant's shop would give lectures on the Code and answer questions. Harmon told the ATOs "to drop a hint here and there about West Point and its honor system."[44] Harmon has been seen as the "driving force" behind the Academy Honor Code, but he did not have to drive very hard: the cadets embraced the concept almost at once. To Harmon's great surprise, the first cadet class voted to accept the Honor Code as written in September 1955—just as they were beginning their academic classes.[45]

Very quickly, however, problems developed over the scope of the honor system and how much it governed cadet activities. In short, would the Code be used to enforce regulations? Harmon was leery of allowing this to happen and quoted Mark Twain to underline his concern: "Honesty is our most cherished possession and we should use it sparingly."[46] By this Harmon meant that the purpose of the Honor Code was to shape and influence a cadet's behavior—to make him want to live an honorable life. The Code should not exist for "easing the authorities' administrative or policing responsibilities."[47]

As it turned out, however, this was indeed a problem. For example, a concept inherited from West Point called the "Five Points" concerned five especially egregious activities: drinking, gambling, narcotics, hazing and limits. (The last referred to certain geographic locations a cadet could or could not visit.) The Air Force Academy adopted the rule that when a cadet signed out and then in again on an off-duty privilege, he was testifying by his signature that he had not violated any of the rules regarding the Five Points. Cadets found this unfair, especially regarding drinking. It happened. To tie a cadet's honor while on a legitimate off-duty privilege to whether or not, in the privacy of a hotel room, he drank a few beers was needlessly invasive. If a cadet were caught in a bar red-handed, then he should be punished accordingly—in the military sphere for violating regulations. Such activities should in no way be considered an honor violation.[48] This provision was eventually removed from the Honor Code, but not until 1960—after the first class had graduated.[49]

Harmon directed the commandant's office to oversee the honor system, but for the cadets actually to run it to the maximum extent possible. In practice this meant that each cadet squadron elected two honor representatives. (As the Wing expanded this was reduced to one first classman and one second classman per squadron—only the first classmen would actually sit on Honor Boards.) Cadets were directed to report any suspected honor infraction to one of these representatives. The "Honor Rep" would then investigate the incident. If he determined it was not a violation, the matter was dropped. If, however, he thought a violation may have occurred, he would refer it to the Honor Committee, which would then schedule a hearing. Lawyers were not used. A cadet merely sat before a group of eight honor representatives to answer questions about his conduct. Witnesses could be called to testify. If all eight found the cadet guilty, he was directed to report to the commandant. If the verdict was not unanimous, the cadet was declared innocent and returned to the Cadet Wing in good standing. All cases, minus names, were briefed to the entire Cadet Wing for instructional purposes and to short-circuit rumors.[50]

A cadet dance held in the social center, Arnold Hall.

The first Honor Board was held one month into the first semester. By the end of the first year at Lowry AFB, eight cadets had been found guilty of honor violations and resigned. Of note, the commandant and superintendent would review the results of all Honor Boards and the latter could reverse a decision. If both officers agreed with the verdict, the case was referred to the secretary of the Air Force, who could also reverse the decision or approve the cadet's resignation.[51] In cases of extreme gravity—or if requested by the cadet—a court-martial was also an option. Cadets who left the Academy as the result of an honor violation were given a general discharge—this was a category less than honorable. It was a controversial decision, but the Academy stuck to this idea, partly because that was the policy at West Point. Even so, several cadet discharges were upgraded by the Air Force secretary during the first year.[52] General O'Donnell, who acted as an Academy go-between with the secretary, believed that it was asking too much of new cadets in a new institution to suffer the serious consequences of a general discharge for the rest of their lives. As a result, he convinced the secretary to decree that cadets leaving on honor violations would receive an honorable discharge. The policy remained in force until the first class graduated in 1959; subsequent honor violations were given a general discharge, as at West Point.[53]

In sum, the Cadet Honor Code was one of the new Academy's most distinctive and unique features. Cadets and staff expressed their approval of it with marked enthusiasm. Yet, time would reveal that some of the systemic problems already noted—the Code's black-and-white nature regarding both degrees of "dishonor" and the severity of punishment, and the issues of toleration, discretion and the enforcement of regulations—would be oft-debated in the years ahead.

The First Stumble

The issue of over-emphasis on athletics, encountered during the cadet selection process for the Class of 1959, arose again when classes began. Cadets, as at West Point, were generally graded daily and their cumulative grades and class standing posted each week. On 16 September, General Stillman sent a memo to General Zimmerman noting that cadets were getting up at 0500 to study, were dragging at football practice, and were staying up beyond taps to study by flashlight to avoid being caught after lights out. Stillman recommended that "we err on the other side for a while; i.e., too light work assignments until such time as we can develop the proper work level that can be supported."[54] Soon after, Colonel Robert Whitlow weighed in with similar complaints. He noted that as of 28 September there were seventy-nine cadets academically deficient. That was over one-quarter of the Cadet Wing. Worse, sixty-four of those cadets were on-season athletes—over 80 percent of all those deficient. Wrote Whitlow: "I can't believe a man is automatically less bright merely because he wants to play a sport. We need to demonstrate to team members that they can participate without being at such a tremendous disadvantage in study time with respect to their classmates." The athletic director continued that the athletes have eight to twelve less hours to study per week than do other cadets. The work load simply had to be reduced.[55]

Zimmerman's response offered little succor, stating simply that an athlete at any institution, including West Point, was always at an academic disadvantage relative to his classmates—"it is the price he pays for fame." There would be no let up.[56]

Over the next two months this issue was watched closely. Athletes, especially football players, continued to struggle, and being rated "academically deficient" meant they could not play on Saturday. McDermott later argued that most of the athletes experiencing difficulty never should have been admitted in the first place, and only gained admission due to the "J Factor" insisted upon by Whitlow that was devised specifically to assist prospective cadets with poor grades but good athletic skills.[57] Even so, further studies by the commandant's office began to paint a somewhat different picture. It soon developed that those cadets arising early were doing so to clean their rooms and polish their shoes—not to study. In addition, athletes still had free time, over seven hours per week, which could be used not only to relax, but also to catch up on their studies.[58] In fact, when interviewing cadets who had decided to resign—Stillman always insisted on seeing them personally—a number told him they were quitting because the program was "too easy" and they were bored.[59] Fortunately, by the end of the first semester, all appeared to be under control. Most cadets were adapting; the initial anxiety experienced by all cadets, and not just athletes, was abating and all were settling in to their rigorous new regime. Regrettably, those who were insufficiently challenged would have to wait several years for major revisions to the curriculum.

This entire incident regarding the cadet academic workload was one of several that pitted Colonel Whitlow against other organizations at the

Academy. There would soon be other missteps that would lead to the athletic director's removal. It is useful to go back and review the background regarding Whitlow's selection.

When looking for an officer to fill the position of athletic director, Harmon had heard a briefing given by Whitlow in 1950 in which he had argued: "Gentlemen, you can't have a circus without the wild animals." An air academy would need some jocks. Whitlow later stated that this briefing and the study he wrote accompanying it landed him the job as the first athletic director. Whitlow's paper began by asserting: "In the current U.S. national outlook, an educational institution primarily contacts the U.S. public not by means of its superior educational program, but by means of its athletic representatives and resulting comment in the sports pages of the nation's newspapers." He noted that Annapolis, which played a tough schedule, received "nothing but praise" for its athletic prowess; whereas, West Point "is treated with decided coolness on all sides for its pantywaist schedule." To ensure a quality program, the air academy would need quality athletes, and he advocated giving the Air Force secretary the authority to appoint forty to fifty cadets each year "to assist the athletic program." Whitlow pushed for a robust recruiting cadre of high school scouts "that will surpass even Notre Dame's holy crusade on the gridiron." Whitlow wanted the air academy to play serious football; his ideal schedule would include every year powerhouses like Alabama, Michigan, Southern Cal, Notre Dame, and, of course, Army and Navy. He concluded:

> It is recognized that intercollegiate athletic competition is by no means the most essential factor in the planning of a future Air Academy; however, its public relations value should dictate that the needs of a well-rounded, top-flight athletic program be considered in all planning. Although realizing athletics are a means and not an end, it is felt that every effort should be made to assure the Academy the best possible advantage in this field.[60]

Whitlow was a believer, and Harmon was forewarned; yet, this study sold Whitlow to the superintendent. Harmon liked his fire and enthusiasm, and upon hiring him in October 1954, gave Whitlow a written directive: "to beat West Point and Annapolis in November 1962 or sooner." To Whitlow the clear implication was that Harmon—as well as Secretary Talbott and General Rosie O'Donnell who were also devoted football fans—was not interested in how Whitlow accomplished the feat.[61]

Upon arriving at Lowry, it soon became apparent that the athletic director was a bit more zealous than was appropriate. One month after his arrival he sent a letter to ROTC programs around the country hoping to stir up interest in the Air Force Academy among prospective athletes. One line caught the attention of several: "The national reputation of an educational institution is rarely determined by academic achievement, but by athletic victories which are highlighted in the public eye by the newspapers, radio and television."[62] This was the same point he had made in his Air Staff briefing in 1950, but now it rang a more discordant note. The president of Kansas State University sent a strongly worded complaint to Harmon, who responded that such a belief was "certainly out of line with our policy."[63] Whitlow was forced to retract his statement. Word of this gaffe reached the Air Staff, and Harmon had to explain: "Obviously, I did not see the original letter, else it would never have gone out."[64]

Whitlow persisted in his aggressive posture, arguing that "unless the Air Force Academy is to be relegated to the stature of the Coast Guard Academy in the eyes of its officers and the general public, the Air Force must move rapidly to have teams capable of competing successfully with the two older services."[65] Harmon's public affairs officer later confessed: "We could not keep Whitlow's mouth shut. He knows this. He would say the damndest things, and then he'd be called on the carpet."[66] Undeterred, Whitlow then proposed the Qualified Candidate Identification Program whereby the Air Force secretary would appoint qualified alternate nominees to Academy vacancies. Whitlow noted that the Naval Academy had such a program—which was permitted by law— and which was used to bring in athletes who would otherwise not have received appointments. The previous year, argued Whitlow, of the Navy secretary's fifty-eight appointments, forty-seven had been athletes. The Air Force should have a similar program.[67] Recall that these were not new ideas: Whitlow had proposed them at least four years earlier. The athletic director also argued that to assist in the grooming of athletic prospects, funds from the Academy's Athletic Association should be used to set up a program at the New Mexico Military Institute (NMMI) for the specific purpose of boosting test scores for athletes so they could get into the Academy. As Whitlow himself phrased it: "NMMI is where I put boys who needed a few more smarts."[68]

Word of all this activity was getting around. In February 1955 the *Cheyenne State Tribune* ran a story ominously titled, "Football Factory?" that lambasted the Academy for releasing "reams and reams of publicity" regarding its nascent football program, but "not a single one" devoted to its academic program.[69] Harmon responded that he was at a loss to understand the editorial: "There have been almost endless releases by the Air Force on the purpose, objectives, curricula, training programs, etc. of the Air Force Academy, none of which have stressed football or any other phase of the athletic program."[70] At the same time, Harmon received a letter from a friend on the Air Staff warning him that several officers from his shop had visited Lowry recently and when asking about cadet entrance qualifications, "were laughingly told that the Athletic Director had more to do with such selections than anybody else."[71] Harmon responded tepidly that "my personal attitude is that athletics and athletes are important—should not be overemphasized, but on the other hand need no apologies."[72]

Harmon continued to maintain this stance, which, frankly, was subject to misinterpretation. For example, he also wrote that "if we play down athletics and make it appear that a coming star will have no chance to glitter in our firmament we will surely fail to attract to our Academy many young men of the type we desire." He then added: "no discrimination was to be made for or against a young man simply because he was an athlete."[73]

There was a razor-thin line in Harmon's reasoning: he wanted quality athletes to choose the Academy, not only because he wanted respectable athletic teams, but also because his own experiences convinced him that athletics, by their very nature, nurtured qualities and characteristics that were highly desirable for future air officers. On the other hand, he was reluctant to institute policies that would ensure the selection and success of cadet athletes. He was reticent to distort unduly the cadet selection process in favor of high school athletes. After the flare up regarding the first class and the "J Factor" issue, Harmon stated that "in the future [we will] give equal weight in extra curriculars to athletic and non-athletic activities."[74] To Whitlow, Harmon wrote that he authorized the Academy Board to *consider* certain high school athletes "who appear to be good prospects and who otherwise could not have been considered." He then reiterated that nothing in this decision "is to be construed as a desire on my part, or on the part of General O'Donnell, to get into the Academy any athlete simply because he is an athlete."[75] It must again be reiterated that Harmon believed that athletics were important but not crucial. His attitude was revealed in events that happened after his death.

The first football coach hired by the Academy was Buck Shaw, a famed professional coach who had led the *San Francisco 49ers* in 1954. Other coaches seriously considered for the job were Vince Lombardi and Ara Parseghian. Harmon insisted on Shaw. Two years later, however, the Academy moved to terminate Shaw's contract. In unraveling the events leading to this decision, the circumstances regarding his original hiring became apparent. Harmon had wanted a part-time coach who would lend prestige to the Academy football program without signaling a concerted effort to build a football factory. For his part, Shaw did not want a full-time job that required year-round recruiting trips all over the country. The desires of Harmon and Shaw converged. After Harmon left, however, the Academy decided it *did* want a full-time individual who would travel extensively during the off-season to recruit players. When pushed to assume these duties, Shaw balked, stating that Harmon had assured him emphatically that he would not have to do such things: "The entire program was based fundamentally upon a recruiting policy which emphasized officer potential first, football second." Harmon "did not want Mr. Shaw in the recruiting business or the intercollegiate policy or politics business."[76] The *act* of hiring Shaw under these conditions seems to speak louder than Harmon's ambiguous *words* regarding the importance of football.

The first varsity football coach—Buck Shaw—flanked by Lt Col Frank Merritt (left) and Colonel Robert V. Whitlow.

In addition, the performance of the Academy's athletic teams that first year certainly did not indicate that it had become a jock factory. The football team went 4-4; baseball was 5-9, and basketball 11-9. Overall, the Academy intercollegiate scorecard for all sports in 1955-56 was a miserable 54-77. Whitlow pushed to improve that record; unfortunately, he pushed too far.

As the Academy geared up for the application process for the Class of 1960, it sent out hundreds of pamphlets describing the test candidates would be required to take and that included sample problems. One of these problems, designed to test depth perception acuity for pilot qualification, gave a picture of a cockpit view of an aircraft in flight, asking what the scene depicted. Whitlow's staff noticed that the picture was the wrong one, and therefore the supposed correct answer was actually incorrect. Whitlow later claimed that he complained of the issue to Harmon, who referred the problem to Colonel Boudreau (the director of admissions). Boudreau told Whitlow to handle the athletes; he would take care of the others.[77] The athletic director then prepared a correct picture, and answer, and sent them to all the high school athletes he was recruiting. Apparently, Boudreau did not send anything to the other applicants, and when a non-athlete saw the corrected exam question, he wrote his congressman in protest. The Air Force Inspector General (IG) conducted an investigation and found Whitlow personally culpable for the error. The IG not only faulted him for the exam question fiasco, but it dug more deeply and chastised Whitlow for his entire attitude towards athletics at the Academy. It stressed in unambiguous terms that "national standing of the teams will be of secondary importance." Also taking a swipe at Whitlow's "cooperative program" at NMMI, funded by Academy boosters, the report concluded: "Policy does not permit the sponsorship, officially or unofficially, by the Air Force or the Air Force Academy of any outside scholarship program or any other course of action aimed at aiding or assisting any particular candidate or select group of candidates in the competitive entrance examinations." The report concluded emphatically: "Considerations of athletic capabilities will not be permitted to compromise an impartial cadet selection and appointment procedure."[78]

Whitlow was fired, and his place taken by Colonel George B. Simler, a former All-American football player at the University of Maryland.[79]

This was not Hubert Harmon's finest moment. As noted, he had been sending decidedly mixed signals to Whitlow from the very beginning regarding the importance he placed on the Academy's athletic program and the lengths to which the Academy should go to ensure that quality athletes were admitted so the school could compete on a national level. Harmon did not exert enough restraint on Whitlow. He had been forewarned. As early as March 1950, Harmon had read and heard Whitlow's ideas on an Academy athletic program, and it is apparent that not only were these ideas a major reason for his hiring, but Whitlow continued to expound them, forcefully, upon arriving at Lowry. Indeed, years later he would use the same arguments to defend his actions at the Academy. When asked in 1979 about his philosophy concerning service academy athletics, he responded by asking two rhetorical questions: "who invented synthetic rubber?" No one he asked ever knew the answer; he then asked if they had ever heard of the Four Horsemen? Of course, most had heard of the famed Notre Dame backfield quartet. His point: the inventor was a faculty member at Notre Dame at the same time the Four Horsemen on Notre Dame's football team dominated headlines. Who, therefore, was more important to the reputation of the school? Whitlow continued that he was enormously proud of his achievements. He pointed to the Academy football team of 1958-59—the first that included seniors—which went undefeated and earned a Cotton Bowl berth. Actually, the football team's success raised as many eyebrows as it did spirits around the Air Force.[80]

Harmon gave Whitlow too much latitude. In latter-day terminology, he "empowered" Whitlow to establish a first-rate athletic program and then stepped back to let his subordinate do his job. Harmon should have been more attentive. There were warning signs—the emphasis on recruiting and complaints from McDermott, the admonitions from the Air Staff, grumbling in the press, and the letter to ROTC instructors. But Harmon failed to take action. Partly this was due to his innate reluctance to come down hard on people. He once freely admitted to a member of his staff that he was not cut out to be a combat commander—unlike his brother Miff—because he was unable "to send people out to die." It would eat away at him too much—he was "too close to his people."[81] In essence, Harmon's good heart would sometimes lead him into difficulties. Brigadier General Don Zimmerman and Colonel Robert Whitlow were bad choices, but Harmon was unable to rein them in firmly or quickly enough. Eventually, he relieved Zimmerman when it was becoming obvious to all that the dean was not up to the task. Harmon never reached that level of awareness with Whitlow, who did damage to the Academy, but who survived Harmon's tenure. Some would argue that the poisonous seeds planted in the Athletic Department during the Academy's first year would later bear bitter fruit in 1965 when the Academy endured a major cheating scandal leading to the expulsion of 109 cadets—44 of whom were athletes and 29 football players.[82]

The reluctance shown by Harmon to deal firmly and quickly with subordinates who stepped out of line was displayed elsewhere as well.

The thread holding the Academy staff together, Harmon's personality, snapped when he retired. Colonel Gideon was blunt: "Without mentioning that perhaps a problem in forceful leadership existed, I will say without qualms or apple-polishing that the assignment of General [James E.] Briggs as Superintendent marked a sharp uptrend in all phases of the Academy…The time had come and it was needed badly." Gideon's opinion was bolstered by actions that Briggs took soon after his assumption of command. He named McDermott the acting dean—he had no intention of being dual-hatted as Harmon had been. McDermott's junior status, however, exacerbated the fractures already evident within the staff. Soon, Briggs would relieve and transfer ten colonels, including Boudreau and several department heads. In an unusually candid letter in April 1958 to General O'Donnell, Briggs explained the moves.

Part of the problem lay in West Point's influence on the Air Force Academy, he began. The professors at the Military Academy had enormous and almost unchecked power, and the professors at Lowry expected to enjoy those same powers and privileges. This sense of entitlement existed despite the fact that all had been clearly told their appointments were not permanent: decisions as to longevity would be made at a later date. Harmon had witnessed the debilitating problem of unchecked power of the permanent professors during his tour at West Point from 1929 to 1932. He did not wish to replicate it. The appointment of McDermott as the acting dean and later as dean caused some of these older, more academically credentialed and more senior officers, to begin a campaign of "slander and innuendo" against the Academy.

At the time he assumed his position as superintendent, talks with Harmon and O'Donnell had alerted Briggs to the problems brewing. In several instances Harmon had acknowledged the deficiencies in several colonels, but he had been unwilling to take action before his retirement. The mess was left for Briggs to clean up.

One colonel had a drinking problem and was "undependable" in public venues as an Academy representative. Another colonel was an outstanding academic and department head, but his wife was "violent and outspoken socially."

Briggs stated that "she borders on being a religious fanatic and thinks herself as an intellectual." Briggs thought she was the main source of the poison pen letters that had been sent anonymously to the General Officers Advisory Board.

A professor in the Philosophy Department thought that "cadets should live by the standards of the society around them and not by the ideals the Academy was attempting to teach." Another professor was "academically unqualified." One colonel had to be corrected by Briggs personally for offensive language and for "loud and unsportsmanlike behavior at Academy athletic events." Another officer, the dean's former executive, gave a very poor public performance at a West Point conference, which generated two letters of complaint from faculty members there; he "could not get along and showed open hostility."[83]

For Briggs to relieve such a large number of senior officers in such a brief period was remarkable and indicates that deep fissures existed within the senior staff. Brigg's assertion that most of these problems were known by Harmon is compelling. Briggs argued that the officers needed to be fired or transferred, but that Harmon was unwilling or unable to do so. Once again, Harmon's generosity of spirit and good nature proved to be a fault. In his position as a senior military commander he simply could not allow such softness to override his responsibility to take actions necessary for the good of his command.

At the same time, however, two points should be noted in Harmon's defense. First, it is clear from reading Rosa-Maye's diary that Hubert's health, never robust, began to deteriorate significantly from January 1956 onwards. This was in fact alluded to above by Colonel Gideon. Second, General Twining had already informed Harmon in December 1955 that Briggs would replace him the following August. It was unusual for a commander to know the identity of his successor nine months in advance. It is therefore possible that the combination of Harmon's poor health and the knowledge of who would replace him as superintendent contributed to his slowness in reacting to the personnel issues noted above.

"Our Goal is to the Stars"
Still, it would be most unfair to conclude this chapter on such a melancholy note. The Academy had a remarkable first year, and Harmon was to a great extent responsible for that success. For example, although he remained mostly in the background, the Academy took important steps towards gaining academic accreditation prior to the graduation of the first class.

Accreditation is a badge of legitimacy. It sends a clear statement to all that an educational institution has passed muster with nationally-known experts in the field. Accreditation grants prestige to a school and its graduates, allowing them to enter civilian universities at a later date to pursue a master's or doctoral degree. The process needed to gain accreditation is long and arduous. A school must prove its worthiness. It must show not only that it has a clear and impartial student admission system, but that its faculty is qualified, the curriculum is well conceived and rigorous, procedures are fair and consistent, college-level laboratories and a library are available for student and faculty use, and that mechanisms are in place to ensure academic freedom and governance responsibilities for the faculty. Many of the steps taken during the first year of the Academy's existence were taken with an eye cast on the officials of the North Central Association of Colleges and Secondary Schools (NCACSS). Would they understand and agree that the Academy, although a military unit, was a first-rate educational institution as well?

The rules of the NCACSS stated that an institution would not qualify for accreditation until it had completed at least four years of instruction. Harmon and the Faculty planned for the Academy to be an exception to that rule. In March 1955, Dr. Manning M. Pattillo, Jr. of the NCACSS met with McDermott, Boudreau and Colonel A.W. Rigsby. Pattillo bluntly told the colonels that at the present stage the Academy was not in compliance—it was still functioning like a military organization rather than an academic institution. The faculty needed to have a greater say over the curriculum. When Academy officials argued that they did not want to "stagnate" like West Point—referring to the perils of the "Academic Board" model—Pattillo told them that such an argument was irrelevant—the Air Force Academy was being discussed, not the Military Academy. It was also noted that "in a good school" at least 30 percent of the faculty had doctorates and the rest a master's degree. The Academy needed to improve the quality of its faculty. The colonels were also warned that the overall academic load on cadets was too heavy, especially for freshmen.[84]

The following month, Dr. Pattillo visited the Academy and met with Harmon. Although saying that he was "deeply impressed" with the sense of mission and the industry of the faculty, he was concerned with the mechanism for determining academic policy: there needed to be a more institutionalized body that could make recommendations to the superintendent for his decision.[85] The Academy Board was not yet in the configuration necessary to meet NCACSS standards. Harmon listened carefully, but responded to Pattillo that although he was in "complete agreement" regarding the need for a more robust academic council, he argued that the time for its actual formation was "not yet ripe." He concluded: "I am confident that an organizational structure similar in design and purpose to that which you outlined will be established as we progress."[86]

There would be many more meetings between Academy and North Central officials. Indeed, General Briggs later commented that he, McDermott and Stillman went to Chicago—home of the NCACSS—"a thousand times" to meet with accrediting officials. Whatever the NCACSS wanted they got—receiving accreditation for the Academy by June 1959 was paramount.[87]

In August 1955, Generals O'Donnell and Stone met with Dr. Pattillo and had a frank talk. Pattillo told them that in his opinion faculty morale was low; faculty organization was not satisfactory; and the dean's [Zimmerman's] leadership was insufficient. As for the curriculum, Pattillo stated that it "did not appear to have sufficient flexibility to permit the exercise of intellectual initiative on the part of the student body." The generals were told, as had been Harmon, that the quality of the faculty was "not up to proper standards." There were several more complaints made regarding the dean's office.[88] This report, added to the other rumblings, was no doubt instrumental in Harmon's decision to relieve Zimmerman three months later.

McDermott later claimed that Harmon was often absent when representatives from the NCACSS called for a meeting.[89] Pattillo himself later commented that he thought it "strange" that Harmon was not more proactive in meeting with him.[90] Although it does appear that Harmon remained in the background during this process, the reason why is not clear. Obviously, Harmon wanted Academy accreditation, but perhaps believed it best to remain silent at this early stage. The Academy was so new perhaps he thought it wise to work some of the bugs out first. His civilian academic advisors were old friends with decades of experience behind them in such matters—Bob Stearns at Colorado, Bruce Hopper at Harvard, Ben Wood at Columbia, and Virgil Hancher at Iowa. It is possible that he was acting on their advice. It may also be that Harmon was simply too exhausted to engage fully with these duties, and was, as noted, already beginning to feel the effects of the cancer that would soon lead to his final illness. In addition, his respect for General Briggs may have convinced him simply to leave this thorny and long-range issue to his successor. In any event, the process continued to move forward, and accreditation *was* granted the Academy in time for the graduation of the first class in June 1959. Harmon's comment to Secretary Talbott—"Our goal is to the stars and they are a long way off"—was true, but the Academy was closing on them rapidly.

Towards the end of the Academy's first academic year, Harmon requested a board of general officers to review the program. This board, which consisted of Major Generals James E. Briggs, Ralph P. Swofford and Matthew K. Deichelmann, examined the curriculum and made several suggestions. They were unanimous that the academic program was too heavy; the maximum load for all four years should not exceed 140 academic semester hours. They suggested new classes in logistics and in aeronautical design. All cadets should receive foreign language instruction, and one of the languages offered should be Russian. The superintendent should remove himself from the Academy Board as a voting member so as to maintain a "reserve position." A permanent dean should be appointed immediately.[91] Overall, it was a complimentary report with useful advice.

The following month the first Board of Visitors (BOV) meeting was held at the Academy. The membership of the Board was glittering: Generals Carl Spaatz and Charles Lindbergh; noted academics Arthur Compton, Virgil Hancher and John Hannah; and several senators and representatives. The members attended cadet classes, and were briefed on plans and operations. In their report, the BOV commended Harmon and his staff for inspired leadership during the Academy's formative years. It thought the curriculum was sound, but recommended against making any significant changes over the next three or four years—"revolutionary changes would be most unwise."[92] The BOV also thought the individual courses could be better integrated into a more comprehensive whole. The classroom instruction was presented with "great enthusiasm and in an interesting manner."[93] As noted earlier, Dr. Hancher also commented to Harmon that he personally was concerned about the quality of the all-military faculty—echoing the concerns of the NCACSS. The Honor Code was hailed as a very positive factor in cadet life. The BOV report concluded: "The Force Academy bears indelibly the stamp of its Superintendent, Lieutenant General Hubert R. Harmon, and his well chosen staff."[94]

Overall, the Academy's first year had been challenging, interesting, exciting and successful. As the BOV acknowledged, much of that success was due to Hubert Harmon.

CHAPTER 12

"The Academy is his Monument"

*I*t had been Eisenhower's plan that Harmon would be superintendent for only two years—until the summer of 1956. At the same time, the president made an exception to the unwritten rule that the position was a two-star slot—he let Harmon keep his third star. Indeed, when West Point nominated a lieutenant general to be its new superintendent in July 1954, Eisenhower sent a sharp rebuke. Although he ultimately relented and allowed the assignment, he wrote a strong memo to all three academies telling them bluntly to plan ahead—he would not again approve a similar request, regardless of the circumstances; Harmon had been an exception to the policy and should not be repeated.[1]

As a consequence, Harmon knew well in advance that he would not shepherd his first class through to graduation, or even to their permanent home near Colorado Springs. That seemed not to bother him. He was ebullient that he was given the opportunity to *begin* the Academy. That was enough. To General Lauris Norstad then stationed at NATO he wrote: "I can only assure you it will receive every ounce of enthusiasm I possess. Along with that I shall pray for a great deal of divine guidance."[2] Enthusiasm he possessed aplenty. To a friend he wrote: "The job of Superintendent is fascinating, and I have grown ten years younger in the assignment."[3] Would only that had been the case.

Harmon had already been planning for his final retirement. The family would move back to their home on Westover Road in San Antonio. He would stay busy. Besides playing golf every chance he got, he would also become president of the new Kelly Field National Bank.[4] To an old friend Harmon wrote that he intended on retiring because of his age, 63; it was too expensive to run households both in Denver and San Antonio; and the job at Kelly National Bank would not wait another year.[5] Even so, leaving his beloved Academy was not easy. To Secretary Talbott, who had become a close personal friend, he wrote: "Needless to say, I would like to stay on here forever. Nevertheless, I feel very definitely that because of my age I should now step down and out and leave the thrilling task to younger hands."[6]

The "younger hands" would be those of Major General James E. Briggs. "Buster" was West Point, Class of 1928. He and Harmon had not crossed paths until Briggs was assigned to the Air Staff. In 1955 Harmon had then asked him to chair the curriculum board that had recommended, among other things, to lighten the load on freshmen. Briggs was offered the job of superintendent on 15 December 1955, and his appointment was announced the following March. It was initially planned that Briggs would not arrive at Lowry until August, but events would necessitate his arrival in June.[7] General Briggs would prove an excellent choice as superintendent.

Harmon had suffered from respiratory problems since he was a child, and these were aggravated by his bouts with influenza and pneumonia in 1918. For most of his adult life he suffered from recurring bouts of bronchitis. In the spring of 1956 these maladies seemed to be worsening. When climbing hills at the permanent Academy site he had become distressingly short of breath. Rosa-Maye's diary during this period refers frequently to her husband being tired and going to bed soon after dinner. On 30 April, Harmon began to feel ill during a briefing on cadet selection procedures for the new class. He left work and went to the base dispensary. The doctors noted a condition of "an increasing harassing cough with associated tiredness and feeling run down."[8] They then sent him to Fitzsimmons Army Hospital, also in Denver. X-rays revealed a tumor in his lungs. The doctors wanted to schedule immediately an exploratory operation, but Harmon demurred. He had promised to give a talk to his cadets on the evening of 7 May. He would not break that date. The doctors agreed that a delay of two weeks would make little difference.[9] Harmon returned to his office and wrote out his will in longhand.[10] At this point, he said nothing to his wife.

On 6 May, Harmon began to get nervous about his upcoming talk to the cadets. What would he say? The man who had been the life of every party suddenly seemed at a loss for words. Rosa-Maye calmed him, telling him simply to be at ease and tell stories about his life and career. Once he began, she knew he would have no trouble connecting with his audience. She was right. His remarks to the cadets, some of their girlfriends, and also some of the Academy staff, were, in Rosa-Maye's words: "The finest talk of my General's career, which went unrecorded." Well, not quite unrecorded.

Several cadets and staff members took notes on what Harmon said that night in Arnold Hall. He began by reminiscing about his career, recalling his time as a cadet and then as a young pilot. He had stories of flying—when he ran out of fuel in Wyoming, crashed his plane in Connecticut, and landed in a park for an ice cream cone. He told the assembled that in 1927 he made the wisest move of his life when he married Rosa-Maye Kendrick. He reminisced about his attaché assignment in England where he studied "rugs, china, silver and various other objects of art as well as worm-infested furniture." There had been many years of schooling, learning about airpower, war planning, and staff duties—all were vital. He skipped lightly over the war years, but emphasized his five-year tour at the United Nations. He told the cadets that his experience there convinced him "that future Air Force officers must be able to express their ideas so clearly and forcibly that they can hold their own with representatives of other nations and other military services."

Turning to the Academy, he said that he expected the cadets would move to the permanent site in the summer of 1958. He noted that the recent curriculum review board had reiterated that foreign language would be mandatory for all and that there would be no electives or academic majors.[11] As faculty members were wont to claim: the unique core curriculum was the Academy's academic major. As for military training, Harmon stated: "It is expected that you will help to indoctrinate the new cadets firmly, though not unkindly. There should and will be no hazing. It is expected that the treatment of freshmen classes will be pleasant, agreeable, and wholesome."

He offered advice based on his own long experience in uniform. He emphasized to his cadets the absolute importance of "complete integrity, both internal and external. In this connection, I can think of no better advice than that of Shakespeare's Polonius to his son: 'This above all: to thine own self be true, and it must follow, as the night the day, thou canst not then be false to any man.'" Harmon stressed the importance of loyalty, but cautioned that this was a two-way street. Too many thought that it only extended upwards, to superiors, but he emphasized that it must also flow downwards, to subordinates. A commander must take care of his personnel. If he did so, they would take care of him. He stressed the need to ensure an attention to detail in all work. As officers, they must always remember to take their duties seriously, but never themselves: "Your reputation will be the sum total of what other people think of you." He concluded by advising his young men to choose very carefully whom they would marry: "A loyal wife with interests similar to her husband's can contribute enormously to success in life; a wrong wife can be a tremendous handicap."[12]

It was a wonderful and inspiring talk, and it was one the cadets would remember and take with them.

The following day, Harmon saw the doctors at Fitzsimmons. He went back a few days later for more tests, but still told Rosa-Maye little—she thought he was merely going in for a checkup. On 14 May, Colonel Max Boyd called Rosa-Maye and advised her to speak to the doctors directly. Hubert could keep the problem secret no longer. On 17 May Harmon underwent surgery; the results revealed that the tumor was malignant and inoperable—it was too close to his heart to risk its removal. The doctors told him that he had perhaps one year to live. Yet, as Rosa-Maye wrote her family and friends, "Hubert refused to be downcast."[13]

Because Harmon believed it was wrong to hide such things, he directed a press release that acknowledged the operation and that he had lung cancer. On 1 June he flew to Walter Reed hospital in Washington DC for further treatment. Initially, he was in high spirits: President Eisenhower was in the hospital at the same time, recovering from a bout of ileitis. The two had a good time catching up and discussing their golf games. The good humor soon passed. Harmon remained at Walter Reed for the next six weeks to undergo radiation treatments. They made him miserable. In a poignant note to Rosa-Maye, Hubert advised his beloved wife not to come to Washington to visit him. The treatments were so debilitating that he would "not be fit company for anyone."[14] Sergeant Wall remembers seeing the large black area on Harmon's side—the effect of the radiation treatments—that was a source of great pain for the general.

He slowly began to mend. In early July he wrote his "Rosie" that he was "living the life of Riley" and that he was eating well and receiving excellent treatment. He received flowers from "our beloved President" and had gotten out a golf club to practice his grip. He was planning on making a comeback and becoming a scratch golfer. There was an endless stream of visitors: Eisenhower, Talbott, Twining, Spaatz, relatives and friends, even Charles Lindbergh stopped in to say hello.[15]

Yet, there was a final military duty that he felt compelled to perform. There would be one last parade and one last chance to review his Cadet Wing. Harmon had recovered sufficiently to return to Colorado on 12 July. He walked off his plane, the *Phoenix Bird*, in uniform, and Rosa-Maye thought he looked stronger than he had in months. Even so, he spent most of the next two weeks in bed, exhausted. On 26 July he ventured into his office to discuss plans for the change of command ceremony scheduled for the following day when he would turn over the Academy to General Briggs.[16]

The following afternoon proved dark, overcast and threatening. Harmon dismissed the weather reports. The new Air Force secretary, Donald Quarles, was on hand, and Harmon wanted to impress him with the professionalism of his cadets. After delaying the start for fifteen minutes, the general directed the band to strike up the music. Minutes later, after the event had already begun, the heavens opened. Briggs later stated that he was "scared to death." He remembered that "thunder and lightning were all over the place, and the kids were out there with their guns, and the lightning arresters, the rifles had bayonets on. I was sure we were going to kill about ten cadets out there, if we didn't kill General Harmon

Harmon's final retirement in July 1956 when the heavens opened after the parade had begun. From left to right: Air Force Secretary Donald Quarles, Harmon (in civilian rain-coat), Briggs, and Stillman.

in the pouring rain."[17] No one died, but the *Denver Post* chided the Academy the next day, noting that the assembled dignitaries and guests largely fled for shelter. The ceremony was cut short, "but not until some 450 cadets training to be air generals of the future sloshed through ankle-deep water as they passed in review like infantrymen."[18] Harmon, Quarles, Briggs, and Stillman stood ramrod straight and reviewed the entire event throughout the deluge. Finally, Sergeant Wall grabbed a civilian raincoat and draped it over Harmon's shoulders.

When the first class was set to graduate three years later, the base newspaper at the permanent site ran an article reminiscing about the send-off parade for General Harmon: "It was not a shower; it was as though the gods had turned their bathtubs upside down." The sky grew so dark that photographers could not get a reading on their light meters. The parade went on. One cadet who marched that day summed the feelings of so many others: "We were in real high spirits that day, all of us were. The parade was for Gen. Harmon and we wanted to be in that parade. The rain didn't make any difference at all. … [we] really wanted to do it for the Old Man."[19]

Because of the storm, the third Distinguished Service Medal that Quarles was to pin on Harmon's blouse was instead given to him at a party that night. A letter from General Twining was read that thanked Harmon for his forty years of conscientious service and devotion to duty. Twining noted that "as important as anything else" is the Academy—"you are the 'father' of the Air Force Academy."[20] Harmon then came to the podium, thanked the secretary, General Twining, and all present. Typically, he brushed-off talk of his achievements: "The Academy is the product of the devoted efforts of several hundred officers, airmen, and civilians." He finished by wishing all, especially the cadets, congratulations and good luck. He said that he hoped to see all of them again in the fall—perhaps at a football game.[21] Many of those who attended that evening were still in uniforms soaked by the storm, but no one's enthusiasm was dampened.

Four days later Harmon's staff held a going-away party for him at the headquarters building. As a retirement present, Harmon's staff bought their boss a golf cart. There were strict rules about giving senior officers presents that exceeded a certain value, but in this instance, no one paid any attention to those rules.

He would get little use of the cart. Hubert and Rosa-Maye flew to their home in San Antonio a few days later, while Sergeant Wall drove their car down

from Denver. Hubert was able to golf on one or two occasions, but less than a month after his retirement he was back in the hospital, this time at Lackland AFB in San Antonio. Constant headaches caused the doctors to do a thorough examination. They found a brain tumor, and they would have to operate. Hubert was "crushed by the verdict" and he, Rosa-Maye and Eula wept together. Soon after, however, their spirits were lifted by the cards, books, and flowers that flooded in by the dozens. Harmon answered nearly all of them, despite his failing health. His spirits remained high.

Harmon, looking tired but proud, in the golf cart given to him by his staff at his going-away party in July 1956.

The brain operation on 5 September prompted Rosa-Maye to write Briggs that this event "obliges us to face the future and make plans and arrangements."[22] Still, the general fought on. The following month he told Rosa-Maye and others that the X-rays of his chest were negative—the doctors told him "they got it all"—so he was now "full of optimism."

It was not to be. In November they operated again and "took a chunk" out of his right shoulder to remove a cancerous tumor; yet, he still wrote a warm letter to Rosie O'Donnell a week later stating: "The privilege of serving with the Academy during its first year more than compensates for any misfortunes which may follow. I am eternally grateful to you and Nate [Twining]."[23]

He continued to see his friends, usually at the Saint Anthony Country Club, although now his activities were confined to cards and domino games. He also wrote short notes to his many friends who continued to wish him well. In mid-November a group of officers flew in from Lowry to visit, and Sergeant Wall brought films of the Academy football team. During December the general was in and out of the Lackland hospital on several occasions, but was home with his family for Christmas. In February, Kendrick, now a first classman at West Point, wrote to his father to tell him that he decided to choose the Infantry upon graduation. He then talked of his hopes for the future. It was the letter of a self-confident and brash young man, but it was one from the heart. He wrote:

> If I have learned the love of life, joviality, keenness of mind, practicality, leadership and the like from me ole Paw (not to mention a few golf and tennis tips), from me ole Maw I have picked up a stubbornness to maintain certain standards and a fastidious attitude toward the accomplishment of certain tasks, not to mention the strong urge to reason deeply, into the various situations that confront me.[24]

It was the type of letter to bring tears to the eyes of any parent.

On 3 February the general entered the Lackland hospital for the last time. Soon after, Kendrick was granted leave by West Point to be with his dad. On 20 February, Hubert slipped into a restless sleep and only awoke occasionally and for brief periods. On Friday afternoon, 22 February 1957, with Rosa-Maye at his side, Hubert Harmon passed away. He was five weeks short of his 65th birthday.

His wishes were that he be cremated and his ashes preserved until the new Academy cemetery was completed. On 28 September 1958, Harmon's remains were the first to be interred at the Air Force Academy. A contingent of cadets,

*The Cadet Wing, resplendent in white parade uniforms, turns out for the internment of
Harmon's remains at the new Academy cemetery on September 28, 1958.*

resplendent in their white parade uniforms, was on hand to see him off. The
minister, Colonel John Bennett, gave a short homily, noting that Harmon had
told him he had but three regrets: leaving his family, leaving projects undone,
and not being able to see the first Academy class graduate. Bennett then made
an appropriate comment—the Air Force Academy was the general's true monument. It was indeed.

Rosa-Maye Harmon never remarried. She remained in San Antonio for
several years, but eventually moved back to Wyoming. She would die there on 5
August 1979. She was buried next to her husband in the Academy cemetery.[25]

Retrospective

Hubert Harmon was the ideal man for the great challenge given to him in 1949
and again in 1954. He was the perfect choice to fight the agonizingly long journey from conception to fulfillment of the Air Force Academy. This was so for
several reasons.

Harmon was a born organizer and administrator. From early in his career
it was obvious that his strength lay in staff work. He was conscientious, dedicated, tireless, and meticulous. He knew how to budget his time and prioritize
so as to get the important things done first. As he advanced in rank his duties
became more complex and demanding—the 1st Wing at March Field and then

the War Department G-1—but he continued to excel. Because of the vast expansion for war in 1940, Harmon was sent to Kelly Field and then Randolph to oversee the dramatic acceleration of the aircrew training program. After unhappy interludes in operational commands—in which he did well but was not exceptional—Harmon returned to the tasks for which he was so well suited—staff and the command of a new personnel organization. For two years, he criss-crossed the country standing up the Personnel Distribution Command from scratch—hiring hundreds of people, taking care of millions, and locating, leasing, and building scores of facilities.

Harmon in one of his last photographs—looking cheerful and upbeat despite his recent brain surgery.

It must be realized that World War II was a relentlessly Darwinian affair. Some officers, like Harmon, but also those like Spaatz, Vandenberg, Twining, LeMay, Doolittle, Quesada, Norstad and many others, were given a chance to perform and exercise an enormous amount of authority that belied their youth and seeming inexperience. Those who rose to the occasion and performed well are those whose names we remember. Those who were not up to the challenge were ruthlessly pushed aside: there was a war to be won. As a consequence, it is no exaggeration to state that the entire academy project—though complex and wide-ranging—was no more difficult and perhaps even less so, than what Harmon had already accomplished during the war.

Second, Harmon was a master of personal relations, and this was not an affectation. He genuinely liked people and their company. It gave him pleasure to please others. He cared. He listened. When writing letters he tried to personalize each one—a reference to a previous meeting, a comment on the school football team, an apposite literary reference. He killed people with kindness. His obvious concern made his subordinates love him so that their worst fear was not that "the boss" would be angry—far worse, that he would be disappointed in them. Because of his sincerity and good will, these same subordinates would not take advantage of him. Repeatedly, in interviews and letters one reads: "I loved that man" or "he was the greatest guy I ever knew." This was not hyperbole or obligatory testimonials given after Harmon had passed away. Rather, these were heartfelt sentiments. McDermott later said: "General Harmon was a prince of a man. I really loved that man."[26] Stillman characterized him as "a lovable man; a fine, human gentleman. He was courteous, thoughtful of other people; he was one of the true gentlemen that it's been my privilege to work for."[27] General Briggs noted that Harmon had a unique relationship with his subordinates: "It was not only one of respect but it was one of true love, affection, and sincere devotion to duty, as General Harmon led them to their duty."[28] Ira Eaker, Harmon's colleague and poker partner for decades, wrote that Doodle was "one of the finest gentlemen with the best balanced personality and character I think I ever knew. He joined the characteristics of gentleness and kindness with great industry and intelligence."[29]

As also noted, however, this gentleness of spirit on some occasions proved a detriment. Harmon gave subordinates room to do their jobs. He expected his senior officers to know their business and to do the right thing. Regarding the first dean and athletic director, however, he obviously was too lax in his oversight. Fortunately, there were others nearby who saw what needed to be done and stepped up. The Academy did not suffer serious damage.

Third, Harmon was intellectually inclined and conditioned to establish and run the Academy. As he himself admitted, he was not an educator, although he had spent a great deal of time during his life as a student at the college level—over nine years—with three more in educational administration and five years in a training environment. Harmon therefore had a well-defined sense of what a quality education entailed and what was required to make it work. He knew and understood what motivated students and how they learned. He recognized the requirement for well-qualified teachers and administrators. Because he was an intelligent and thoughtful man, he had given much reflection to the subject and the problems of education.

In addition, of course, his four years as the Special Assistant for Air Academy Matters made him the unquestioned expert on the subject of an academy. To be sure, this had never been the expectation—of either Harmon or the Air Force leadership. When Vandenberg named him the Special Assistant all believed that Congress would act quickly and the school would open in a year—another officer had already been identified to be the first superintendent. Harmon's role in the academy project was thus initially seen merely as a temporary "additional duty" to handle the paper work in the project's initial stages. As we have seen, this turned out not to be the case. For reasons that were beyond the control of Harmon or anyone else in the Air Force, Congress and the Truman administration simply did not act. There were significant reasons for this lack of aggressiveness—the Korean War, the West Point cheating scandal, and funding problems—but there were also reasons, equally out of Harmon's control, which were less weighty—political maneuverings over the academy's location, and simple bureaucratic inertia. The result of all of this tardiness, whether justified or not, meant that the path to an Air Force Academy would be long and tortuous.

The unintended effect of this slow-moving process was that Harmon had the time to think through all aspects of an air academy in great depth —its curriculum, disciplinary system, organization, location, personnel requirements, and construction. He was able to dwell on details. Because his job at the United Nations did not require much of his time, Harmon was able to focus on one project and *become* the educator that the situation demanded.

And so, for over six years Hubert Harmon spent the majority of his working day dealing with the possibilities and challenges of an Air Force Academy. In a very real sense, there was no other officer in the country who knew more about the issue. Harmon was the unquestioned expert.

Fourth, Harmon well understood the political environment in which he had to work. His education began with Air Service staff experience in Washington from 1921 to 1927. His duties included working closely with Congress, especially when he was named chief of the Information Division. Another of his obligations during that period was working as a White House aide, which gave him another opportunity to mingle with politicians and better understand the government process. And then of course there was his marriage to Rosa-Maye and the association with her father, Senator John Kendrick. The letters between Harmon and his father-in-law reflect a close and respectful relationship. Given Rosa-Maye's political awareness, as well as Hubert's, the contacts with the Kendrick family sharpened Harmon's budding instincts.

Hubert Harmon's political education was further advanced by subsequent tours as an air attaché in London, command in Texas that involved a great deal of interaction with local politicians during World War II, and his tours in Panama and at the United Nations following the war. All of these assignments gave him a deepening appreciation for the intricacies, complications, and contradictions of the political process. In addition, as we have seen, this experience caused him to push hard for a strong, internationalist approach in the Air Force Academy curriculum.

Even this lengthy exposure to the political scene, however, was insufficient to prepare him adequately for his tenure as Special Assistant for Air Academy Matters. The unpredictable nature of his Congressional dealings between 1949 and 1954 was enormously frustrating. Yet, the ingenuity and sheer endurance he displayed during this period were impressive. This extended apprenticeship also meant that Harmon became well and personally acquainted with a number of congressmen and their staffs, as well as officials in the Bureau of the Budget. All of this added up and contributed to a certain amount of capital he held in account with people who mattered. By 1954 he was an old hand in Washington. His performance during the House and Senate hearings, which earned the praise of Chairman Dewey Short, was flawless and reflected his long participation in the legislative arena.

Once the Academy was actually authorized, Harmon's warm relations with President Eisenhower became a factor. To a great extent, this closeness was merely a function of their having been West Point classmates and team-mates. It is difficult to exaggerate the importance of the Academy connection. By 1954 there were slightly over one hundred men left from the Class of 1915; they had been through two world wars together as well as the Korean War; they had endured the long peace between the world wars when the military was neglected and in the doldrums. These men knew each other, and in most cases, liked and respected one another. This was certainly true of Eisenhower and Harmon, as the unusually warm and personal letter written by Ike when he was the NATO commander in 1952 illustrates. There is no evidence whatsoever that Harmon ever attempted to trade on this friendship. In one sense, that was not necessary: the president's support for Harmon, and by extension the Academy, was known and understood by all. In June 1954 the Eisenhowers threw a party in the White House for the Class of 1915. In the group photo taken of all attendees on the back staircase, the Harmons are in the front row with the president and first lady. Harmon was the only member still on active duty.

After his friend's death, Eisenhower wrote Rosa-Maye a moving tribute: "Hubert was loved and admired by many; to Mamie and me he always seemed the ideal classmate and so for him we had a boundless affection … He lived by the motto of his Alma Mater [duty, honor, country] and so he was a loyal friend, a great and gallant soldier, a distinguished citizen of our country."[30]

Fifth and finally, Harmon succeeded with the Air Force Academy simply because he loved it; he loved the idea of an academy; and, most importantly, he loved cadets. As noted at the beginning of this study, the Harmon clan was an unusually strong military family. Most especially, it was a strong West Point family with thirty-one of its members being graduates. Throughout his life Hubert Harmon harbored a deep attachment and appreciation for the Military Academy. It shaped his life, teaching and reinforcing inherited traits of character, integrity

The Class of 1915 gathers at the White House in June 1954. Hubert and Rosa-Maye (with her face averted) are in the front row. Harmon was the only member of his class still on active duty at the time.

and dedication. His return to West Point as a tactical officer in 1929 increased his endearment for the Military Academy, while at the same time putting him in a position as a commander of cadets. He relished the experience.

It should also be noted that he was a decent man who believed in equality. He was insistent that the Air Force Academy should never be a school for the privileged. It was to be a leveler. One aspect of this belief was expressed in his directive to Colonel Whitlow regarding the scheduling of football games. Many Southern schools were still segregated. For Harmon that presented insurmountable obstacles. Although the first class did not contain any black cadets, Harmon expected that future classes would. As a result, it would be unacceptable to play schools that would not permit visiting black athletes to use the same facilities and hotels as the white cadets. Teams in such states would therefore not be scheduled. Harmon would not permit discrimination against any of his cadets.[31]

By the time the first air cadets arrived at Lowry AFB, Harmon was already 63 years old—an age when most men are already grandfathers. He looked the part. It is therefore understandable that he was seen as a warm and paternal figure to cadets—there were plenty of others around with stern miens who could impose discipline. Such warm feelings were reciprocated. Harmon drew strength and energy from his association with these young men. It was not unusual for him to leave his office and walk outside between class periods, just so that he might meet and talk to the cadets. When General Ed Rawlings (the Air Force comptroller) came to speak to the Cadet Wing, the cadets "flocked" around Harmon in the lobby of Arnold Hall after the presentation, and Rosa-Maye had a hard time getting him away from them and back home.[32] A story that epitomizes the relationship between Harmon and cadets was later recalled by his wife.

One afternoon the general returned to his quarters after work and Rosa-Maye noticed the smile on his face and that her husband was in an unusually upbeat mood. She asked him why. Harmon responded that when he left the office and stepped out onto the sidewalk he encountered two cadets who were passing by. Upon seeing him, they snapped to attention, saluted smartly, smiled, and exclaimed: "Hi, General Harmon!"[33] It made his day. It summed his life.

The combination of respect and affection this incident reveals says much about Harmon and the impact that he had on the Academy and its personnel. In the words of old friend Bruce Hopper, he had become "immortal." Hubert Harmon was indeed the Father of the Air Force Academy, the ideal man for the job.

Endnotes

Chapter 1

1 John Honeycutt, "The Harmon Clan at West Point," December 15, 1976, located in Hubert R. Harmon Collection (HRHC) at the Air Force Academy, Addendum (A) 3, Box (B) 1, Folder (F) 6. The oldest graduate listed was Amiel W. Whipple, Class of 1841, who died at the Battle of Chancellorsville. He was the great-grandfather of Sallie Whipple, who married Cornelius Lang (Class of 1935), who was Hubert's nephew.

2 Ltr., Eula Harmon Hoff (Hubert Harmon's daughter; hereinafter, EHH) to author, June 23, 2007; genealogy data prepared by the Harmon family and provided by EHH.

3 US Military Academy, "Official Register of the Officers and Cadets," 1877–1880, various pages each year.

4 Genealogy material provided by EHH.

5 PMA was a venerable military school, and in 1869 it was the first in the country to be assigned a US Army detail. Although at one point they flogged wayward cadets at PMA, by the time Millard Harmon arrived that practice had ended; however, they still did lock cadets in "dark prison" on a diet of bread and water! Ruth Henderson Moli, "Decades of Dedication," March 24, 1955, paper presented at a meeting of the PMA Ladies. Copy located in HRHC, B4, F4.

6 The Reillys were a Philadelphia family who were quite close to the Harmons, and when Hubert was born Millard and Madelin asked the Reillys if they could use their name for their new son.

7 A letter from Millard Harmon to his wife, dated October 21, 1892, notes that the child died the day before and was laid to rest in Oak Ridge Cemetery. She was only two and a half at her "release from bondage." Copy of letter provided by EHH.

8 "Slip in Etiquette Sends Colonel Off," *New York Times*, June 23, 1913, 7.

9 Much of the foregoing is derived from US Military Academy, "Annual Report, June 11, 1930," 149–52; and George W. Cullum, *Biographical Register of the Officers and Graduates of the U.S. Military Academy at West Point,* *New York* (Saginaw, MI: Sherman and Peters, multiple volumes and publication years), IV, 327; V, 305; VI, 291. Hubert Harmon would later note on a medical form that his father suffered from aphasia. Millard Harmon's grandchildren state they heard that "Gampy" was suffering from what today would be termed Alzheimer's disease.

10 Much of this material is derived from notes written by Rosa-Maye Harmon in the early 1960s. At that point she attempted to gather information regarding her late husband's early life from Hubert's surviving brother and sister and his West Point classmates. These notes are extensive and are located in HRHC, A4, B21, F2. (Hereinafter, Notes by RMH.) The story of the history reading is from a phone conversation with EHH on June 14, 2007.

11 US Military Academy, *The Howitzer*, Cadet Yearbook, 1910, 65. Handwritten notes by EHH, November 1989, HRHC, A4, B19, F1. Kenneth graduated twenty-third in a class of eighty-three—better than either of his brothers.

12 Ltr., K. Harmon to Rosa-Maye Harmon, (RMH), June 12, 1961, HRHC, A4, B20, F6. The Academy archives contain an entire file of such puzzles that Hubert Harmon had collected over the years. Incidentally, I have no idea what the solution is to the "girls in column" puzzle.

13 In a letter from Millard Harmon to Madelin, the colonel instructed his wife to give Hubert money to find an "entirely respectable" boarding house in Brooklyn. Ltr., M.F. Harmon to Madelin Harmon, August, 25, 1909, copy supplied by EHH.

14 Ltr., HRH to "Papa," June 28, 1907, contained in "West Point Scrapbook" held by Kendrick Harmon.

15 Though dated, an interesting and insightful account of the war remains Walter Millis, *The Martial Spirit: A Study of Our War with Spain* (NY: Viking, 1965), chapters 6 and 8.

16 Russell F. Weigley, *History of the United States Army* (NY: Macmillan, 1967), chapter 14; Philip C. Jessup, *Elihu Root* (NY: Dodd, Mead, 1938), Part III.

17 In the Army, the percentage of officers who were West Point graduates hovered around 25 percent in 1900. Army leaders wanted that percentage increased to 50 percent. In 1915 the percentage had grown to 44 percent, but then dropped back to around 30 percent by 1920. US Military Academy, "Annual Report of the Superintendent," 1915, 4; same Report for 1920, 4.

18 Theodore J. Crackel, *West Point: A Bicentennial History* (Lawrence: University Press of Kansas, 2002), 169–78.

19 Roger H. Nye, "The United States Military Academy in an Era of Educational Reform, 1900–1925," PhD Dissertation, Columbia University, 1968, 351.

20 Gen Omar N. Bradley and Clay Blair, *A General's Life* (NY: Simon & Schuster, 1983), 30.

21 Nye, 38–39; Crackel, 163.

22 There were a few civilians on the Academy staff, such as the chaplain, dentist and bandleader, but it was not until 1904–05 that three civilian instructors were hired to teach foreign language. US Military Academy, "Official Register of the Officers and Cadets," 1905, 7.

23 Crackel, 197; US Military Academy, "Annual Report of the Superintendent," 1915, 19.

24 Nye, 47.

25 The seven "charter" departments employing permanent professors were Civil and Military Engineering, Natural and Experimental Philosophy, Chemistry and Electricity, Modern Languages, Mathematics, Drawing, and English and History. The other departments, headed by officers (usually lieutenant colonels) "detailed" on temporary duty from the Army were Military Hygiene, Practical Military Engineering, Law, and Ordnance and Gunnery.

26 Nye, 49.

27 Capt Robert C. Richardson, *West Point: An Intimate Portrait of the National Military Academy and the Life of the Cadet* (NY: G.P. Putnam's Sons, 1917), 177.

28 Stephen E. Ambrose, *Eisenhower, Vol. I: Soldier* (NY: Simon & Schuster, 1983), 47.

29 Nye, 354.

30 Crackel, 160, 162, 181. Of note, Larned was the Professor of Drawing when Millard Harmon, Sr. arrived as a cadet in 1876. He was still there when Millard, Jr. arrived thirty-two years later.

31 Nye, 361. An academic presence was always small. Prior to 1907 the Board of Visitors, usually containing around a dozen members, was composed almost entirely of active-duty and retired generals and serving representatives and senators. The Board, whose composition changed each year, only contained a single university professor. After 1907, however, even that minor academic influence was removed. The Board of Visitor reports for each year, which list the members, are available on line through the Military Academy's library website: http://www.library.usma.edu/archives.asp.

32 Crackel, 182–84. The extra two votes were

taken away in 1911, restoring unquestioned dominance to the permanent professors.

33 Crackel, 181–82. Because of the virtual impossibility of finding a serving officer with the appropriate credentials, the new department head chosen was a Yale PhD with no military experience—Lucius Holt. He was immediately commissioned into the Army as a lieutenant colonel. It is illustrative that the Academy had offered courses in English and history for its entire existence, but they were generally taught by the chaplain. Crackel, 163.

34 Notable exceptions were Major Generals John Logan for the North and John B. Gordon for the South.

35 The first four Air Force chiefs of staff were Carl A. Spaatz (Class of 1914), Hoyt S. Vandenberg (Class of 1923), Nathan F. Twining (Class of 1918), and Thomas D. White (Class of 1920). The string was broken by Curtis E. LeMay, an ROTC graduate.

36 US Military Academy, "Official Register of the Officers and Cadets," 1911, 5.

37 Nye, 15–25.

38 US Military Academy, "Official Register of the Officers and Cadets," 1912, 54. Crackel argues that by 1900 the test was "elementary" compared to that of leading schools like Yale, Columbia and MIT, 164.

39 Notes by RMH. Presumably, Rosa-Maye was told this story by Hubert. She later wrote his older brother Kenneth asking for more details; he confirmed the story. Notes and correspondence between Rosa-Maye and Kenneth Harmon, HRHC, A4, B20, F6.

40 Ltr., Gen L. Wood to HRH, September 21, 1910, HRHC, A4, B20, F6. In his letter, Wood wrote a postscript in his own hand: "If you can get an appointment from Mr. Oliver, by all means get it." Presumably, Wood was referring to George T. Oliver, the Republican senator from Pennsylvania. The chances of Harmon getting an appointment from Oliver were slim: according to the rules, a candidate had to reside in the same state as the senator who appointed him. (In the case of a Congressional appointment, the candidate had to reside in the same district.) Although born in Chester, Pennsylvania, Hubert had not lived in the state for years. Wood had been the commanding general of the Eastern Division, headquartered on Governor's Island, immediately preceding his elevation to chief of staff in April 1910; he knew the Harmon family well.

41 Notes by RMH.

42 Congress had authorized the growth of the Cadet Battalion to 748 cadets by 1914. Harmon's class of 252 was the largest to enter in Academy history to that point. In fact, the freshman class made up 44 percent of the entire Cadet Battalion in 1911. By 1916, the year after Harmon graduated, the number of cadets authorized would nearly double to 1332 cadets. Crackel, 179. By then there were three battalions—so it was now termed the Corps of Cadets.

43 Francis T. Miller, *Eisenhower: Man and Soldier* (Philadelphia: John C. Winston, 1944), 135. Of interest, Eisenhower, also Harmon's classmate, thought all of this was infantile; whereas, Bradley "loved every minute of it." Dwight D. Eisenhower, *At Ease: Stories I Tell to Friends* (Garden City, NY: Doubleday, 1967), chapter 1; Bradley and Blair, 30.

44 Richardson, 118; US Military Academy, "Annual Report of the Superintendent," 1911, 4.

45 The term "plebe" comes from the Roman term "plebian" or commoner. The cadet yearbook, *The Howitzer*, defines plebe as: "a fourth classman. An insignificant member of W.P. society. Scum of the earth." US Military Academy, *The Howitzer*, 1915, 355.

46 US Military Academy, "Official Register of the Officers and Cadets," 1912, 63; Richardson, 134–35. In the cadet argot, a cadet's roommate was his "wife."

47 The superintendent in 1914–15, Col Clarence P. Townsley, noted the problem of over-zealous cadets who used excessive "discipline" with the plebes, but he opined that the problem was, for the time being at least, solved. US Military Academy, "Annual Report of the Superintendent," 1915, 12. One of the more famous epidemics of hazing occurred at the turn of the century. The story is told in Philip W. Leon, *Bullies and Cowards: The West Point Hazing Scandal, 1898–1901* (Westport, CT: Greenwood, 2000). In his biography of Eisenhower, Ambrose states that in 1911 "hazing was more widely practiced than at any time in the Academy's history." This seems an exaggeration, but undoubtedly hazing still occurred far more often than it should have. Ambrose, 44.

48 Bradley and Blair, 31.

49 Notes by RMH. He had been warned. After visiting West Point in 1906 to bring a sword up to Kenneth, Hubert was told by an upperclassman that if he became a cadet, "we will try to be as mean to you as we were to your brother."Ltr., HRH to "Papa," June 30, 1906, contained in "West Point Scrapbook" held by Kendrick Harmon.

50 Richardson, 151.

51 It was a measure of the Academy's outdated curriculum that these subjects—which should have been mastered in high school—were still required for all cadets.

52 US Military Academy, "Official Register of the Officers and Cadets," 1912, 24.

53 "Cadet Disciplinary Record for Cadet Hubert R. Harmon," copy provided to author by the USMA archivist.

54 It was one of the peculiarities of the Academy system that cadets on furlough could only stay with family or close friends—presumably to avoid the dens of iniquity in New York City. Those cadets from far away were thus often doomed to stay in the barracks over the holidays and summer. If fortunate, they would be invited home by other cadets whose families lived closer.

55 "Turnout exams" were also administered in June before graduation.

56 Richardson reports that there were a total of 170,835 minutes of academic classroom instruction in the four-year curriculum; 76,555—45 percent—were devoted to mathematical subjects. Richardson, 174–75.

57 US Military Academy, "Official Register of the Officers and Cadets," 1913, 71, 77. According to *The Howitzer*, a yearling was "a member of the third class. An unsophisticated mortal who dreams of furloughs, babbles foolishness, and howls at the moon." US Military Academy, *The Howitzer*, 1915, 355.

58 US Military Academy, "Official Register of the Officers and Cadets," 1914, 16–17.

59 US Military Academy, "Official Register of the Officers and Cadets," 1915, 71.

60 Crackel, 166–67. Of course, that equality did not extend to what were then termed Negroes, and indeed, there were very few Jews or Catholics at West Point during this era. One source notes that the vast majority of cadets were white, Anglo-Saxon, and Episcopalians from the South or from rural areas in the North. Peter Lyon, *Eisenhower: Portrait of the Hero* (Boston: Little, Brown, 1974), 43; Edward M. Coffman, *The Regulars: The American Army, 1898–1941* (Cambridge, MA: Belknap, 2004), 235–37.

61 "Cadet Disciplinary Record for Cadet Hubert R. Harmon," provided to author by the USMA archivist.

62 Of note, during his sophomore year, West Point played the Indian School at Carlisle Barracks. The star player on Carlisle's team was the legendary Jim Thorpe—he ran roughshod over the cadets, and the final score was 27–6.

63 Interview with Kendrick Harmon and Eula Harmon Hoff, by Col James C. Gaston, August 29, 2002, contained in James C. Gaston (ed.) *US Air Force Academy, 1954–2004: 50th Anniversary Oral History* (USAF Academy, CO: Friends of the Air Force Academy Library, 2005), 5.

64 Eisenhower had shown early promise as an outstanding running back, until severely injuring his knee. He remained on the team as a coach.

65 The year after MacArthur left West Point, the new superintendent, Maj Gen Fred Sladen, returned the summer camps to Academy grounds.

66 Crackel, 91. During the academic year, hops were held two Saturday evenings each month.

67 US Military Academy, *The Howitzer*, 1915, 355.

68 Interview with Brig Gen Hume Peabody, by Hugh Ahman, September 13–16, 1975, 61, located in Air Force Historical Research Agency (AFHRA), File K239.0512–867.

69 US Military Academy, *The Howitzer*, 1915, 101. The roommate was "Buddy" Cronkhite, who he had known for years; his father was an Army colonel—West Point Class of 1882—who had

been stationed at Governor's Island. Tragically, Buddy would die of an accidental gunshot wound in October 1918. Joe McNarney, George Stratemeyer and Joe Swing were, like Harmon, "clean sleeves" throughout their cadet careers.

70 Ltr., H. Peabody to RMH, April 29, 1961, HRHC, A4, B20, F6.

71 Ltr., J. Wogan to RMH, June 27, 1965, HRHC, A4, B20, F6. Although a good story, and no doubt essentially true, Harmon's cadet disciplinary record shows no entry for ten demerits received for using profanity during his entire four years. In fact, the only time he received that many demerits was for the wagering incident noted above. McGuire was turned back and graduated with the Class of 1916; Wogan retired as a major general in 1946 after a career in the Field Artillery. Other members of "the squirrels" were George Stratemeyer, Clifford King, Buddy Cronkhite, Sammy Cousins and H.J.F. Miller—the last two becoming major generals.

72 "Graduation Exercises, Class of 1915," Remarks by L.M. Garrison, HRHC, A4, B19, F6.

Chapter 2

1 Summary of Efficiency Reports, no specific dates, but months and years listed; this entry unsigned but dated 1915, HRHC, A4, B20, F5.

2 US Military Academy, "Five Year Book, Class of 1915," June 1921, 59. Actually, thirty of Harmon's classmates joined him in the Coast Artillery branch.

3 Summary of Efficiency Reports, no specific dates, but months and years listed; period covering 12 September to 30 November, 1915, signed by Capt J.C. Ohnstad, HRHC, A4, B20, F5.

4 "Five Year Book," 59; notes of a talk given by Lt Gen Harmon to cadets at the Air Force Academy, Lowry AFB, May 7, 1956, HRHC, B4, F5. (Hereinafter, Harmon talk to cadets.) Cannings were a type of artillery piece then in use.

5 Eula would note that her father always loved classical music and would often play it on the phonograph during dinner. Ltr., EHH to author, September 30, 2007.

6 Summary of Efficiency Reports, November 1916, signed by Lt Col W. Chamberlaine, HRHC, A4, B20, F5.

7 John Garry Clifford, *The Citizen Soldiers: The Plattsburg Training Camp Movement, 1913–1920* (Lexington: University Press of Kentucky, 1972), 159. Wood, not a West Point graduate, believed in universal military training for all American males—a stance that most regular Army officers opposed because they saw their own influence being diluted. See Penelope D. Clute, "The Plattsburg Idea," *New York Archives,* 5 (Fall 2005): 9–15.

8 Ralph Barton Perry, *The Plattsburg Movement* (NY: E.P. Dutton, 1921), 111–12.

9 Donald M. Kington, "The Plattsburg Movement and its Legacy," *Relevance,* 6 (Autumn 1997): 4.

10 In 1917 a "Junior Plattsburg Camp" was held on Plum Island off northern Long Island for boys of high school age. Of interest, Hoyt S. Vandenberg—who would play a significant role in Harmon's career many years later—attended this camp in 1917.

11 Perry, 117.

12 Clifford, 80; Jack C. Lane, *Armed Progressive: General Leonard Wood* (San Rafael, CA: Presidio Press, 1978), see chapter 14 for a good discussion of Wood's role and motives.

13 Clifford, 17.

14 Perry, 119.

15 Kington, 4. It also appears that some who had attended the earlier businessmen camps in 1916 returned after the US entered the war so they could earn commissions in the Army.

16 Ltr., Maj Gen L. Wood to HQ Eastern Department, September 12, 1916, HRHC, A4, B21, F4; notes by RMH.

17 Tom D. Crouch, *The Bishop's Boys: A Life of Wilbur and Orville Wright* (NY: W.W. Norton, 1989), 268–72.

18 "The Signal Corps Specification, No. 486" for a Flying Machine, dated December 23, 1907, is contained as an appendix in Charles deF. Chandler and Frank P. Lahm, *How Our Army Grew Wings: Airmen and Aircraft before 1914* (NY: Ronald, 1942), 295–98.

19 Crouch, 376–78. Selfridge Field near Detroit was named after the first military aviator to die in an airplane crash. There would be many more to follow; most of the early Army airfields were named after aircraft crash victims: Kelly, Brooks and Randolph (all near San Antonio), March (Riverside), Maxwell (Montgomery), Ellington (Houston), Barksdale (Shreveport), Love (Dallas), Rockwell (San Diego), Scott (Belleville), McChord (Tacoma), Clark (Philippines), and Albrook (Panama Canal Zone). Indeed, of the first twenty-four Army pilots, eight died in plane crashes.

20 The best description of early Army aviation remains the memoirs of its chief participants: Chandler and Lahm; Benjamin D. Foulois with Col C.V. Glines, *From the Wright Brothers to the Astronauts: The Memoirs of Major General Benjamin D. Foulois* (NY: McGraw-Hill, 1968); and H.H. Arnold, *Global Mission* (NY: Harper, 1949).

21 C.R. Rosenberry, *Glenn Curtiss: Pioneer of Flight* (Garden City, NY: Doubleday, 1972), 317.

22 Maj H.H. Arnold, "The History of Rockwell Field," 1923, 38–19, AFHRA File 168.65041.

23 Rebecca Hancock Cameron, *Training to Fly: Military Flight Training, 1907–1945* (Washington DC: Air Force History and Museums Program, 1999), 63.

24 Seth Shulman, *Unlocking the Sky: Glenn Hammond Curtiss and the Race to Invent the Airplane* (NY: HarperCollins, 2002), 227.

25 Maurer Maurer (ed.) *The U.S. Air Service in World War I,* 4 vols. (Washington DC: Office of Air Force History, 1978–79), II, 60–61. Miff

received his pilot certificate in July 1916—he was the 101st Army aviator. In 1937, Carl Spatz changed the spelling of his name to Spaatz because it was so often mispronounced. To avoid confusion, I will use Spaatz throughout.

26 US Army, "Report of the Chief Signal Officer to the Secretary of War, 1917," Washington DC, 1917, 7.

27 Cameron, 121. West Point classmates of Harmon who had already graduated from North Island included George Stratemeyer and Joe McNarney. Juliette A. Hennessy, *The United States Army Air Arm: April 1861 to April 1917* (Washington DC: Office of Air Force History, 1985), 241.

28 US Military Academy, "Five Year Book, Class of 1915," June 1921, 59; Peabody interview, 140. Most of those mentioned would remain life-long friends. Sammy Cousins was to be a groomsman at Hubert's wedding, and Earl Naiden was Hubert's chief of staff at Thirteenth Air Force during World War II. Of interest, upon being named as the first superintendent of the Air Force Academy, Harmon received a letter from a man who had been with him on North Island in 1917 and who remembered him well. He was pleased to see that Harmon had done alright for himself. Ltr., 1lt G.D. Litherland to HRH, August 2, 1955, HRHC, B1, F4.

29 Harmon talk to cadets.

30 Arnold, "History of Rockwell Field," 59.

31 Ibid., 59–62; Hennessy, 189–91. The incident occurred soon after Harmon's arrival, not before as he recollected forty years later. Glassford's deputy was Capt Frank Lahm, who backed his boss, thus earning the lasting enmity of a number of young flyers.

32 Hennessy, 91–94. Other aircraft then at North Island were Martins, Standards and Sturtevants.

33 Harmon talk to cadets.

34 Cameron, 77–78.

35 In 1916 the First Aero Squadron under the command of Maj Benjamin Foulois accompanied Brig Gen John Pershing into Mexico on his unsuccessful attempt to capture the bandit Pancho Villa. The handful of obsolescent aircraft that were sent into Mexico broke down frequently and earned little praise. These operations were a far and embarrassing cry from the serious combat then evolving over France. Foulois and Glines, chapter 8; Roger G. Miller, "A Preliminary to War: The 1st Aero Squadron and the American Punitive Expedition of 1916," Air Force History and Museums Program pamphlet, 2003.

36 Maurer, *Air Service in World War I*, II, 101; Hennessy, 196–97. According to Hennessy's detailed records, 139 regular Army pilots had completed pilot training prior to America's entry into the war. There were also Reservists and Guardsmen who had finished training, but many of the total number had either been killed or left flying prior to the war. Frederic

Humphreys, for example, the Army's second pilot, resigned his commission in 1910. Hennessy, 236–48.

37 US Military Academy, "Five Year Book, Class of 1915," June 1921, 59.

38 Notes by RMH.

39 Efficiency Report, January 5, 1918, signed by Brig Gen J.W. Ruckman; another dated March 5, 1918 and signed by Maj J.W. Heard, HRHC, A4, B20, F5.

40 This package of letters and telegrams dating from February 9, 1918 to March 7, 1918, includes several endorsements from officers in Harmon's chain of command—but does not include the actual efficiency report that started it all—is located in AFHRA, File 141.290–37.

41 The history of Kelly Field during this period mentions Harmon's tenure as engineer officer only in passing, while lauding the activities of his successor. Henry D. Kroll (ed.), *Kelly Field in the Great War* (San Antonio, TX: San Antonio Printing Co., 1919), 101–03.

42 Efficiency Report, September 3, 1918, signed by Lt Col T.C. Turner, HRHC, A4, B20, F5.

43 Harmon talk to cadets.

44 Notes by RMH. There was a host of officers stationed at Kelly Field while Harmon was there who would continue to play important roles in his future career: James Fechet, Conger Pratt, Henry Clagett, Gerald Brant, Carl Spaatz, George Brett, and Bart Yount.

45 Carol R. Byerly, *Fever of War: The Influenza Epidemic in the U.S. Army during World War I* (NY: New York University Press, 2005), 6–10. Wartime censorship in the belligerent countries kept much of the news regarding the flu's devastation among the troops from the public. In Spain, which was neutral, censorship was not a factor, so when King Alfonso caught the flu, it became widely known, and this led to the disease being referred to as the Spanish Influenza.

46 One source gives the astounding statistic that 99.4 percent of all US soldiers dying from the flu were actually victims of pneumonia. Byerly, 81. The Army doctor most involved in attempting to combat the flu was W.C. Gorgas, who had already attained fame for conquering Yellow Fever in Panama. This was the same Dr Gorgas who had treated young Hubert Harmon when he had fallen down the cellar steps and cracked his head at Fort Barrancas twenty years earlier.

47 Although the chances of catching the flu were extremely high, the morbidity rate was only 2–4 percent. The horrible death toll was due to the high infection rate. Byerly, 90.

48 My treatment of this pandemic is taken from John M. Barry, *The Great Influenza: The Epic Story of the Deadliest Plague in History* (NY: Viking, 2004); Pete Davies, *The Devil's Flu: The World's Deadliest Influenza Epidemic and the Scientific Hunt for the Virus that Caused It* (NY: Henry Holt, 2000); Lynette Iezzoni, *Influenza*

1918: The Worst Epidemic in American History (NY: TV Books, 1999); and Byerly. Harmon's classmate and fellow pilot, William Peebles, died of the flu on September 30, 1918, infected while en route to France on a troopship.

49 "History of Issoudun Training Center," part of the Col Edgar Gorrell "History of the Air Service in the World War" account, 1919, series J: "Training," microfilm reels 35 and 36 located at Air University Library, Maxwell AFB, Al.

50 David R. Mets, *Master of Airpower: General Carl A. Spaatz* (Novato, CA: Presidio, 1985), 26. Spaatz had been the commander at Issoudun just prior to Harmon's arrival.

51 This illness episode is based on the Notes by RMH, but Harmon's own account in the West Point Class of 1915 Reunion Book confirms the story. Harmon later recalled that he would have died earlier, before the flight, but a fellow officer rescued him from the wet and drafty barracks and brought him to live in a warm building near headquarters. Ltr., HRH to C.A. Hill, November 16, 1954, HRHC, B3, F1.

52 The virus causing influenza was not isolated until the 1930s, and the actual Spanish Influenza strain was not determined until the late 1990s.

53 Davis, 103. Harmon's complete medical records, which note his childhood illnesses, including pneumonia at age 10, are in AFHRA, File 141.290–37.

54 Gen John J. Pershing, *My Experiences in the World War*, 2 vols. (NY: Frederick Stokes, 1931), I, 33.

55 For a discussion of this controversy, see Donald Smythe, *Pershing: General of the Armies* (Bloomington: University of Indiana Press, 1986), 67–72; David R. Woodward, *Trial by Friendship: Anglo-American Relations, 1917–1918* (Lexington: University Press of Kentucky, 1993), chapters 4, 7 and 11; and David F. Trask, *The AEF and Coalition Warmaking, 1917–1918* (Lawrence: University Press of Kansas, 1993), chapter 2.

56 Keith L. Nelson, *Victors Divided: America and the Allies in Germany, 1918–1923* (Berkeley: University of California Press, 1975), chapters 1–4.

57 One American serving at Coblenz later recalled being told by a French officer not to worry: "When we march into Germany, you will find that all the men will be on their bellies, and all the women on their backs." Interview with Maj Gen Howard C. Davidson, by Hugh Ahman, December 5–8, 1974, 262, AFHRA, File K239.0512–817.

58 Ibid., 132–37; Nelson, 49; Erika Kuhlman, "American Doughboys and German *Fräuleins*: Sexuality, Patriarchy, and Privilege in the American-Occupied Rhineland, 1918–23," *Journal of Military History*, 71 (October 2007): 1077–1106.

59 For a discussion, see Bruce Kent, *The Spoils of War: The Politics, Economics, and Diplomacy of Reparations, 1918–1932* (Oxford: Clarendon Press, 1989).

60 Allen, 63.

61 US Military Academy, "Five Year Book, Class of 1915," June 1921, 60.

62 Notes by RMH.

63 Ibid. Harmon had a substitute West Point ring made, which is now located in the Special Collections branch at the Air Force Academy's McDermott Library.

64 Maj Ira B. Joralemon, "At Coblentz [sic] Bridgehead," *U.S. Air Services*, April 1919, 23–27.

65 One source also notes that the newspapers for the American Occupation Force, the *Amaroc News*, were usually delivered to various spots in the American zone by Air Service aircraft. Harmon may have been involved. Alfred E. Cornebise, *The Amaroc News: The Daily Newspaper of the American Forces in Germany, 1919–1923* (Carbondale: Southern Illinois University Press, 1981), 27.

66 Efficiency Reports, September 30, 1919, signed by Col J.C. Montgomery, and December 31, 1919, signed by Lt Col H. Fowler, HRHC, A4, B20, F5.

67 US Army American Forces in Germany, "American Military Government in Occupied Germany, 1919–1920," 85, bound typescript in Air University Library, Maxwell AFB, AL.

68 Maurer Maurer, *Aviation in the U.S. Army, 1919–1939* (Washington DC: Air Force History Office, 1987), 11.

69 Harmon talk to cadets.

70 The telegram's date is smudged, but appears to be July 23, 1920. Rosa-Maye would later note Hubert's fondness for the high-bred and charming English ladies he met during this assignment.

71 Notes by RMH.

72 Efficiency Report, May 31, 1920, signed by Lt Col J. Pierce. A second report during his stay in London was not quite as laudatory, ranking Harmon "below average" in "physical energy and endurance" but noting that this was a result of his near-fatal bout with double pneumonia. Efficiency Report, October 19, 1920, signed by Col R.H. Rolfe, HRHC, A4, B20, F5. Like many others in the Army, as a result of rapid demobilization Harmon dropped in rank temporarily; he was reduced to captain in January 1920 but promoted back to major the following March.

73 Of interest, two men about to become key players in Harmon's career were also in Europe at the same time: Billy Mitchell was at Coblenz and Mason Patrick in London as head of the Aviation Liquidation Mission. Given the small size of the American aviation contingent in Europe after the Armistice, it is probable Harmon met both. Other airmen at Coblenz who Harmon would serve with in the future were Bill Streett and Jack Curry.

Chapter 3

1 Maj Gen Mason Patrick, *The United States in the Air* (Garden City, NY: Doubleday, Doran, 1928), 5–7; Robert P. White, *Mason Patrick and the Fight for Air Service Independence* (Washington DC: Smithsonian, 2001), 18–19.

2 Both men wrote their memoirs and, not surprisingly, their antagonist usually comes out far the worse. For Foulois' side of the story see his *From the Wright Brothers to the Astronauts*, and for Mitchell's version, see his *Memoirs of World War I* (NY: Random House, 1960).

3 Patrick, 52–53; White, 36.

4 Maurer, *Aviation in the U.S. Army*, 5, 48; White, 63.

5 During this period Mitchell's duty title would vary between chief of the Air Service Training and Operations Division, assistant chief of the Air Service, and director of Military Aeronautics.

6 Mitchell wrote three books on aviation and scores of articles expressing these ideas. His most famous book was *Winged Defense* (NY: G.P. Putnam's Sons, 1925). In many ways his best book, however, was his first: *Our Air Force: Keystone of National Defense* (NY: E.P. Dutton, 1921). The best discussion of Mitchell's aeronautical ideas remains Alfred F. Hurley, *Billy Mitchell: Crusader for Air Power* (NY: Franklin Watts, 1964).

7 For personnel statistics see "Report of the Secretary of War to the President," published annually from 1923–1941. For budget figures see *The Army Almanac: A Book of Facts Covering the Army of the United States* (Washington DC: GPO, 1950), 692 (foldout).

8 The first airman to achieve permanent brigadier general rank was Frank Andrews in 1939. See *Official Army Register* (Washington DC: GPO, 1939), 2.

9 Initially, Mitchell lauded aircraft carriers as the future of the Navy. Later he would see them as a threat to an independent Air Force, so he branded them as little more than "floating targets." William L. Mitchell, "Look out Below!" *Collier's*, April 21, 1928, 42; "General Mitchell tells House Committee Airplanes can Destroy Battleships," *U.S. Air Services*, February, 1921, 22.

10 In June 1944 Streett would succeed Harmon as commander of the Thirteenth Air Force.

11 Douglas Waller, *A Question of Loyalty: Gen Billy Mitchell and the Court-Martial that Gripped the Nation* (NY: HarperCollins, 2004), 153.

12 Isaac D. Levine, *Mitchell: Pioneer of Air Power* (NY: Duell, Sloan and Pearce, 1958), 257.

13 The Navy demanded a rematch, and in September 1923 it made two more battleships available—the Air Service sank both of those as well. Maurer, *Aviation in the U.S. Army*, 126–27.

14 Menoher returned to the Infantry and eventually retired as a lieutenant general.

15 White, 52–53.

16 Patrick, 86.

17 Menoher was West Point, Class of 1886, and his son, Pearson, was Hubert Harmon's classmate.

18 Ira C. Eaker, "As I Remember Them: Air Chiefs Patrick and Fechet," *Aerospace Historian*, June 1973, 57–61. Harmon initially moved in with his parents on Lanier Place in Washington; his father was not well and would die the following year. Harmon then took an apartment on 18th St.

19 Notes by RMH. This event occurred in December 1923.

20 Efficiency Report, October 4, 1921, signed by Maj Gen C.T. Menoher, HRHC, A4, B20, F5.

21 Efficiency Report, June 30, 1922, signed by Maj W.H. Frank, HRHC, A4, B20, F5. The list of officers assigned to the Air Service staff during this period was a veritable "who's who" of future air leaders: Hap Arnold, Oscar Westover, James Fechet, Ira Eaker, Bart Yount, Bert Dargue, Horace Hickam, Tony Frank, Walter Weaver, Ken Walker, Bill Streett and Clayton Bissell.

22 Ltr., Maj Gen J.L. Hines, to Maj Gen M.M. Patrick, November 3, 1923, HRHC, A1, B21, F4.

23 Efficiency Report, June 30, 1924, signed by Maj W.H. Frank and endorsed by Maj Gen M.M. Patrick, HRHC, A4, B20, F5.

24 This story is told in an amusing fashion, complete with drawings, in a letter to Rosa-Maye Kendrick (RMK), November 1, 1922, HRHC, A1, B1, F1; ltr., HRH to Commanding Officer, Mitchel Field, October 31, 1922, AFHRA, File 141.290–37.

25 Ltr., HRH to RMK, November 9, 1922, HRHC, A2, B1, F1.

26 Copy of this report included in ltr., HRH to RMK, April 1924, HRHC, A4, B3, F4.

27 Ltr., HRH to RMK, October 10 and 15, 1922, both in HRHC, A2, B1, F1.

28 Maurer, *Aviation in the U.S. Army*, 65.

29 Interview, Col Edwin E. Aldrin, by Arthur Marmor, February 1967, 1–6, AFHRA, File K239.0512–573. Aldrin was the first head of the Engineering Section; he was also the father of astronaut "Buzz" Aldrin.

30 Efficiency Report and "Certificate of Proficiency," August 14, 1925, signed by Maj J.F. Curry, HRHC, A4, B20, F5. Curry had been at North Island when Harmon was there in 1917, and would later serve as commandant of the Air Corps Tactical School when Harmon was a student in 1932.

31 "List of Officer Graduates attaining Rank of General," USAF Historical Division study, July 22, 1952, AFHRA, File K110.7027–7. Graduates included George Kenney, Santy Fairchild, Ben Chidlaw, Jimmy Doolittle, Ennis Whitehead and Jack Curry.

32 Notes by RMH. Harmon's flight log from the last six months of his time at McCook Field is in the possession of his grandson, Paul Hoff, and the log shows several flights each month, with most lasting around an hour to check out radios, armaments, engines, etc.

33 James J. Cooke, *Billy Mitchell* (Boulder, CO: Lynne Rienner, 2002), 169–78; Patrick, 180.

34 A copy of the statement is on line at: http://www.afa.org/magazine/july2006/keep_billy.pdf.

35 Dik A. Daso, *Hap Arnold and the Evolution of American Airpower* (Washington DC: Smithsonian, 2000), 111–13; Thomas Coffey, *Hap: The Story of the US Air Force and the Man who Built It* (NY: Viking, 1982), 119–27; White, 118–20.

36 Eaker, "As I Remember Them," 58.

37 Harmon testified on November 11, 1925, and his testimony is contained on a series of microfilm reels that cover the Mitchell court-martial. The National Archives publication number is M1140, covering the years 1919–1927, roles 9–12; the relevant pages for Harmon's testimony are 645–52.

38 White, 126–27; Coffey, 126, Daso, 113. Patrick thought highly of both men—Dargue had taught him how to fly—but disciplinary action was necessary. Patrick does not mention any of this in his memoirs. Arnold implies in his that the transfer was due to his support for Mitchell; this seems doubtful given Patrick's directions to Eaker noted above. Arnold, *Global Mission*, 122.

39 Efficiency Reports, March 10, 1926, signed by Maj H.H. Arnold; June 30, 1926 and February 24, 1927, both endorsed by Maj Gen M.M. Patrick, HRHC, A4, B20, F5.

40 Ltr., Maj Gen M.M. Patrick to HRH, February 24, 1927, HRHC, A4, B21, F4.

41 Ltr., I.C. Eaker to RMH, April 3, 1957, copy supplied by EHH.

42 Ltr., I.C. Eaker to RMH, May 10, 1962, HRHC, A4, B2, F6.

43 Notes by RMH. At the time of the wedding, Gene Vidal was an instructor at West Point. Nina Gore was the daughter of Thomas Gore, the US senator from Oklahoma. The product of the Vidal-Gore marriage was Eugene Luther Vidal, who later changed his name to Gore Vidal. Nina later divorced Gene Vidal and in 1935 married another Air Corps officer named Robert Olds, an extremely capable man of whom great things were expected. Tragically, Olds died of a heart attack in May, 1943. Olds had been married earlier, but his wife had died in 1926. Their son—Nina's stepson—was Robin Olds, who went on to become a West Point graduate, All-American football player, and pilot. He was a double ace in World War II, married actress Ella Raines, fought in Vietnam—where he shot down four MiGs—and was then appointed the commandant of cadets at the Air Force Academy in 1967.

44 John B. Kendrick was a fascinating individual. He began as a simple cowboy in Texas, moving the herd of his boss, Charles Wulfjen, to Wyoming. He stayed there and began to grow an empire. Along the way he married Eula Wulfjen, the daughter of Charles, and the two settled in the Sheridan area. The mansion he built in Sheridan, *Trail End,* is now a state historic site. For his biography see Cynde A. Georgen, *One Cowboy's Dream: John B. Kendrick, His Family, Home, and Ranching Empire* (Sheridan, WY: Donning, revised edition, 2004).

45 I owe Rosa-Maye an enormous debt; her voluminous diaries and letters have proven invaluable in writing the biography of her husband.

46 RMK Diary, HRHC, A3, B1. Rosa-Maye kept a diary most of her life. A copy of the first volume, covering the years 1922–1927, is located in HRHC, but the subsequent diaries are in the possession of EHH. Several entries in the first diary refer to visiting the White House to work with Mrs. Harding and Mrs. Hoover on Girl Scout issues and other volunteer projects. Other entries speak of her attendance at lectures, plays, and concerts. Later, she would refer to several discussions with Harmon regarding the stock market and other financial matters. The later diaries, as well as many other family papers, will eventually be donated to the American Heritage Center at the University of Wyoming.

47 The Army encouraged its officers to engage in some athletic activity twice each week. Equitation was a popular option, and the Army pushed it by granting officers $150 per year for the upkeep of a horse and $50 more if they kept a second horse. Hennessy, 158.

48 Poem, HRH to RMK, no date, but probably from 1922 or 1923, HRHC, A4 B2, F2. Rosa-Maye kept all of these letters from Hubert, and all are now in HRHC, both on microfilm and in hard copy, A2, B1, F1, A3, B1, and A4, B1 through 6.

49 Alfred Ollivant, *Redcoat Captain: A Story of That Country* (NY: Macmillan, 1907).

50 Rosa-Maye later related to her daughter that when she told her father that Doodle had proposed to her, he replied that he approved, but she must promise not to call him by that silly name thereafter! Ltr., EHH to author, June 18, 2007.

51 Ollivant, 64–65.

52 Ltr., RMK to HRH, n.d., but sometime in 1922, HRHC, A4, B1, F13.

53 RMK Diary, various entries during January 1922. Lem Shepherd, a Marine Corps officer who later wore four stars, was the most serious of these suitors.

54 Ibid., June 16 and July 13, 1922.

55 Ibid., September 15, 1922.

56 Ibid., December 10, 1922.

57 Ibid., January 6, 1923.

58 Ibid., April 30, 1923.

59 Ibid., December 30 and 31, 1923.

60 Ibid., March 21, 1924. Actually, Harmon proposed to Rosa-Maye on a dozen occasions over the years, but she kept putting him off.

61 Coffman, 233, 242.

62 RMK Diary, June 10, 1924. Harmon was a student at the Air Service Engineering School in Dayton, Ohio, at the time, and his flight to Wyoming was approved for the purposes of flight-testing a new compass. It appears that the only other aircraft mishap involving Harmon—aside from the crash at New Haven already mentioned—occurred in July 1936 when he ground-looped his B-18 upon landing and damaged the propeller. "Accident Report," July 14, 1936, AFHRA, File 141.290–37; RMH Diary, July 1, 1936.

63 RMK Diary, June 20, 1924; EHH and Kendrick Harmon interview in Gaston, *50th Anniversary Oral History,* 17. The clock from the

aircraft's control panel remains a Harmon family heirloom. The plane was shipped back east by flatcar.

64 RMK Diary, April 5, 1926.

65 Ibid., September 6, 1926.

66 Ibid., July 10, 1924; undated news clipping from the *Denver Herald*, copy supplied by EHH.

67 Tinker got out of the initial crash all right, but then went back to the burning wreckage to rescue another crewmember, and was severely burned in the process. He received the Army Medal for his heroism. In June 1942, Tinker, by then a major general, was killed in action at the Battle of Midway. For his biography, see James L. Crowder, Jr., *Osage General: Maj. Gen Clarence L. Tinker* (Tinker AFB: Air Logistics Center History Office, 1987).

68 Rosa-Maye Kendrick/Harmon Engagement and Wedding Book, in possession of EHH.

69 Ibid.

70 Nina Gore, an actress, for stage purposes continued to use her maiden name. At the time, Miff was stationed in Washington on the War Department General Staff.

71 From a newspaper clipping pasted into the Wedding Book. The gold dollar is noted in a letter from Grace Coolidge to RMK, February 17, 1927, copy provided by Helen Harmon.

72 Rosa-Maye Kendrick Harmon (RMKH), *Intimate Letters from London* (Denver: Welch-Haffner, 1928).

73 RMKH, "A Letter from London," *Goucher College Alumnae Quarterly*, no date, but probably 1928 or 1929, HRHC, A4, B5, F10. Rosa-Maye soon dropped the Kendrick from her name.

74 Harmon talk to cadets.

75 Ltr., Adj Gen to HRH, March 18, 1927, AFHRA, File 141.290–37.

76 RMKH, *Intimate Letters*, 102.

77 Ibid., 95.

78 Coffman, 256.

79 Chamberlain was the first man to cross the Atlantic non-stop with a passenger—Charles Devine. The flight was in June 1927—two weeks after Lindbergh's flight—and went from New York to Berlin. Chamberlain's aircraft was a Wright-Bellanca WB-1.

80 RMKH, *Intimate Letters*, 62–69.

81 Ibid., 126. Balbo would later gain fame for leading twenty-four Italian flying boats on a roundtrip flight from Rome to Chicago for the World's Fair in July–August 1933.

82 RMH Diary, June 23, 1928.

83 RMKH, *Intimate Letters*, 153–54.

84 Lecture by Maj HRH to RAF Staff College, no date but presumably 1928, HRHC, A4, B6, F2.

85 For accounts of these air operations, see David E. Omissi, *Air Power and Colonial Control: The Royal Air Force, 1919–1939* (NY: St. Martin's, 1990), and Philip A. Towle, *Pilots and Rebels: The Use of Aircraft in Unconventional Warfare, 1919–1988* (London: Brassey's, 1989).

86 Harmon's diplomatic passport is located in HRHC, A5, B8, Package 1. See also RMH Diary

for June through August, 1929.

87 These reports are in AFHRA, File 200–3912.

88 All reports from Harmon to the Military Intelligence Division in Washington—with information copies to the Air Staff—are contained in AFHRA, File 248.501–53.

89 Efficiency Reports, June 30, 1927 and August 29, 1927, both signed by Lt Col K.A. Joyce; and June 30, 1929 and May 21, 1929, both signed by Col J.R. Thomas, HRHC, A4, B20, F5.

90 On one trip to Oxford, Rosa-Maye was particularly anxious for Hubert to tour the Bodelian Library and walk among the various colleges. RMKH, *Intimate Letters*, 173.

91 US Military Academy, "Annual Report of the Superintendent," 1929, 1. Stewart Field, where pilot training was conducted for cadets during World War II, would be built on this land parcel.

92 RMH Diary, September 8, 1929, February 20 and July 6, 1930. When Senator Kendrick visited his daughter and son-in-law in July 1930, Hubert showed him around the campus but also took him out to view the area when he wanted the Academy to build an airfield for cadet flying training. Kendrick enthusiastically supported the idea, which certainly helped the legislation's chances when it came before Congress the following year.

93 US Military Academy, "Annual Report of the Superintendent," 1930, 1.

94 There remained three civilians teaching in the Foreign Language Department.

95 US Military Academy, "Annual Report of the Superintendent," 1930, 3 and 1931, 4.

96 US Military Academy, "Official Register of the Officers and Cadets," 1930, 18 and 1931, 19; Crackel, 203. The main textbooks used included the Bible, Shakespeare, and English literature to Thomas Hardy. There were no modern novels read, and the only American works were those of Ralph Waldo Emerson and Stephen Vincent Benet. US Military Academy, "Official Register of the Officers and Cadets," 1932, 24.

97 D. Clayton James, *The Years of MacArthur, Volume I: 1880–1941* (Boston: Houghton Mifflin, 1970), 268. See chapter 10 for the complete story.

98 Ltr., HRH to E.W. Kendrick, October 28, 1929, HRHC, A4, B6, F5.

99 Of note, the commandant was the same Robert C. Richardson, Jr. who had published *West Point: An Intimate Portrait*, cited in the chapter on Harmon's cadet days.

100 Ltr., HRH to E.W. Kendrick, October 28, 1929, HRHC, A4, B6, F5. During his three-year tour at West Point there were generally only three or four other aviators on post, all on the faculty. One of these was 1Lt Earle "Pat" Partridge, who would later rise to full general after World War II; another was 1Lt Russell Randall, who would serve under Harmon in Panama in 1942–43.

101 "The Battalion Board," *The Howitzer*, 1932, 68. Harmon took all of this very seriously and never relished having to discipline cadets. Rosa-Maye recorded in her diary one day when he returned from work "solemn" over the fact that a cadet had been caught "under the influence" and would have to face a court martial. RMH Diary, January, 13, 1930.

102 On one trip to New York City, Rosa-Maye confessed that they had their first experience with a "speakeasy'—a bar then illegal due to Prohibition. RMH Diary, November 8, 1930.

102 Because of all this help for just the two of them, Rosa-Maye was not all that accomplished around the house. She wrote in her diary that one day "the girls" were off to Newburgh and she was forced to make both lunch and supper by herself. She confessed that it was not very good, largely because she did not know how to turn on the oven! RMH Diary, April 15, 1930.

104 Notes by RMH. Eula Wulfjen was Rosa-Maye's mother's maiden name; ltr., EHH to author, September 30, 2007.

105 Efficiency Report, June 30, 1931, signed by Lt Col R.C. Richardson, Jr., HRHC, A4, B20, F5.

106 Efficiency Report, June 30, 1932, signed by Lt Col R.C. Richardson, Jr., HRHC, A4, B20, F5.

107 Notes by RMH.

108 Ibid; ltr., Maj Gen B.D. Foulois to Lt Col R.C. Richardson, Jr., January 18, 1932, HRCH, A4, B21, F4.

109 Ltr., HRH to Eula Cumming, November 24, 1931, HRHC, A4, B6, F9; ltr., EHH to author, September 30, 2007.

Chapter 4

1 Maj William Sherman, *Air Warfare* (NY: Ronald Press, 1926), chapter 7.

2 Thomas H. Greer, "The Development of Air Doctrine in the Army Air Arm, 1917–1941," AF Historical Study no. 89, 1955 (republished by Air University Press in 1985), 81.

3 Donald Wilson, an instructor at Maxwell while Harmon was a student there, claims to have invented this idea—although evidence confirming this is scanty. For his story, see Maj Gen Donald Wilson, "Origin of a Theory for Air Strategy," *Aerospace Historian*, March 1971, 19–25.

4 Arnold, *Global Mission*, 154.

5 RMH Diary, September 6 and October 9, 1932.

6 Lt Col J.F. Curry, "Annual Report," July 11, 1933, AFHRA, File 245.111.

7 Pursuit was the term then used to denote fighter operations or fighter aircraft—as in the "P" designation for aircraft. Fighter pilots were termed "pursuiters."

8 *Air Corps News Letter*, April 15, 1936, 3.

9 Robert T. Finney, "The History of the Air Corps Tactical School, 1920–1940," AF Historical Study no. 100, 1955 (republished by Air University Press in 1992), 37–38. Harmon's class was unusual because most of the students flew

out to California for maneuvers, increasing their flying time to over 140 hours.

10 Maj Gen Donald Wilson, *Wooing Peponi: My Odyssey Thru Many Years* (Monterey, CA: Angel Press, 1973), 241.

11 For a typical map problem, see "Solution to Problems," February 24, 1933, AFHRA, File 248.101–18.

12 The six men who served on the ACTS faculty and later became full generals were Joe McNarney (HRH's West Point classmate), George Kenney, Hoyt Vandenberg, Santy Fairchild, Pat Partridge and Larry Kuter.

13 Finney, 122. In the appendices are rosters of students and faculty members for all classes.

14 1Lt Kenneth N. Walker, "Bombardment Aviation—Bulwark of National Defense," *U.S. Air Services*, August 1933, 15–19. This article was a copy of one of Walker's ACTS lectures. Walker had been an aide to Billy Mitchell in Washington, so it is likely that Harmon knew him from his time on the Air Staff. Walker would later be killed-in-action while leading a bombing mission over Rabaul, New Guinea, on January 5, 1943. He was posthumously awarded the Medal of Honor. For his biography, see Martha Byrd, *Kenneth N. Walker: Airpower's Untempered Crusader* (Maxwell AFB, AL: Air University Press, 1997). For the bombardment lectures during Harmon's year at ACTS, see AFHRA, File 248.2202A.

15 ACTS Lecture, "Pursuit Aviation," September 1933, AFHRA, File 248.101–8. See also, Capt Claire Chennault, "Special Support for Bombardment," *U.S. Air Services*, January 1934, 18–21. In a show of ambivalence not uncommon for other pursuit advocates at the time, Chennault rejected the concept of fighter escort for the bombers. To him, this was a defensive mission not suitable for offensive-minded and aggressive pursuit pilots. Instead, Chennault argued, a bit strangely, that the only solution was to build more bombers to compensate for the attrition that enemy fighters would cost an attacking force!

16 For Chennault's memoirs, which discuss in some detail these arguments at the Tactical School in the early 1930s, see *Way of a Fighter* (NY: G.P. Putnam's Sons, 1949). There have been a number of biographies of Chennault, but the best is Martha Byrd, *Chennault: Giving Wings to the Tiger* (Tuscaloosa: University of Alabama Press, 1988).

17 "GHQ Air Force (Prov) Command and Staff Exercises, Critique," May 8–26, 1933, AFHRA, File 248.2122–3.

18 Notes by RMH.

19 Efficiency Report, July 1, 1933, signed by Lt Col J.F. Curry, HRHC, A4, B20, F5.

20 Finney, 43.

21 Efficiency Report, August 21, 1933, signed by Lt Col. J.F. Curry, HRHC, A4, B20, F5.

22 The Command and General Staff School was a two-year program between 1928 and 1935.

Before and after that period it was a one-year course.

23 Philip C. Cockrell, "Brown Shoes and Mortar Boards: U.S. Army Officer Professional Education at the Command General Staff School Fort Leavenworth, Kansas, 1919–1940," PhD Dissertation, University of South Carolina, 1991, 139.

24 Boyd L. Dastrup, *The US Army Command and General Staff College: A Centennial History* (Manhattan, KS: Sunflower University Press, 1982), 74–75.

25 US Army Command and General Staff School, "Summary of Schedule," 1935, copy provided by archivist at Fort Leavenworth; Cockrell, 143–46.

26 Timothy K. Nenninger, "The Fort Leavenworth Schools: Postgraduate Military Education and Professionalism in the U.S. Army, 1880–1920," PhD Dissertation, University of Wisconsin, 1974, 357–58.

27 US Army Command and General Staff School, "Summary of Schedule," 1935. Equitation was accorded twice as much time as war planning and six times as much as military intelligence.

28 Cockrell, 200.

29 Dastrup, 71.

30 RMH Diary, February 23, 1934.

31 Coffman, 282.

32 Maj Ira C. Eaker, "Now it Can be Told," *Air Corps Newsletter*, July 15, 1937, 1–3. In the School's Annual Report, the commandant complained of the academic and housing facilities that were much in need of repair and remodeling. US Army Command and General Staff School, "Annual Report," 1935, 10–11.

33 Col Orville Z. Tyler, Jr., Col Elvid Hunt and Capt Walter E. Lorence, "The History of Fort Leavenworth, 1827–1951," The Command and General Staff College, 1951, 1–3.

34 Efficiency Report, June 30, 1935, signed by Col Troup Miller, HRHC, A4, B20, F5.

35 As noted in chapter one, the son was Robin Olds, destined to become a fighter ace in World War II, wing commander in Vietnam, and commandant at the Air Force Academy in 1967.

36 RMH Diary, December 17, 1934 and February 20, 1935.

37 R. Earl McClendon, "A Question of Autonomy for the United States Air Arm, 1907–1945," Air University Documentary Research Study, 1950 (republished by Air University Press in 1996 as "Autonomy of the Air Arm"), 59–60.

38 McClendon, 61–70. A dissenting opinion that *did* call for an independent Air Force was submitted by Jimmy Doolittle.

39 John F. Shiner, *Foulois and the U.S Army Air Corps, 1931–1935* (Washington DC: Office of Air Force History, 1983), 207.

40 Maurer, *Aviation in the U.S. Army*, 330.

41 DeWitt S. Copp, *Forged in Fire* (Garden City, NY: Doubleday, 1982), 331; Cameron, 339.

42 Coffey, 168.

43 Maurer, *Aviation in the U.S. Army*, 339.

44 Efficiency Report, January 10, 1936, signed by Brig Gen H.H. Arnold, HRHC, A4, B20, F5.

45 Efficiency Reports, July 1, 1936, signed by Col H.B. Clagett, and August 20, 1936, signed by Brig Gen D.C. Emmons, HRHC, A4, B20, F5.

46 Notes by RMH.

47 War Department, "Medical Records of Major Hubert R. Harmon," June 24, 1936, AFHRA, File 141.290–37.

48 For an account of the crash, see Phillip S. Meilinger, "When the Fortress Went Down," *Air Force Magazine*, October 2004, 78–82.

49 Maurer, *Aviation in the U.S. Army*, 360–61.

50 All of the new bombers went to the 2nd Bomb Group of the 2nd Wing for operational testing. The commander of the 2nd Bomb Group was Bob Olds.

51 Craven, Wesley Frank and James L. Cate (eds.) *The Army Air Forces in World War II.* 7 vols. (Chicago: University of Chicago Press, 1948–58), VI, 176.

52 Maurer, *Aviation in the U.S. Army,* 381.

53 *Air Corps News Letter*, June 15, 1936, 23; *Air Corps News Letter*, November 1, 1936, 5.

54 "GHQ Air Force Thirty-Day Exercise on West Coast," *U.S. Air Services*, June 1937, 11–12; notes by RMH.

55 Efficiency Report, June 29, 1937, signed by Col J.H. Pirie and endorsed by Brig Gen D.C. Emmons, HRHC, A4, B20, F5.

56 RMH Diary, June 22, 1936.

57 Coffman, 285.

58 Harry P. Ball, *Of Responsible Command: A History of the U.S. Army War College* (Carlisle Barracks, PA: Alumni Association of the Army War College, 1983), 233–45; George S. Pappas, *Prudens Futuri: The US Army War College, 1901–1967* (Carlisle Barracks, PA: Alumni Association of the Army War College, 1967), 97–101. For a critical discussion of the deficiencies of the branch schools, see David E. Johnson, *Fast Tanks and Heavy Bombers: Innovation in the U.S. Army, 1917–1945* (Ithaca, NY: Cornell University Press, 1998).

59 Lt Col H.R. Harmon, "A Current International Estimate," US Army War College paper, January 29, 1938, HRHC, A4, B20, F4. It would have been interesting if Harmon had taken Britain's maritime situation and drawn parallels to the US as a global power that relied on airpower.

60 There was also a tour of Civil War battlefields to "study the terrain"; such anachronistic events are still a part of the Army War College curriculum. Pappas, 102.

61 Harmon's later tours in the Panama Canal Zone and the South Pacific gave these map exercises special significance. The US war plans developed during the interwar years were color-coded based on projected adversaries: Japan was designated as orange, Germany was black, Italy was silver, etc. The collective plans written to deal with these various enemies and their combination were termed "Rainbow Plans." For a discussion, see Kent Roberts Greenfield (ed.)

Command Decisions (Washington DC: Office of Chief of Military History, 1960), 12–19.

62 Ball, 240–41.

63 Ibid., 246.

64 Lt Col H.R. Harmon, "The Recording and Analysis of Bombing Results," US Army War College paper, May 7, 1938, HRHC, A4, B20, F4.

65 For an overview of the problem, see Phillip S. Meilinger, "A History of Effects-Based Air Operations," *Journal of Military History* 71 (January 2007): 139–68.

66 The classmate was Joe Collins. He would have an extremely distinguished combat career during World War II and afterwards would be named Army chief of staff. The senior airman referred to was probably Lewis Brereton; he would rise to the rank of lieutenant general in the AAF. Gen Joseph L. Collins, *Lightning Joe: An Autobiography of General J. Lawton Collins* (Baton Rouge: Louisiana State University Press, 1979), 92.

67 Notes by RMH; Efficiency Report, July 1, 1938, signed by Maj Gen C.L. DeWitt, HRHC, A4, B20, F5.

68 William Wallace Whitson, "The Role of the United States Army War College in the Preparation of Officers for National Security Policy Formulation," PhD Dissertation, Fletcher School of Law and Diplomacy, 1958, 158. Two West Point classmates of Harmon were students at the War College that year, including football teammate Tom Larkin who, like Harmon, would eventually wear three stars.

69 The five divisions were G-1, personnel and administration; G-2, intelligence; G-3, operations and plans; G-4, logistics; and war plans, which was unnumbered.

70 US Army, AR 10-15, "General Staff: Organization and General Duties," August 18, 1936, 34; War Department General Staff, "Personnel Rosters," April–November 1940, copies provided by US Army Center of Military History (CMH).

71 Brig Gen L.D. Gasser, "The War Department General Staff," lecture delivered at the Army War College, September 16, 1939, copy provided by CMH.

72 Notes by RMH. Harmon's efficiency reports for his two years on the War Department General Staff were unusually bland, simply noting that he was a "thorough, energetic, and capable officer" who took his work "seriously." In fact, the report for his second year on the job was less laudatory—and that term is used loosely—than the one before it. Efficiency Reports, June 30, 1939 and June 12, 1940, both signed by Col E.B. Colladay, HRHC, A4, B20, F5.

73 Frederick J. Shaw (ed.) *Locating Air Base Sites: History's Legacy* (Washington DC: Air Force History and Museums Program, 2004), 6–8, 19, 23; Jerold E. Brown, *Where Eagles Land: Planning and Development of U.S. Army Airfields, 1910–1941* (Westport, CT: Greenwood, 1990), 101–14. All four of these airbases are still active.

The General Staff, which was largely a product of World War I, proved inadequate in World War II, and underwent a wide-ranging reorganization in March 1942. Harmon was instrumental in establishing the site of Westover Field in Massachusetts. RMH Diary, October 17 and 25, 1938.

74 Arnold, *Global Mission*, 179.

75 "Organization of AAF Training Activities, 1939–1945," AAF Historical Study no. 53, June 1946, 1–13.

76 Craven and Cate, VI, 131.

77 Ibid., 151.

78 Robert L. Thompson, "Initial Selection of Candidates for Pilot, Bombardier, and Navigation Training," AAF Historical Study no. 2, November 1943, 17.

79 Ibid., 19.

80 Craven and Cate, VI, 512.

81 Norman H. Caldwell, "Preflight Training in the AAF," AAF Historical Study no. 48, November 1946, 9–11, 54.

82 In 1943 the AAF turned out 65,797 pilots. *The Official World War II Guide to the Army Air Forces* (NY: AAF Aid Society, 1944), 103.

83 Willard Wiener, *Two Hundred Thousand Flyers: The Story of the Civilian-AAF Training Program* (Washington DC: Infantry Journal Press, 1945), ix. For a more sober rendition see Dominick A. Pisano, *To Fill the Skies with Pilots: The Civilian Pilot Training Program, 1939–1946* (Urbana: University of Illinois Press, 1993).

84 *Randolph Field: A History and Guide* (NY: Devin-Adair, 1942), 47–48; Cameron, 566.

85 Efficiency Report, October 23, 1940, signed by Brig Gen M.F. Harmon; Efficiency Reports, July 10 and September 22, 1941, signed by Brig Gen G.C. Brant, HRHC, A4, B20, F5.

86 Of note, also on the same promotion list to brigadier was Harmon's West Point classmate and football teammate, Dwight Eisenhower.

87 Gen George Marshall wrote the president suggesting the move due to Lahm's "recognition of past service." Larry I. Bland, Sharon R. Ritenour, and Clarence E. Wunderlin, Jr. (eds.) *The Papers of George Catlett Marshall: "We Cannot Delay" July 1, 1939–December 6, 1941* (Baltimore, MD: Johns Hopkins University Press, 1986), 592. There are several news clippings and photographs of this event in a large scrapbook, HRHC, A2, B1. See also "General Harmon Molds Army Air Corps Pilots," *Form One*, January 1942, 1–2.

88 Ltr., HRH to E.W. Kendrick, November 12, 1941, copy supplied by EHH.

89 Ltr., RMH to Col W.A. Robertson, June 4, 1958, HRHC, A4, B14, F13.

90 Ltr., HRH to Mr and Mrs Francis Williams, December 25, 1942, HRHC, A4, B7, F4.

91 "History of the Army Air Forces Flying Training Center, 7 December 1941–31 December 1942," 18–19, AFHRA, File 223.01; same history, dates "1 January 1939–7 December 1941," 394.

92 Ibid., 106–07.

93 All speeches were given during 1942 and copies are in HRHC, A4, B7, F4. Harmon did not always look forward to such duties. Rosa-Maye noted for example: "In spite of Hubert's prayers the day dawned fair and he had to go to Dallas to the live stock fair to make a speech." RMH Diary, October 1, 1941.

94 Visitors noted in letters of appreciation and newspaper clippings located in a large scrapbook, HRHC, A2, B1, and in other material in A4, B7, F4-7; RMH Diary, October 31, 1942.

95 News Release, December 20, 1942, HRHC, A4, B7, F7. On the other hand, a cynic would have noted that the president's son was commissioned into the Air Corps as a captain, not as a second lieutenant like most everyone else.

96 Efficiency Report, November 21, 1942, signed by Maj Gen B.K. Yount, HRHC, A4, B20, F5. Yount had been Harmon's classmate at the Engineering School in 1924–25.

Chapter 5

1 Daniel P. Hagedorn, *Alae Supra Canalem—Wings over the Canal* (Paducah, KY: Turner, 1995), 8.

2 Arnold, *Global Mission*, 46–47.

3 John Major, *Prize Possession: The United States and the Panama Canal, 1903–1979* (Cambridge: Cambridge University Press, 1993), 182, 189.

4 Major, 293.

5 Hagedorn, 21; Major, 281, 293.

6 Hagedorn, 25; Kathleen Williams, "Air Defense of the Panama Canal, January 1937–December 1941," AAF Historical Study no. 42, January 1946, 19. Oscar Westover had been killed in an airplane crash in September 1938. Arnold was then promoted to take his place.

7 Stetson Conn, Rose C. Engelman, and Byron Fairchild, *Guarding the United States and Its Outposts*, in United States Army in World War II series (Washington DC: Army Historical Office, 1964), 302–08.

8 Thomas M. Leonard and John F. Bratzel (eds.) *Latin America during World War II* (Lanham, MD: Rowman & Littlefield, 2007), 59.

9 Thomas L. Pearcy, *We Answer Only to God: Politics and the Military in Panama, 1903–1947* (Albuquerque: University of New Mexico Press, 1998), 91.

10 Bland, Ritenour, and Wunderlin, 380.

11 Ibid., 257.

12 Major, 297.

13 Craven and Cate, VI, 300.

14 The official US Navy historian, himself a rear admiral, concluded bluntly: "This unpreparedness was largely the Navy's own fault." Samuel Eliot Morison, *History of United States Naval Operations in World War II*, 14 vols. (Boston: Little, Brown, 1954–66), I, 200.

15 Morison, I, 144; A. Timothy Warnock, *The Battle against the U-Boat in the American Theater* (Maxwell AFB, AL: Air Force Historical Research Agency, 1995), 16–17.

16 Morison, I, 200. The Panama Canal was never seriously threatened during the war, and between July 1941 and June 1945 there were over 23,000 successful transits of the Canal—an average of sixteen per day. Leonard and Bratzel, 71.

17 Ltr., HRH to RMH, November 26, 1942, HRHC, A5, B7, F10.

18 Ltr., HRH to RMH, March 7, 1943, HRHC, A5, B7, F10.

19 Ltr., HRH to RMH, March 6, 1943, HRHC, A5, B7, F10.

20 Hagedorn, 40; "Report on the Sixth Air Force," Air Staff Historical Study, September 24, 1943, 3, AFHRA, File 105.2–6B.

21 Arnold, *Global Mission*, 186.

22 Hagedorn, 41.

23 Ibid., 44, 106, 108. The official designation of the BT–13 was the "Valiant," but it tended to rattle so loudly in flight it was known universally to pilots as the "Vibrator."

24 "Chronology of Events in Sixth Air Force since Pearl Harbor," September 1943, AFHRA, File 105.2–6A.

25 Hagedorn, 44.

26 Ibid., 73.

27 Ltr., HRH to RMH, March 8, 1943, HRHC, A5, B7, F10. Adm Ernest King was chief of naval operations, succeeding Adm Stark in March 1942.

28 Ltr., HRH to RMH, March 15, 1943, HRHC, A5, B7, F10.

29 Sixth Air Force Public Affairs press release, May 5, 1943; ltr., Maj Gen Harry Johnson to RMH, no date, HRHC, A4, B13, F 4; Air Medal citation for this event, HRHC, A4, B20, F6.

30 Hagedorn, 190–92.

31 Ltr., HRH to RMH, July 9, 1943, HRHC, A5, B7, F10. The "friend" was presumably Maj Gen Edwin J. House who took over the Antilles Air Command. "Tommy" was Lt Col Thomas Musgrave, Harmon's chief of staff, who had also been with him at Randolph.

32 For the story, see Douglas A. Cox, *Airpower Leadership on the Front Line: Lieutenant General George H. Brett and Combat Command* (Maxwell AFB, AL: Air University Press, 2006), chapter 5.

33 Efficiency Report, June 30, 1943, signed by Lt Gen G.H. Brett; Efficiency Report, November 10, 1943, signed by Maj Gen W.E. Shedd and endorsed by Brett, HRHC, A4, B20, F5. Harmon also received a Legion of Merit for his activities at Sixth Air Force.

34 RMH Diary, July 24, 1953; ltr., HRH to RMH, August 22, 1943, HRHC, A4, B7, F10. The AAF personnel chief at this time was old friend and West Point classmate Sammy Cousins.

35 Ltr., HRH to RMH, August 24, 1943, HRHC, A4, B7, F10.

36 Ltr., HRH to RMH, September 1, 1943, HRHC, A4, B7, F10.

37 One of those lost was Maj Gen Clarence Tinker, the man Harmon had succeeded as air attaché to London in 1929. Shortly before that, another

old colleague from Air Staff days, Maj Gen Bert Dargue, died in a plane crash en route to Hawaii.

38 For an overview of the air campaigns in the South Pacific, see Eric M. Bergerud, *Fire in the Sky: The Air War in the South Pacific* (Boulder, CO: Westview, 2001); and for the Guadalcanal campaign in particular see Richard B. Frank, *Guadalcanal* (NY: Random House, 1990).

39 Bergerud., xix. See also Robert Sherrod, *History of Marine Corps Aviation in World War II* (Washington DC: Combat Forces Press, 1952), 170–71.

40 Clark G. Reynolds, *The Fast Carriers: The Forging of an Air Navy* (NY: McGraw-Hill, 1968), 31.

41 James A. Winnefeld and Dana J. Johnson, *Joint Air Operations: Pursuit of Unity in Command and Control, 1942–1991* (Annapolis, MD: Naval Institute Press, 1993), 33–34. This statement is an exaggeration: George Kenney's operations in the Southwest Pacific and the Allied Expeditionary Air Force established for the Normandy invasion were joint/combined organizations that were also quite impressive.

42 Kenn C. Rust and Dana Bell, *Thirteenth Air Force Story in World War II* (Terre Haute, IN: Sunshine House, 1981), 16; Sherrod, 172.

43 United States Strategic Bombing Survey (USSBS), "The Thirteenth Air Force in the War against Japan," September 30, 1946, 1–5; Rust and Ball, 16–18. The COMAIRSOLS staff was composed of personnel from all the US services plus New Zealand, and it remained reasonably constant to ensure a degree of continuity between the rotating commanders.

44 For a good discussion of Millard Harmon's role in the South Pacific, see Major Robert G. Novotny, "Tarmacs and Trenches: Lieutenant General Millard Fillmore Harmon, Jr., USAAF," Master's Thesis, School of Advanced Air and Space Studies, Maxwell AFB, AL, June 2007.

45 Ltr., HRH to RMH, November 26, 1943, HRHC, A4, B7, notebook binder. Fitch's headquarters, as well as that of Millard Harmon, was on the island of Noumea in the New Caledonia chain.

46 Ltr., HRH to RMH, November 26, 1943, HRHC, A4, B7, notebook binder. Despite his words to Rosa-Maye, Harmon did fly combat on several occasions, as when he flew in a B-25 over Rabaul on March 8, 1944, and on a Marine "Avenger" a week later. He would later receive a Distinguished Flying Cross for these combat missions.

47 Maj John N. Rentz, *Bougainville and the Northern Solomons* (Washington DC: US Marine Corps, 1948), 122.

48 Ltr., HRH to RMH, December 25, 1943, HRHC, A4, B7, notebook binder.

49 Both Bong and McGuire flew with the Fifth Air Force. The top ace of the Thirteenth Air Force was Bob Westbrook with twenty kills—he also flew a twin-engine P-38.

50 Kramer J. Rohfleisch, "The Thirteenth Air Force, March–October 1943," AAF Historical Study no. 20, September 1946, 212–13. Significantly, when Harmon took over the Thirteenth Air Force a month later, one of his first priorities was to improve the living conditions of his personnel. See Benjamin Lippincott, "History of Headquarters, Thirteenth Air Force, January–March 1944," HRHC, A4, B7, F15.

51 USSBS, "Thirteenth Air Force against Japan," 18. Harmon's bombers were B-24s and B-25s, his fighters were P-38s and one squadron of P-61 night interceptors, and his transports were C-47s.

52 Ltrs., HRH to RMH, November 29, 1943, and to Eula Harmon, December 13, 1943, HRHC, A4, B7, notebook binder.

53 Efficiency Report, June 30, 1944, signed by Gen H.H. Arnold, HRHC, A4, B20, F5.

54 USSBS, "Thirteenth Air Force against Japan," 7; Sherrod, 212. Although Rabaul was soon neutralized, it remained in Japanese hands. Allied aircraft continued to bomb it periodically for the rest of the war, eventually dropping over twenty thousand tons of bombs, most by the AAF.

55 Ltr., HRH to RMH, January 6, 1944, HRHC, A4, B7, notebook binder.

56 "Operations Analysis Report," Historical Branch, Thirteenth Air Force, April 10, 1944, AFHRA, File 750.303.

57 Ltr., HRH to RMH, May 9, 1944, HRHC, A4, B7, notebook binder. One of his actions at Thirteenth Air Force headquarters was to beef up the Public Relations section so his airmen would get more press in the US. Lippincott, "Thirteenth Air Force Headquarters history," 5.

58 USSBS, "Thirteenth Air Force against Japan," 8.

59 Ibid., 9.

60 Ibid., 17–18 and Charts IV and V in appendix.

61 The message was sent on April 3, 1944. Larry I. Bland and Sharon Ritenour Stevens (eds.) *The Papers of George Catlett Marshall, Vol. 4: "Aggressive and Determined Leadership," June 1, 1943–December 31, 1944* (Baltimore, MD: Johns Hopkins University Press, 1996), 385. Of interest, the Army introduced the 24th Regiment into combat on Bougainville—the first American black unit to see action in the Pacific.

62 Ltr., HRH to RMH, April 21, 1944, HRHC, A4, B7, notebook binder. Actually, his letter was indeed darn amusing.

63 Ltr., HRH to RMH, February 25, 1944, HRHC, A4, B7, notebook binder.

64 Lippincott, "Thirteenth Air Force Headquarters history," 3.

65 Ltr., HRH to Lt Gen G.C. Kenney, April 18, 1944, AFA, Huston/Kenney papers, B3, F4.

66 Ltr., HRH to RMH, May 9, 1944, HRHC, A4, B7, notebook binder.

67 Ltr., HRH to RMH, May 14, 1944, HRHC, A4, B7, notebook binder. Although Harmon was a major general, his permanent rank was that of

colonel. In February 1944 Kenney was a lieutenant general, but also only a colonel on the
permanent list; moreover, his date of rank to
colonel on the permanent list was later than
that of Harmon and thus Kenney was, technically, his junior.

68 Ibid.

69 Ltr., HRH to RMH, May 24, 1944, HRHC, A4,
B7, notebook binder. Harmon and Streett had
crossed paths numerous times throughout
their careers—at Coblenz in 1919, on the Air
Service Staff in 1921, at Fort Leavenworth, and
now in the Pacific.

70 Ltr., HRH to RMH, May 20, 1944, HRHC, A4,
B7, notebook binder; ltr., HRH to Lt Gen G.C.
Kenney, May 24, 1944, AFA, Huston/Kenney
papers, B3, F4.

71 Efficiency Report, December 31, 1943, signed
by VAdm A.W. Fitch, HRHC, A4, B20, F5.

72 Efficiency Report, June 30, 1944, signed by Gen
H.H. Arnold, HRHC, A4, B20, F5. (Emphasis added.) Arnold did, however, authorize the
award to Harmon of a Distinguished Service
Medal—the Army's highest non-combat decoration—for his tour in the South Pacific.

73 Efficiency Report, June 13, 1944, signed by Lt
Gen M.F. Harmon, HRHC, A4, B20, F5.

74 Ltr., Lt Gen M.F. Harmon to Gen H.H. Arnold,
May 17, 1944, HRHC, A4, B21, F4.

75 Ltrs., HRH to RMH, January 21 and April 21,
1944, HRHC, A4, B7, notebook binder.

76 Ltr., HRH to RMH, May 20, 1944, HRHC, A4,
B7, notebook binder.

77 HRHC, A4, B7, F11. The meaning of Bonnie
Paidie is unknown; given the context it could be
the local name for a foreigner, neophyte, youngster, or even ne'er do well. "Vulcan's Lady" was
the name of the B-24 he would be flying; DFC =
Distinguished Flying Cross; [Al]berta Harmon
was Miff's wife; Rennell was an island southwest
of Guadalcanal.

78 R.L. Jones and Chauncey E. Sanders, "Personnel Problems Related to AAF Commissioned
Officers, 1939–1945," AAF Historical Study no.
11, [1946], 10–11.

79 "History of the Personnel Distribution Command," January 1946, AFHRA, File 254.1–1.

80 Ltr., HRH to RMH, May 24, 1944, HRHC, A4,
B7, notebook binder.

81 Jones and Sanders, 165.

82 "History of the Medical Department, Personnel Distribution Command," January 1945,
1–10, AFHRA, File 254.3–1.

83 Ltrs., HRH to S. Streett, August 12 and 25,
1944, HRHC, A4, B7, F18.

84 Ltr., HRH to S. Streett, December 4, 1944,
HRHC, A4, B7, F18.

85 Ibid.

86 Chauncey E. Sanders, "Redeployment and Demobilization," AAF Historical Study no. 77,
June 1953, 7.

87 Jones and Sanders, 166.

88 Ibid., 167–68.

89 Alfred Goldberg (ed.), *A History of the United*
States Air Force, 1907–1957 (Princeton, NJ: Van
Nostrand, 1957), 105.

90 US Military Academy, "Thirty-five Year Book,
Class of 1915," 1950, 41.

91 Press Release, HQ AAF, February 27, 1945, located in HRHC, A4, B8, F4.

92 Ltr., HRH to RMH, February 23, 1945, located
in HRHC, A4, B8, F1.

93 Ltr., HRH to RMH, March 11, 1945, located in HRHC, A4, B8, F1. Millard Harmon's
plane was lost on 3 March. His daughter re-
lates that her husband, then-Colonel Joe
Nazarro, ran into his father-in-law unexpectedly on Kwajalein. Harmon suggested that Nazarro come with him on his plane to Hawaii, but
Nazarro said he needed to go elsewhere. That
decision saved his life. Nazarro later became
commander in chief of Strategic Air Command. Email, Kendrick Harmon to author,
June 23, 2007. For a good discussion of this final flight and the resulting search see Novotny,
chapter one. Novotny claims that Harmon was
going back to Washington to confront Arnold
over the command and control arrangements
of the Twentieth Air Force.

Chapter 6

1 Ltr., HRH to RMH, March 11, 1945, HRHC,
A4, B8, F1.

2 Ltr., HRH to RMH, March 6, 1945, HRHC, A4,
B8, F1.

3 Twining and LeMay served in both theaters,
but the former's greatest success was as commander of the Fifteenth Air Force in Italy,
while LeMay was chosen to command the B-
29s in the Mariana Islands because of his great
success in Europe—and also as a way of keeping the "very heavy bombers" out of the hands
of Kenney, Miff Harmon, and Chennault. Also
of note, this same battle was taking place
in the Army as a whole, with the same results.
The leaders of the postwar Army would be
Eisenhower, Bradley, Collins, and Ridgway—
not MacArthur, Stilwell, Krueger, Wedemeyer
and Eichelberger. In a revealing letter, Arnold
wrote Kenney in September 1944 chastiz-
ing him for his press releases that talked frequently of the "remarkable achievements" of
MacArthur and Halsey without mentioning
airpower. To Arnold, this was unpardonable
and reflected on Kenney's loyalty to his service. Ltr., Gen H.H. Arnold to Lt Gen G.C.
Kenney, September 26, 1944, AFA, Huston/
Kenney papers, B3, F2.

4 Ltr., HRH to RMH, March 17, 1945, HRHC, A4,
B8, F1. Hubert conceded that his brother's loss
also hurt his own career because he would not
be able to count on Miff's support in the AAF's
highest councils.

5 Ltr., HRH to RMH, March 21 and 27, HRHC,
A4, B8, F1.

6 With Millard's loss, Barney Giles left Washington to take his place in the Pacific, and Eaker
returned from the Mediterranean (he had been

the commander-in-chief of Allied Air Forces there) to become Arnold's deputy.

7 Ltr., HRH to RMH, April 28, 1945, HRHC, A4, B8, F1.

8 Ltrs., HRH to RMH, June 7 and 28, 1945, HRHC, A4, B8, F1.

9 Ltr., RMH to E. Kendrick, January 6, 1946, HRHC, A6, B1, F1.

10 Ltr., HRH to RMH, July 16, 1945, HRHC, A4, B8, F1.

11 Ltr., HRH to RMH, July 20, 1945, HRHC, A4, B8, F1. According to Eula Hoff, her father later confessed that he had been offered a job in Hawaii after the war, but had turned it down because it meant having to work with the Navy—the commander at the time was Admiral John Tower, a notoriously parochial and difficult sailor. Harmon knew that Hawaii would be the family's first choice, so he didn't tell them about it until years later! Ltr., EHH to author, June 9, 2007.

12 Ltr., HRH to RMH, July 24, 1945, HRHC, A4, B8, F1.

13 Ibid. Harmon had known Royce almost his entire career; the two men had been at North Island together in 1917. Harmon had also worked for Royce during the air maneuvers of 1933.

14 Ltr., HRH to RMH, October 3, 1945, HRHC, A4, B8, F1. Harmon had worked for Arnold in the Information Division of the Air Service staff in 1925–26; RMH Diary, January 22, 1946.

15 "Citation for the Distinguished Service Medal, First Oak Leaf Cluster," HRHC, A4, B19, F5.

16 Ltr., HRH to Gen H.H. Arnold, October 26, 1945, located in Volume VI of "History of the AAF Personnel Distribution Command," January 1946, AFHRA, File 254.1–1.

17 Efficiency Report, February 11, 1946, signed by Gen C.A. Spaatz, AFHRA, File 147.290–37.

18 RMH Diary, January 16, 1947.

19 Ltr., RMH to E.W. Kendrick, January 25, 1946, HRHC, A6, B1, F1.

20 R.A. Humphreys, Latin America in the Second World War, 2 vols. (London: Athlone, 1981), I, 310–13.

21 "Commanders Stress Defenses of Panama," New York Times, August 13, 1946, 4.

22 Pearcy, 114.

23 Ibid., 104.

24 Walter LaFeber, The Panama Canal: The Crisis in Historical Perspective (NY: Oxford University Press, 1978), 99–101.

25 Maj Gen H.R. Harmon, "Caribbean Air Command," Army and Navy Journal, December 28, 1946, 1.

26 These monthly histories are quite entertaining, and one wonders if the anonymous author was trying to be humorous or if it just turned out that way for modern readers. For all these reports, see AFHRA, File 464.01.

27 Ibid.

28 Interview with Kendrick Harmon and Eula Harmon Hoff, by James C. Gaston, August 29, 2002, contained in Gaston 50th Anniversary Oral History, 16.

29 Ltr., HRH to Eula Harmon, June 16, 1947, HRHC, A2, B1, F2. This was not a make-work project. Dad wrote out a detailed three-page list of Eula's duties, to include planning meals, buying groceries, paying all household expenses, and managing and paying the servants. His final words are interesting: "Conduct yourself with dignity and restraint in dealings with the servants and with Corporal Sharp. If any of them evidence any familiarity or lack of proper respect, let me know instantly."

30 Photos and news clippings, some undated, HRHC, A4, B8, F9. The "Frolics" was such a great success, the entire cast was flown to Puerto Rico to give two more performances.

31 Ltr., RMH to E.W. Kendrick, July 14, 1947, HRHC, A6, B1, F16.

32 Ltr., R.M. McGrath to HRH, July 21, 1953, HRHC, A1, B1, F7. George Brett was also mentioned for the post, but Harmon was told that he was "completely unacceptable" to the Panamanians.

33 Ltr., EHH to author, June 23, 2007. Eula also contends that her mother never let on regarding her wealth. To Eula and Kendrick, the family seemed always one step ahead of the poor house, and they were told to live their lives accordingly. Ltr., EHH to author, June 9, 2007.

34 RMH Diary, July 17, 1946.

35 RMH Diary, February 10, 1947.

36 Ltr., HRH to RMH, June 22, 1947, HRHC, A4, B8, F10. As the AAF moved towards an independent Air Force, inequities in airmen promotions finally began to be addressed. This was why the permanent major general's list followed closely on the heels of the permanent brigadier general's list.

37 After the Air Force became independent in September 1947, a number of officers were promoted one rank in order to establish parity with the other services. Harmon pinned on a third star in February 1948. Harmon's place as commander in Panama was taken by Maj Gen Willis Hales.

38 Ltr., Maj J.L. Peeler to EHH, February 19, 1948, HRHC, A4, B9, F3.

39 Notes by RMH.

40 For the League, see F.S. Northedge, The League of Nations: Its Life and Times, 1920–1940 (NY: Holmes & Meier, 1986), and George Scott, The Rise and Fall of the League of Nations (NY: Macmillan, 1973).

41 For the origins and organization of the UN, see Leland M. Goodrich, The United Nations (NY: Thomas Y. Crowell, 1959); Charles Patterson, The Oxford 50th Anniversary Book of the United Nations (NY: Oxford University Press, 1995); and Paul Kennedy, The Parliament of Man: The Past, Present, and Future of the United Nations (NY: Random House, 2006).

42 US Department of State, Foreign Relations of the United States, 1947, Volume I: General; The

United Nations (Washington DC: GPO, 1973), 665–70.

43 US Department of State, "Arms for the United Nations," June 1948, 4. The estimates of military forces submitted by the UK, France, and China were closer to the Soviet submissions in quantity—though not composition—than they were to the US. These countries no doubt feared that because the permanent members would be required to supply the bulk of the forces, the cost could quickly get out of hand.

44 Ibid., 13–14.

45 Stephen C. Schlesinger, *Act of Creation: The Founding of the United Nations* (Boulder, CO: Westview Press, 2003), 165.

46 Lt Gen H.R. Harmon, untitled speech to Town Hall Meeting, December 20, 1947, 7, HRHC, B4, F1.

47 Ibid., 8.

48 A.M. Rosenthal, "U.S. Aide Suggests U.N. Isolate Russia," *New York Times*, December 21, 1947, 26.

49 Lt Gen H.R. Harmon, "Outline of Talk on Military Staff Committee," March 29, 1949, 1–5, HRHC, B4, F1. Harmon also provided comments regarding the Soviets on the Committee: Lt Gen Sharopov was a "fastidious, peasant type" and Lt Gen Vasiliev was "an intellectual."

50 Gen Matthew B. Ridgway, *Soldier* (NY: Harper, 1956), 165.

51 "Outline of Talk on Military Staff Committee, 15–16.

52 Lt Gen H.R. Harmon, "Talk to Air War College," no date but the context of his remarks places it in late 1950, 4–5, HRHC, B4, F1.

53 Ibid., 7. In April 1952 Harmon gave a similarly "Cold Warrior" perspective in a speech in Dayton, Ohio. HRHC, B4, F2.

54 Harmon talk to cadets.

55 For the unification controversy see Demetrios Caraley, *The Politics of Military Unification* (NY: Columbia University Press, 1966); Steven L. Rearden, *History of the Office of the Secretary of Defense, Volume 1: The Formative Years, 1947–1950* (Washington DC: GPO, 1984); and *Chronology, Functions and Composition of the Joint Chiefs of Staff,* JCS Historical Study (Washington DC: Joint Chiefs of Staff, 1979).

56 For the roles and functions debate see Alice Cole, et. al. (eds.) *The Department of Defense: Documents on Establishment and Organization, 1944–1978* (Washington DC: GPO, 1978).

57 Louis Galambos (ed.) *The Papers of Dwight David Eisenhower, Columbia University: X* (Baltimore, MD: Johns Hopkins University Press, 1984), 448–49. The new bomber was the B-36; the new carrier was a flush-decked vessel to be named the *United States*; Radford was then a vice admiral on the Navy staff.

58 For the official transcript of the hearings, see US Congress, House, hearings before the Armed Services Committee, *Investigation of the B-36 Bomber Program*, 81st Congress, 1st Session (Washington DC: GPO, 1949).

59 For these hearings, see US Congress, House, hearings before the Armed Services Committee, *The National Defense Program—Unification and Strategy*, 81st Congress, 1st Session (Washington DC: GPO, 1949).

60 Ltr., Gen H.S. Vandenberg to Lt Gen C.E. LeMay, February 15, 1949, Vandenberg papers, Library of Congress, box 45; RMH Diary, February 9, 1949.

61 An important consideration that was not mentioned by the Harmon Board was the exact number of atomic weapons available at the time. This number was so highly classified it is doubtful the Board was provided this information. It therefore *assumed* there were enough atomic bombs in the stockpile to hit all of the assigned targets. In retrospect, that was a debatable assumption. For statistics on the number of weapons available—in June 1948 there were only fifty—see David Alan Rosenberg, "U.S. Nuclear Stockpile, 1945–1950," *Bulletin of the Atomic Scientists*, May 1982, 25–30.

62 Most of the Harmon Report, which was classified Top Secret at the time, has been reproduced in Stephen T. Ross and David Alan Rosenberg, *America's Plans for War against the Soviet Union, 1945–1950. Volume 11: The Limits of Nuclear Strategy* (NY: Garland, 1989). This volume itself is not paginated; however, the pages on the original document are usually legible. The conclusions of the report, which are given first, are on pages 3–6 of the original.

63 Ibid.

64 Ibid. Vandenberg's memo is dated July 8, 1949, and its pages in the original, reproduced in Ross and Rosenberg, are 279–83.

65 Bradley and Blair, 501.

66 Hanson W. Baldwin, "Secret Report Backs Navy," *New York Times*, October 14, 1949, 3.

67 Hanson W. Baldwin, "The Reply to the Navy," *New York Times*, October 19, 1949, 13.

Chapter 7

1 Unless otherwise noted, this section is derived from letters, emails, and phone calls with EHH and Kendrick Harmon, and interviews with EHH and Kendrick Harmon, August 29, 2002, and with MSgt Frank P. Wall, April 19, 2005, both contained in Gaston, *50th Anniversary Oral History*. My views are also based on the hundreds of letters and memos in the Harmon collection.

2 Ltr., RMH to E. Kendrick, January 11, 1934, copy supplied by EHH.

3 Ltr., HRH to K. Harmon, November 4, 1955, HRHC, B2, F6.

4 Ltr., HRH to and from K. Harmon, September 22, 1953, HRHC, A5, B5, F14.

5 Ltr., HRH to E. Kendrick, November 12, 1941, copy supplied by EHH.

6 RMH Diary, May 15, 1953.

7 Ltr., HRH to J.H. Hinemon, October 22, 1954, HRHC, B3, F1.

8 Ltr., RMH to G.C. Wood, n.d. but apparently written in mid-July 1958, HRHC, A4, B13, F4.

9 Ltr., HRH to "Papa," June 20, 1906, contained in "West Point Scrapbook" held by Kendrick Harmon.

10 RMH Diary, July 17, 1948.

11 Ltr., HRH to T. Bryan, September 4, 1954, HRHC, B3, F1. Howard Davidson, a retired major general, had been a classmate of Harmon's at Leavenworth and the next-door neighbor at March Field.

12 Interview with Col Thomas J. Hanley, Jr., by EHH, November 10, 1989, contained in HRHC, unprocessed material.

13 M. Hamlin Cannon and Henry S. Fellerman, "Quest for an Air Force Academy," USAF Academy Historical Study, 1974, 10.

14 It was also the case, however, that many equated educating airmen with training men to fly. It was no coincidence that the flying school at Randolph Field between the wars was referred to as "The West Point of the Air"—as if the two types of schools, one for training and one for educating, were analogous.

15 AC/AS Study, "Establishment of Separate Air Academy," July 7, 1945, AFA, Record Group (RG) 102, Microfilm Cartridge (MC) 302.

16 Cannon and Fellerman, "Quest," 90–91.

17 Interview with Lt Gen David M. Schlatter, by Maj E.A. Holt, October 24, 1956, contained in Lt Col Edgar A. Holt, M. Hamlin Cannon, and Carlos R. Allen, Jr., "History of the United States Air Force Academy, 27 July 1954–12 June 1956," VII vols., USAF Academy Historical Study, 1 August 1957, III, Document (D) 10, 2. [Hereinafter, "AFA Official History."] This history covers events well before 1954.

18 Cannon and Fellerman, "Quest," 89–93; ltr., W.S. Symington to P.J. Kilday, November 24, 1947, AFA, RG 103, A1, B1, F4.

19 Cannon and Fellerman, "Quest," 97.

20 Air Training Command, "United States Air Force Academy Plan," April 1948, AFA, Vertical Files.

21 Ltr., F. Pace to W.S. Symington, June 24, 1948, AFA, RG 103, A1, B2, F11.

22 Cannon and Fellerman, "Quest," 72.

23 "AFA Official History," I, 12–13, 27; memo, CSAF to SECAF, October 8, 1947, "AFA Official History," IV, D174.

24 Ltr., CSAF to DCS/P, August 2, 1948, AFA, RG 102, MC 302.

25 Ltr., Maj Gen M. Taylor to Gen H.S. Vandenberg, August 10, 1948, AFA, RG 103, A1, B1, F3.

26 Copy of letter from Vandenberg contained in Air Force Planning Board, "A Plan for an Air Force Academy," III vols., Air University, January 1949, I, iii. [Hereinafter, "Planning Board Study."] General Edwards felt so strongly about the inadvisability of a composite plan, despite not being an Academy graduate himself, that he went directly to Vandenberg to argue against the idea. Interview, Lt Gen Idwal H. Edwards,

by Maj E.A. Holt, October 26, 1956, contained in "AFA Official History," III, D3, 5. See also Cannon and Fellerman, "Quest," 107–08.

27 Phillip S. Meilinger, Hoyt S. Vandenberg: The Life of a General (Bloomington: Indiana University Press, 1989), 8–9. It is also interesting to note that 1923 was the first year that West Point cadets could choose the Air Service directly after graduation. Before 1923, graduates like Hubert Harmon would enter another branch first, and then request a transfer to the Air Service at a later date. Vandenberg chose the Air Service upon his graduation in 1923.

28 "Planning Board Study," I, xii–xiii. Of note, one of the Board's members was Col Robert M. Stillman, later to be the Air Force Academy's first commandant of cadets. Also of note, Beukema was Hubert Harmon's West Point classmate; he too would play a significant role in the years ahead.

29 In fact, the Navy gave the Air Force none of its Annapolis graduates in 1948; the 7 percent quota was to begin in 1949. Cannon and Fellerman, "Quest," 110.

30 "Planning Board Study," I, chapter 15, gives a detailed analysis of the expansion issue.

31 Ibid., I, 4–5.

32 Ibid., I, 7.

33 Ibid., I, 47–51.

34 Ibid., I, 53–55.

35 Ibid. These courses are outlined in the first volume of the Report, but given in detail in volume two.

36 Ibid., I, chapters 6 and 7.

37 As an AFA cadet in 1966 I did very poorly in freshman chemistry, so I was "re-sectioned" to the very bottom of the class. At the beginning of the second semester a crusty major breezed into the classroom the first day and told us that he had been stuck with attempting to teach us "knuckle-draggers" something about chemistry. He didn't think that was possible and we had not a prayer, but he "knew chemistry inside and out" and would do the best he could to get us all a passing grade. He did.

38 "Planning Board Study," I, 13–15.

39 Of the ten general officers serving as consultants to the Planning Board, only three were West Point graduates: Maxwell Taylor, Bart Yount, and Maj General Robert W. Harper, the commander of Air University. This fact, plus the large number of civilian consultants, indicates that all were extremely impressed by the West Point model and wished to emulate it.

40 Gen H.S. Vandenberg, "Remarks before the West Point Society of New York," March 16, 1949, AFA, RG 102, MC 102.

41 Ltr., Gen D.D. Eisenhower to J. Forrestal, January 13, 1949, AFA, RG 103, A1, B2, F11.

42 Department of Defense, "A Report and Recommendation to the Secretary of Defense by the Service Academy Board," January 1950, 17–19. An interim report was filed in April 1949. [Hereinafter, "Stearns-Eisenhower Report."]

A cynic would no doubt argue that given the Board's composition, it was most unlikely its conclusions would be other than a ringing endorsement of West Point and Annapolis.

43 Schlatter became commander of the Research and Development Command in February 1950.

44 "Stearns-Eisenhower Report," 2.

45 Ibid., 3.

46 Ibid., 4, 6.

47 Schlatter interview, 3.

48 "Stearns-Eisenhower Report," 9.

49 There are dozens of such bills contained in AFA, RG 100, MC 299.

50 Cannon and Fellerman, "Quest," 132–33; memo, M. Leva to Army, Navy and Air Force, December 19, 1949, AFA, RG 101, MC 302.

51 Ltr., F. Pace to W.S. Symington, July 11, 1949, "AFA Official History," IV, D138. Pace's letter strongly implied that he was satisfied with the Air Force proposal; he just did not think that Congress would be.

52 Ltr., Lt Gen J.K. Cannon to SECAF, March 25, 1948, "AFA Official History," IV, D174.

53 Ltr., W.S. Symington to W.G. Andrews, March 31, 1948, "AFA Official History," IV, D170.

54 Memo, CSAF to SECAF, March 26, 1948, "AFA Official History," IV, D174.

55 Memo, W.S. Symington to J.H. Sullivan, May 7, 1948, AFA, RG 103, A1, B1, F3.

56 Ltr., Brig Gen J.B. Newman to HRH, February 17, 1950, "AFA Official History," IV, D120.

57 Memo, Lt Gen L. Norstad to SECAF, February 20, 1948, "AFA Official History," IV, D174. It is not known how Norstad came up with the figure of 605 officers—most studies called for between 500 and 575 Academy graduates for the Air Force each year. In addition, the Army disputed the figures produced by Norstad, but after some lobbying by Symington, it acquiesced, telling Congress that it had "no objection" to the air academy proposal. Cannon and Fellerman, "Quest," 96.

58 "Planning Board Study," III, passim. Initially, it had been intended for the Board to look at several possible sites for an academy, but it ran out of time and money.

59 Edward A. Miller, Jr., "The Founding of the Air Force Academy: An Administrative and Legislative History," PhD Dissertation, Denver University, 1969, 239–40.

60 Edwards interview, 5–6. Harmon had worked in personnel both for the Army and the AAF for over four years, so his offer to Edwards made much sense. Edwards' reaction was similarly logical.

61 Ibid., 6; RMH Diary, November 29, 1949.

62 Ibid., 11. Edwards did not give a date for this conversation between Vandenberg and Harmon, but my guess would be that it occurred in September 1952 when Harmon raised the issue of his mandatory retirement date and the possibility of his being recalled to active duty shortly thereafter.

63 Ltr., HRH to Lt Gen I.H. Edwards, July 8, 1948.

Chapter 8

1 AF DCS/P, "Office Memo No. 50," December 19, 1949, AFA, RG 103, A1, B2, F11; Paul T. Ringenbach, *Battling Tradition: Robert F. McDermott and Shaping the U.S. Air Force Academy* (Chicago: Imprint, 2006), 38. Stone would become the third superintendent of the AFA in 1959.

2 Memo, HRH to CSAF, January 20, 1950, AFA, RG 103, MC 303.

3 Miller, 298–99. The opening statement regarding the importance of a beautiful site was derived from the 1948 Planning Board Report, of which Newton was a member. It was an important criterion to Harmon.

4 Interview with Col Arthur J. Boudreau, by Maj E.A. Holt, October 10–11, 1956, "AFA Official History," III, D1, 9–10.

5 Cannon and Fellerman, "Quest," chapter 3; Edwards interview, 7–8.

6 Miller, 306.

7 For Harmon's thoughts on flying training at the academy, see his letter to SECAF, June 4, 1950, AFA, RG 104.4, MC 305. In a letter to Spaatz in July, Harmon expressed the hope that despite the new guidelines, they would be able to complete the project by November. Ltr., HRH to C. Spaatz, July 6, 1950, AFA, RG 103, MC 303.

8 Miller, 308.

9 Ltr., HRH to CSAF, April 26, 1950, "AFA Official History," IV, D113.

10 Ltr., HRH to B.D. Wood, September 5, 1950, HRHC, B3, F1. Actually, Spaatz remained on the Board through the conclusion of its work in May 1951.

11 HRH, "Memorandum for Minister Ross," August 8, 1952, HRHC, A4, B11, F3.

12 Ibid.

13 "List of Criteria," December 1950, AFA, RG 120.2, "Site Selection" box.

14 Memo, HRH to CSAF, October 31, 1950, AFA, RG 103, A1, B2, F12.

15 Miller, 315.

16 DoD Release, "List of 354 Sites Narrowed to 29 for Air Force Academy," November 17, 1950, AFA, RG 103, A1, B2, F13.

17 Miller, 317–18; ltr., HRH to RMH, November 25, 1950, HRHC, A4, B10, F5.

18 Boudreau interview, 10–11.

19 Miller, 319.

20 MFR, HRH, January 5, 1951, AFA, RG 103, MC 303; MFR, HRH, January 24, 1951, AFA, RG 101, MC 300.

21 Ltr., HRH to AF/JAG, February 2, 1950, and ltr., AF/JAG to HRH, February 23, 1950, both in "AFA Official History," IV, D118, 121. The following October, Secretary Finletter raised this idea again. Memo, HRH to SECAF, October 9, 1951, RG 102, MC 302.

22 Miller, 321.

23 Memo, HRH to SECDEF, March 21, 1951, AFA, RG 101, MC 300.

24 Miller, 330–31.

25 Ibid.; Cannon and Fellerman, "Quest," 133. Memo, Lt Col D.H. Reed to HRH, December 21, 1950, AFA, RG 101, MC 300, gives a depressing history of the slow progress of the omnibus bill.

26 Interview with James F.C. Hyde, Jr., by Maj E.A. Holt, October 19, 1956, contained in "AFA Official History," III, D5, 5–7; see also the MFR regarding this meeting, February 23, 1951, "AFA Official History," IV, D109. This memo puts most of the blame for delay on the omnibus bill with the Navy.

27 Memo, HRH to CSAF, September 27, 1951, AFA, RG 103, MC 303.

28 Edwards interview, 8–11; Boudreau interview, 11–12; ltr., C. Vinson to W.S. Symington, March 20, 1950, AFA, RG 100, MC 300.

29 Memo, HRH to CSAF, February 2, 1951, "AFA Official History," IV, D110.

30 Ltr., B.D. Wood to HRH, with attached essay, February 11, 1952, AFA, RG 101, MC 301.

31 Ibid.

32 HRH, "Statement before the Committee on Armed Services, House of Representatives," August 8, 1950, AFA, RG 101, MC 300.

33 "Press Release," March 1, 1951, AFA, RG 120.2, "Site Selection" box.

34 MFR, OSAF, January 24, 1951, AFA, RG 101, MC 300.

35 Miller, 339–40; MFR, Lt Col J.J. Easton, May 23, 1951, AFA, RG 101, MC 300.

36 Vinson's article, "For a 'West Point' of the Air," was published in the New York Times Magazine on June 22, 1952.

37 MFR, Col D.M. Reed, June 1, 1951, "AFA Official History," IV, D104; interview with Col William Barrett Taylor, by Lt Col E.A. Holt, January 13, 1958, 1–2, AFA, RG 101, MC 301.

38 Memo, Brig Gen R.E. Eaton to Lt Gen W. McKee, June 18, 1951, "AFA Official History," IV, D102.

39 Ltr., D.K. Edwards to Speaker, June 20, 1951, "AFA Official History," IV, D101.

40 Miller, 342.

41 Ibid., 344. Once the Korean War broke out, the Navy decided it needed the Bainbridge site after all, so it withdrew its offer to the Air Force.

42 Ltr., C. Vinson to T.K. Finletter, July 3, 1952, AFA, RG 101, MC 301.

43 Memo, CSAF to All Deputy Chiefs of Staff, September 27, 1951, AFA, RG 103, MC 303.

44 Miller 347; memo, SECAF to CSAF, March 3, 1952, AFA, RG 101, MC 301; MFR, HRH, March 10, 1952, AFA, RG 101, MC 301.

45 MFR, Lt Col T.L. Sheldrake, August 6, 1952, "AFA Official History," IV, D92.

46 MFR, HRH, December 23, 1952, AFA, RG 101, MC 301.

47 Memo, VCSAF to CSAF, December 1952, "AFA Official History," IV, D84. Vandenberg decreed that cadets would carry rifles. Memo, DCS/P to VCSAF, January 17, 1953, AFA, RG 103, MC 303.

48 MFR, HRH, February 6, 1953, AFA, RG 101, MC 301.

49 Memo, HRH to CSAF, March 4, 1953, AFA, RG 101, MC 301.

50 HRH, "Speech to the USAF Personnel Conference," March 2, 1953, HRHC, B4, F2.

51 Memo, HRH to VCSAF, March 13, 1953, AFA, RG 101, MC 301; MFR, Col R.E. Masters, February 2, 1953, "AFA Official History," IV, D80.

52 Ltr., R. Kent to Speaker, January 5, 1953, "AFA Official History," IV, D83.

53 Memo, Maj Gen R.E.L. Eaton to CSAF, February 2, 1953, AFA, RG 101, MC 301.

54 Ltr., D.D. Eisenhower to HRH, April 1, 1952, HRHC, A4, B11, F3. The letter from Harmon to Eisenhower that prompted this warm response is not in Harmon's papers.

55 Public Papers of the Presidents of the United States: Dwight D. Eisenhower, 1953 (Washington DC: GPO, 1960), 31; MFR, HRH, March 25, 1953, AFA, RG 101, MC 301. The question came from Sarah McClendon of the San Antonio Light.

56 Ltr., HRH to Lt Gen L.S. Kuter, September 24, 1952, AFA, RG 103, MC 103.

57 Ltr., HRH to E. Kendrick, January 7, 1953, HRHC, A4, B11, F7.

58 Memo, Maj Gen R.E.L. Eaton to SECAF, April 9, 1953, AFA, RG 103, MC 303. The assistant secretary referred to was John A. Hannah. See also memo, HRH to SECAF, May 14, 1953, AFA, RG 103, MC 304.

59 MFR, Col A.E. Boudreau, April 23, 1953; and MFR, Col W.G. Hipps, April 28, 1953, both in AFA, RG 101, MC 301.

60 Press Release, SECAF, May 21, 1953, AFA, RG 101, MC 301.

61 Memo, SECAF to Dep Sec Kyes, May 12, 1953, AFA, RG 103, MC 303.

62 Ltr., HRH to Lt Gen E. O'Donnell, July 1, 1953, AFA, RG 103, MC 303. Wilson was then commandant of the Air War College at Maxwell AFB. For his replacement at the UN, Harmon recommended Maj Gen Leon Johnson, a Medal of Honor winner at Ploesti during World War II.

63 See leather binder in HRHC, A4, B11, F11.

64 Memo, B. Harlow to Gen Persons, August 1, 1953, AFA, RG 127, MC 812. The memo begins: "The President asked Dewey Short two or three weeks ago to do something about the Air Force Academy."

65 MFR, Maj Gen R.E.L. Easton, August 1, 1953, AFA, RG 101, MC 301; Miller, 377.

66 Memo, CSAF to SECAF, no date but context indicates it was written in July or August 1953, AFA, RG 103, MC 303.

67 Ltr., Lt Gen L.S. Kuter to VCSAF, July 16, 1953, AFA, RG 303, MC 303; ltr., E. Husted to HRH, December 15, 1953, AFA, RG 104.4, MC 305.

68 Ltr., Lt Gen L.S. Kuter to Lt Gen E. O'Donnell, October 6, 1953, and ltr., Lt Gen E. O'Donnell to Lt Gen L.S. Kuter, October 27, 1953; ltr., Lt Gen E. O'Donnell to HRH, November 27, 1953, all in AFA, RG 103, MC 303.

69 Ltr., HRH to Brig Gen D.O. Smith, December 15, 1953, "AFA Official History," IV, D69.

70 MFR, HRH, October 21, 1953, AFA, RG 103, MC 303.

71 Ltr., Sec J.H. Douglas to the President, November 3, 1953, AFA, RG 127, MC 812.

72 US Congress, House, hearings before the Armed Services Committee, *To Provide for the Establishment of a United States Air Force Academy*, 83rd Congress, 1st session (Washington DC: GPO, 1954), 14–15.

73 Ibid, 65–66.

74 Ibid.

75 Ibid., 67–68.

76 Ibid., 66–67.

77 Ibid., 69.

78 Ibid., 70–71.

79 Ltr., HRH to RMH, January 15, 1954, HRHC, A4, B11, F7.

80 US Congress, Senate, hearings before the Armed Services Committee, *An Act to Provide for the Establishment of a United States Air Force Academy and for Other Purposes*, 83rd Congress, 2nd session (Washington DC: GPO, 1954), 35–56.

81 Miller, 403–05.

82 Ltr., H. Talbott to HRH, April 2, 1954, HRHC, B1, F5.

83 Cannon and Fellerman, "Quest," iii.

Chapter 9

1 Cannon and Fellerman, "Quest," 218.

2 "Minutes of the Commission by the Secretary of the Air Force Appointed under the Provisions of the Air Force Academy Act to Advise him in Connection with Selection of a Permanent Location for the Academy," n.d., but presumably May 1954, "AFA Official History," III, D31, 1–2. [Hereinafter, "Minutes of the Site Commission."] "Primary Factors Considered by the Commission in Evaluating Proposed Locations," June 9, 1954, "AFA Official History," IV, D51.

3 Robert Bruegmann, (ed.) *Modernism at Mid-Century: The Architecture of the United States Air Force Academy* (Chicago: University of Chicago Press, 1994), 59.

4 Miller, 413; "Minutes of the Site Commission," 3–4. The higher the altitude the less oxygen is available for man and machine. In the case of an aircraft engine, it means that as an aircraft climbs it suffers from an increasing loss of power—a potentially dangerous condition for student pilots prone to making errors.

5 "Minutes of the Site Selection," 7–8.

6 "Minutes of the Site Selection," 9; interview with Merrill C. Meigs, by Maj E.A. Holt, May 21, 1956, contained in "AFA Official History," III, D7, 2. Ever since the kidnapping of Lindbergh's son in 1932 and the resulting media circus, the aviator had avoided newsmen.

7 Interview with Gen Carl A. Spaatz, by Maj E.A. Holt, June 13, 1956, contained in "AFA Official History," III, D13, 7.

8 Interview with Charles A. Lindbergh, by Maj E.A. Holt, January 3, 1957, contained in "AFA Official History," III, D6, 3.

9 "Minutes of the Site Commission," 5–8; Meigs interview, 6.

10 Ltr., W. Darley to HRH, April 16, 1954, AFA, RG 104.4, MC 305; "Minutes of the Site Commission," 12–14.

11 Miller, 417.

12 Ltr., CSAF to AASC, May 26, 1954, "AFA Official History," III, D52. Harmon confided to Rosa-Maye that he favored the Colorado Springs site and had pushed Twining to make a decision on the altitude issue once and for all. Ltr., HRH to RMH, May 21, 1954, HRHC, A4, B11, F14.

13 Lindbergh interview, 3; Meigs interview, 7–8.

14 Meigs interview, 3; Miller, 419. The city quickly grew north towards the Academy; today the metropolitan area begins immediately outside the south gate. For the official Commission report see "Report to the Secretary of the Air Force by the Air Force Academy Site Selection Commission," June 3, 1954, "AFA Official History," III, D52.

15 Cannon and Fellerman, "Quest," 226.

16 Telegram, Geneva Lake Civic Association to H.E. Talbott, June 3, 1954, and ltr., F. Walsh to D.D. Eisenhower, June 19, 1954, both in AFA, "Site Selection" box.

17 Miller, 431–32.

18 Diary entry, Lt Col W. G. Draper, June 19, 1954, AFA, RG 120, MC 812. Draper was the military aide to the president.

19 Ltr., HRH to V.M. Hancher, July 26, 1954, HRHC, B3, F1.

20 Memo, HRH to SECAF, July 19, 1954, HRHC, B6, F2; interview with Col Arthur G. Witters, by Maj E.A. Holt, July 9, 1956, contained in "AFA Official History," V, D17, 5.

21 Cannon and Fellerman, "Quest," 270.

22 Several other smaller homes were also left standing and used as base housing units.

23 Fact Sheet, "Site and Plan Data, United States Air Force Academy," May 14, 1955, AFA, RG 120, MC 812. The 4,650-acre Cathedral Rock Ranch, owned by L.B. Lehman, dominated this ridge.

24 Memo, HRH to DCS/O, November 18, 1953, AFA, RG 104, MC 304; memo, HRH to DCS/O, November 23, 1953, AFA, RG 104.4, MC 305.

25 Bruegmann, 22, 59; "Report of Group Visit to University City, Mexico City," July 9, 1955, AFA, RG 104, MC 304.

26 General Order no. 32, "Establishment of the Air Academy Construction Agency," June 9, 1954, "AFA Official History," V, D101.

27 Memo, HRH to SECAF, March 31, 1954, "AFA Official History," IV, D58.

28 MFR, HRH, March 12, 1954, "AFA, RG 104.1, MC 304; memo, HRH to Maj Gen L.B. Washbourne, March 31, 1954, "AFA Official History," IV, D57.

29 Bruegmann, 29.

30 Bruegmann, 43. This confirmed what one architect had noted: the Air Force wanted to deal

with "rational businessmen," not "temperamental artists."

31 Memo, CSAF to the President, March 9, 1955, AFA, RG 120, MC 812.

32 Bruegmann, 30–31.

33 Bruegmann, 177. The architects did draw up plans for the Cadet Area to be in a valley, but by that point Harmon had agreed the ridge top made more sense. Witters interview in "AFA Official History," 7.

34 Highway 85/87 was soon replaced by Interstate 25; a remnant of the old highway can still be seen between the interstate and the airfield. A small, gravel airstrip already existed on the site, but was far too small for what the Academy intended.

35 MFR, HRH, August 6, 1954, HRHC, A4, B12, F7.

36 Bruegmann, 62, 188.

37 Bruegmann, 16.

38 Memo, HRH to N. Owings, March 31, 1955; memo, HRH to J.M. Ferry, April 12, 1955; and memo, HRH to CSAF, n.d., but about this same time, all located in AFA, RG 120, MC 812.

39 News Release, "Air Force Secretary Talbott Unveils Architecture Models of Air Academy," May 14, 1955, "AFA Official History," V, D69; interview with Col Max Boyd, by Maj E.A. Holt, July 24, 1956, contained in "AFA Official History," V, D14, 103.

40 Interview with Walter A. Netsch, by Col James C. Gaston, May 15–16, 2002, 19, located in *50th Anniversary History,* 102; Richard G. Powers, "The Cold War in the Rockies: American Ideology and the Air Force Academy Design," *Art Journal,* 33 (Summer 1974): 304; "AFA Official History," I, 278–82.

41 David Boroff, "Air Force Academy: A Slight Gain in Altitude," *Harper's Magazine,* February, 1963, 86. In cadet lore, the seventeen spires represent the twelve apostles and five joint chiefs of staff.

42 The cardinal of New York City tried to put Walter Netsch's mind at rest on the issue: "Walter, don't worry. We can beat the Protestants to heaven anytime. Seventeen feet means nothing." Netsch interview, 114.

43 Bruegmann, 44–46.

44 Bruegmann, 45.

45 Ltr., HRH to H.C. Price, August 18, 1954, HRHC, B3, F2.

46 "Too Many Amateurs," *Denver Post,* July 14, 1955, 32.

47 Bruegmann, 46.

48 Netsch Interview, 99.

49 Bruegmann, 32; "AFA Official History," I, 294–95.

50 Netsch interview, 99.

51 Interview with Col Gordon P. Culver, by Maj Russell Mank and Capt Phillip Meilinger, June 16, 1979, 24, Air Force Academy Oral History Collection (AFAOHC).

52 Bruegmann, 21–22.

53 Ltr., HRH to Lt Gen L. Kuhn, March 1, 1954, HRHC, B6, F1.

54 Interview with Lt Col Virgil J. O'Connor, by Maj E.A. Holt, November 27, 1956, contained in "AFA Official History," V, D7, 4.

55 Netsch interview, 103. Spiral staircases were also placed in the dining hall (Mitchell Hall) and the cadet social center (Arnold Hall).

56 Netsch interview, 104.

57 Netsch interview, 103; Witters interview in "AFA Official History," 8–9.

58 Bruegmann, 150; "AFA Official History," I, 261–62.

59 "AFA Official History," II, 866–68; memo, HRH to VCSAF, August 3, 1954, HRHC, B6, F1; ltr., HRH to DCS/O, February 7, 1955, "AFA Official History," VII, D12.

60 Ltr., C.B. DeMille to Maj Gen J.E. Briggs, July 30, 1956, AFA, RG 403, MC 604. Actually, at one point Harmon thought DeMille was stalling and recommended to Talbott that the contract be terminated. He wanted a presentation of the new designs by February 1956. DeMille made this deadline. Memo, HRH to SECAF, November 23, 1955, AFA, RG 610, MC 1163.

61 Ltr., Brig Gen R.M. Stillman to HRH, October 29, 1956, HRHC, A4, B13, F1.

62 Bruegmann, 145; Donald Hayne (ed.) *The Autobiography of Cecil B. DeMille* (NY: Garland, 1985), 197–205. De Mille had attended the Pennsylvania Military Academy from 1896 to 1898. Recall that First Lieutenant Millard Fillmore Harmon had been commandant of the Academy from 1890–1893, and Hubert had been born while his father was assigned there.

63 Bruegmann, 109.

64 If the Academy were being built today, it is unlikely that the more secularized American society and its architects would make a religious building the centerpiece of the Air Force Academy's public image.

65 A beautiful golf course (two of them actually) was added later, appropriately named after one of Hubert Harmon's favorite golf partners—Dwight D. Eisenhower.

66 "Study of Movement of USAF Academy to Permanent Site," June 30, 1956, AFA, Gen E. O'Donnell papers, B28, F8. The delay caused the second class, that of 1960, to be cut from 400 to 300 due to space constraints at Lowry.

67 Memo, HRH to CSAF, October 12, 1951, AFA, RG 103, MC 303.

68 Ibid. Col Schlatter was the younger brother of the first Academy superintendent designate, Maj Gen David M. Schlatter.

69 Ringenbach, 42.

70 Memo, HRH to DCS/P, November 20, 1952, AFA, RG 1904, MC 305.

71 See for example, ltrs., HRH to Col D.O. Smith, February 16 and November 18, 1953, both in HRHC, B3, F1.

72 Interview with Brig Gen Dale O. Smith by Maj E. A. Holt, April 18, 1956, in "AFA Official History," III, D12, 2.

73 Col Robert R. Gideon "Historical Record," n.d., but presumably late 1957, contained in "AFA Official History," V, D8, 2.

74 Interview with Myra Stone, by Capts Russell Mank and Fred Shiner, March 20, 1973, 14, AFAOHC; memo, HRH to DCS/P, February 19, 1954, AFA, RG 104, MC 305. Stone had been White's executive officer for three years in the early 1950s.

75 Ringenbach, 45; "AFA Official History," I, 395; ltr., HRH to Col W.M. Bessell, January 29, 1954, HRHC, B3, F1.

76 Ltr., Col P.M. Hoisington to Brig Gen R.C. Wilson, AFA, RG 101, MC 301. Zimmerman was one of fifteen individuals recommended, but he was near the bottom of the list.

77 Ringenbach, 48.

78 Ltr., HRH to CSAF, July 20, 1954, AFA, Brig Gen D.Z. Zimmerman papers, F1.

79 Interview with Brig Gen Don Z. Zimmerman, by Maj Russell Mank and Capt Phillip Meilinger, September 7, 1979, 1, AFAOHC.

80 Ringenbach, 48.

81 Ltr., Lt Col R.F. McDermott to USAF/MPC, March 2, 1954, AFA, Brig Gen R.F. McDermott papers, B3, Envelope 1; Ringenbach, 48–49; memo, HRH to CSAF, August 27, 1954, HRHC, B6, F2. By using the phrase "a career basis" McDermott presumably meant he had no desire to return to a flying assignment.

82 Interview with Lt Col Thomas F. Corrigan, by Maj Russell Mank and Capt Phillip Meilinger, January 24, 1979, 4, AFAOHC.

83 Ltr., HRH to RMH, March 11, 1954, HRHC, A4, B11, F14. Stillman had been on Harmon's list as one of his top three choices. Memo, HRH to DCS/P, February 18, 1954, AFA, RG 104, MC 305.

84 US Air Force Academy, "Morning Report," August 14, 1954, HRHC, B6, F2.

85 Zimmerman interview, 5.

86 Ringenback, 47.

87 In June 1979 Maj Russell Mank and I interviewed Brig Gen Robin Olds at his home in Steamboat Springs, Colorado. Over lunch he mentioned his role as a personnel officer in 1954. There were indeed numerous West Point athletes on the initial Academy staff. Besides Harmon, Stillman, Zimmerman and Whitlow, other letter-winners included Colonels Francis E. Merritt (football), Robert R. Gideon (polo), Benjamin B. Cassiday (track), Louis T. Seith (football), Henry L. Hogan (track), Thomas J. Hanley (golf), and William C. McGlothlin (boxing).

88 Ltr., Col T.J. Gent to HRH, December 28, 1954, HRHC, B4, F3; O'Connor interview, 3.

89 Ltr., HRH to L.B. Charney, November 22, 1954, HRHC, B6, F1.

90 Interview with Lt Col George C. Cooke, by Maj E.A. Holt, July 11, 1956, located in "AFA Official History," III, D2, 7.

91 Interview with Brig Gen Benjamin B. Cassiday, Jr., by EHH, June 3, 1989, HRHC, A4, B17, F8.

92 Gideon, "Record," 1.

93 "AFA Official History," II, 703–05.

94 William T. Woodyard, "A Historical Study of the Development of the Academic Curriculum of the United States Air Force Academy," PhD Dissertation, University of Denver, 1965, 52.

95 Woodyard, 106. Note also the Board did not include the athletic director.

Chapter 10

1 Anonymous poem found in HRHC, A4, B13, F7.

2 Notes by RMH.

3 "AFA Official History," I, 461–62; Boudreau interview, 13.

4 "Planning Board Study," I, 13–15.

5 "AFA Official History," I, 463. These detailed syllabi are in AFA, RG 103, MC 304 and 305.

6 There are over a dozen of these theses located in AFA, RG 103, MC 304.

7 Woodyard, 29–30.

8 "AFA Official History," I, 465–66. Harmon and Spaatz had become quite close after World War II. Harmon wrote Rosa-Maye in 1954: "Tooey has helped me immeasurably"—he was responsible for getting him promoted to permanent brigadier and major general, the assignment to the UN that earned him a third star, and "who now says I must be the first Superintendent." Ltr., HRH to RMH, January 29, 1954, HRHC, A4, B11, F14.

9 Ltr., HRH to Brig Gen D.Z. Zimmerman, November 22, 1954, "AFA Official History," VI, D46; Cannon and Fellerman, "Quest," 186.

10 The science/humanities split at West Point was 65/35 percent, and at Annapolis it was 76.8/23.2 percent in favor of science. Ltr., Col G.A. Lincoln to Col A. Boudreau, November 10, 1952, AFA, RG 104.2, MC 304.

11 Woodyard, 58.

12 Ltr., HRH to Lt Gen L.S. Kuter, May 18, 1954, "AFA Official History," IV, D53. Kuter had complained about this issue to Ira Eaker who in turn passed the comments on to Harmon.

13 "AFA Official History," I, 503–08.

14 "AFA Official History," I, 461; Woodyard, 51–60. Plans called for twelve hours of class time in academic courses to equal one semester hour; lab courses were pegged at twenty-four class hours per one semester hour; athletics, military training and airmanship ranged from forty-two to eighty-four hours of contact time for every one semester hour granted. These would be very busy young men. Woodyard, 64.

15 "AFA Official History," I, 511–13.

16 Cannon and Fellerman, "Quest," 189.

17 Woodyard, 59.

18 Zimmerman interview, 10–12, 14.

19 Ltr., HRH to Col G.A. Lincoln, August 17, 1955, HRHC, B3, F3.

20 "AFA Official History," I, 552; Zimmerman interview, 14.

21 Cannon and Fellerman, "Quest," 190. Hopper, who Harmon generally called Dr. Whopper, had been on the Spaatz Site Selection Board in 1950–51.

22 Although not occurring until after Harmon was gone, McDermott, who eventually succeeded

Zimmerman as dean, pushed through major changes in the Academy curriculum, including validation credit for those with prior college, electives, academic majors, and even a cooperative master's degree program for select cadets. For the story of the Air Force Academy's "enrichment" program, see Ringenbach, chapter 5.

23 Spaatz interview, 7. Spaatz implied that a light aircraft would fulfill that requirement.

24 Cannon and Fellerman, "Quest," 194–95; "AFA Official History," I, 475–80.

25 "AFA Official History," II, 817.

26 Smith interview, 1; ltr., Col D.O. Smith to HRH, December 22, 1952, "AFA Official History," IV, D86.

27 Memo, HRH to CSAF, December 29, 1952, AFA, RG 104.4, MC 305; memo, DCS/P to VC-SAF, January 10, 1953, AFA, RG 104.3, MC 304; Boudreau interview, 16.

28 Cannon and Fellerman, "Quest," 199.

29 "United States Air Force Academy Catalogue, 1954–1955," 39–40.

30 "Planning Board Study," I, 50.

31 Cannon and Fellerman, "Quest," 203.

32 Memo, Col D.O. Smith to HRH, March 5, 1953, "AFA Official History," IV, unnumbered document following D77.

33 Ltr., HRH to Col G.A. Lincoln, March 2, 1953, HRHC, A1, B1, F11. Harmon also proposed this idea to Talbott, but again, nothing happened. Memo, HRH to SECAF, July 19, 1954, "AFA Official History," III, D46.

34 Ltr., HRH to Col H. Beukema, April 13, 1953, HRHC, A1, B1, F11.

35 Ltr., Col H. Beukema to HRH, April 14, 1953, HRHC, A1, B1, F11.

36 HRH, "Speech to USAF Personnel Conference," March 2, 1953, HRHC, B4, F2.

37 Ringenbach, 51; Zimmerman interview, 14.

38 Cannon and Fellerman, "Quest," 205. Academic rank was based on military rank and responsibility, teaching experience, and academic credentials.

39 Ltr., HRH to V. Hancher, September 9, 1954, "AFA Official History," III, D41.

40 Cannon and Fellerman, "Quest," 207; "AFA Official History," I, 409–11.

41 Ltr., HRH to Lt Gen B.M. Bryan (West Point superintendent), March 31, 1955, AFA, RG 322, MC 688.

42 Cannon and Fellerman, "Quest," 207–10.

43 Woodyard, 99; "AFA Official History," II, 693–97.

44 Woodyard, 99.

45 Interview with Lt Gen James E. Briggs, by Capts Timothy E. Kline, Robert Bartanowicz and Robert Wolff, February 24, 1973, 5, AFAOHC.

46 Ltr., Brig Gen R.M. Stillman to Commander, Flying Training Air Force, November 16, 1954, contained in "Official History of the Commandant of Cadets, 1 September 1954–12 June 1956" by Joseph G. Michaloski, 1957, D16.

47 "AFA Official History," I, 585–86.

48 Aloysius G. Casey and Patrick A. Casey, *Velocity—Speed with Direction: The Professional Career of Gen Jerome F. O'Malley* (Maxwell AFB, AL: Air University Press, 2007), 54–58.

49 Interview with Col Richard J. Coffee, by Col James C. Gaston, June 17, 2002, in Gaston, *50th Anniversary History*, 142.

50 Smith interview, 3; ltr., Lt Gen E. O'Donnell to CSAF, July 8, 1954, HRHC, B6, F2.

51 Witters interview, 6.

52 Gideon, "Record," 4. The Academy's materiel officer felt similarly. Interview with Maj R.C. Hutto, by Maj E.A. Holt, July 5, 1956, contained in "AFA Official History," V, D18, 4; Cooke interview, 5.

53 Ltr., HRH to Lt Gen T.H. Landon, July 25, 1956, HRHC, B1, F2.

54 MFR, Maj R.C. Hutto, December 17, 1954, AFA, DCS/M "Funds" box, "Funds" file.

55 Anthony Leviero, "School for Jet Age Leaders," *Nation's Business*, October 1954, 61.

56 "AFA Official History," I, 348.

57 Ltr., HRH to CSAF, June 22, 1954; memo, Maj Gen J.S. Mills to CSAF, July 2, 1954; and MFR, HRH, September 21, 1954, all in HRHC, B6, F2.

58 Memo, HRH to DCS/O, July 29, 1954, "AFA Official History," III, D43; ltr., HRH to Gen L. Norstad, August 21, 1954, "AFA Official History," V, D94; interview with Lt Col Thomas F. Corrigan, by Maj E.A. Holt, July 12, 1956, contained in "AFA Official History," V, D16, 3.

59 Corrigan interview with Mank and Meilinger, 22.

60 "Many Seek Air Training," *New York Times*, February 19, 1956, 36.

61 "United States Air Force Academy Catalogue, 1954–1955," 9–10; Fact Sheet, "Data on the Curriculum, History and Admission Procedures, USAF Academy," May 14, 1955, "AFA Official History," V, D70. If a cadet lost his pilot qualification while at the Academy, he could continue on to graduation. In addition, all cadets had a three-year service commitment upon graduation.

62 "Selection for Candidates for the Air Force Academy," April 6–7, 1954, "AFA Official History," IV, D55; "United States Air Force Academy Catalogue, 1954–1955," 15; interview with Brig Gen Benjamin B. Cassiday, by Col James C. Gaston, October 6, 2002, in Gaston, *50th Anniversary History*, 141; MFR, Brig Gen D.Z. Zimmerman, September 20, 1954, "AFA Official History," V, D49.

63 Interview with Brig Gen Robert F. McDermott, by Maj Paul T. Ringenbach and Capt Russell Mank, June 1, 1971, AFA, Ringenbach papers, B44, F15, 6. See also memo, Col R. Gideon to DCS/P, April 29, 1955, Gen E. O'Donnell papers, AFA, B28, F4; "AFA Official History," I, 356–58. The selection board lasted five days.

64 "AFA Official History," I, 334; memo, Col B.B. Cassiday to HRH, January 17, 1956, "AFA Official History, VII, D59. As at West Point, there was an unlimited quota for the sons of Medal of Honor recipients—if one of them passed the exams, he was in and did not need an appointment from his senator or representative.

65 Interview with Lt Col William C. Cox, by Maj E.A. Holt, September 12, 1956, contained in "AFA Official History," V, D11, 4, 7.

66 One cadet, due to medical issues, received a diploma but not a commission.

67 Data provided by Air Force Academy Association of Graduates.

68 Memo, HRH to CSAF, July 5, 1955, and MFR, HRH, July 9, 1955, both in AFA, Superintendent's files, MC 606.

69 Culver interview, 18–20; Corrigan interview with Mank and Meilinger, 10. In May 1968 an F-105 "Thud"—a veteran of the Vietnam War—was being officially dedicated as a static display on the cadet mall. As the visiting generals finished their speeches, a flight of four F-105s in arrowhead formation moving from south to north was scheduled to roar over the Cadet Wing assembled in ranks. The lead aircraft was moving significantly faster than the rest. In fact, it was going supersonic. The result was a sonic boom that blew out hundreds of windows in Mitchell Hall, Fairchild Hall, and Vandenberg Hall. Legend has it that the F-105 pilot was "Black Bart."

70 H.E. Talbott, "Air Age Just Beginning," *The Army and Navy Courier*, September 1955, 3–4.

71 Cannon and Fellerman, "Quest," 277.

72 Ltr., D. Benedict to HRH, July 15, 1955, HRHC, B1, F2.

Chapter 11

1 "… The Devil is an ATO…" *Flying*, March 1956, 20–22, 58–59.

2 MFR, Stillman, January 11, 1955, "Official History of the Commandant of Cadets," 1957, D5.

3 Interview with Col Herman L. Gilster, by Col James C. Gaston, March 22, 2002, in Gaston, *50th Anniversary History*, 160. Gilster was an ATO.

4 Interview with Maj Gen Robert M. Stillman, by Maj Russell Mank and Capt Phillip Meilinger, April 3, 1979, 9, AFAOHC.

5 "AFA Official History," II, 820–22.

6 Ringenbach, 60.

7 Woodyard, 95–96.

8 Ibid., 94.

9 Ibid., 93. For engineering and scientific subjects, the Air Force Institute of Technology, located at Wright-Patterson AFB, Ohio, was often the most practical choice.

10 For an excellent overview of the curriculum for this first year, as well as the philosophy behind it, see Col John L. Frisbee, "Educational Program of the Air Force Academy," *Higher Education*, 13 (December 1956): 60–65. Frisbee was the first head of the Academy's History Department.

11 Ltr., K.D. Metcalf to HRH, April 26, 1955, HRHC, B6, F1; "AFA Official History," I, 413–18, 439–41.

12 Interview with Col Francis E. Merritt, by Capts Robert Bartanowicz and Robert Wolff, December 30, 1976, 2–4, AFAOHC. Merritt was the Academy's first assistant athletic director.

13 Ringenbach, 60. There were a series of Dean's Policy Files that were promulgated that first semester dealing with everything from grading policies to extra instruction for cadets to graduate school for faculty members. See "AFA Official History," VI.

14 Ringenbach, 61.

15 Interview with Maj J. Robert Gibson, by Maj E.A. Holt, July 26, 1956, contained in "AFA Official History," III, D4, 3; interview with Brig Gen Robert F. McDermott, by Col James C. Gaston, March 19–20, 2002, contained in Gaston, *50th Anniversary Oral History*, 183.

16 Ringenbach, 62.

17 McDermott interview with Gaston, 173.

18 Interview with Col George V. Fagan by Col James C. Gaston, February 27, 2002, in Gaston, *50th Anniversary History*, 209. Fagan initially was in the History Department but later became head of the Academy Library.

19 Gideon, "Record," 1.

20 RMH Diary, March 16, 1955; Zimmerman interview, 25.

21 McDermott interview by Ringenbach and Mank, 10.

22 Ltr., Brig Gen H. Beukema to Col G.A. Lincoln, July 19, 1956, AFA, Ringenbach papers, B6, F11.

23 Fagan interview, 213.

24 "AFA Official History," I, 587; Air Force Cadet Manual, "The Operation and Administration of the Aptitude for Commissioned Service System," August 16, 1955.

25 "AFA Official History," I, 587–604. A "confinement" meant a cadet had to stay in his room for a specific period of time, usually around two hours, and could have no visitors. Confinements were generally served on Wednesday afternoons after class, and on Saturday and Sunday. "Restriction" meant a cadet could leave his room but was limited to certain areas on base: the library, gym, chapel, etc. It must be noted that the punishments assigned for various offenses have varied widely over the past fifty years. See also Lawrence C. Landis, *The Story of the Air Force Academy* (NY: Rinehart, 1960), 100–103.

26 "AFA Official History," II, 869–71.

27 Interview with Harold M. Webster, by Col James C. Gaston, January 7, 2003, in Gaston, *50th Anniversary History*, 92; "AFA Official History," II, 895; memo, Capt H.H. Heiberg to Asst Chief of Staff, December 15, 1955, "AFA Official History," VII, D64.

28 Memo, HRH to Commandant, April 3, 1956, HRHC, B6, F1.

29 "AFA Official History," II, 858.

30 Ibid., 897.

31 Ltr., HRH to Col H.E. Kloepfer, March 16, 1955, "AFA Official History," V, D75.

32 Ltr., HRH to Rev J.S. Minnis, August 23, 1955, "AFA Official History," V, D58.

33 Gideon, "Record," 3.

34 Memo, Col B.B. Cassiday to Dir of Flying Training, November 15, 1955, "AFA Official History," VII, D75.

35 Memo, Col R.F. McDermott to Brig Gen R.M. Stillman, January 11, 1955, "AFA Official History," VI, D37.

36 Memo, HRH to VCSAF, October 1, 1954, HRHC, B6, F2.; "AFA Official History," I, 247–48.

37 *New York Times*, September 12, 1955, 27C; ltr., Pres D.D. Eisenhower to HRH, September 12, 1955, "AFA Official History," VII, D85. According to tradition, a visiting chief of state can grant amnesty to cadets. Other names suggested for the permanent site were "Cathedral Rock" and "Ramparts." No such name was ever made official.

38 "AFA Official History," II, 907; Peggy Leigh Sherman Ball, "The Evolution of the Honor Code at the United States Air Force Academy: An Historical Case Study Analysis," PhD dissertation, University of Texas, 1997, 68.

39 The First Captain/Honor Chairman/Class President was George H. Olmsted, one of the more remarkable cadets ever to attend the Military Academy. He graduated second in his class, was chosen as First Captain for *two* years, and was a champion boxer. The day of his graduation in 1922, MacArthur reinstated his rank of cadet captain and allowed him to march with his chevrons. The identity of the shanghaied cadet is not known. Phillip S. Meilinger, "George Hamden Olmsted: The Life and Legacy of a Citizen Soldier," Olmsted Foundation, 2007, 20–21. I would also note that "silencing" was used for other purposes. Benjamin O. Davis, Jr., who graduated in 1936, was the first black cadet to attend West Point in decades. He was not welcomed and was strongly encouraged to resign. He refused to do so and was therefore silenced. No cadet spoke to him except in an official capacity for his entire four-year cadet career. After graduation he went on to a distinguished career in the Air Force, leading the Tuskegee Airmen during World War II and retiring as a lieutenant general in 1970. His time as cadet did not overlap with Harmon's tour. The practice of silencing was abandoned at West Point in 1973. It was never used at the AFA.

40 Cassiday interview with EHH, 8–10. The final clause of the Code was changed to "or anyone who does" in 1961.

41 Ltr., HRH to Brig Gen O.J. Gatchell, August 3, 1954, HRHC, B1, F4.

42 Memo, Brig Gen R.M. Stillman to Prof of Mathematics, November 16, 1955, "AFA Official History," VII, D74.

43 Barry D. Watts, "The History of the Honor Code: 1955–1965," Cadet Term Paper, USAF Academy, 1965, 35; Cassiday interview, 10. In fact, over the years relatively few cadets have been expelled for toleration.

44 "Instruction Handbook, The Honor Code, Military Training Course, Freshman Summer Training Period," May 16, 1955, "AFA Official History," VII, D55.

45 Watts, 36.

46 "AFA Official History," II, 909–10.

47 Ball, 69.

48 "AFA Official History," II, 912–16.

49 Watts, 49–50.

50 AFCM 30–1, "Procedures for Handling Violations of the Honor Code," July 1, 1955.

51 Ibid.

52 Ltr., Brig Gen R.M. Stillman to HRH, July 7, 1955, "AFA Official History," VII, D94; memo, Col N.D. Janney to HRH, April 23, 1956, "AFA Official History," VII, D42.

53 "AFA Official History," II, 622.

54 Memo, Brig Gen R.M. Stillman to Brig Gen D.Z. Zimmerman, September 16, 1955, "AFA Official History, VI, D13.

55 Memo, Col R.V. Whitlow to Brig Gen D.Z. Zimmerman October 3, 1955, "AFA Official History," VII, D81.

56 "AFA Official History," I, 718.

57 Ltr., Col R.F. McDermott to Col G.A. Lincoln, October 6, 1955, AFA, Ringenbach papers, B4, F1.

58 "AFA Official History," II, 675, 723–26.

59 Memo, Brig Gen R.M. Stillman to Brig Gen D.Z. Zimmerman, November 15, 1955, "AFA Official History," VI, D9.

60 Memo, Col G.W. Martin to HRH, March 17, 1950, with attached study, AFA, RG 104.1, MC 812.

61 Interview with Col Robert V. Whitlow, by Maj Russell Mank and Capt Phillip Meilinger, April 5, 1979, 9, AFAOHC. At the interview, Whitlow provided the interviewers with the original directive, signed by Harmon. Briggs later confirmed the pressure from the secretary's office, stating: "Talbott didn't have much of an idea of NCAA or collegiate rules. He only wanted to win football." Briggs interview, 14.

62 Ltr., Col R.V. Whitlow to ROTC Instructors, November 12, 1954, "AFA Official History," VII, D132.

63 Ltr., HRH to J.A. McCain, March 25, 1954, "AFA Official History," V, D74; Whitlow interview, 3.

64 Ltr., HRH to Brig Gen M.K. Deichelmann, November 13, 1954, VI, D130.

65 "AFA Official History," II, 1003.

66 Corrigan interview with Mank and Meilinger, 25.

67 "AFA Official History," II, 1004–05; Whitlow interview, 12.

68 Whitlow interview, 46. At the time, Whitlow denied running a "farm system" for prospective cadets. "AFA Denies Subsidizing Cadets," *Denver Free Press*, March 21, 1957, 1.

69 "Football Factory?" *Cheyenne State Tribune*, February 25, 1955, n.p., clipping in AFA, RG 350, B1, F1.

70 Ltr., HRH to T.S. McCracken (editor of the *Tribune*), March 25, 1955, AFA, RG 350, B1, F1. Note that it took Harmon a month to respond to this editorial.

71 Ltr., Brig Gen B.E. Allen to HRH, February 21, 1955, "AFA Official History," VII, D119.

72 Ltr., HRH to Brig Gen B.E. Allen, March 4, 1955, "AFA Official History," VII, D114.

73 "AFA Official History," II, 1013, 1016.

74 "AFA Official History," I, 358.

75 Memo, HRH to Col R.V. Whitlow, May 1, 1956, "AFA Official History," VII, D41. The reference to O'Donnell implies that he was involved in recruiting athletes as well, or at least that he was in contact with Whitlow on the matter.

76 Ltr., Maj Gen J.E. Briggs to Lt Gen E. O'Donnell, December 17, 1958; ltr., Col G.B. Simler to Col R.V. Whitlow, December 31, 1957; and ltr., Col R.V. Whitlow to Col G.B. Simler, January 11, 1958, all in AFA, Gen E. O'Donnell papers, B28, F2. Shaw was bought out of his contract, and he was replaced as head coach by Ben Martin.

77 Whitlow interview, 79–81.

78 Ltr., Acting CSAF (Gen T.D. White) to AFA Superintendent (Maj Gen J.E. Briggs), April 24, 1957, AFA, Gen E. O'Donnell papers, B28, F4.

79 Simler eventually wore four stars but died in an airplane crash in September 1972. Whitlow later claimed that the athletic director position was first offered to Col Robin Olds, who declined. Whitlow interview, 81.

80 Whitlow interview, 23–24, 27–28. The AFA played TCU to a 0–0 tie on 1 January 1959.

81 Witters transcribed memoir in Gaston, *50th Anniversary History*, 32.

82 "Report to the Secretary and Chief of Staff of the Air Force by the Special Advisory Committee on the United States Air Force Academy," [White Report], May 5, 1965, 14–15, 53. A contrary view: one faculty member present during the cheating scandal in 1965 maintained that the problem lay largely in the faculty and the Academy's over-emphasis on academics and its dysfunctional academic policies. J. Arthur Heise, *The Brass Factories: A Frank Appraisal of West Point, Annapolis, and the Air Force Academy* (Washington DC: Public Affairs, 1969).

83 Ltr., Maj Gen J.E. Briggs, to Lt Gen E. O'Donnell, April 10, 1958, AFA, Gen E. O'Donnell papers, B28, F4.

84 Memo, Col R.F. McDermott to Brig Gen D.Z. Zimmerman, March 9, 1955, "AFA Official History," VI, D31. Rigsby was the head of the Law Department.

85 "AFA Official History," II, 808–09.

86 Ltr., HRH to M.M. Pattillo, n.d., but apparently late April or early May 1955, AFA, Ringenbach papers, B3, F2.

87 Briggs interview, 6.

88 MFR, Maj Gen W.S. Stone, August 1, 1955, AFA, Gen E. O'Donnell papers, B28, F4.

89 McDermott interview, 183; Ringenbach, 70–72.

90 Interview with M.M. Pattillo, Jr., by Col Paul T. Ringenbach, September 9, 1999, AFA, Ringenbach papers, B44, F20.

91 "Report of USAF Curriculum Review Board," to HRH, March 7, 1956, "AFA Official History," VI, D8; ltr., Col R.F. McDermott to D.H. Morgan, March 26, 1956, AFA, RG 321, MC 688.

92 "Report of the Board of Visitors to the United States Air Force Academy, 1956," April 15, 1956, 9, HRHC, A1, B1, F13. Compton was a noted nuclear physicist who had worked on the Manhattan Project; Hancher was still the president of the University of Iowa; and Hannah had left government to return to the presidency at Michigan State University.

93 Ibid., 10.

94 Ibid., 11, 16.

Chapter 12

1 Memo, President to SECDEF, July 16, 1954, HRHC, B1, F5.

2 Ltr., HRH to Gen L. Norstad, August 21, 1954, "AFA Official History," V, D94.

3 Ltr., HRH to G.S. Carrell, December 13, 1954, HRHC, B1, F4.

4 Ltr., B.P. McGimsey to HRH, May 3, 1956, HRHC, B2, F1.

5 Ltr., HRH to L.B. Cuyler, November 7, 1955, HRHC, B3, F3.

6 Ltr., HRH to H. Talbott, December 28, 1955, HRHC, B3, F3.

7 Ltr., HRH to Lt Gen E. O'Donnell, February 23, 1956, AFA, Superintendent's Files, MC 606; Briggs interview, 2.

8 HRH Medical Records, AFHRA, File 341.290–37.

9 Notes by RMH.

10 Wall interview, in Gaston, *50th Anniversary History*, 82.

11 The deputy director of the Central Intelligence Agency, Air Force Lt Gen Pierre Cabell, had strongly urged foreign language training for all cadets, and Harmon agreed with him. Ltrs., Lt Gen C.P. Cabell to HRH, January 31, 1956, and HRH to Lt Gen C.P. Cabell, February 3, 1956, both in AFA, RG 321, MC 688.

12 Harmon talk to cadets.

13 Undated news clipping in HRHC, A4, B19, F4; ltr., RMH to Cuylers, May 17, 1956, HRHC, A4, B18. See also Rosa-Maye's diary for the months of April and May 1956.

14 Ltr., HRH to RMH, June 20, 1956, HRHC, A4, B12, F9.

15 There are dozens of Harmon's letters to Rosa-Maye and his many friends in HRHC, B2 and B12, several different folders.

16 RMH Diary for July 1956.

17 Briggs interview, 3.

18 *Denver Post* news clipping, July 28, 1956, HRHC, A4, B12, F8.

19 *Falconews* news clipping, May 29, 1959, HRHC, A4, B12, F8.

20 Ltr., CSAF to HRH, July 27, 1956, AFA, Superintendent's Files, MC 606.

21 HRH, "Outline of Remarks," July 27, 1956, AFA, Superintendent's Files, MC 606.

22 Ltr., RMH to Maj Gen J.E. Briggs, September 3, 1956, HRHC, B2, F7.

23 Ltr., HRH to Lt Gen E. O'Donnell, December 2, 1956, AFA, Gen E. O'Donnell papers, B7, F3.

24 Ltr., K. Harmon to HRH, February 11, 1957, HRHC, A5, B5, F14.

25 Eula Wulfjen Kendrick, who was staying with her daughter in San Antonio when Hubert died, passed away in June 1961 at the age of 89.

26 McDermott interview, in Gaston, *50th Anniversary History*, 184.

27 Stillman interview, 6.

28 Comments made by Maj Gen J.E. Briggs to Radio Station KIMN, Denver, February 27, 1957, HRHC, B2, F2.

29 Ltr., I.C. Eaker to RMH, April 3, 1957, copy supplied by EHH.

30 Ltr., D.D. Eisenhower to RMH, February 29, 1957, copy supplied by EHH. This two-page letter is written in longhand by the president and signed "Ike."

31 Ltrs., Col R.V. Whitlow to B. Dodd (Georgia Tech), January 18, 1956 and to J. Corbett (LSU), January 23, 1956, both in AFA, RG 350, B1, F1.

32 RMH Diary, March 30, 1956.

33 Notes by RMH.

Glossary

Below is a list of acronyms used in the text, footnotes and bibliography

AACA .... Air Academy Construction Agency
AASC .... Air Academy Site Commission
AAF .... Army Air Forces
ACTS .... Air Corps Tactical School
AEF .... American Expeditionary Force (World War I)
AFA .... Air Force Academy
AFAOHC .... Air Force Academy Oral History Collection
AFB .... Air Force Base
AFHRA .... Air Force Historical Research Agency
AOC .... Air Officer Commanding
ATC .... Air Training Command
ATO........................ Air Training Officer
BOV .... Board of Visitors
CDC........................ Caribbean Defense Command
COMAIRSOPAC ..... Commander, Aircraft, South Pacific
COMAIRSOLS .... Commander, Aircraft, Solomons
CONAC .... Continental Air Command
CSAF .... Chief of Staff, Air Force
DCS/O .... Deputy Chief of Staff, Operations
DCS/P .... Deputy Chief of Staff, Personnel
DoD .... Department of Defense
EHH........................ Eula Harmon Hoff
GCTC...................... Gulf Coast Training Center
GHQ .... General Headquarters
GPO .... Government Printing Office

HRH..........................Hubert R. Harmon
HRHC......................Hubert R. Harmon Collection (at the Academy)
IG ....Inspector General
JAG...........................Judge Advocate General
JCS ....Joint Chiefs of Staff
MFR ....Memo for Record
MIT ....Massachusetts Institute of Technology
MPC.......................Military Personnel Center (at Randolph AFB)
MSC ....Military Staff Committee (of the UN)
NCACSS   North Central Association of Colleges and Secondary
                    Schools
NMMI......................New Mexico Military Institute
OSAF.......................Office of the Secretary of the Air Force
OCS..........................Officer Candidate School
OSD ....Office of the Secretary of Defense
PDC ....Personnel Distribution Command
PMA.........................Pennsylvania Military Academy
RAF ....Royal Air Force (Great Britain)
RG ....Record Group
RMK/RMH..............Rosa-Maye Kendrick/Harmon
ROTC.......................Reserve Officers Training Corps
SAC ....Strategic Air Command
SECAF......................Secretary of the Air Force
SECDEF...................Secretary of Defense
SECNAV...................Secretary of the Navy
SOM..........................Skidmore, Owings and Merrill
USMA ....United States Military Academy
USSBS ....United States Strategic Bombing Survey
VCSAF ....Vice Chief of Staff, Air Force

Bibliography

Official Sources

US Air Force, Air Force Planning Board, "A Plan for an Air Force Academy," III vols., Air University, January 1949.

US Air Force Academy, "Catalogue, 1954–1955."

US Army, Air Corps Tactical School, "Annual Report," 1933.

_____, "Official Army Register," various years.

_____, "Report of the Secretary of War to the President," various years.

_____, "Report of the Chief Signal Officer to the Secretary of War, 1917."

US Army Command and General Staff College, "Annual Reports," 1934–1936.

US Congress, House, hearings before the Armed Services Committee, *Investigation of the B-36 Bomber Program*, 81st Congress, 1st Session. Washington DC: GPO, 1949.

_____, House, hearings before the Armed Services Committee, *The National Defense Program—Unification and Strategy*, 81st Congress, 1st Session. Washington DC: GPO, 1949.

_____, House, hearings before the Armed Services Committee, *To Provide for the Establishment of a United States Air Force Academy*, 83rd Congress, 1st session. Washington DC: GPO, 1954.

_____, Senate, hearings before the Armed Services Committee, *An Act to Provide for the Establishment of a United States Air Force Academy and for Other Purposes*, 83rd Congress, 2nd session. Washington DC: GPO, 1954.

US Department of Defense, "A Report and Recommendation to the Secretary of Defense by the Service Academy Board," [Stearns-Eisenhower Report], January 1950.

US Department of State, *Foreign Relations of the United States, 1947, Volume I: General; The United Nations*. Washington DC: GPO, 1973.

_____, "Arms for the United Nations," June 1948.

US Joint Chiefs of Staff, "Chronology, Functions and Composition of the Joint Chiefs of Staff," JCS Historical Study, 1979.

US Military Academy. "Annual Report," 1930.

_____, "Annual Report of the Superintendent," various years.

_____, "Board of Visitors Report," various years.

_____, "Five Year Book, Class of 1915," June 1921.

_____, "Thirty-five Year Book, Class of 1915," 1950.

_____, "Official Register of the Officers and Cadets," various years.

_____, *The Howitzer*, Cadet Yearbook, various years.

United States Strategic Bombing Survey, "The Thirteenth Air Force in the War against Japan," September 1946.

Secondary Sources

"Air Academy: A Better Man for a Better Plane," *Newsweek*, June 6, 1955, 59–65.

Allen, Maj Gen Henry T. *The Rhineland Occupation*. Indianapolis, IN: Bobbs-Merrill, 1927.

Ambrose, Stephen E. *Eisenhower, Vol. I: Soldier*. NY: Simon & Schuster, 1983.

The Army Almanac: A Book of Facts Covering the Army of the United States. Washington DC: GPO, 1950.

Arnold, Gen H.H. *Global Mission.* NY: Harper, 1949.

Ball, Harry P. *Of Responsible Command: A History of the US Army War College.* Carlisle Barracks, PA: Alumni Association of the US Army War College, 1983.

Barry, John M. *The Great Influenza: The Epic Story of the Deadliest Plague in History.* NY: Viking, 2004.

Bergerud, Eric M. *Fire in the Sky: The Air War in the South Pacific.* Boulder, CO: Westview Press, 2001.

Bland, Larry I., Sharon R. Ritenour, and Clarence E. Wunderlin, Jr. (eds.) *The Papers of George Catlett Marshall, Vol. 3: "We Cannot Delay," July 1, 1939–December 6, 1941.* Baltimore, MD: Johns Hopkins University Press, 1986.

Bland, Larry I. and Sharon Ritenour Stevens (eds.) *The Papers of George Catlett Marshall, Vol. 4: "Aggressive and Determined Leadership,"* June 1, 1943–December 31, 1944. Baltimore, MD: Johns Hopkins University Press, 1996.

Boroff, David. "Air Force Academy: A Slight Gain in Altitude," *Harper's Magazine,* February, 1963, 86.

Bradley, Gen Omar N. and Clay Blair. *A General's Life.* NY: Simon & Schuster, 1983.

Brown, Jerold E. *Where Eagles Land: Planning and Development of U.S. Army Airfields, 1910–1941.* Westport, CT: Greenwood, 1990.

Bruegmann, Robert (ed.) *Modernism at Mid-Century: The Architecture of the United States Air Force Academy.* Chicago: University of Chicago Press, 1994.

Byerly, Carol R. *Fever of War: The Influenza Epidemic in the U.S. Army during World War I.* NY: New York University Press, 2005.

Byrd, Martha. *Chennault: Giving Wings to the Tiger.* Tuscaloosa: University of Alabama Press, 1988.

_____. *Kenneth N. Walker: Airpower's Untempered Crusader.* Maxwell AFB, AL: Air University Press, 1997.

Cameron, Rebecca Hancock. *Training to Fly: Military Flight Training, 1907–1945.* Washington DC: Air Force History and Museums Program, 1999.

Caraley, Demetrios. *The Politics of Military Unification.* NY: Columbia University Press, 1966.

Casey, Aloysius G. and Patrick A. Casey. *Velocity—Speed with Direction: The Professional Career of Gen Jerome F. O'Malley.* Maxwell AFB, AL: Air University Press, 2007.

Chandler, Charles deF. and Frank P. Lahm. *How Our Army Grew Wings: Airmen and Aircraft before 1914.* NY: Ronald, 1942.

Chennault, Capt Claire. "Special Support for Bombardment," *U.S. Air Services,* January 1934, 18–21.

_____, Maj Gen. *Way of a Fighter.* NY: G.P. Putnam's Sons, 1949.

Clifford, John Garry. *The Citizen Soldiers: The Plattsburg Training Camp Movement, 1913–1920.* Lexington: University Press of Kentucky, 1972.

Clute, Penelope D. "The Plattsburg Idea," *New York Archives,* 5 (Fall 2005): 9–15.

Coffey, Thomas. *Hap: The Story of the US Air Force and the Man Who Built It: Henry H. Arnold.* NY: Viking, 1982.

Coffman, Edward M. *The Regulars: The American Army, 1898–1941.* Cambridge, MA: Belknap, 2004.

Cole, Alice, et. al. (eds.) *The Department of Defense: Documents on Establishment and Organization, 1944–1978.* Washington DC: GPO, 1978.

Collins, Gen Joseph L. *Lightning Joe: An Autobiography of General J. Lawton Collins.* Baton Rouge: Louisiana State University Press, 1979.

Conn, Stetson, Rose C. Engleman, and Byron Fairchild, *Guarding the United States and its Outposts, in United States Army in World War II* series. Washington DC: Army Historical Office, 1964.

Cooke, James J. *Billy Mitchell.* Boulder, CO: Lynne Rienner, 2002.

Copp, DeWitt S. *Forged in Fire.* Garden City, NY: Doubleday, 1982.

Cornebise, Alfred E. *The Amaroc News: The Daily Newspaper of the American Forces in Germany,*

1919–1923. Carbondale: Southern Illinois University Press, 1981.

Cox, Douglas A. *Airpower Leadership on the Front Line: Lieutenant General George H. Brett and Combat Command.* Maxwell AFB, AL: Air University Press, 2006.

Crackel, Theodore J. *West Point: A Bicentennial History.* Lawrence: University Press of Kansas, 2002.

Craven, Wesley Frank and James L. Cate (eds.) *The Army Air Forces in World War II,* 7 vols. Chicago: University of Chicago Press, 1948–1958.

Crowder, James L. Jr. *Osage General: Maj. Gen. Clarence L. Tinker.* Tinker AFB: Oklahoma City Air Logistics Center, 1987.

Crouch, Tom D. *The Bishop's Boys: A Life of Wilbur and Orville Wright.* NY: W.W. Norton, 1989.

Cullum, George W. *Biographical Register of the Officers and Graduates of the U.S. Military Academy at West Point, New York.* Saginaw, MI: Sherman and Peters, multiple volumes and publication years.

Daso, Dik A. *Hap Arnold and the Evolution of American Airpower.* Washington DC: Smithsonian, 2000.

Dastrup, Boyd L. *The U.S. Army Command and General Staff College: A Centennial History.* Manhattan, KS: Sunflower University Press, 1982.

Davies, Pete. *The Devil's Flu: The World's Deadliest Influenza Epidemic and the Scientific Hunt for the Virus that Caused It.* NY: Henry Holt, 2000.

Eaker, Maj Ira C. "Now it Can be Told," *Air Corps Newsletter,* July 15, 1937, 1–3.

_____, Lt Gen. "As I Remember Them: Air Chiefs Patrick and Fechet," *Aerospace Historian,* June 1973, 57–61.

Eisenhower, Gen Dwight D. *At Ease: Stories I Tell to Friends.* Garden City, NY: Doubleday, 1967.

Fischer, Conan. *The Ruhr Crisis, 1923–1924.* Oxford: Oxford University Press, 2003.

Fleming, Thomas. *The Illusion of Victory: America in World War I.* NY: Basic Books, 2003.

Foulois, Maj Gen Benjamin D. with Col C.V. Glines. *From the Wright Brothers to the Astronauts: The Memoirs of Major General Benjamin D. Foulois.* NY: McGraw-Hill, 1968.

Frank, Richard B. *Guadalcanal.* NY: Random House, 1990.

Frisbee, Col John L. "Educational Program of the Air Force Academy," *Higher Education,* 13 (December 1956): 60–65.

"GHQ Air Force Thirty-Day Exercise on West Coast," *U.S. Air Services,* June 1937, 11–12.

Galambos, Louis (ed.) *The Papers of Dwight David Eisenhower, Columbia University: X.* Baltimore, MD: Johns Hopkins University Press, 1984.

Gaston, Col James C. (ed.) *US Air Force Academy, 1954–2004: 50th Anniversary Oral History.* USAF Academy, CO: Friends of the Air Force Academy Library, 2005.

"General Harmon Molds Army Air Force Pilots," *Form One,* January 1942, 1–2.

Georgen, Cynde A. *One Cowboy's Dream: John B. Kendrick, His Family, Home, and Ranching Empire.* Sheridan, WY: Donning, revised edition, 2004.

Goldberg, Alfred (ed.) *A History of the United States Air Force, 1907–1957.* Princeton, NJ: Van Nostrand, 1957.

Goodrich, Leland, *The United Nations.* NY: Thomas Y. Crowell, 1959.

Greenfield, Kent Roberts (ed.) *Command Decisions.* Washington DC: Office of Chief of Military History, 1960.

Hagedorn, Daniel P. *Alae Supra Canalem—Wings over the Canal.* Paducah, KY: Turner, 1995.

Harmon, Maj Gen Hubert R. "Caribbean Air Command," *Army and Navy Journal,* December 28, 1946, 1.

Harmon, Rosa-Maye Kendrick. *Intimate Letters from London.* Denver: Welch-Haffner, 1928.

_____. "A Letter from London," *Goucher College Alumnae Quarterly,* [1928], 34–39.

Hayne, Donald (ed.) *The Autobiography of Cecil B. DeMille.* NY: Garland, 1985.

Heise, J. Arthur. *The Brass Factories: A Frank Appraisal of West Point, Annapolis, and the Air Force Academy.* Washington DC: Public Affairs, 1969.

Hennessy, Juliette A. *The United States Army Air Arm: April 1861 to April 1917.* Washington DC: Office of Air Force History, 1985.

Humphreys, R.A. *Latin America and the Second World War.* 2 vols. London: Athlone, 1981.

Hurley, Alfred F. *Billy Mitchell: Crusader for Air Power.* NY: Franklin Watts, 1964.

Iezzoni, Lynette. *Influenza 1918: The Worst Epidemic in American History.* NY: TV Books, 1999.

James, D. Clayton. *The Years of MacArthur, Volume I: 1880–1941.* Boston: Houghton Mifflin, 1970.

Jessup, Philip C. *Elihu Root.* NY: Dodd, Mead, 1938.

Johnson, David E. *Fast Tanks and Heavy Bombers: Innovation in the U.S. Army, 1917–1945.* Ithaca, NY: Cornell University Press, 1998.

Johnson, Kenneth M. *Aerial California: An Account of Early Flight in Northern and Southern California, 1849 to World War I.* Los Angeles: Dawson's Book Shop, 1961.

Joralemon, Maj Ira B. "At Coblentz [sic] Bridgehead," *U.S. Air Services,* April 1919, 23–27.

Kennedy, Paul. *The Parliament of Man: The Past, Present, and Future of the United Nations.* NY: Random House, 2006.

Kent, Bruce. *The Spoils of War: The Politics, Economics, and Diplomacy of Reparations, 1918–1932.* Oxford: Clarendon Press, 1989.

Kington, Donald M. "The Plattsburg Movement and its Legacy," *Relevance,* 6 (Autumn 1997): 1–7.

Kroll, Henry D. (ed.) *Kelly Field in the Great War.* San Antonio, TX: San Antonio Printing Co., 1919.

Kuhlman, Erika. "American Doughboys and German *Fräuleins*: Sexuality, Patriarchy, and Privilege in the American-Occupied Rhineland, 1918–23," *Journal of Military History,* 71 (October 2007): 1077–1106.

LaFeber, Walter. *The Panama Canal: The Crisis in Historical Perspective.* NY: Oxford University Press, 1978.

Landis, Lawrence C. *The Story of the Air Force Academy.* NY: Rinehart, 1960.

Lane, Jack C. *Armed Progressive: General Leonard Wood.* San Rafael, CA: Presidio Press, 1978.

Leon, Philip W. *Bullies and Cowards: The West Point Hazing Scandal, 1898–1901.* Westport, CT: Greenwood Press, 2000.

Leonard, Thomas M. and John F. Bratzel (eds.) *Latin America during World War II.* Lanham, MD: Rowman & Littlefield, 2007.

Leviero, Anthony. "School for Jet Age Leaders," *Nation's Business,* October 1954, 32–35, 59–61.

Levine, Isaac D. *Mitchell: Pioneer of Air Power.* NY: Duell, Sloan and Pearce, 1958.

Lowell, John P. *Neither Athens nor Sparta? The Service Academies in Transition.* Bloomington: University of Indiana Press, 1979.

Lyon, Peter. *Eisenhower: Portrait of the Hero.* Boston: Little, Brown, 1974.

Major, John. *Prize Possession: The United States and the Panama Canal, 1903–1979.* Cambridge: Cambridge University Press, 1993.

Maurer, Maurer (ed.) *The U.S. Air Service in World War I,* 4 vols. Washington DC: Office of Air Force History, 1978–79.

_____. *Aviation in the U.S. Army, 1919–1939.* Washington DC: Office of Air Force History, 1987.

Meilinger, Phillip S. *Hoyt S. Vandenberg: The Life of a General.* Bloomington: Indiana University Press, 1989.

_____. (ed.) *The Paths of Heaven: The Evolution of Airpower Theory.* Maxwell AFB, AL: Air University Press, 1997.

_____. "When the Fortress Went Down," *Air Force Magazine,* October 2004, 78–82.

_____. "A History of Effects-Based Air Operations," *Journal of Military History* 71 (January 2007): 139–68.

Mets, David R. *Master of Airpower: General Carl A. Spaatz.* Novato, CA: Presidio, 1985.

Miller, Francis T. *Eisenhower: Man and Soldier.* Philadelphia: John C. Winston, 1944.

Miller, Roger G. "A Preliminary to War: The 1st Aero Squadron and the American Punitive Expedition of 1916," Air Force History and Museums Program pamphlet, 2003.

Millis, Walter. *The Martial Spirit: A Study of our War with Spain.* NY: Viking, 1965.

Mitchell, Brig Gen William L. *Our Air Force: Keystone of National Defense.* NY: E.P. Dutton, 1921.

_____. *Winged Defense.* NY: G.P. Putnam's Sons, 1925.

_____. "Look Out Below!" *Collier's,* April 21, 1928, 40–44.

_____. *Memoirs of World War I: From Start to Finish our Greatest War.* NY: Random House, 1960.

Morison, Samuel Eliot. *History of United States Naval Operations in World War II,* 14 vols. Boston: Little, Brown, 1954–66.

Nelson, Keith L. *Victors Divided: America and the Allies in Germany, 1918–1923*. Berkeley: University of California Press, 1975.

Northedge, F.S. *The League of Nations: Its Life and Times, 1920–1940*. NY: Holmes & Meier, 1986.

Official World War II Guide to the Army Air Forces. NY: AAF Aid Society, 1944.

Ollivant, Alfred. *Redcoat Captain: A Story of That Country*. NY: Macmillan, 1907.

Omissi, David E. *Air Power and Colonial Control: The Royal Air Force, 1919–1939*. NY: St. Martin's, 1990.

Pappas, George S. *Prudens Futuri: The US Army War College, 1901–1967*. Carlisle Barracks, PA: Alumni Association of the US Army War College, 1967.

Patrick, Maj Gen Mason. *The United States in the Air*. Garden City, NY: Doubleday, Doran, 1928.

Patterson, Charles. *The Oxford 50th Anniversary Book of the United Nations*. NY: Oxford University Press, 1995.

Pearcy, Thomas L. *We Answer Only to God: Politics and the Military in Panama, 1903–1947*. Albuquerque: University of New Mexico Press, 1998.

Perry, Ralph Barton. *The Plattsburg Movement*. NY: E.P. Dutton, 1921.

Pershing, John J. *My Experiences in the World War*. 2 vols. NY: Frederick Stokes, 1931.

Pisano, Dominick A. *To Fill the Sky with Pilots: The Civilian Pilot Training Program, 1939–1946*. Urbana: University of Illinois Press, 1993.

Powers, Richard G. "The Cold War in the Rockies: American Ideology and the Air Force Academy Design," *Art Journal*, 33 (Summer 1974): 304.

Public Papers of the Presidents of the United States: Dwight D. Eisenhower, 1954. Washington DC: GPO, 1960.

Randolph Field: A History and Guide. NY: Devin-Adair, 1942.

Rearden, Steven L. *History of the Office of the Secretary of Defense, Volume 1: The Formative Years, 1947–1950*. Washington DC: GPO, 1984.

Rentz, Major John N. *Bougainville and the Northern Solomons*. Washington DC: US Marine Corps, 1948.

Reynolds, Clark G. *The Fast Carriers: The Forging of an Air Navy*. NY: McGraw-Hill, 1968.

Richardson, Capt Robert C. *West Point: An Intimate Portrait of the National Military Academy and the Life of the Cadet*. NY: G.P. Putnam's Sons, 1917.

Ringenbach, Paul T. *Battling Tradition: Robert F. McDermott and Shaping the U.S. Air Force Academy*. Chicago: Imprint, 2006.

Ridgway, Gen Matthew B. *Soldier*. NY: Harper, 1956.

Rosenberg, David Alan. "U.S. Nuclear Stockpile, 1945–1950," *Bulletin of the Atomic Scientists*, May 1982, 25–30.

Rosenberry, C.R. *Glenn Curtiss: Pioneer of Flight*. Garden City, NY: Doubleday, 1972.

Ross, Stephen T. and David Alan Rosenberg. *America's Plans for War against the Soviet Union, 1945–1950. Volume 11: The Limits of Nuclear Strategy*. NY: Garland, 1989.

Rust, Kenn C. and Dana Bell. *Thirteenth Air Force Story in World War II*. Terre Haute, IN: Sunshine House, 1981.

Schlesinger, Stephen C. *Act of Creation: The Founding of the United Nations*. Boulder, CO: Westview Press, 2003.

Scott, George. *The Rise and Fall of the League of Nations*. NY: Macmillan, 1973.

Shaw, Frederick J. (ed.) *Locating Air Base Sites: History's Legacy*. Washington DC: Air Force History and Museums Program, 2004.

Sherman, Maj William C. *Air Warfare*. NY: Ronald Press, 1926.

Sherrod, Robert. *History of Marine Corps Aviation in World War II*. Washington DC: Combat Forces Press, 1952.

Shiner, John F. *Foulois and the U.S. Army Air Corps, 1931–1935*. Washington DC: Office of Air Force History, 1983.

Shulman, Seth. *Unlocking the Sky: Glenn Hammond Curtiss and the Race to Invent the Airplane*. NY: HarperCollins, 2002.

Simons, William E. *Liberal Education in the Service Academies*. NY: Institute of Higher Education, 1965.

Smythe, Donald. *Pershing: General of the Armies*. Bloomington: Indiana University Press, 1986.

Talbott, H.E. "Air Age Just Beginning," *The Army and Navy Courier*, September 1955, 3–4.

"... The Devil is an ATO ..." *Flying*, March 1956, 20–22, 58–59.

Towle, Philip A. *Pilots and Rebels: The Use of Aircraft in Unconventional Warfare, 1919–1988.* London: Brassey's, 1989.

Trask, David F. *The AEF and Coalition Warmaking, 1917–1918.* Lawrence; University Press of Kansas, 1993.

Walker, 1lt Kenneth N. "Bombardment Aviation—Bulwark of National Defense," *U.S. Air Services,* August 1933, 15–19.

Waller, Douglas. *A Question of Loyalty: Gen Billy Mitchell and the Court-Martial that Gripped the Nation.* NY: HarperCollins, 2004.

Warnock, A. Timothy. *The Battle against the U-Boat in the American Theater.* Maxwell AFB, AL: Air Force Historical Research Agency, 1995.

Weigley, Russell F. *History of the United States Army.* NY: Macmillan, 1967.

White, Robert P. *Mason Patrick and the Fight for Air Service Independence.* Washington DC: Smithsonian, 2001.

Wiener, Willard. *Two Hundred Thousand Flyers: The Story of the Civilian-AAF Training Program.* Washington: Infantry Journal Press, 1945.

Wilson, Maj Gen Donald. "Origin of a Theory for Air Strategy," *Aerospace Historian*, March 1971, 19–25.

_____. *Wooing Peponi: My Odyssey Thru Many Years.* Monterey, CA: Angel Press, 1973.

Winnefeld, James A. and Dana J. Johnson. *Joint Air Operations: Pursuit of Unity in Command and Control, 1942–1991.* Annapolis, MD: Naval Institute Press, 1993.

Woodward, David R. *Trial by Friendship: Anglo-American Relations 1917–1918* Lexington: University Press of Kentucky, 1993.

Unpublished Sources

Air Corps Newsletter, various issues, various years.

Ball, Peggy Leigh Sherman. "The Evolution of the Honor Code at the United States Air Force Academy: An Historical Case Study Analysis," PhD Dissertation, University of Texas, 1997.

Caldwell, Norman H. "Preflight Training in the AAF," AAF Historical Study no. 48, November 1946.

Cannon, M. Hamlin and Henry S. Fellerman, "Quest for an Air Force Academy," USAF Academy Historical Study, 1974.

Cockrell, Philip C. "Brown Shoes and Mortar Boards: U.S. Army Officer Professional Education at the Command General Staff School Fort Leavenworth, Kansas, 1919–1940," PhD Dissertation, University of South Carolina, 1991.

Finney, Robert T. "The History of the Air Corps Tactical School, 1920–1940," AF Historical Study no. 100, 1955. (Reprinted by the Air University Press in 1992.)

Greer, Thomas H. "The Development of Air Doctrine in the Army Air Arm, 1917–1941," AF Historical Study no. 89, 1955. (Reprinted by the Air University Press in 1985.)

Holt, Lt Col Edgar, M. Hamlin Cannon, and Carlos R. Allen, Jr., "History of the United States Air Force Academy, 27 July 1954–12 June 1956," VII vols., USAF Academy Historical Study, 1 August 1957.

Jones, R.L. and Chauncey E. Sanders. "Personnel Problems Related to AAF Commissioned Officers, 1939–1945," AAF Historical Study no. 11, [1946].

McClendon, R. Earl. "A Question of Autonomy for the United States Air Arm, 1907–1945," Air University Documentary Research Study, 1954. (Reprinted by the Air University Press in 1993 as "Autonomy of the Air Arm.")

Meilinger, Phillip S. "George Hamden Olmsted: The Life and Legacy of a Citizen Soldier," Olmsted Foundation, 2007.

Miller, Edward A. Jr. "The Founding of the Air Force Academy: An Administrative and Legislative History," PhD Dissertation, Denver University, 1969.

Nenninger, Timothy K. "The Fort Leavenworth Schools: Postgraduate Military Education and Professionalism in the U.S. Army, 1880–1920," PhD Dissertation, University of Wisconsin, 1974.

Novotny, Major Robert G. "Tarmacs and Trenches: Lieutenant General Millard Fillmore Harmon,

Jr., USAAF," Master's Thesis, School of Advanced Air and Space Studies, Maxwell AFB, AL, June 2007.

Nye, Roger H. "The United States Military Academy in an Era of Educational Reform, 1900–1925," PhD Dissertation, Columbia University, 1968.

"Organization of AAF Training Activities, 1939–1945," AAF Historical Study no. 53, June 1946.

Rohfleisch, Kramer J. "The Thirteenth Air Force, March–October 1943," AAF Historical Study no. 20, September 1946.

Sanders, Chauncey E. "Redeployment and Demobilization," AF Historical Study no. 77, June 1953.

Thompson, Robert L. "Initial Selection of Candidates for Pilot, Bombardier, and Navigation Training," AAF Historical Study no. 2, November 1943.

Tyler, Col Orville Z., Jr., Col Elvid Hunt and Captain Walter E. Lorence, "The History of Fort Leavenworth, 1827–1951," The Command and General Staff College, 1951.

Watts, Cadet Barry D. "The History of the Honor Code: 1955–1965," Cadet Term Paper, USAF Academy, CO, 1965.

Whitson, William Wallace. "The Role of the United States Army War College in the Preparation of Officers for National Security Policy Formulation," PhD Dissertation, Fletcher School of Law and Diplomacy, 1958.

Williams, Kathleen, "Air Defense of the Panama Canal, January 1937–December 1941," AAF Historical Study no. 42, January 1946.

Woodyard, William T. "A Historical Study of the Development of the Academic Curriculum of the United States Air Force Academy," PhD Dissertation, University of Denver, 1965.

Interviews

There are a number of sources for interviews regarding the Air Force Academy. The US Air Force has an oral history program that contains hundreds of interviews, and these are located in the Air Force Historical Research Agency (AFHRA), located at Maxwell AFB in Montgomery, Al. Included below is their file number. Other interviews were conducted by the AFA historian, usually Maj/Lt Col Edgar Holt in the early years of the Academy. Most of these interviews are contained as appendices in the Academy Official History and are so noted below by volume; also included is the document (D) number. There were a number of other interviews that were conducted by members of the AFA History Department and are in the AFA Oral History Collection (AFAOHC). Finally, to commemorate the 50th anniversary of the opening of the Academy, James C. Gaston conducted a number of interviews—several with early Academy personnel—and these were bound by The Friends of the Library. All of the interviews used for this study, except some of those done at Maxwell, are contained in AFA Special Collections.

Aldrin, Col Edwin E., by Arthur Marmor, February 1967, AFHRA, File K239.0512–573.

Briggs, Lt Gen James E., by Capts Timothy E. Kline, Robert Bartanowicz and Robert Wolff, February 24, 1973, AFAOHC.

Boudreau, Col Arthur J., by Maj E.A. Holt, October 10–11, 1956, in "AFA Official History," III, D1.

Boyd, Col Max, by Maj E.A. Holt, July 24, 1956, in "AFA Official History," V, D14.

Briggs, Lt Gen James E., by Capts Timothy Kline, Robert Bartanowicz, and Robert Wolff, February 24, 1973, AFAOHC.

Cassiday, Brig Gen Benjamin B. Jr., by Eula Harmon Hoff, June 3, 1989, HRHC, A4, B17, F8.

_____, by Col James C. Gaston, October 6, 2002, in Gaston, *50th Anniversary Oral History*.

Coffee, Lt Col Richard J., by Col James C. Gaston, June 17, 2002, in Gaston, *50th Anniversary Oral History*.

Cooke, Lt Col George C., by Maj E.A. Holt, July 11, 1956, in "AFA Official History," III, D2.

Corrigan, Lt Col Thomas F., by Maj E.A. Holt, July 12, 1956, in "AFA Official History," V, D16.

_____, by Maj Russell Mank and Capt Phillip Meilinger, January 24, 1979, AFAOHC.

Cox, Lt Col William C., by Maj E.A. Holt, September 12, 1956, in "AFA Official History," V, D11.

Culver, Col Gordon P. by Maj Russell Mank and Capt Phillip Meilinger, June 16, 1979, AFAOHC.

Davidson, Maj Gen Howard C., by Hugh Ahman, December 5–8, 1974, AFHRA, File K239.0512–817.

Edwards, Lt Gen Idwal H., by Maj E.A. Holt, October 26, 1956, in "AFA Official History," III, D3.

Fagan, Col George V., by Col James C. Gaston, February 27, 2002, in Gaston, *50th Anniversary Oral History.*

Gibson, Maj J. Robert, by Maj E.A. Holt, July 26, 1956, in "AFA Official History," III, D4.

Gilster, Col Herman L., by Col James C. Gaston, March 22, 2002, in Gaston, *50th Anniversary Oral History.*

Hanley, Col Thomas J. Jr., by Eula Harmon Hoff, November 10, 1989, HRHC, unprocessed material.

Harmon, Kendrick and Eula Harmon Hoff, by Col James C. Gaston, August 29, 2002, in Gaston, *50th Anniversary Oral History.*

Hutto, Maj R.C., by Maj E.A. Holt, July 5, 1956, in "AFA Official History," V, D18.

Hyde, James F.C., Jr., by Maj E.A. Holt, October 19, 1956, in "AFA Official History," III, D5.

Lindbergh, Charles A., by Maj E.A. Holt, January 3, 1957, in "AFA Official History," III, D6.

McDermott, Brig Gen Robert F., by Maj Paul T. Ringenbach and Capt Russell Mank, June 1, 1971, AFA, Ringenbach papers, B44, F15.

_____, by Col James C. Gaston, March 19–20, 2002, in Gaston, *50th Anniversary Oral History.*

Meigs, Merrill C., by Maj E.A. Holt, May 21, 1956, in "AFA Official History," III, D7.

Merritt, Col Francis E., by Capts Robert Bartanowicz and Robert Wolff, December 30, 1976, AFAOHC.

Netsch, Walter A., by Col James C. Gaston, May 15–16, 2002, in Gaston, *50th Anniversary Oral History.*

O'Connor, Lt Col Virgil J., by Maj E.A. Holt, November 27, 1956, in "AFA Official History," V, D7.

Olds, Brig Gen Robin, by Maj Russell Mank and Capt Phillip Meilinger, June 5, 1979, AFAOHC.

M.M. Pattillo, Jr., by Col Paul T. Ringenbach, September 9, 1999, AFA, Ringenbach papers, B44, F20.

Peabody, Brig Gen Hume, by Hugh Ahman, September 13–16, 1975, AFHRA, File K239.0512–867.

Schlatter, Lt Gen David M., by Maj E.A. Holt, October 24, 1956, in "AFA Official History," III, D10.

Smith, Brig Gen Dale O., by Maj E. A. Holt, April 18, 1956, in "AFA Official History," III, D12.

Spaatz, Gen Carl A., by Maj E.A. Holt, June 13, 1956, in "AFA Official History," III, D13.

Stillman, Maj Gen Robert, by Maj Russell Mank and Capt Phillip Meilinger, April 3, 1979, AFAOHC.

Stone, Myra, by Capts Russell Mank and Fred Shiner, March 20, 1973, AFAOHC.

Taylor, Col William Barrett, by Lt Col E.A. Holt, January 13, 1958, AFA, RG 101, MC 301.

_____, by Col James C. Gaston, June 4, 2002, in Gaston, *50th Anniversary Oral History.*

Wall, MSgt Frank P., by Col James C. Gaston, April 19, 2005, in Gaston, *50th Anniversary Oral History.*

Webster, Harold M., by Col James C. Gaston, January 7, 2003, in Gaston, *50th Anniversary Oral History.*

Whitlow, Col Robert V., by Maj Russell Mank and Capt Phillip Meilinger, April 5, 1979, AFAOHC.

Witters, Col Arthur G., by Maj E.A. Holt, July 9, 1956, in "AFA Official History," V, D17.

_____, transcribed memoir, in Gaston, *50th Anniversary Oral History.*

Zimmerman, Brig Gen Don Z., by Maj Russell Mank and Capt Phillip Meilinger, September 7, 1979, AFAOHC.

Appendix One
Key Staff Personnel, Academic Year 1955–56

Command Section

Lt Gen Hubert R. Harmon ....Superintendent
Col Robert R. Gideon ....Chief of Staff
Col William B. Taylor III................................Assistant Chief of Staff
Col Thomas J. Hanley, Jr...............................Deputy Chief of Staff/Operations
Col William W. Converse...............................Deputy Chief of Staff/Comptroller
Col Wingate B. Jones.....................................Deputy Chief of Staff/Materiel
Lt Col Gilbert C. Cooke ....Deputy Chief of Staff/Personnel
Col Max B. Boyd..Chief of Information Services
Lt Col Arthur G. Witters................................Director of Installations
Lt Col James D. Hunter.................................Academy Registrar
Col Levi M Browning.....................................Academy Surgeon
Col Chaplain John S. Bennett........................Protestant Chaplain
Col Chaplain Constantine E. Zielenski..........Catholic Chaplain
MSgt Harry S. Parnell ....Sergeant Major
Mrs. Gail McComas ....Academy Hostess

Commandant of Cadets

Brig Gen Robert M. Stillman..........................Commandant
Col Benjamin B. Cassiday, Jr.........................Deputy Commandant
Col Carl C. Barthel...Director of Flying Training
Col H.L. Hogan III ....Director of Military Training
Col Arthur W. Holderness ....Director of Operations and Training
Lt Col William C. McGlothlin, Jr...................Director of Physical Training
Lt Col James B. Townsend ....Air Officer Commanding, 1st Group
Capt Raymond O. Barton, Jr..........................Air Officer Commanding, 1st Squadron
Major William B. Yancey, Jr...........................Air Officer Commanding, 2nd Squadron

Major Henry L. Warren ....Air Officer Commanding, 3rd Squadron

Capt Arnold W. Braswell...................................Air Officer Commanding, 4th Squadron

Dean of Faculty

Brig Gen Don Z. Zimmerman.........................Dean

Col Robert F. McDermott...............................Vice Dean

Col Arthur E. Boudreau..................................Assistant Dean

Col Ward T. Abbot..Professor of Mechanics

Col James S. Barko ....Professor of Graphics

Col Josephus A. Brown ....Professor of Geography

Col Edwin Watson Brown ....Professor of Physics

Lt Col Gerhardt C. Clementson ....Professor of Aerodynamics

Col Thomas L. Crystal ....Professor of Philosophy

Col Howard Dane ....Professor of Thermodynamics

Col John L. Frisbee...Professor of History

Col Archie Higdon ....Professor of Mathematics

Lt Col Fred E. Holdredge, Jr............................Professor of Psychology

Col Peter R. Moody...Professor of English

Col Allen W. Rigsby..Professor of Law

Col James V. G. Wilson ....Professor of Chemistry

Lt Col Arthur J. Larsen...................................Director of Library

Athletic Department

Col Robert V. Whitlow....................................Athletic Director

Lt Col Francis E. Merritt.................................Assistant Athletic Director

Buck Shaw (a/o 1 Jan 1956)............................Football Coach

Maj Robert Spear ....Basketball Coach

Capt Glenn Mackie ....Baseball Coach

Capt Richard Bowman....................................Fencing Coach

Capt Frank Lee ....Golf Coach

1Lt Anthony Biernacki....................................Soccer Coach

1Lt Nick Fenney ....Tennis Coach

1Lt Byron Gillory ....Track Coach

1Lt Dorrence Sandfort.....................................Rifle, Pistol Coach

1Lt Robert Sullivan ....Gymnastics Coach

1Lt Russell Thoburn ....Cross-Country Coach

Appendix Two
Class of 1959 Graduating Class

Adamson, Herbert A.
Akers, Howard T.
Anderson, David D.
Anderson, Thomas I.
Archino, David T.
Axlund, Roger C.
Barnard, Robert K.
Barnwell, Ules, L. Jr.
Bartholomew, James O.
Beckel, Robert D.
Bender, Charles G. Jr.
Bigelow, Richard M.
Black, Jon D.
Blackwell, James R.
Blake, Robert E.
Bobko, Karol J.
Bowen, Thomas G.
Brooks, Don L.
Brown, James W. III
Browning, Robert L.
Bryan, Jack B.
Buckles, Robert C.
Burch, George W.
Burghardt, Stanley K.
Burton, James G.
Buss, Marvin W.
Canterbury, Henry D.
Carns, Michael P.C.
Carpenter, James T.
Carr, Richard E.
Chapman, James E.
Chase, Donald T.
Chepolis, Robert J.
Clark, George C.
Conant, Roger G.
Connally, James W.
Cook, Curtis G.

Cotton, Lawrence F.
Counts, Roger L.
Culler, Harry H. Jr.
Cwach, Emil E.
Davey, John M.
Davis, Charles R.
Davis, Howard D.
Davis, William S. III
Delligatti, Robert S.
Derrickson, Thomas G. II
DeSantis, Joseph G.
Dolan, John W.
Dorey, Lee R.
Douskey, Paul T.
Dwyer, Robert J.
Elsbernd, Gerald F.
Elser, Arthur G.
Fay, Robert H. Jr.
Ferrari, Charles J.
Finneran, Gerard B.
Fletcher, James K.
Fortner, Larry D.
Fox, Ronald C.
Gagliardi, Albert A. Jr.
Galios, Stephen E.
Gallo, Jon a.
Garber, Gares Jr.
Garvey, Gerald J.
Gaunt, John J. Jr.
Givens, Walter C.
Goetze, Richard B. Jr.
Gold, William H.
Goodrich, David M.
Grafflin, Douglas G. Jr.
Griffin, David E.
Groark, David H.
Gulledge, John F.

Gunter, James P. Jr.
Halbower, Harlow K.
Hamer, Stephen A.
Hammond, Flaye M. III
Hardage, Daniel, W.
Harnitchek, Joseph A.
Hayes, John G. Jr.
Hayes, John R. Jr.
Hester, Floyd R.
Hilbert, Richard M.
Holmes, Ransom S. III
Hosmer, Bradley C.
House, Thomas D. Jr.
Houston, John G.
Howell, John M. Jr.
Hundemer, John R.
Hunt, Leigh H. Jr.
Hurley, Robert L.
Hutchinson, John F. Jr.
Inness, Roy G. Jr.
Jay, Jimmie L.
Jefferson, Wayne O. Jr.
Jennings, Robert S.F.
Johnson, Hansford T.
Johnson, Theodore B.
Jolly, Lawrence M.
Josephson, Edward H.
Jozwiak, Thomas J.
Kaake, Charles A. Jr.
Kay, Conrad M.
Keezell, Nathaniel H. Jr.
Kingsland, Louis Jr.
Kozelka, Robin M.
Krueger, Lorin B. II
Lankenau, Edward F. III
Lanman, Ronald T.
Lasen, Paul S.

Lee, John E.
Lee, Richard D.
Lentz, Dana C.
Livingston, Donald B.
Lofton, Charles M. Jr.
Loveridge, Robert T.
Lovrien, Clark E. Jr.
Lowe, Robert E.
Lynch, Edward J.
Madonna, Donald E.
Mahony, Leonard J. Jr.
Mantei, John E.
Mason, Richard A.
May, Charles A. Jr.
McDonald, Gerald B.
McLain, William L. Jr.
McMonigal, James C.
Meier, Charles H. Jr.
Melancon, John M.
Merz, Melvin J.
Miholick, James I.
Miller, Craig V.
Miller, Donald W.
Miller, Max I. Jr.
Milligan, John C.
Miltner, John H.
Mitchell, Jay N.
Montavon, Kent
Montgomery, Edwin J. Jr.
Morgan, Joseph D. III
Murphy, Michael C.
Musmaker, Patrick L.

Oaks, Robert C.
Oberdier, Lyn D.
Olson, John A.
Olson, Norris, O.
Oneil, James F.
Page, William E. Jr.
Parker, Brian T.
Penn, Richard L. Jr.
Peterson, Roger H.
Phillips, David J.
Pittman, Wayne C. Jr.
Pollard, Melvin E.
Prescott, Leo L. Jr.
Quigley, Norman P.
Reardon, Michael P.
Reed, James M. Jr.
Reeves, John M.
Rhodes, James M. Jr.
Richart, David K.
Richers, Sherwood A.
Roberts, Roscoe R. III
Rodgers, Charles S.
Rosane, Edwin L.
Schaum, Craig O.
Schemenaur, Roger E.
Schmidt, Karl W.
Schmidt, Walter E.
See, Dennis R.
Seizys, Anthony W.
Shafer, Jonathan S.
Shaffer, Jon G.
Shearin, David R.

Shumate, Arthur K.
Siteman, Robert H.
Smith, Jimmie L.
Smith, Kenneth R.
Smothermon, Philip R.
Stack, Thomas P.
Starrett, Samuel D.
Stevens, John R.
Strom, Brock T.
Telford, William D.
Thomas, Eugene A.
Thompson, Kenneth R.
Thomson, Laurence J.
Todd, Harold W.
Toney, William M.
Tracey, Richard E.
Trail, Richard L.
Ulmer, John W. Jr.
Vance, James C.
Vosika, Eugene L.
Warren, James E.
Waters, Albert L.
Weaver, James R.
Welch, James C.
West, James E.
Wideman, Hubert G. II
Wilder, Robert L.
Williams, Robert F.
Winters, Charles P.
Wood, Dean C.
Wynn, Frederick, B.
Zaleski, Charles D.

Appendix Three
Air Training Officers, Academic Year 1955–56
(All First Lieutenants)

Adams, William T.
Atwell, Alfred L.
Bassett, Kimbrough S.
Battle, Benjamin R.
Biernacki, Anthony J.
Biersack, Elmer R.
Calvert, John W.
Caudell, Colvin E.
Clendenen, James D.
Cole, Charles W.
Collins, James Q.
Coon, Richard D.
Coulter, Herschel E.
Dalton, William M.
Day, Richard D.
Dengler, Reese L.
Doran, John J. Jr.
Drew, Frank M.
Englehart, John R.
Fenney, Nicholas W.
Frederick, George A.
Fredlund, William A.

Garey, George F.
Gilster, Herman L.
Gornto, Harry C. III
Greaves, George H.
Haight, Herbert B.
Hall, Allen W.
Harre, Arthur F.
Hennessey, Charles B.
Koch, Edwin E.
Kuester, Keith C.
Loper, Joseph R.
Lorigan, James W.
Loufek, Matthew E.
Mattson, Matt C.
McFarlan, Edward R.
McFaull, John J. Jr.
Michler, Earl E.
Nial, George A.
O'Donnell, John F.
O'Hare, John A.
Oliver, Kenneth D.
O'Malley, Jerome F.

Ortiz-Benitez, Rafael
Pedjoe, John P.
Peloquin, Dale B.
Penola, Charles R.
Petersen, Carl D.
Puryear, Edgar F.
Sanders, Ned M.
Sandfort, Dorrence O.
Sciarroni, Robert F.
Smith, Doss L.
Steward, Charles R.
Stewart, Bobbie L.
Strain, Robert B.
Taylor, Charles D.
Thoburn, Russell E.
Till, Jerald, J.
Vigee, Edward E.
Wilkerson, Frank S.
Wilson, Alan D.

Appendix Four
Academic Curriculum, Academic Year 1955–56

Freshman Year

1st Semester	Semester Hours	2nd Semester	Semester Hours
Mathematics	4	Mathematics	4
Chemistry	$3^1/_2$	Chemistry	$3^1/_2$
History	3	History	3
English	3	English	3
Philosophy/Geography	$2^1/_2$	Philosophy/Geography	$2^1/_2$
Physical Training	1	Physical Training	1
Graphics	$1^1/_3$	Airmanship	$^2/_3$
TOTAL	**$18^1/_3$**		**$17^2/_3$**

Sophomore Year (Proposed)

1st Semester	Semester Hours	2nd Semester	Semester Hours
Mathematics	$3^1/_2$	Mathematics	$3^1/_2$
Physics	$3^1/_2$	Physics	$3^1/_2$
History	3	History	3
Graphics	$1^1/_3$	Airmanship	2
Psychology	$2^1/_2$	Law	$1^1/_2$
English	$2^1/_2$	Psychology	$2^1/_2$
Law	$1^1/_2$	English	$2^1/_2$
Airmanship	$^2/_3$		
TOTAL	**$18^1/_2$**		**$18^1/_2$**

Junior Year (Proposed)

1st Semester	Semester Hours	2nd Semester	Semester Hours
Mechanics	$3^1/_2$	Mechanics	$3^1/_2$
Electrical Engineering	$3^1/_2$	Electrical Engineering	$3^1/_2$
Economics	3	Economics	3
Government	$2^1/_2$	Government	$2^1/_2$
English	$2^1/_2$	English	$2^1/_2$
Law	$2^1/_2$	Military History	$2^1/_2$
Airmanship	$1^2/_3$	Airmanship	$1^2/_3$
TOTAL	**$18^5/_6$**		**$18^5/_6$**

Senior Year (Proposed)

1st Semester	Semester Hours	2nd Semester	Semester Hours
Thermodynamics	$3^1/_2$	Thermodynamics	$3^1/_2$
Aeronautics	$3^1/_2$	Aeronautics	$3^1/_2$
Foreign Language	6	Foreign Language	6
Nuclear Physics	$2^1/_2$	Military History	$2^1/_2$
International Relations	$2^1/_2$	International Relations	$2^1/_2$
Airmanship	$^2/_3$	Airmanship	$^2/_3$
TOTAL	**$18^2/_3$**		**$18^2/_3$**

Total Academic Hours: 148

Index

* **Boldface pages** indicate illustrations.

A

A-1s, 139, 146
A-17s, 120
A-18s, 120
A-19s, 120
AAF. *See* Army Air Forces (AAF)
Academic Board at West Point, 10–11, 76
Aden, RAF air policing operations in, 72–73
Admiralty Islands, 133
Adolfo de la Guardia, Ricardo, Panama under, 117
Advanced flying schools, 108
Aeronautical Academy, importance of, 174
Aeronautical engineers of England, 72
Afghanistan, RAF air policing operations in, 72–73
Air academy. *See* Air Force Academy
Airbases as key to control of South Pacific, 127
Air Command and Staff College, establishing, 176
Air Corps
  expansion plans for, 92, 104, 105–6
  name change for, 92
  training activities for, 104–5
  as under-manned and under-funded, 92–93
Air Corps Act (1926), 92, 175
Air Corps Tactical School (ACTS), 99, 101–2
  curriculum at, 83–87
  at Maxwell Field, Alabama, 81–82
Air Corps Training Centers, 104
Aircraft, accidents in early, 32–33

Air Force
  Army and Navy opposition to independent, 92
  desire for thorough planning study on Air Force Academy, 194
  establishment of, 160–61
  independence of, 160, 166, 175, 185
  leaders of the postwar, 145
  as reality, 176
  strategic air warfare and, 161
Air Force Academy
  academic program at, 217–18, 284–85
  Academy Board at, 248
  airmanship program at, 276–77
  air observer program at, 277
  Air Training Officers at, 260–61, 270
  Annapolis midshipmen at, 192
  approval of, 221
  architectural design of, 231–48, **234**
  athletics at, 246–47, 271–72, 283–91
  bureaucracy and, 174–75
  Bureau of Budget in establishing, 200
  cadet airsickness at, 277
  Cadet Area at, xiii, xiv, 231, 232–33, 236, 238–39, **239–40**, 241
  Cadet Chapel at, 235–36, 237–38, 240–41
  Cadet Corps at, 74
  cadet dance at, **282**
  cadet military training at, 74–75
  cadet schedule at, 270–71
  cadet selection at, 218–19, 262–67
  cadet's order of merit at, 25
  cadet uniforms at, 208, 239, 241
  Cadet Wing at, 260

Air Force Academy, *continued*
  Cathedral Rock at, **239**
  cheating scandal of 1965 at, 291
  class makeup and, 192
  classrooms at, 238–39
  construction on permanent site, 276
  criteria in site selection, 222
  curriculum at, 181, 249–56, 272–73
  Dedication Ceremony at, 266, **267**, 270
  discipline and cadet activities at, 274–77
  "Doolies" at, 270
  engineering and science laboratories at, 272
  entrance requirements at, 181
  establishment of, 133, 191
  faculty at, 256–61, 271
  Fairchild Hall at, **239–40**
  finalizing initial site and generating momentum, 205–16
  first cadet class of, 265, **266**
  flag and seal of, 275
  flying training program at, 193–94, 208–9, 217, 253–56
  football program at, 288–89
  funds available for and, 198–200
  Harmon Hall at, 241
  Harmon in establishment of, 191–220
  Headquarters Building at, **239–40**
  hiring of Academy hostess, 275–76
  Honor Code at, xvii, 181, 278–83
  House Armed Services Committee in establishment of, 200
  instruction at, 178–79, 181, 270–71
  interim academy at Lowry AFB, 261–62

Air Force Academy, *continued*
  interim site selection of, 229–30
  internment of Harmon's
    remains, 303–4, **304**
  Library at, 271–72
  location of, 176, 186–87, 202–3
  mascot of, 275
  mission of, 180–81, 269
  Mitchell Hall at, **239–40**
  nearing reality status, 166
  need for separate, 176
  organization of, 208
  origin of idea, 174
  philosophy of, 189
  planning for, 175
  procurement of students,
    175–76
  Protestant chapel services and,
    276
  quest for, 174–84
  Rampart Range of, 241
  reasons for choosing, 184
  rigidity of academic program
    at, 253
  selecting team, 242–48
  site of, 189, 221–30
  Site Selection Board and,
    192–93, 194, 196–99, 200
  size of, 186
  stagnation in Congress and,
    200–205
  start-up challenges for, 276–77
  steps toward gaining academic
    accreditation, 292–95
  textbooks at, 272
  Vandenberg Hall at, **239–40**
  West Point model at, 182
  West Point's influence on,
    192, 291
Air Force Academy compound at
  Lowry AFB, **261**
Air Force Academy Planning
  Board, 179–84
  establishment of, 179
  report on, 179–80
Air Force Aid Society, 153
Air Force Council, 208
Air Force Frolics, 153
Air Force Institute of Technol-
  ogy, 271
Air Force ROTC programs, 213
Airlift (poodle), 170
Air operations, uniqueness of, 175
Air power doctrine, 72
  Douhet on, 81
  Mitchell on, 48–51, 56, 81, 124
  as response in World War II,
    118–19
  Slessor on, 81
  Trenchard on, 81
Air races of 1924, 57
Air Service, 175
  opening of Tactical School
    by, 81

Air Service, *continued*
  as under-manned, 49
  value of Arnold in expansion
    of, 114
Air Staff Personnel Division
  (A-1), planning for, 175
Air Task Group, 137
Air Training Command (ATC),
  194
  preparation of study on struc-
    ture of air academy, 177
  site selection and, 225–26
Air Training Officers (ATOs),
  260–61
Air University
  on Air Force Academy cur-
    riculum, 250
  board of, on air academy,
    178–79
  establishment of Air Force
    Academy Planning Board,
    179–84
Air University Academy Plan-
  ning Board, 179–84, 186,
  249–50
Air War College (Maxwell Air
  Force Base)
  establishing, 176
  Harmon's speeches at, 158–60
Air Warfare (Sherman), 81
Aitape, 133
Alaska, purchase of, 7
Albrook Field, Hubert's com-
  mand of Sixth Air Force
  based at, 119–24
Allen, Henry T., on fraterniza-
  tion between soldiers and
  German women, 42
All Souls Unitarian Church
  (Washington, DC), wedding
  of Harmon and Rosa-Maye
  at, 68
Alton, Illinois, as possible site of
  Air Force Academy, 226, 227
American Expeditionary Force,
  38, 41–45
American Occupation Forces,
  41–45
Anderson, Frederick, 146
  on air academy, 178
Anderson, G. W., 163
Anderson, Orville, testimony of,
  at Mitchell's court-martial, 57
Andrews, Frank
  as Brigadier General, 92
  as commander General Head-
    quarters Air Force, 96
  as commander in Caribbean
    Defense Command, 117, 118
  as key player in the war, 97
  as poker buddy of Harmon,
    xi, 97
Andrews, W. G., 185
Anglophiles, 69

Annapolis midshipmen, 217. *See
  also* Naval Academy
  transfer of, to Air Force Acad-
    emy and, 192
Antilles, 116
Antilles Air Command, formation of, 122–23
Anti-Submarine Command,
  formation of, 119
Area Tactical Commander, 137
Arias, Arnulfo, 117
Armistice for World War I, 42–43
Armstrong, H. G., site selection
  and, 223
Army
  allocation of academy graduat-
    ing classes to Air Force, 177
  on establishment of air acad-
    emy, 200–201
  establishment of Air Corps
    within, 175
  fight against Air Force inde-
    pendence, 160
  flying school at North Island, 33
  opposition to independent Air
    Force, 92
  purchase of plane from Wright
    Brothers, 29
  VIII Corps area of, 56
Army Air Forces (AAF), 127–28,
  175
  drop-in number of combat-
    ready groups, 143
  future of, 145
  growth of officer corps, 179–80
  planning for independence,
    175
  productivity in, 148
Army Corps of Engineers,
  screening of site for Air
  Force Academy, 193, 194, 196
Army G-1, Harmon as chief of,
  103–4
Army-Navy football game, 19, 25
Army War College, Washington,
  DC, 96
  Harmon at, 96–104
Army-Yale football game, 53–54
Arnold, Henry "Hap," xv, 12,
  83, 129
  advancement of, 48
  in air academy, 177
  as Air Corps chief, 104
  buildings named after, xiv
  as "clean sleeve," 22
  as commander of 7th Aero
    Squadron and, 113–14
  as commanding general of
    Army Air Forces, 111
  creation of Training Group, 104
  as deputy chief of the Air
    Corps, 94
  evaluation of Harmon's physical
    activity and endurance, 137

Arnold, Henry "Hap," *continued*
  firing of, 58
  on flight training at Air Force
    Academy, 194
  friendship between Spaatz
    and, 154
  Harmon, Hubert, and, 32, 121
  as head of Information Divi-
    sion, 57
  as key player in the war, 97
  letter from Harmon to, on AAF
    personnel policies, 148
  letter from Miff to, on Hubert,
    137
  at March Field, California,
    91, 93
  at North Island, 30
  as peacetime flying mate, xi
  problems with Roosevelt, 120
  taking over of Personnel Dis-
    tribution Command, 139–44
  talk of retirement and, 146
  training of, as pilot, 29
  value of, in expansion of Air
    Service, 114
  visit to Canal Zone, 116
  war plans division on the Air
    Staff, 87
Arnold Hall, cadet dance in, **282**
Aruba, airfields in, 116
AT-6 "Texans," 107, 120
AT-17s, 107
AT-24s, 107
Atlanta as possible site of Air
  Force Academy, 198
Atomic disarmament, Harmon
  on, 196
Atomic offensive, Harmon on,
  164
Aurand, Henry, 21
Australia in World War II, 125,
  127
Austria, 100
Aviation Cadet Program, 180
Aviation School, purchase of
  Curtiss JN series aircraft
  by, 30
AWPD-1, 87

B

B-10 bombers, 85, 95
B-12 bombers, 95
B-17Bs, 120
B-17s, 95, 121, 128
B-24s, 121
B-36, 162–63
  debate over, versus super car-
    rier, 201
Badger, Charles J., 4
Bainbridge, Maryland, 202–3
  as possible site for Air Force
    Academy, 209
Baker, Newton D., 93
Balbo, Italo, 72

Baldwin, Hanson, 165
Bargue, Bert, testimony of, at
  Mitchell's court-martial, 57
Barksdale Field, Louisiana, 93
Barron Field (Fort Worth,
  Texas), 36–37
Barry, Thomas H., 8, 14
Basic flying schools, 108
Bataan Peninsula, 124
  MacArthur's retreat into, 124
Battalion Board, 78
Battle Creek, Michigan, as pos-
  sible site of Academy, 226
Becket, Welton, architectural
  design of academy and, 233
Belluschi, Pietro, architectural
  design of academy and,
  233
Bennett, John, homily of, for
  Harmon, 304
Bergen, Edgar, 263
Bernhard, Prince of the Nether-
  lands, 111
Beukema, Herman, 179, 242
  on faculty of West Point, 191
  faculty selection and, 257–58
  team selection and, 244
  Zimmerman and, 274
Bishop, H. G., 32
Bissell, Clayton, at Wright Field
  air maneuvers, **59**, 59–60
Black Bart, 267
Blackburn, Jane, 2
Blackburn, Thomas, 2
Blitz (dachshund), 170–71
"Bobby" (horse), 62
  Rosa-Maye (wife) with, **88**
Boeing B-17s, 83
Boeing P-12Es, 116
Boeing P-26s, 83, 116
Bolling Field, 64
  Air Force Academy and, 191
Bolo, 95
Bomber Command in
  COMAIRSOLS, 129
Bomb Group, Harmon's com-
  mand of, 94–97
Bong, Dick, 130–31
Boots, Bill, 31
Boston Harbor, 26
Boudreau, Arthur E., 179
  accreditation and, 293
  as assistant dean, 245
  athletic program and, 289
  establishment of Air Force
    Academy and, 191
  site selection and, 186, 198,
    221–22, 224
Bougainville, fighting on, 129,
  134, 137
Boyington, "Pappy," as member
  of first cadet class, 265
Bracing, 15

Bradley, Omar, 8–9, 16, 19
  in football, 19
  golf and, 170
  letters of congratulations to
    Harmon from, 213
  as major general, 111
  memoirs of, 165
  at West Point, xi, 21
Brant, Gerald C.
  at Barksdale Field, Louisiana, 93
  Hubert serving under, 108
Brett, George H., 89, 91, 116,
  146, 149
  Harmon and, 123, **124**
  at North Island, 30
  problems with MacArthur,
    123–24
Briggs, James E., 306
  accreditation and, 295
  Harmon's final retirement and,
    301, **301**
  as superintendent, 291–92,
    294, 298
Britain, Battle of, Joseph Ken-
  nedy and, 110–11
Brooks Field, 105
Brown, Josephus A., curriculum
  design and, 251
BT-9s, 107
BT-13s, 107, 120
Buck Buck (game), 45
Bureau of Budget, 201
  on establishment of Air Force
    Academy, 200
  site selection and, 206–7
Buress, Withers A., **164**
Burma, fall of, 124–25
Burwell, Harvey, officer in charge
  of flying at Kelly Field, 36

C

C-79, 120
Calder, William M., 14
California Edison Company, 96
Camp Beale, as possible site for
  Air Force Academy, 205
Camp Funston, influenza out-
  break at, 38
Cannon, Joe, as commander
  of Air Training Command,
  185
Capital crimes, 274
Caribbean Air Command, xvi
  under Harmon, xvi, 149–55,
    150. *152*, 153, **154**
  morale and, 151–52
  reduction in military person-
    nel, 151
  social functions hosted at, **152**,
    152–53
Caribbean basin, 113
Caribbean Defense Command
  (CDC), formation of, 117
Carlton House, 238

Carns, Michael, as member of
　　first cadet class, 265
Caroline Islands, 133
Cassiday, Ben
　as deputy commandant, 247
　faculty selection and, 260–61
　study of Honor Code by, 280
Cavalry, 25
Chamberlain, Clarence, 71
Chamberlaine, William, 26
Charleston, SC, as possible site
　　for Air Force Academy,
　　224–25
Charlotte, NC, as possible site
　　for Air Force Academy, 205
Cheating scandal
　at Air Force Academy in 1965,
　　291
　at West Point, 207
Chelsea Park Gardens, 70, **71**
Chennault, Claire, 86
　passing over, as postwar leader,
　　145
Cheyenne Mountain, 237
Chiang Kai-shek, 156
Chidlaw, Benjamin, site selection
　　and, 225
China
　as present member of Security
　　Council, 156
　representation in United
　　Nations, 195
Churchill, Winston, 72
Civil War, 2
　military commanders in, 12
Clagett, Henry B., 94, 96
Clark, Harold L., Site Selection
　　Board and, 187
Clark, Mark, at Leavenworth, 91
Class III offenses, 274
Clean sleeve, 22
Coast Artillery, 25
Coblenz, Germany, Harmon as
　　part of American occupation
　　force in, 41–45
Cold War, 203–4, 216
College Park, Maryland, training
　　airdrome at, 29
College Training Detachments,
　　105–6
Colorado Springs, CO, as
　　possible site for Air Force
　　Academy, 198, 205, 210, 221,
　　222–23, 225–26, 227–30
Colorado Springs Fine Arts
　　Center, 235
COMAIRSOLS, Harmon's tour
　　at, 134, 137
COMAROLS, functional sub-
　　commands in, 129
Command and General Staff
　　School, Harmon at, 123
Compton, Arthur, as member of
　　Board of Visitors, 295

Congress, U. S., establishment
　　of Air Force Academy and,
　　194–95, 200–205
Connally, Thomas, 176
Consolidated-Vultee, 162
Continental Air Command
　　(CONAC), 202, 208
Cooke, George C., as staff mem-
　　ber, 245, 246
Coolidge, Calvin, 56
　at Harmon's wedding, 69
Coolidge, Grace, at Harmon's
　　wedding, 69
Corps of Engineers, 25, 47
Corregidor, fall of, 124
Corrigan, Tom, as staff member,
　　245
Corruption in contract for B-36,
　　162
Cousins, Sammy
　as aviator, 31, **44**
　as major general, 111
Crittenberger, Willis D., 149
Cronkite, Walter, Dedication Day
　　and, 266
Cross City, Tallahassee, as pos-
　　sible site and, 225
Croydon Airfield, 71
Cs in Panama, 120
Culver, Gordon, as Academy
　　protocol officer, 267
Cummings, Eula, as matron of
　　honor at Harmon wedding,
　　68
Cupina, Virginia, establishment of
　　Air Force Academy and, 191
Curry, Jack, at North Island, 30
Curtis, Tom, as fighter pilot, 173
Curtiss, Glenn, 29–30
Curtiss aircraft, 30
　Aviation School's purchase
　　of, 30
Czechoslovakia, German take-
　　over of, 100, 103

D

Dargue, Bert
　air academy and, 174
　passage of Air Service bill
　　and, 58
Darley, Ward, site selection and, 225
Dawes, Mrs. and Mrs. Charles, at
　　Harmon's wedding, 69
Defense, U.S. Department of,
　　93, 161
　Air Force Academy and, 206–7,
　　212
Deichelmann, Matthew K.
　accreditation and, 295
　as possible dean of faculty
　　and, 242
DeMille, Cecil B., design of
　　parade uniforms by, 239–40,
　　241

Denfeld, Louis on naval opera-
　　tions, 165
Denver University as possible
　　interim site, 230
Devine, Charles, as aviator who
　　crossed the Atlantic, 71
Dewey, letters of congratulations
　　to Harmon from, 213
Dodge, Joseph, Air Force Acad-
　　emy and, 210–11
Doolittle, Jimmy, 146
　bombing of Tokyo by, 125
Douglas, James
　as Acting Air Force Secretary, 216
　approval of Air Force Academy
　　and, **220**
Douglas B-18 bombers, 95
Douglas Valley, 230, 233, 238
Douhet, Giulio, on air power, 81
Ds in Panama, 120
Duchess of Gloucester, visit to
　　Panama, 153
Dutch East Indies, 125, 127

E

Eaker, Ira, 51, 57, 90–91
　as aide in Air Service maneu-
　　vers, 59–60
　Harmon and, 145–46
　as key player in the war, 97
　as leader of postwar Air Force,
　　145
　parachute jumps of, 60, **60**
　as peacetime flying mate, xi
　as poker buddy of Harmon, 59
　rank ordering of, 145
　Spaatz and, 146
　at Wright Field air maneuvers,
　　59, 59–60
Earhart, Amelia, 72
Easton, Arthur, establishment of
　　Air Force Academy and, 191
Echols, Oliver, 91
Edwards, Daniel, site selection
　　and, 206–7
Edwards, Idwal H., 91
　delegation of academy respon-
　　sibilities, 187
　as poker buddy of Harmon, 59
　preparation of legislative
　　language of, 177
Egypt, RAF air policing opera-
　　tions in, 72–73
Eighth Air Force, 146
　deployment to Okinawa, 142
Eisenhower, Dwight
　appointment of Harmon as
　　superintendent of Air Force
　　Academy, xvi, 297
　as Army chief of staff, 152–53
　as chairman of Joint Chiefs of
　　Staff, 161–62
　decision to run for presidency,
　　211

Eisenhower, Dwight, *continued*
  establishment of Air Force
    Academy by, 191, 210–11,
    219–20, **220,** 221
  golf and, 170
  Harmon and, xvi, 21, 213,
    300, 308
  as letter-winner in football, 19
  on need for air academy, 211
  as new president, 209
  as president of Columbia
    University, 183–84
  recall of Harmon to active
    duty, 216
  site selection and, 229
  as Supreme Allied Commander
    Europe, 211
  unifying of command under,
    160
  visit to Air Force Academy, 277
  at West Point, xi
Ellington Field, 106, 107
Emmons, Delos C., 91, 94
  as key player in the war, 97
Empress Augusta Bay on Bou-
    gainville, 130
England. *See* Great Britain
Es in Panama, 120
Espiritu, airfield at, 131
"Evaluation of Effect on Soviet
    War Effort Resulting from
    the Strategic Air Offensive"
    (Harmon), 163–66
Excess personnel, problem of,
    140–41

F

Fagan, George, Zimmerman
    problem and, 273
Fairchild, Muir "Santy," xiv, 178
Falconry, 275
Fechet, James
  Mitchell's replacement as
    deputy, 59–60
  at Wright Field air maneuvers,
    59, 59–60
Fédération Aéronautique Inter-
    nationale Certificate test,
    33–34
Fernandina Beach, Florida, as
    possible site for Air Force
    Academy, 225
Field artillery, 25
Fifth Air Force, 133, 134
Fiji, airfield at, 131
Finletter, Thomas
  academy affairs and, 196–97
  establishment of Air Force
    Academy and, 199, 201
  letters of congratulations to
    Harmon from, 213
  site selection and, 198, 205,
    206, 207, 208, 221–22
Finley, Bob, 63–64

First Class Club, 18
Fitch, Admiral
  Harmon as deputy com-
    mander under, 130, 131, 137
  Harmon's fondness for, 137–38
Flight training, at Air Force
    Academy, 253–56
Flying Fortress, 83
Flying Tigers, Chennault's com-
    mand of, 86
Flying Training Command, 104
Foch, Ferdinand, command of, 42
Fogarty, John, architectural
    design of Air Force Academy
    and, 235, 236
Folies Bergère, 111
Formosa, representation of, in
    United Nations, 195
Forrestal, James, 176–77
  as secretary of defense, 183, 201
Fort Andrews, 25–26
Fort Benning, 153
Fort Leavenworth, 94, 102
Fort Logan, site selection and,
    229, 230
Fort McNair, 97
Fort Monroe, 25
Fort Myer, 29
Fort Riley, 58
Fort Rosecrans, 29
Fort Sam Houston, 34, 56
Foulois, Benjamin, 80
  Dedication Day and, 266
  quarrel with Mitchell in France,
    47
  training of, as pilot, 29
France
  desire for buffer zone with
    Germany, 41–42
  Harmon, Hubert Reilly in,
    37–40
  as present member of Security
    Council, 156
Frank, W. H. "Tony"
  as graduate of Engineering
    School, 54
  as poker buddy of Harmon, 59
  ranking of Harmon by, 52, 53
  French Indochina, fall to Japan,
    125

G

Gainesville, Florida, as possible
    site for Air Force Academy,
    225
Galapagos Islands
  airfields in, 116
  military personnel's possession
    of liquor in, 152
Garrison, Lindley M., 23
Gasser, Lorenzo D., 103–4
General Headquarters (GHQ)
  Air Force, 93, 175
  under Andrews, 96

General Headquarters (GHQ)
  Air Force, *continued*
  formation of, 93
  maneuvers to, 94
George (friend of Rosa-Maye), 68
George, Hal
  on industrial web, 82
  on strategic bombing cam-
    paign, 87
  testimony of, at Mitchell's
    court-martial, 57
German JU-52, 120
Germany
  American occupation forces
    in, 41–45
  collapse of Nazi, 142
  desire for buffer zone with
    France, 41–42
  reparations payments of, 42
  as threat, 100
Gettysburg, 2
Gideon, Robert, 291
  as Academy chief of staff, 243,
    262
  as staff member, 246
  Zimmerman and, 273
Glassford, William, 32
Gore, Nina, 91, 246
  as bridesmaid at Harmon's
    wedding, 68
  marriage of, 61
Grapevine Lake, TX, as possible
    site for Air Force Academy,
    205
Grayson County, TX, as possible
    site for Air Force Academy,
    205
Great Britain
  aeronautical engineers of, 72
  Battle of Britain and, 110–11
  Harmon in, 67–70
  as member of Security Council,
    156
  RAF operations and, 45, 72–73
  signing of Atlantic Charter
    by, 156
  sinking of capital ships of, 124
Great Salt Lake, 19th Group
    simulated attack on, 96
Gropius, Walter, architectural
    design of Air Force Academy
    and, 236
Grubbs, Sydney D., as possible
    commandant, 242
Grumman OA-9, 122
Guadalcanal
  airfield at, 131
  battle for, 127, 128, 129
  Harmon at, **131**
  Japanese landing on, 125
Guam, fall of, 124
Guidoni, Alessandro, 72
Gulf Coast Training Center
    (GCTC), 104, 106, 107–8

Gulf Coast Training Center
(GCTC), *continued*
Harmon at, 105–6
mission of, 110

H

Hale, Willis, instructors at Tactical School, 91
Hall, Admiral, as superintendent
of Coast Guard Academy, 222
Halsey, Bull, 129, 133–34
Harmon and, xi, 131, 137–38
visit to Panama, 153
Hamilton AFB as possible site
for Air Force Academy, 226
Hancher, Virgil
faculty selection and, 260
as member of Board of Visitors,
295
site selection and, 221–22, **223,**
226, 229
Handley Pages, 50
Hanley, Thomas J., Jr., 90, 91
at aviation school with Harmon, 31
as Harmon's aide, 155
as staff member, 246
Hanlon, A. J., 174
Hannah, John, as member of
Board of Visitors, 295
Hansell, Haywood "Possum"
B-29s and, 136
on industrial web, 82
on strategic bombing cam-
paign, 87
Harding, Florence, 61
Harman, Ann Blackburn, 1–2, **3**
Harman, George Washington, 1–2
Harmon, Banny (grandmother),
70, 169–70
Harmon, Don Z., on curriculum,
257
Harmon, Edith (aunt), 2
Harmon, Edith (sister), 3, **5**
Harmon, Eula Wulfjen (daughter),
119
birth of, 79
correspondence with, 131, 168
Harmon's brain tumor and, 303
hiring of, to run household, 153
horseback riding and, 170
hosting of Mamie Eisenhower
at Officers' Club, 152–53
at Leavenworth, 91
at Madeira School, 153
memories of Banny (grand-
mother), 169–70
move to Louisville, 147
move to Maxfield Field, 83
personality of, 80
social upbringing of, 155
Harmon, Hubert Reilly, 3, **5,** 6,
17, **212**
at A-1, 146

Harmon, Hubert Reilly, *continued*
abilities as staff officer and
administrator, 167
academic performance of, xv,
16–17, 18, 21–22
Academy Board and, 248
at Academy headquarters, **260**
accreditation and, 293–95
addiction to games, 171
admission to Engineering
School, 54–55
as Aeronautical Officer of the
Army's Southern Depart-
ment, 34
as aide in Air Service maneuvers, 59–60
as air attaché, 73–74
at Air Corps Tactical School
at Maxwell Field, Alabama,
xv, 80
on the Air Service staff, 51–59,
52
at Air War College, 158–60
alcohol and, 168
anecdotes about, 22–23
approval of Air Force Academy
and, **220**
architectural design of academy and, 233–36, 238
at Army War College, xv,
96–104
at Army-Yale football game,
53–54
arrangements for "Air Force
Frolics," 153
art skills of, **18,** 21
assignment to England, 67–68
assignment to G-3 (Opera-
tions) division, 86
as assistant commandant of
West Point, 78–80
athletics and, xiv, 17, 19, 43,
285–92
in Atlantic City, New Jersey, 139
on atomic disarmament, 196
on atomic offensive, 164
on balanced curriculum, 204,
250–53, **257**
at Barron Field, 36–37
as battalion tac, 78–79
at Beast Barracks, 15–16
birth of, 3
birth of daughter, Eula, 79
as boss, 172–73
brain tumor and, 302–3, **305**
Brett, George H. and, 123, **124**
on broad education, 45, 79–80,
204
at Brooklyn's Polytechnic
Preparatory School, 6
"Buzzie" as nickname for, 3
as cadet at West Point, 1, 6–7,
13–14, 15
cadet selection and, 264–65

Harmon, Hubert Reilly, *continued*
cadet uniform design and, 240
as candidate for US ambassador, 154
carpentry as hobby of, 171–72
as chairman of board on TRO-
JAN, 163–64
Chamberlaine, William, and, 26
at Chelsea Park Gardens, 70, **71**
as chief of Army G-1, 103–4
as chief of Information Division, 58–59
classes of, 19
class ranking of, 18, 19
as "clean sleeve," 22
at coastal gun batteries at Fort
Andrews, 25–26
in Coast Artillery, xiv, 25
in cockpit of DH-4, **44**
at COMAIRSOLS, 132–33,
134, 137
combat associates of, xi
at Command and General Staff
School, xv, 87–91, 123
with commandant, **246**
as commander of 19th Bomb
Group, 94–97
as commander of major air
unit in combat, xvi
as commander of Second Air
Force, 124
as commander of the Gulf
Coast Training Center, xv
as commander of the Sixth
Air Force in Panama Canal
Zone, xv, 111, 119–24
as commander of the Thir-
teenth Air Force in the
Solomon Islands, xv–xvi,
131–32, **132**
commissioning from West
Point, 167
concern over current AAF
personnel policies, 148
concerns over rank, 154–55
congratulating of Roosevelt,
Elliott, by, **110**
considered "The Right Man," xii
correspondence with Arnold,
121
correspondence with Rosa-
Maye, 121–22, 123–24, 129,
134, 135, 140, 145, 146, 147,
172, 198
courtship of Rosa-Maye, 61–69
daily routine of, 119–20
death of, 303–4
death of Millard and, 144, 145
at Dedication Day, 267
defining characteristics of,
73–74
demand for Court of Inquiry
to clear name, 35–36
demerits of, 18, 22, 23

Harmon, Hubert Reilly, *continued*
  as deputy commander of aircraft under Admiral Fitch, 130
  desire for active duty, 37, 122
  as devoted Army football fan, 170
  Distinguished Service Medal and, 302
  "Doodle" as nickname for, 63, 174
  as draftsman with the Corps of Engineers in New York City, 6–7
  dreams of being soldier, **12**
  Eaker and, 145–46
  Earhart, Amelia, and, 72
  early collective insight to, xi
  education of, 5, 6
  as educator, 249
  efficiency reports for, 79, 87, 94, 96–97, 137, 148
  Eisenhower and, 308
  elevation to A-1, 143
  at Engineering School in Dayton, Ohio, xv
  in establishment of Air Force Academy, 166, 191–220, 245, 269
  establishment of Cadet Honor Code, xvii
  as executive officer for Menoher and Patrick, xv
  as expert on military education and requirements for Air Force Academy, xvi
  "Expert" rifleman designation of, 21
  extended honeymoon of, 69–74
  on faculty, 271
  faculty selection and, 256–61
  F.A.I. (flight license) of, 34, **34**
  family of, xiv, 1–4
  family pets and, 170–71
  as father, 80, 168–69, 169–70
  as Father of the Air Force Academy, xi, xiv, xvii, 306–10
  as field grade officer, 37
  as first classman, 18–19
  before first haircut, **3**
  as First Lieutenant, 27, 31
  as first superintendent of the new Air Force Academy, xvi, 191–92, 261, **272**
  flight training of, xiv, 31–34, 254, 255–56
  formation of lifetime friendships at Military Academy and, 21
  at Fort DuPont, Delaware, 86
  at Fort Monroe in Virginia, 25
  in France, 37–40
  as frustrated architect, 237
  Garrison as speaker at graduation exercises, 23

Harmon, Hubert Reilly, *continued*
  at George Washington University night school, 54
  golf and, 120, 153, 170, **174, 188,** 297, 302, **302**
  in Guadalcanal, **131,** 134
  at Gulf Coast Training Center, 105–6, **109,** 109–11
  as head of Caribbean Air Command, xvi, 149–55, **150, 152, 153, 154**
  health problems of, 40, 120, 144, 167, 292, 294–95, 298, 302–3, **304**
  in his CH-4, **64**
  with his mother, **114**
  Honor Code and, 278–83
  as Hop Manager, 20
  horseback riding and, 170
  as I Company tactical officer, 77–78
  illness and death of mother, 153
  importance of War College in intellectual development of, 102–3
  in Information Division, xv
  infractions of, 17
  inquisitiveness of, 137
  as instructor at Plattsburg, 27–28
  interim site for academy and, 229–30
  interpersonal skills of, 160
  on interservice squabbling, 121–22
  as joint officer, 135
  at Kelly Field, xv, 33, 34, 35–36, **106**
  as key player in the war, 97
  leaving of Personnel Distribution Command, 147–48
  legislative development on academy and, 197
  leisure activities and, 171–72
  letter of Miff's, on, 137
  letters of, 119, 135–36, 138, 140, 141
  as Lieutenant General, **176**
  Lindbergh, Charles, and, 71–72
  as Little Doodle, 16, 17
  in Louisville, 147
  at Lowry AFB, 262
  loyalty of, 58
  as major general, 111
  at March Field, 91–92, 94
  marriage of, xv, 5, 168, 299
  as master of personal relations, 305–6
  mathematics skills of, 6
  maturing of, 34–35, 45, 53
  at Maxwell Field, 83–87
  as member of 12" mortar company, 26
  as member of *Howitzer* staff, 21

Harmon, Hubert Reilly, *continued*
  as member of Spoonoid Club, 20–21
  as member of the US Embassy staff, 70–71
  as member of Vidal-Gore wedding party, 61
  in Middle East, 72–74
  Miff (brother) and, 28, 30–31, 136, 138–39
  military career of, 19–20, 167
  military conduct of, 17, 18
  military family of, 1, 4–5
  missing of family by, 119
  on mission statement for new Air Force Academy, 269
  on need for air academy, 203–5
  on need for strict commanding officer, 25
  on need for strong recruiting devices, 148
  1956 speech to cadets, 298–300
  19th Bombardment Group under, 136
  as not on permanent brigadier general list, 154
  on occasion of Academy's first birthday, **254**
  order of merit on graduation, 25
  organizational and administrative skills of, 140
  over Thirteenth Air Force, 134–35
  in Panama, 149–55
  parachute jumps of, 60, **60**
  participation in poker game, 59
  as part of American occupation forces, 41–45
  peacetime flying mates of, xi
  performance level of, 34–35, 43–44, 45, 123
  personality of, xi, 22, 131–32, 153–54, 167, 172, 173–74
  at Personnel Distribution Command (PDC), xv, **141,** 147
  physical activity and endurance of, xiv, 40, 43, 45, 137
  plan for selecting cadets, 262–63
  Plattsburg Movement and, 27
  as plebe, 17–18
  poker circle of, xi, 97
  political education of, 307–8
  political leanings of, 174
  posting to Air Service Staff in Washington, DC, xv
  preparation of annual report in 1925, 53
  in preparing defense for Mitchell, 57
  as president of Kelly Field National Bank, 297

Harmon, Hubert Reilly, *continued*
profound sense of duty and
service of family of, 1
as protégé of Mitchell, 57
as pursuit pilot, 86
at RAF College at Andover, 72
ranking of, as average, 52
rankings of, from Kenney,
Spaatz and Eaker, 145
at Ranleagh Country Club in
England, 70
rating of, 58
reading and, 171
receipt of adverse report, 35
receipt of Air Medal, 122
receipt of Distinguished Service Medal, 147–48
relief from command of Thirteenth Air Force, 136–37
religion of, 5
relishing of experience of command, 95
reluctance of, to deal with subordinate problems, 291–92
reporting for duty, 12
restiveness of, 120
retirement of, xvi, 120, 145–46,
154, 212, 213, 297–98, **301**
retrospective on, 304–10
return to Air Service staff in
Washington, 55–56
return to West Point, 74–80
reversion to captain in 1922, 53
review of Cadet Wing by, 300
Roosevelt, Elliott, and, 111
in San Antonio, xvi, 144, 213,
297, 302
as Second Lieutenant, 27
selection of Air Training Officers (ATOs) and, 270
selection of Shaw as football
coach, 288
as semi-mythic figure, xiii–xiv
as senior U.S. airman on
United Nations Military
Staff Committee, xvi
sense of humor of, 22, 169
sense of integrity of, 23
signing of order standing up
Academy, **247**
site selection and, 186, 221–22,
223, 224, 226
skills of, 25
smoking habit of, 167–68
socializing by, 20–21, 78–79
social summertime process of,
20–21
solidification of professional
knowledge and abilities as
officer, administrator and
airman, xv
in Solomons, 130
son's attendance at West Point,
169

Harmon, Hubert Reilly, *continued*
in South Pacific, 129–30, 137
as Special Assistant for Air
Academy Matters, xvi, 5,
187–89, 194–95, 214, 216,
306–7
on SS *Republic,* 97
staff selection and, 247
stature of, 167
at summer encampment, 15–16
as tactical officer, xv, 76–77, 279
taking of Fédération Aéronautique Internationale
Certificate test, 33–34
at Taliaferro Field, 36
testimony of, at Mitchell's
court-martial, xv, 57–58
toleration clause in Honor
Code, 280–81
at training camp for learning
military fundamentals, 26–27
transfer out of Coast Artillery, 28
transfer to Aviation Section of
Signal Corps, 31
at United Nations, 155–60,
173, 187, 191, 195–96
with Van Fleet, Struble, and
Buress, **164**
as victim of influenza pandemic of 1918, 37–40
wedding to Rosa-Maye, 66–69,
68
in West Point Class of 1915, xi,
20–21, 23, **23**
as White House aide, 52
Whitlow and, 289–91
winning of wings by, 28–34
work with Royal Air Force
officers, 80
work with surplus war equipment in London, 44–45
in World War I, xiv
at Wright Field air maneuvers,
59, 59–60
writing of poetry by, 62
as yearling, 18
Zimmerman problem and,
273–74
Harmon, John Bell (uncle), 2
Harmon, Kendrick (son), 95
birth of, 92
death of father, 303
on father, 172
letter to Rosa-Maye, 119
memories of Banny (grand-
mother), 169–70
quality time together, 168
at West Point, 168–69
Harmon, Kenneth (brother), 1,
3, **5,** 6
closeness of Harmon to, 144
illness and death of mother, 153
influenza of Hubert and, 40
mechanical inclination of, 5–6

Harmon, Kenneth, *continued*
in Ordnance Corps, 6
as outdoorsman, 171
retirement of, 6
at West Point, 6, 13, 14
Harmon, Madelin (sister), 3
death of, 3
Harmon, Madelin Kendig
(mother), **2,** 3
death of, 4
move to Washington, DC, 4
with sons, **114**
Harmon, Millard, Jr. "Miff"
(brother), xiv, xv, 1, 3, **5,** 16,
86, 135
as Army commander in the
South Pacific area, 6, 129
at Aviation Section of Signal
Corps, 6
as best man at Harmon's wedding, 68
death of, 6, 144, 145
Harmon and, 28, 30, 136, 137,
138–39
with his mother, **114**
Hubert under, 108, 124
at Kelly Field, **106,** 108
learning to fly, 30
letter to Arnold on his brother,
137
as lieutenant general, 6
New Caledonia's home of, 130
as outdoorsman, 171
poetry of, 138–39
return to Washington from
France, 37
temporarily stationed in Washington, 133
as three star general, 84
at West Point, 13, 14
Harmon, Millard Fillmore
(father), 1, **2,** 2–3
with the Coast Artillery, 4
at Corregidor, 4
death of, 4
at Fort Adams, 4
at Fort Barancas, 3
at Fort Caswell, 4
at Fort Du Pont, 4
at Fort Hamilton, 4
at Fort Mason, 3
at Fort McHenry, 4
at Fort Monroe, 3, 4
at Fort Stevens, 3
health problems of, 4
marriage to Kendig, Madelin, 3
move to Washington, DC, 4
at Narragansett Bay, Rhode
Island, 4
at Pennsylvania Military Academy in Chester, 3
at Port Canaby, Washington, 3
at Presidio, San Francisco, 3
retirement of, 4

Harmon, Millard Fillmore,
 continued
 at Sandy Hook, New Jersey, 3
 in Spanish-American War, 4
 at Sullivan's Island, 3–4
 using of sword of, to cut the
  wedding cake, 69
 at West Point, 2–3, 13
Harmon, Rosa-Maye Kendrick
 (wife), xv, 111, 130, 237, 310
 with "Bob" (horse), **88**
 ca. 1920, **63**
 correspondence with Harmon
  and, 119, 121–22, 123–24,
  129, 131, 133, 134, 135, 140,
  145, 146, 147, 155, 198, 245
 death of, 304
 death of father, 87
 diaries of, 64–66, 86, 91, 171,
  292, 298
 in England, 69–70
 golf and, 170
 Harmon's courtship of, 61–69
 Harmon's health problems
  and, 303. *300*
 on Harmon's support for
  broad curriculum, 204
 horseback riding and, 170
 Hubert's letters to, 123
 income of, 154
 at Leavenworth, 91
 letter from Eisenhower to, 308
 literary bent of, 174
 in Louisville, 147
 marriage to Harmon, 168, 299
 in Maxfield Field, 83
 in 1930s, **83**
 opposition to post-war European assignment, 146
 in Panama, 149
 political learning of, 174
 in San Antonio, 212, 302
 social upbringing of, 78–79, 155
 trying to break smoking habit
  of Harmon, 167–68
 visiting Great Quadrangle of
  Christ Church, 238
 wedding to Harmon, 66–69, **68**
Harmon family at Fort Leavenworth, **92**
Harmon method, 170
Harmon Report, 163–66
Hawaiian Islands, 113
Haynes, Caleb, at Wright Field
 air maneuvers, **59**, 59–60
Hazing, 16
Heard, Jack, 36
Hemisphere-defense mindset,
 101
Henderson Field, 128, 130
Hickam, Horace
 as poker buddy, 59
 testimony of, at Mitchell's
  court-martial, 57

Higdon, Archie, curriculum
 design and, 251
Hill, James T., site selection and,
 208
Hill, T. B., 163
Hill airbase, 104
Himmler, Heinrich, 109
Hines, John L., 53
Hirohito, 125
Hitler, Adolf, 100, 110, 117
Hoboken, 37
Hogan, Ben, golf and, 170
Hollandia, 133, 134
Holt, Lucius, 75
Honeycutt, Francis W. (brother-
 in-law), 1
Honeycutt, John (nephew), 1, 78
Honeycutt, Margaret Harmon
 (sister), 1, **5,** 78
Hong Kong, fall of, 124
Honor Code, xiv, 5, 295
Hoover, Mrs. Herbert, 61, 68
Hopper, Bruce
 accreditation and, 294
 curriculum design and,
  252–53
 site selection and, 186, 208
Hosmer, Bradley, as member of
 first cadet class, 265
House, U. S., hearings on Air
 Force Academy, 219–20
House Armed Services Commit-
 tee on establishment of Air
 Force Academy, 200
The Howitzer (cadet yearbook),
 19, 20, 22, 78
H.R. 2328, 210
H.R. 5337, 219
Humphreys, Frederic, training
 of, as pilot, 29
Husted, Ellery, architectural
 design and, 231
Hutto, Robert, Air Force Acad-
 emy as staff member, 245

I

India
 RAF air policing operations
  in, 72–73
 in World War II, 125
Industrial web, 82
Infantry, 25
Influenza pandemic of 1918,
 37–40
Instrument flying, 32
Interservice rivalry, problems of,
 117–18, 121–22
Iraq, RAF air policing operations
 in, 72–73
Irwin, Sam, architectural design
 and, 232
Irwin, Stafford, athletic team-
 mate of Harmon, 21
Issoudun, 39, 40

I Wanted Wings (propaganda
 movie), 111

J

Jackson, Andrew, 12
Jack's Valley, 230, 233
Jamaica, airfields in, 116
Japan
 bombing of Tokyo and, 125
 invasion of Manchuria in 1937,
  116–17
 invasion of Pearl Harbor, 124
 invasion of Philippines, 124
 surrender of, 143
Jennies, 32, 39
J Factor, 284, 287
 cadet selection and, 264
JN-4 Jenny, 30
Johnson, Hansford T., as mem-
 ber of first cadet class, 265
Johnson, Herschel V., 157
Johnson, Louis, 199–200
 as secretary of defense, 201
Johnson, Lyndon B., 219, 221
Joint Chiefs of Staff, 157, 158
Jutland, Battle of (1916), 50

K

Kay, Harry, friend of Rosa-Maye
 Kendrick, 63–64
Kelly Field, 105, 106
 Harmon's service at, xv, 33, 34,
  35–36, **106**
Kelly Field National Bank, 297
Kendig, Henry, 3
Kendrick, Eula Wulfjen (mother-
 in-law), 61, **67**, 68, 170
Kendrick, John B. (father-in-
 law), 61, 66, **67**, 67–68
 death of, 87
 long career of, 174
Kendrick, Manville (brother-in-
 law), 62
Kennedy, John, architectural
 design and, 232
Kennedy, Joseph, Battle of Britain and, 110–11
Kenney, George
 as combat associate of Harmon, xi
 Fifth Air Force and, 133
 as full general, 87
 letters between Harmon and,
  135
 passing over, as postwar leader,
  145
 rank ordering of, 145
Kent, Roger, 210
Kilday, Paul J., 176–77
Kittyhawk Associates, design
 of, 232
Knerr, Hugh, service academies
 and, 178
Koehler, Henry, sketch by, **267**

Korea, fall to Japan, 125
Korean War, xvi, 166, 210
    start of, 159, 195
Krause, Walt, 86
Ks in Panama, 120
Kuter, Larry
    as Air University commander,
        214
    curriculum design and, 250–51
    on industrial web, 82
    as personnel chief on Air Staff,
        211
    on strategic bombing, 87
    team selection and, 242
Kwajalein, 144

L

Lahm, Frank
    Dedication Day and, 266
    at North Island, 30
    Roosevelt's promotion of, 108
    training of, as pilot, 29
Lake Champlain, 27
Lake Geneva, Wisconsin, as pos-
    sible site, 226, 227
Lakeland, Florida, as possible site
    and, 225
Lampert Committee (1925), 56
Landry, Robert B., as possible
    commandant, 242
Lang, Edith Harmon (sister), 1
Lang, John W. (brother-in-law), 1
Langley Field, Virginia, 74, 78
Lansdowne, Zachary, as *Shenan-
    doah* skipper, 56
Larkin, Tomon, 21
Larned, Charles, 11
League of Nations, 155
Leahy, William, visit to Panama,
    153
Leavenworth, 123
Lehman ridge as overly dramatic
    design, 233
Lehman Valley, 230
Lem, friend of Rosa-Maye Ken-
    drick, 64
LeMay, Curtis, 163
    consolidating of B-29s and, 136
    as leader of postwar Air Force,
        145
    letters of congratulations to
        Harmon from, 213
    site selection and, **223**
Lincoln, George "Abe"
    curriculum design and, 252
    faculty selection and, 257
    Zimmerman problems and, 274
Lindbergh, Charles, 71
    as member of Board of Visi-
        tors, 295
    site selection and, 221–22, **223**,
        224, 225, 226
Lombardi, Vince, 288
Long Island, 202

Los Negros, 133
Lowry AFB as interim site, 230

M

M1 bombsight, 94
MacArthur, Douglas, 20, 110
    air forces under, 123
    as Army chief of staff, 93, 96
    Harmon's blaming for poor
        publicity, 135
    as Military Academy superin-
        tendent, 17, 76, 179, 278–79
    in Philippines, 124
    problems with Brett, George,
        123–24
    success at Inchon and, 198
    Thirteenth Air Force and, 134
    unifying of command, against
        global war enemies, 160
    westward shift of war and, 134
MacDill AFB, 104
    as possible site of Air Force
        Academy, 225
Madison, IN, as possible site for
    Air Force Academy, 205, 226
Magna Carta of airpower, 104
Manchuria, Japan's invasion of,
    in 1937, 116–17
Manifest Destiny, 7
Manila as open city, 124
Manus Island, fighting on, 134
March Field, California, 91–92,
    94
Mariana, Florida, 134
    as possible site of Air Force
        Academy, 225
Marine Corps, 92
Marshall, George, 129
    as Army chief of staff, 111,
        117, 194
    concerns over interservice
        rivalry, 117–18
    letters of congratulations to
        Harmon from, 213
    message to Admiral Halsey,
        133–34
    replacement of, 200
    as secretary of defense, 201
Martin, Joseph W., 210
Martin B-10, flight of, 82–83
Martin MB-2 bombers, 50
Mason, Charles P., 129
Massive retaliation, national
    strategy of, 166
Maxwell Field, Alabama, 83,
    94, 105
    Air Corps Tactical School
        located at, 81–82
McCarthy, Charlie, 263
McChord airbase, 104
McDermott, Robert F.
    accreditation and, 293
    as acting dean, 291–92
    athletic program and, 284

McDermott, Robert F., *continued*
    curriculum design and, 251,
        252–53
    faculty selection and, 258
    in front of Academy headquar-
        ters, **260**
    instruction and, 271
    staff selection and, 247
    as vice dean, 244–45
    Zimmerman problem and,
        273–74
McGuire, Ed, 22–23
McGuire, Tommy, as air ace AAF
    pilot, 130–31
McNarney, Joseph, xi
    as full general, 87
    as West Point classmate of
        Harmon, xi, 21, 155
Meigs, Merrill C., site selection
    and, 221–23, **223**, 224, 226
Meneely, Jake, as classmate of
    Harmon, 22
Menoher, Charles T., xv, 51
    as chief of Air Service, 48
    as commander of 42nd Divi-
        sion, 47–48
    prediction that the Navy would
        get airplane carriers soon,
        50–51
    ranking of, 52
    transfer of, back to Real Army, 51
Merrill, Jack G., for comman-
    dant, 242
Merritt, Frank, **288**
Mexico, U-boat operations in
    Gulf of, 118
Midway Island, capture of, 125
Military Academy, 175. *See also*
    West Point, US Military
    Academy at
    importance of, 174
    laws pertaining to, 216–17
Military Affairs Committee, air
    academy and, 216
Military camps, influenza out-
    break at, 38–39
Milling, Thomas, training of, as
    pilot, 29
Mills, Albert L., 7–8, 11
Mitchel AFB, as possible site
    for Air Force Academy, 207,
        208, 209
Mitchell, William L. "Billy," 72
    air academy and, 174
    as air commander during
        World War I, 47
    on air power, 48–51, 55–56,
        81, 124
    attacks on the Navy, 49–51
    building named after, xiv
    court-martial of, xv , 56,
        57–58, 92
    as deputy chief of the Air
        Service, 56

Mitchell, William L. "Billy,"
    continued
  goal of, 92
  personality of, 47
  revolutionary ideas of, 85
  theories of, 87
Mitchell Field, 202
Mitscher, Marc A., COMAIR-
    SOLS position of, 129
Moffett Field, California, 105
Monument Creek, 230
Monument Valley, 230
Moody, Peter R., curriculum
    design and, 251
Morane aircraft, 39
Morgenthau, Henry, as Treasury
    Secretary, 111
Mousoulini's [sic], 100
Munda, airfield at, 131
Muroc, Lake, 96
Musgrave, Thomas C., 132–33, 138
  job offer to, 245
  as possible commandant, 242

N

Naiden, Earl, 133, 138
  at Aviation School with Har-
    mon, 31
National Combined Academy,
    175, 177
National Security Act (1947), 160
Naval Academy, 175
  cost for expanding, 186
  importance of, 174
  legislation governing, 188
  reasons for choosing, 184
  selection process for cadets
    and, 218
Navy
  adoption of airpower theory, 50
  B-36 and, 162
  on establishment of air acad-
    emy, 200–201
  experiments with aircraft car-
    riers, 49, 50
  Mitchell's attacks on, 49–51
  opposition to independent Air
    Force, 92, 160
  strategic air warfare and, 161
Navy's Postgraduate School
    (Monterey, California),
    design of, 232
Netsch, Walter, architectural
    design of Air Force Academy
    and, 236, 238–39
New Britain, 134
  fighting on, 134
  naval base on, 129
New Caledonia, Miff's house
    in, 130
New Georgia, fighting on, 129
New Guinea, 133, 134
New Ireland, 134
Newman, James B., 185, 186

Newman, James B., *continued*
  as head of Planning Board's
    site committee, 192
New Mexico Military Institute
    (NMMI), 286
  funding of, by Academy boost-
    ers, 289
Newport, Rhode Island, 98
Newton, Quigg, site selection
    and, 225
Nieuports, 39
Nimitz, Chester, 129, 134, 144,
    160, 213
19th Bombardment Group, 101,
    242
  under Harmon, 136
Norden, 94
Noriega, Manuel, Panama under,
    151
Norstad, Lauris, 297
  cost for expanding West Point
    and, 186
  as leader of postwar Air Force,
    145
North Central Association of Col-
    leges and Secondary Schools
    (NCACSS), 293–94, 295
North Island, 29–30
  Army flying school at, 32, 33
Nugent, Richard, academy
    responsibilities and, 187

O

Oaks, Robert, as member of first
    cadet class, 265
Ocala, Florida, as possible site for
    Air Force Academy, 225
O'Donnell, "Rosie," 214, 244, 303
  accreditation and, 294
  athletic program and, 285, 287
  cadet selection and, 263
  Honor Code and, 283
  as Lieutenant General, 213
  Zimmerman problem and, 273
Officer Candidate School, 180
  Plattsburg Camps as origin
    of, 28
Okinawa, Eighth Air Force
    deployment to, 142
Olds, Robert, 91, 246
Olds, Robin, 246
O'Malley, Jerry, faculty selection
    and, 260–61
Ondonga, airfield at, 131
Ostfriesland (battleship), attack
    on, 50
Owings, Nathaniel, architectural
    design of, 234

P

P-12 bomber, 86
P-26s in Panama, 120
P-36s in Panama, 120
P-38s, 130–31

P-39Ds in Panama, 120
P-40s, 107, 128
  in Panama, 120
Pace, Frank
  declining of prepared legisla-
    tive language proposal, 177
  as director of Bureau of Bud-
    get, 185–86
Palatka, Florida, as possible site
    for Air Force Academy, 225
Palau, 133
  naval and air strikes on, 134
Palestine, RAF air policing
    operations in, 72–73
Panama
  under Arias, 117
  under Guardia, 117
  Harmon's return to, 149–55
  under Noriega, 151
  7th Aero Squadron in, 113–14
  strategic value of, 149–50
  venereal disease in, 152
Panama Canal
  lease renewal and, 150–51
  Rio Hato airbase and, 150–51
  as strategic asset, 113
  threat to, 114, 116
  in World War II, 118
Parseghian, Ara, 288
Patrick, Mason, xv, 57
  air academy and, 174
  as chief of Air Service, 51–52
  endorsing of report by, 53–54
  enrollment in pilot training
    school, 51
  as member of Corps of Engi-
    neers, 47–48
  testimony on affairs in military
    aviation, 56
Patronage, academy appoint-
    ment system and, 218
Pattillo, Manning M., 293–94
Patton, George, 99
Pay Act, 187
Peabody, Hume
  assistant commandant of
    Tactical School, 83
  as classmate of Harmon, 22, 31
Pearl Harbor, 95
  attack on, 118, 124
Peashooter, 83
Peddocks Island, 26
Pershing, John J., 41
  as commander of American
    Expeditionary Force, 47
  installation of Menoher as
    chief of the Air Service, 48
Personnel Distribution Com-
    mand (PDC)
  under Arnold, 139–44
  Harmon at, 147
Petit, Robert L., as Special
    Assistant for Air Academy
    Matters, 261

Philippine Islands, 113, 134
  Japan's invasion of, 124
Phoenix Bird, **144,** 300
Pickford, Mary, 45
Pike National Forest, 230
Pike's Peak, 230
Pinecastle AFB as possible site
  and, 225
Pine Valley, 230, 233, 238
Plattsburg, Harmon as active in
  setting up athletic programs
  at, 43
Plattsburg, New York, 27–28
Plattsburg Camps as origin of
  Officer Candidate School, 28
Plattsburg Movement, 27
Policing duties, RAF operations
  in, 72–73
Power, Tyrone, 153
Pratt, Conger
  Air Force Academy curriculum
    and, 250
  as Fechet's temporary staff, 59–60
  at Langley Field, 93
Primary flying schools, 108
Prince of Wales (British capital
  ship), sinking of, 124
PT-17 "Stearman Flight training,
  107
Public Law 325, 219, 230
Puerto Rico, airfields in, 116
Pursuit School (Issoudun), 39
  Hubert's graduation from, 40

Q

Qualified Candidate Identification Program, 286
Quarles, Donald
  as Air Force secretary, 301
  Harmon's final retirement
    and, **301**

R

Rabaul, naval base at, 129, 133
  air battle over, 132
  naval and air strikes on, 134
  neutralization of, 131
Radford, Arthur, 166
Rampart Range, 230
Randall, Russell, 122
Randolph AFB, 104–5, 107, 186,
  203
  architectural design of, 231
  as possible site for Air Force
    Academy, 176, 205, 207, 209
Ranleagh Country Club, Har-
  mon joining, in England, 70
Rawlings, Ed, 310
Rayburn, Sam, site selection
  and, 207
RedCoat Captain, 63, 70
Redistribution Center, 139
Repulse (British capital ship),
  sinking of, 124

Rhineland
  French desire for, 41–42
  Germany occupation of, 42, 100
  United States Third Army in,
    43–44
Rice, J. K., 163
Richardson, Robert C., 77, 79
Rickenbacker, Eddie, testimony
  of, at Mitchell's court-
  martial, 57
Ridgway, Matthew, 91, 159
Rigsby, A. W., accreditation and,
  293
Robbins, Warner, key player in
  the war, 97
Robertson, W. A., 32
Rock Creek Park, 62
Rockwell Field in San Diego, 29, 94
Rogner, Harris E., as possible
  commandant, 242
Romero, Cesar, visit to Panama, 153
Roosevelt, Elliott
  Harmon's congratulating of, **110**
  pinning of wings on, by Har-
    mon, 111
Roosevelt, Franklin D., produc-
  tion of 10,000 new aircrafts
  and, 104
Roosevelt, Theodore, 19, 57
  demerits of, 19
  problems with Hap Arnold
    and, 120
Root, Elihu, as secretary of war,
  7, 8
Roper, H. McK., 163
ROTC, 178, 180
Round the World Flight of Air
  Service aircraft, 54
Royal Air Force (RAF) officers, 45
Royal Air Force (RAF) operations
  in policing duties, 72–73
Royal Air Force (RAF) Staff Col-
  lage (at Andover), 72
Royce, Ralph, 86, 147
  at North Island, 30
Ruckman, John W., 34–35, 36
"Rummy Mare" (horse), 62
Rumpf, Clarice B., 122

S

Saarinen, Eero, architectural
  design of academy and, 231,
  233
Saint Anthony Country Club, 303
St. Clair Streett, "Bill," 50
  Air Force Academy curriculum
    and, 250
  letters from Harmon to, 141
  passing over, as postwar leader,
    145
  on permanent brigadier gen-
    eral list, 154
  as personnel expert, 139–44
  as Tactical School instructor, 91

Thirteenth Air Force under, 136
St. Maixent, 37
  hospital at, 39
San Diego Bay, 29
San Francisco, California, as
  possible site for Air Force
  Academy, 226
San Francisco Conference, 156
Santo, airfield at, 131
Schlatter, David M., 183
  Site Selection Board and, 186–87
Schlatter, George F., as possible
  commandant, 242
Scott, Hugh L., 8, 14
Search Command in COMAIR-
  SOLS, 129
Second Air Force, Harmon as
  commander of, 124
Secretary of Commerce and
  Mrs. Hoover, attendance at
  Harmon's wedding, 69
Security Council, 157
Selfridge, Thomas E., 29
Selfridge AFB as possible site for
  Air Force Academy, 207, 209
Senate, U.S., hearings of Air
  Force Academy, 219–20
Service Academy Board, forma-
  tion of, 183
Service academy education, 183
Shaw, Buck, 288, **288**
Sheldrake, Thomas, establish-
  ment of Air Force Academy
  and, 191
Shenandoah (Navy airship), 56
Sherman, William, as writer of
  Air Warfare, 81
Short, Dewey, 210, 308
  approval of Air Force Academy
    and, 214, 216, 219, **220**
  site selection and, 208
Signal Corps, 29
  administration of aviation
    school, 30
  directional controls and, 30
  encouragement by Miff to
    join, 28
  establishment of training
    airdrome at College Park,
    Maryland, 29
  movement of training facility
    to North Island, 29–30
Simler, George B., athletic pro-
  gram and, 289
Singapore, fall of, 124
"Sink the ship" drinking game, 45
Site Selection Board, 196–99,
  205–16
Sixth Air Force, 136
  at Albrook Field in the Canal
    Zone, 119–24
Skidmore, Owings and Merrill
  (SOM), architectural design
  and, 232, **234,** 236, 237–38

Slessor, John, on air power, 81
Smith, Dale O.
  faculty selection and, 256–57
  flight training and, 255
  for possible dean, 242–43
Smith, William R., 74
Solomon Islands
  Harmon in, 137
  Japanese landings on, 125
  Thirteenth Air Force arrival
    in, 129
South America's Cape Horn, 113
Southeast Training Center, 105
South Pacific
  airbases as key to control of, 127
  strategic value of, 127
  World War II in, 125–27
Soviet Union
  atomic bombs and, 149
  Cold War and, 164–65
  effectiveness of air defenses,
    163–64
  industrial production and, 164
  Naval fleet of, 149
  problems with, 203–4
  United Nations and, 156–57,
    158, 159–60
Spaatz, Carl "Tooey," 178, 185
  Air Force Academy curriculum
    and, 250
  as "clean sleeve," 22
  as commanding general of
    AAF, 148
  as Fechet's temporary staff,
    59–60
  flight training at Academy
    and, 254
  as full general, 87
  Harmon's preparing for cross-
    country flight with, 33
  key player in the war, 97
  as leader of postwar Air Force,
    145
  letters of congratulations to
    Harmon from, 213
  as member of Board of Visi-
    tors, 295
  at North Island, 30
  as poker buddy of Harmon, xi, 59
  rank ordering of, 145
  site selection and, 194, 208,
    210, 221–22, **223,** 224, 226
  testimony of, at Mitchell's
    court-martial, 57
  visit to Panama, 154–55
  at Wright Field air maneuvers,
    59, 59–60
Spanish-American War, 113
The Spirit of St. Louis, 71–72
Spivey, Delmar T., as possible
  dean of faculty and, 242
Spoonoid Club, 20–21
Squier, George, as Signal Corps'
  Aviation Section, 31

SS *Northern Pacific,* 51
SS *Republic,* Harmon on, 69,
  97
Stark, Harold R., as chief of
  naval operations, 117–18
Stearns, Robert L.
  accreditation and, 294
  as combat associate of Harmon,
    xi
  as president of University of
    Colorado, 183–84
  site selection and, 225
  on training effectiveness,
    tactics etc., 133
Stearns-Eisenhower Board's
  report, 183–84
Stennis, John, architectural
  design and, 235
Sterling, airfield at, 131
Stewart Field, flight lessons at, 193
Stillman, Robert M.
  Academy Board and, 248
  athletics and, 283–84
  cadet tradition and, 275
  cadet uniforms and, 239, 240
  as commandant, **246**
  faculty selection and, 260
  as first commandant of cadets,
    245
  flight training at Academy
    and, 254
  in front of Academy headquar-
    ters, **260**
  Harmon's final retirement
    and, **301**
  responsibility for military and
    physical training, 274
  staff selection and, 247
Stilwell, Joe, 122, 124–25
Stimson, Henry, as Secretary of
  War, 111, 118
Stinson, Eddie, 37
Stone, William S.
  accreditation and, 294
  curricular design and, 249
  on faculty of West Point, 191
  as possible dean of faculty and,
    242, 243
  as superintendent, 243
  team selection and, 242
Strategic air warfare, 161
Strategic bombing, 72, 102
  theory of, 82, 84–85
Stratemeyer, George, 90
  as athletic teammate of Harmon,
    21
  leaving job as chief of staff for
    assignment to China, 122
  as major general, 111
  on permanent brigadier gen-
    eral list, 154
  in West Point Class of 1915, xi
Strike Command in COMAIR-
  SOLS, 129

Strom, Brock, as member of first
  cadet class, 265
Struble, Arthur D., **164**
Sudan, RAF air policing operations in, 72–73
Sudentenland, German takeover
  of, 103
Swing, Joseph, athletic teammate
  of Harmon, 21
Swofford, Ralph P., Jr.
  accreditation and, 295
  as possible dean of faculty and,
    242
Symington, Stuart, 162, 185
  Air Force Academy and, 193,
    194
  on cost for expanding West
    Point, 186
  letter explaining cost for
    expanding Annapolis, 186

T

Tactical School, move to Maxwell
  from Langley Field, 83
Taft, William Howard, 14
Taiwan, representation in United
  Nations, 195
Talbott, Harold
  approval of Air Force Academy
    and, 209, 213, **220,** 230
  architectural design and, 232
  athletic program and, 285
  cadet selection and, 263
  cadet uniforms and, 239
  at Dedication Day, 267, **267**
  golf and, 170
  Harmon's retirement and,
    297–98
  site selection and, 210, 214–15,
    221–22, 225, 226–27, 229, 230
  team selection and, 243
Taliaferro Field (Hicks, Texas), 36
Taylor, Maxwell, 91, 178
Thayer, Sylvanus, 11
Thirteenth Air Force, 129, 183
  destroying of 130 Japanese
    aircraft at Truk, 133
  under Harmon, 134–37
  improvement in discipline
    of, 137
  in the Solomons, 129
  under Streett, 136
  under Twining, 128
Thornton, Dan
  golf and, 170
  site selection and, 225
Thunderbirds, Dedication Day
  and, 266–67
Tinker, Clarence, as air attaché to
  London, 67, 69
Tokyo, bombing of, by Jimmy
  Doolittle, 125
Torokina, Cape, 130
  airfield at, 131

Trail End (Kendrick mansion in Sheridan, Wyoming), 61–62, **65,** 87
Transjordan, RAF air policing operations in, 72–73
Trenchard, Hugh, 72
on air power, 81
Trinidad, 119, 120
airfields in, 116
TROJAN, 163–64
Troop ships, influenza outbreak on, 38–39
Truk Atoll
Japanese bastion at, 133
naval and air strikes on, 134
transfer of aircraft to, 132
Truman, Harry, 166, 201
Truscott, Lucian, at Leavenworth, 91
Tulagi, Japanese landings on, 125
Twain, Mark, 281
Twining, Nathan F., 213–14
approval of Air Force Academy and, **220**
Bolling AFB and, 213
cadet selection and, 265
cadet uniform design and, 240
COMAIRSOLS position of, 129
as combat associate of Harmon, xi
departure to Europe, 131
faculty selection and, 260
as leader of postwar Air Force, 145
letters of congratulations to Harmon from, 213
site selection and, 210, 225, 227
Thirteenth Air Force under, 128

U

U-boats, 120–21, 122, 137
in Gulf of Mexico, 118
Unification, concept of, 161
Uniform Code of Military Justice, 279
United Nations (UN), 155
Article 43 of Charter of, 156
Atomic Energy Commission and, 160
Economic and Social Council of, 156
General Assembly of, 156
Harmon as U.S. Air Force representative to, 155–60
International Court of Justice of, 156
military forces to be supplied by, 157
Military Staff Committee of, xvi, 156–57, 158–59
Secretariat of, 156
Security Council of, 156, 157, 195
signing of charter, 156
Trusteeship Council of, 156

United States
entry into World War I, 31, 33
as present member of Security Council, 156
signing of Atlantic Charter, 156
US Joint doctrine, 128–29
USS *Maine*, explosion of, 7
Uvalde, Texas, Primary flying school located in, 110

V

Vandenberg, Hoyt S., 162, 165, 166
academy affairs and, 196–97
on Air Force Academy and, 166, 191–92, 199
as Air Force chief of staff, xiv, xvi
buildings named after, xiv
as "clean sleeve," 22
convening of board at Air University, 178–79
flight training and, 194, 255
funeral of, 222
as leader of postwar Air Force, 145
letters of congratulations to Harmon from, 213
reservations over atomic war plan, 187–88
site selection and, 186, 198, 207
Twining as replacement for, 213–16
Vandenberg Hall, xiii
Van Fleet, James, **164**
as athletic teammate of Harmon, 21
in West Point Class of 1915, xi
Van Voorhis, Daniel, 117
Venereal disease in Panama, 152
Versailles Treaty, 100
"Vibrator," 120
Vidal, Gene, marriage of, 61
Vinson, Carl, 198–99, 200
on Air Force Academy, 194, 199, 201, 207–8, **220**
as chairman of House Armed Services Committee, 185
site selection and, 206

W

Wake Island, fall of, 124
Walker, Ken, 85
on industrial web, 82
as instructor at Tactical School, 91
on strategic bombing campaign, 87
Wall, Frank, 172–73, 300
badgering of Harmon to quit smoking, 167–68
Harmon's illness and, 301–2
War College, goal of, 96–97, 101
War Plan Orange, 101

Washington Barracks, 97
Wedemeyer, Al, at Leavenworth, 91
Weeks, John, as Secretary of War, 56, 58
Westbrook, Bob, 138, 144
West Coast Training Center, 104–5
Wester, Harold M., 275
Western Costume Company, 240
Westover, Oscar, 86
visit to Panama Zone, 116
Westover airbase, 104
West Point, US Military Academy at, 7–13, 175
Academic Board at, 10–11, 76
academic curriculum of, 9, 16–17, 75–76, 217
attrition rate of, 263
under Barry, 8, 14
Board of Visitors at, 11
Cadet Chapel at, 8
cadet rooms at, 16
cadets at, 76–77, 217
cheating scandal at, 207, 210
Christmas leave of, 17
Class of 1915 at, 21
"Collegiate Gothic" motif of, 8
cost for expanding, 186
educational philosophy at, 9–10
First Class Club at, 18
Five Points of, 281–82
grading of cadet performance, 10
growth of, 7
Harmon, Kendrick, at, 168–69
Harmon's return to, in 1929, 74–80
hazing at, 16
Honor Code at, 278–80
infantry training at, 16
influence on Air Force Academy, 291
intercollegiate competition at, 8–9
intramural sports at, 17
legislation governing, 188
under MacArthur, 17, 76, 179, 278–79
under Mills, 7–8, 11
mission of, 12–13, 74–75
as new approach to military training, 8
organization of, 208
physical appearance of, 9
reasons for choosing, 184
reforms at, 11–12, 75–76
requirements for attendance, 13
under Scott, 8, 14
selection process for cadets and, 218
Spoonoid Club at, 20–21
stipends for cadets at, 18–19
summers at, 17, 20–21
teaching of foreign language at, 11

West Point, US Military Academy at, *continued*
 transfer of cadets to Air Force Academy and, 192
 turnout exams at, 17
 Vigilance Committee at, 278–79
West Point model, 217
Wewak, naval and air strikes on, 134
White, Tommy
 as Air Force legislative liaison, 199
 cadet uniform design and, 240
 as new vice chief, 214
 team selection and, 243
Whitehead, Ennis, 90
 as combat associate of Harmon, xi
 Fifth Air Force under, 134
 handling combat ops, 136
 key player in the war, 97
 passing over, as leader of postwar, 145
White House, Class of 1915 at, **309**
Whitlow, Robert V., **288,** 310
 as athletic director, 285–87
 athletic program and, 284, 289
 cadet academic workload and, 284–85
 cadet selection and, 264–65
 firing of, 289–90
Whole-man system in cadet selection, 264
Wilcox Act (1935), 104
Wilson, Charles, Air Force Academy and, 209, 210–11
Wilson, Don
 on industrial web, 82
 instructors at Tactical School, 91
Wilson, Roscoe, recommendation for job as academy superintendent-designate, 213
Wing-warping, method of, by Wright Brothers, 30

Witters, Arthur J., 262
 as staff member at Air Force Academy, 245, 246
Wogan, John B., 23
 as staff member, 246
Woleai, naval and air strikes on, 134
Wolfe, Ken, as heading of B-29s arrival, 136
Wood, Ben, 203
 accreditation and, 294
Wood, Leonard, 14
 letter or commendation to Harmon, 28
 on training camp for future officers, 26
World War I
 Armistice in, 42–43
 end of, 40
 Panama Canal Zone and, 114
 propaganda in, 42
 start of, 113
 strategic bombing in, 82
 United States entry into, 31, 33, 114
World War II, 113–44
 Anti-Submarine Command in, 119
 attack on Pearl Harbor, 118, 124
 climax of, in Europe, 141
 collapse of Nazi Germany in, 142
 COMAIRSOLS in, 128–29, 132–33
 COMAIRSOPAC in, 128
 defense of Panama Zone, 116–17, 118
 end of, 143
 fundamental problems plaguing airmen throughout, 102
 Japanese invasion of Manchura and, 116–17
 Pacific front in, 124–38
 in South Pacific, 125–27, 137
 start of, 116
 submarine activity in, 118, 120–21, 122–23

World War II, *continued*
 surrender of Japan, 143
Worldwide Service Golf Tournament, 153
Wright, Frank Lloyd, architectural design and, 232, 234, 235, 236
Wright, Orville, 28–29
 flying trials and, 29
Wright, Wilbur, 28–29
Wright brothers
 method of "wing-warping" of, 30
 offering of "Flyer" to Army, 29

X

XB-15, 120
XC-105, 120

Y

Yancey, William B., as officer-in-charge of Honor Code, 281
Yount, Barton K.
 air academy and, 174
 as general officer, 55
 as major general, 111
 as peacetime flying mate of Harmon, xi

Z

Zimmerman, Don Z.
 Academy Board and, 248
 Air Force Academy as staff member, 245
 athletics and, 283–84
 cadet selection and, 264–65
 curriculum design and, 252, 272–73
 as dean, 243–44
 faculty selection and, 258
 Harmon and, 290
 on mission of Academy, 269
 problems of, as dean, 273–74
Zuckert, Eugene, as Air Force assistant secretary, 199

PHILLIP S. MEILINGER

graduated from the US Air Force Academy in 1970 and over the next thirty years served in a number of operational assignments as an instructor pilot in Air Training Command and as a C-130 and HC-130 pilot in both Europe and the Pacific. He was also an action officer on the Air Staff in the Pentagon during Desert Storm. Meilinger earned a doctorate at the University of Michigan, taught in the History Department at the Academy, and was dean of the School of Advanced Airpower Studies at Maxwell AFB, the Air Force's only graduate school for the education of air strategists. He finished up his career as a professor of strategy at the US Naval War College in Newport, RI. Upon retirement as a colonel in 2000, Meilinger served as a defense analyst in the Washington DC area for six years. He is now a freelance writer living in the Chicago area with his wife, Barbara. Over the years he has written five books and seventy-five articles dealing with airpower theory and operations.